THE ROMAN OCCUPATION OF BRITAIN AND ITS LEGACY

THE ROMAN OCCUPATION OF BRITAIN AND ITS LEGACY

Sir Rupert Jackson

BLOOMSBURY ACADEMIC
LONDON • NEW YORK • OXFORD • NEW DELHI • SYDNEY

BLOOMSBURY ACADEMIC
Bloomsbury Publishing Plc
50 Bedford Square, London, WC1B 3DP, UK
1385 Broadway, New York, NY 10018, USA
29 Earlsfort Terrace, Dublin 2, Ireland

BLOOMSBURY, BLOOMSBURY ACADEMIC and the Diana logo are trademarks of Bloomsbury Publishing Plc

First published in Great Britain 2021
Reprinted 2021 (three times), 2022

Copyright © Sir Rupert Jackson, 2021

Sir Rupert Jackson has asserted his right under the Copyright, Designs and Patents Act, 1988, to be identified as the author of this work.

Cover image: The north wall of the Frigidarium, Viroconium Cornoviorum. Jon Lewis / Alamy Stock Photo

All rights reserved. No part of this publication may be reproduced or transmitted in any form or by any means, electronic or mechanical, including photocopying, recording, or any information storage or retrieval system, without prior permission in writing from the publishers.

Bloomsbury Publishing Plc does not have any control over, or responsibility for, any third-party websites referred to or in this book. All internet addresses given in this book were correct at the time of going to press. The author and publisher regret any inconvenience caused if addresses have changed or sites have ceased to exist, but can accept no responsibility for any such changes.

A catalogue record for this book is available from the British Library.

Library of Congress Cataloging-in-Publication Data
Names: Jackson, Rupert M, author.
Title: The Roman occupation of Britain and its legacy / by Sir Rupert Jackson.
Description: London ; New York : Bloomsbury Academic, 2020. | Includes bibliographical references and index. | Summary: "This book tells the fascinating story of Roman Britain, beginning with the late pre-Roman Iron Age and ending with the province's independence from Roman rule in AD 409. Incorporating for the first time the most recent archaeological discoveries from Hadrian's Wall, London and other sites across the country, and richly illustrated throughout with photographs and maps, this reliable and up-to-date new account is essential reading for students, non-specialists and general readers alike. Writing in a clear, readable and lively style, Rupert Jackson draws on current research and new findings to deepen our understanding of the role played by Britain in the Roman Empire, deftly integrating the ancient texts with new archaeological material. A key theme of the book is that Rome's annexation of Britain was an imprudent venture, motivated more by political prestige than economic gain, such that Britain became a 'trophy province' unable to pay its own way. However, the impact that Rome and its provinces had on this distant island was nevertheless profound: huge infrastructure projects transformed the countryside and means of travel, capital and principal cities emerged, and the Roman way of life was inseparably absorbed into local traditions. Many of those transformations continue to resonate to this day, as we encounter their traces in both physical remains and in civic life"– Provided by publisher.
Identifiers: LCCN 2020019024 (print) | LCCN 2020019025 (ebook) | ISBN 9781350149380 (hardback) | ISBN 9781350149373 (paperback) | ISBN 9781350149397 (ebook) | ISBN 9781350149403 (epub)
Subjects: LCSH: Great Britain–History–Roman period, 55 B.C.–449 A.D. | Great Britain–Civilization–Roman influences.
Classification: LCC DA145 .J28 2020 (print) | LCC DA145 (ebook) | DDC 936.2/04–dc23
LC record available at https://lccn.loc.gov/2020019024
LC ebook record available at https://lccn.loc.gov/2020019025

ISBN: HB: 978-1-3501-4938-0
       PB: 978-1-3501-4937-3
       ePDF: 978-1-3501-4939-7
       eBook: 978-1-3501-4940-3

Typeset by RefineCatch Limited, Bungay, Suffolk
Printed and bound in Great Britain

To find out more about our authors and books visit www.bloomsbury.com and sign up for our newsletters.

*For my grandchildren Beatrix, Clemmie, Elsie, Freddie, Leo and Zahra
in the hope that they will read this book when they are older*

CONTENTS

List of Illustrations		viii
Preface		x
1	Introduction and Background	1
2	Britain in the Iron Age	17
3	The First Invasions: Julius Caesar	37
4	The Invasion of Southern Britain: The Emperor Claudius	47
5	Britain in the Mid-First Century	67
6	Boudica's Rebellion and Its Aftermath	81
7	The Flavian Period	95
8	Life on the Northern Frontier	119
9	The Romanization of Britain in the First Century	131
10	The Emperor Hadrian Visits Britain	143
11	Britain in the Second Century	161
12	The Emperor Severus Arrives and Stays	175
13	The Third Century	187
14	The Emperor Constantine Launches His Career in Britain	209
15	Turmoil in the Mid-Fourth Century	223
16	The Final Years of Roman Britain	239
17	Towns and Urban Life	251
18	Life in the Countryside	269
19	Religion in Roman Britain	283
20	The Romano-British Legacy	305
Bibliography		327
Index		339

Appendix available online only at https://www.bloomsbury.com/uk/the-roman-occupation-of-britain-and-its-legacy-9781350149373/

ILLUSTRATIONS

Maps

2.1	British communities in the late Pre-Roman Iron Age	27
10.1	Hadrian's Wall and Stanegate Road	150
11.1	Britain in the mid-second century	166

Tables

5.1	First-Century AD Civitas Capitals in Southern England	71
17.1	Civitas Capitals Throughout Roman Britain	256

Figures

2.1	Snettisham Hoard	19
2.2	Maiden Castle hillfort	22
2.3	Iron currency bars – perhaps not convenient small change	34
3.1	Julius Caesar	45
4.1	Claudius' triumphal arch in Rome, as sketched in 1756	58
4.2	Tombstone of Marcus Favonius Facilis, Colchester	62
5.1	Cartimandua hands Caratacus over to the Romans	74
6.1	Statue of Boudica by Westminster Bridge	88
6.2	Bloomberg tablet WT45	92
7.1	Colchester, Balkerne Gate	115
7.2	Caerleon amphitheatre	118
8.1	Vindolanda tablet (*Tab Vindol* II 343, two complete diptychs) referring to 'bad roads'	127
9.1	Dolaucothi, gold mine	141
10.1	First coins showing Britannia, *c.* AD 119	145
10.2	Hadrian's Wall at Greenhead Lough	154
10.3	Wroxeter	157
11.1	The Bridgeness slab, a distance slab in Antonine Wall	165
13.1	Coin showing Carausius with his two 'brothers' RIC 1[mdc]	205
13.2	The Arras Medallion	207
14.1	Bronze statue of Constantine I at York	213
15.1	Crambeck pottery	229
17.1	Tombstone of Volusia Faustina, Lincoln	254
17.2	Roman arch, now known as Newport Arch, Lincoln	258

17.3	York, Roman wall and tower	260
17.4	The great bath at Bath	267
18.1	Dolphin mosaic at Fishbourne palace	274
18.2	Chedworth villa	275
19.1	Gorgon's head, Bath	293
19.2	Marble relief of Mithras slaying the bull, found at Bloomberg site, London	295
19.3	Curse tablet, Tab Sulis 10	301
20.1	Pevensey shore fort: Second World War pillbox built into the Roman wall	319

PREFACE

Roman Britain is a fast-moving subject, with a constant stream of investigation reports, research papers, new discoveries, books and scholarly articles pouring into the public domain. I have (so far as the word limit allows) drawn upon this material in attempting to provide an up-to-date account. I have integrated the archaeological material with the ancient texts.

The history of Britain between the late Iron Age and the first Brexit in AD 409 is a fascinating one. This book tells the story concisely, in a clear and user-friendly way. It is targeted at general readers, students and everyone with an interest in the ancient world. There are three themes. First, the Roman invasion of Britain and subsequent crushing of dissent was a brutal exercise of imperialism. Tacitus' description of the scene after the battle of Mons Graupius epitomizes this (see Chapter 7). Second, Rome's annexation of Britain was an unprofitable venture, but the possession of this distant island brought some prestige. We were a 'trophy province', which did not pay its way for the first two centuries and possibly longer. Third, and contrary to the view of most modern scholars, Romanization is a useful concept and an ongoing process. The impact of Rome and its provinces upon Britain has been and still is profound: our capital city, infrastructure, language, alphabet, religion and culture are all part of the Roman heritage.

My thanks go to Anthony Bowen, Mark Hassall and Peter Jones for looking at the drafts which I produced six years ago and for their advice. I am grateful to Alan Bowman for a helpful discussion about the Vindolanda tablets; to Sam Moorhead for his advice; to Rose Ferraby for guiding me round her work at Aldborough; to Michael Fulford for showing me round his excavations at Silchester; to the three anonymous reviewers who commented on my text; to Alice Wright, Lily Mac Mahon and Georgina Leighton at Bloomsbury for their wise input and tolerance.

Above all, I am grateful to Martin Millett, the Laurence Professor of Classical Archaeology at Cambridge, for reading and commenting on all the first draft chapters. Martin and I have had many enjoyable meetings, discussions, lunches and dinners over the last six years. He has an encyclopaedic knowledge of Roman Britain and a lively sense of humour. Martin has pointed me towards relevant material and made many incisive criticisms of my efforts. I alone am responsible for the errors and heresies that remain.

I thank my wife Claire, and various friends who have accompanied me on visits to Roman sites around the country; my daughters Chloe, Corinne and Tamsin who encouraged me to start this project when convalescing from a serious illness; my cousin, Geoffrey May, for his considerable help.

Some additional material, for which there is not space in the printed book, is available in the Appendix, which is online only. In future years the Appendix may contain some updating material.

All the net royalties from this first edition will go to Classics for All, a charity which promotes and funds the teaching of classics in state schools.

Rupert Jackson
30 September 2019

CHAPTER 1
INTRODUCTION AND BACKGROUND

1. Introduction
2. A brief account of the Roman Empire
3. The Roman army
4. How do we know what happened?
   (i) Contemporaneous historians
   (ii) Official records
   (iii) Archaeological evidence

1. INTRODUCTION

This book is an account of Britain under the Roman Empire. It is written for students and general readers.

The ancient texts tell the story from the perspective of the conquerors and colonizers. There is now a (long overdue) move to decolonize the curriculum. Much modern scholarship has focused on cultural questions in a post-colonial context. There is a vast mass of literature on indigenous motivations, experience and cognitive process in negotiations with empire.[1] This book is not, and could not be, a digest of all that material. Instead it provides a clear account of what the ancient texts say, integrated with the principal archaeological evidence. Any interested reader will require this before they delve into the broader literature.

2. A BRIEF ACCOUNT OF THE ROMAN EMPIRE

Roman Britain did not exist in isolation. It was part of an Empire that dominated Europe, the Near East and North Africa for several centuries. A basic understanding of that Empire and its institutions is essential. Many of those institutions were adapted and replicated in the provinces, including Britain. The institutions evolved over four hundred years, both in the mother city and across the Empire. But the interaction between the centres of imperial administration and

---

[1] Versluys (2014) notes that this approach, which has developed since the mid-1990s in Anglo-Saxon scholarship, departs from the approach of French, German and Italian scholars. This work should enrich academic debate, rather than lead to jettisoning earlier scholarship.

the provinces continued. Any account of Britain between the first century BC and the fifth century AD that ignored what was happening on the Continent would be myopic.

Rome, a city on the River Tiber in central Italy, was traditionally founded in 753 BC. Initially a kingdom, it developed into a Republic[2] and gradually gained control of Italy, in due course making all Italians Roman citizens. In the third century BC Rome was engaged in a series of foreign wars, principally against Carthage in North Africa, from which it emerged victorious. During these wars Rome annexed overseas territories and put them under the control of governors. During the second century pressures of survival and military necessity gradually led Rome to expand its Empire.[3] Thus by 100 BC Rome found itself as the dominant power in the region, controlling a ring of provinces around the Mediterranean coast. This arrangement was not viable in the long term, because hostile peoples were massed in the hinterlands behind each of these provinces. In the first century BC a series of Roman generals entrusted with super-commands and vying with one another won spectacular victories in those hinterlands.

The Empire came to embrace most of Europe, the Near East and North Africa. Rome secured this domination through the discipline of its armies, the brilliance of its generals and its intelligent provincial administration.[4] Internal strife within the territories that Rome invaded also played a part. One of those generals, Julius Caesar, mounted the first recorded attack on Britain. After leaving Britain, he effectively became a dictator and dominated Rome until his assassination in 44 BC.

By the late first century BC the Empire and the Roman road system extended up to the north coast of Gaul (modern France and Belgium). Britain was still nominally independent and remained so for a few more years, but southern Britain had become part of the 'Roman world'. Latin was appearing on coinage and cross-Channel trade was increasing with customs duties going to the Roman treasury.

After thirteen years of political compromise and civil war Caesar's great nephew and heir, Octavian, emerged as sole ruler of the Roman Empire in 31 BC. As the first Roman Emperor, Octavian was given the title Augustus.[5] The eighth month of the year was named after him. Ironically, August is now the month when most people go on holiday, but this frivolity was not foreseen at the time. Augustus described his status as *princeps*, meaning leader or first minister, since this term was less offensive than *dictator*, the word traditionally used for individuals who exercised supreme power as had Caesar. Augustus died in AD 14. Many emperors followed in his path. Some were good, some were bad. Some were sane, others were less so. Some emperors enjoyed long reigns, but many were quickly despatched, usually by poison or the dagger. In all there were 66 emperors between 30 BC and AD 284. This period is known as the 'Principate'.

Climate change may have been a factor in these events.[6] There was a warm period from about 200 BC to AD 150, known as the 'RCO' (Roman Climate Optimum). The RCO coincided with the high point of Roman imperial expansion. Favourable climate was possibly one of the

---

[2] For a concise and readable history of the Roman Republic, see Southern (2009).
[3] As described in Woolf (2012).
[4] This sentence is not a justification of Roman imperialism, which was morally indefensible. It is a factual summary of how Rome accomplished what no other European power has managed to do.
[5] For a clear account of Augustus' reign, see Wallace-Hadrill (2018).
[6] Scheidel (2018) chapter 1.

reasons for the growth of the Empire. During the turbulent third century, the weather became a bit chillier. Some warming occurred in the north-western part of the Empire during the fourth century. That was the golden age of villa culture in Britain.

The 'later Roman Empire' or 'late antiquity' are terms used to describe the period[7] starting in AD 284 when Diocletian became Emperor and introduced a new form of imperial rule, the 'tetrarchy'. 'Tetrarchy' is a Greek word meaning rule by four people. Under this system power was shared between two senior emperors and two junior emperors. The two senior emperors each had the title 'Augustus' and the two junior emperors had the title 'Caesar'. The tetrarchic system did not last long. Four men with large egos are hardly likely to share out power amicably. Nevertheless, the administrative reforms that Diocletian initiated and his successor, Constantine, carried through substantially re-shaped the Roman Empire.

Quite when the 'later Roman Empire' ended is a moot point. Italy was subject to successive invasions by barbarians[8] in the fifth century. The last Emperor in Rome was deposed in AD 476. But by then the capital of the Empire had been moved to Constantinople (formerly called Byzantium, now Istanbul). The Eastern Empire centred on Constantinople continued for another thousand years until it fell to the Ottomans in 1453. For present purposes it is unnecessary to identify the end point of the later Roman Empire, since Britain dropped out of the Roman Empire when it was definitely still in existence, namely in AD 409.

After this brief historical summary, we must look at the main institutions of the Roman state. These institutions formed the backbone of the Empire and will often feature in the later chapters.

Under the Republic popular assemblies had limited law-making powers. They elected magistrates, who served in pairs for a year at a time and carried out the administration. These magistrates have a pre-eminent place in the history of the Roman Republic,[9] although later they were subordinate to the emperors. They possessed a range of executive, legal, military and religious functions. These included maintaining the city, managing public finances, sometimes determining foreign policy, commanding armies and of course sitting as judges. Each magistrate held office for a year. The top magistrates were two consuls. Below them came praetors and then quaestors. The Romans established a similar hierarchy of magistrates in Britain.

The leading men of the state formed the Senate, which was in origin an advisory body. The Senate was the most senior and prestigious council under the Roman constitution. Having been established early in Rome's history, its role evolved over time. The Senate acquired supervisory, executive and judicial functions. It remained in existence after the demise of the Republic, but with reduced powers. The Senate legitimized emperors by ratifying their appointment. Usually it had no option.

Once again, the institutions of Roman Britain mirrored those of the mother city. As areas attained self-government, they elected their own 'senates'. If you go to the village church at Caerwent in Monmouthshire, in the porch you can see a third-century inscription[10] recording decisions taken by the local senate.

---

[7]See generally Mitchell (2011) and Johnson (2012).
[8]The Romans described everyone outside the Empire as barbarians. This became a difficult concept when foreigners started adopting Christianity: Maas (2012).
[9]See Lushkov (2015).
[10]*The Roman Inscriptions of Britain* (hereafter, RIB) 311.

The institutions of the Roman state were reflected in its social structure. Senators and their families formed the upper class. Below them came the equites or equestrians. Senators were drawn from the equites, but after 129 BC senators were required to surrender their membership of the equestrian order.[11] The equites were originally citizens rich enough to own horses and thus to serve in the cavalry. By the period with which we are concerned the equites were citizens whose wealth put them in the top 1 per cent of society. Under the Empire the equites became highly influential. They served as administrators or financiers both in Rome and the provinces.[12] In the later Roman Empire the equites were graded, with *perfectissimus* being the top rank. You can see a fourth-century column erected by a *perfectissimus* called Lucius Septimius[13] in the Corinium Museum at Cirencester.

The mass of the population were the plebs. They gained political power through electing or serving as tribunes. Confusingly, there were two sorts of tribunes. Tribunes of the plebs were powerful officials under the Republic. They were elected by the plebeian assembly and represented the interests of the plebs. The office continued under the Principate. Military tribunes were senior army officers, as explained in the next section. Hadrian, the founder of Hadrian's Wall, served as both a tribune of the plebs and as a military tribune at different stages of his career.

The acquisition of overseas provinces made new demands on Rome's political institutions. The term *provincia* originally meant a task entrusted to a commander. As Rome acquired overseas territories, the word came to mean an area in which a governor held sway. That meant both territory under formal Roman administration and any wider area in which the governor was entitled to operate.[14] Thus, the governor of Britannia, the province roughly equating to modern England and Wales, had freedom to campaign in Scotland whenever he saw fit.

If the area was turbulent, a governor with consular powers was needed. If it was more peaceful, like Sicily, someone with praetorian powers would do. Britain required a governor with consular powers. The expanding Empire gave rise to the need for more magistrates to run provinces. Rome met that need by the device of prorogation. A formal decision of the people (or later the Senate) enabled a consul or praetor to continue to perform his military responsibilities after the expiration of his office. As a result there were plenty of pro-consuls and pro-praetors. They had all the necessary powers to govern provinces.[15]

Another key position was held by the procurator. He was the chief financial officer of a province. His job was to collect taxes from the local population and to pay the troops. The procurator was not universally loved. He reported directly to the emperor and so was not subordinate to the provincial governor. The procurator and the governor each had their own teams of officials and clerks. As we shall see in Chapter 6, this split in responsibilities caused serious problems in the governance of Britain.

Our discussion so far has focused on the ruling layers of society. But ordinary people, self-evidently, were vital to the functioning of provinces. Their co-operation in paying taxes and supplying foodstuffs to the military was essential to the imperial administration. They seldom feature in the ancient texts except in the context of revolts, principally in the case of Britain in

---

[11]Cicero, *De Re Publica* 4.4.2; Davenport (2019) 58–60.
[12]Davenport (2019) chapters 4–7.
[13]RIB, 103.
[14]Famously, Julius Caesar as governor of Provence ranged across the whole of Gaul and conquered it in the process.
[15]Drogula (2015).

the Boudican rebellion. The curse tablets from Bath, Uley and elsewhere give us glimpses of their lives. There is little other written evidence. The research summarized in Chapter 18 provides an indication of life in the deep countryside.

We should now turn to a specific category of people, who were also crucial to the functioning of the Empire, slaves. Slavery[16] was an accepted fact in the ancient world. The Romans made extensive use of slave labour. It has been estimated that during the Principate there were approximately 6.5 million slaves within the Empire, out of a total population of some 64 million.[17] The average slave served for about 20 years. Thus, there was a requirement for 300,000 to 400,000 new slaves each year. Individuals could be enslaved if they were captured in war or seized by pirates. Roman citizens were occasionally enslaved as a punishment for crimes, becoming *servi poenae*. That was better than the alternative, a death sentence.

Slaves were classified as items of property (*res mancipi*) in the same category as land, houses, furniture and farm animals. They could be bought and sold at will. Slave dealing across the Empire was big business, involving both wholesalers and middlemen. The major slave markets were at Rome, Ephesus (on the west coast of modern Turkey) and – most famously – the Mediterranean island Delos. Delos during the Principate was probably similar to Zanzibar in the nineteenth century.[18] Prosperous Romans and provincials usually acquired slaves by purchase from slave traders. Pliny the younger, an otherwise liberal minded lawyer, discusses how to make a good slave purchase in a letter to his father.[19] Apparently you should examine the slave physically and also enquire about his/her reputation. Any child born to a slave woman automatically became a slave.

The less fortunate slaves were sent to work in mines or on large agricultural estates. Others were attached to the villas of wealthy citizens and provided domestic services. Good order and discipline among slaves were maintained by flogging anyone who stepped out of line.[20] Human rights were not an issue. If slaves had the requisite skills, they could be set to work as secretaries, doctors, goldsmiths, stone masons, librarians, architects, teachers or in a host of similar occupations. Some of the slaves belonging to senators or the Emperor performed important roles in financial or general administration.

The evidence relating to slavery in Britain is sparse. A small number of slave chains have been found. The phrase 'whether slave or free' appears in some of the curse tablets discussed in Chapter 19. An early second-century tablet found in London records the sale of a slave girl called Fortunata, whom we shall meet in Chapter 10. Enslaved people had their own hierarchy of status and identities. The owner of Fortunata was himself a slave, but in a senior position.

Owners could free their slaves by a process known as 'manumission'. The ex-slave or freedman (*libertus*) then became a Roman citizen. In practice such individuals usually remained under the patronage of their former owners, often doing much the same work as before. Some ex-slaves held responsible positions in government. A good example is the freedman Polyclitus, a senior civil servant whom the Emperor Nero sent over to Britain to investigate alleged misconduct by the governor.

---

[16] Cartledge (2011) chapters 14 and 19.
[17] Cartledge (2011) 292.
[18] See Hazell (2011) and Ruete (1998).
[19] *Epistulae* 1.21.2.
[20] Quintilian, *Institutio Oratoria* 1.3.14.

Stable political institutions and an abundance of free labour were part of the reasons for Rome's success. But there were many other factors at work. First, Rome developed a remarkably mature legal system,[21] including a law of contract. This underpinned economic growth, because traders and contractors had a means of enforcing their agreements. Javolenus, who served as a judge in Britain, was one of Rome's greatest jurists. Second, Roman designers and builders had astonishing engineering skills. It was these two assets that enabled the Roman government to create a durable infrastructure across the Empire. The network of Roman roads, drains, viaducts and monumental buildings has left an imprint on modern Europe, including Britain. Roman law is the foundation of modern jurisprudence.

Perhaps the most important factor of all in the creation and maintenance of the Empire was the Roman army. The army was a permanent presence in Britain for four centuries. It is to that we must now turn.

3. THE ROMAN ARMY

Rome's army[22] originally comprised units conscripted from citizens modelled on Greek phalanxes.[23] During the late third century BC there were 16 legions which, after a life-and-death struggle, managed to defeat Carthage. In the second century BC the number of legions was reduced, and tribunes played a vital role in the command structure. In the early first century BC, a consul called Marius established the permanent structure described below. By now the legions were regular fighting units, rather than farmers who enrolled at the beginning of each campaigning season.

The backbone of the Roman army was the legion.[24] Throughout the Principate there were about thirty legions. They were stationed in different parts of the Empire, mainly in troublesome provinces. Three were permanently based in Britain. There were ten cohorts in each legion. Initially a cohort comprised six centuries of 80 men, i.e. 480 soldiers in all. Later a cohort comprised five centuries of 160 men, i.e. 800 soldiers in all. The officer commanding a legion was a legate. One legate who served with distinction in Britain was Vespasian, who later became Emperor. Below the legate came six tribunes. The *tribunus laticlavius* (tribune with a broad stripe) was second in command of the legion.[25] The officer commanding a century was a centurion. There was also a contingent of cavalry in each legion, usually about 120 men. This was divided into smaller groups, each commanded by a decurion. A detachment from a legion sent to perform a specific task was a vexillation (*vexillatio*).

A typical legion had both a name and a number. For example, the legion that Vespasian commanded during the invasion of Britain was the Second Legion Augusta or II Augusta

---

[21] For a helpful overview, see Du Plessis et al. (2016) and Nicholas (1987).
[22] See generally Breeze (2016). In the later Roman Empire, the army underwent major reorganization: see Chapter 14.
[23] Greek phalanxes comprised heavily armed soldiers, 'hoplites', standing shoulder to shoulder with the commander leading from the front: Hornblower (1991) 160.
[24] For a more detailed account, see Goldsworthy (2011) 50–8.
[25] The legate and the tribunus laticlavius were members of the Senate. The other tribunes were equites. A senator had a broad stripe on his toga, an equestrian had a narrow stripe: Davenport (2019) 118.

(meaning the Second Legion, which was established by Augustus). A legion that provided additional support in Britain during the tumultuous post-conquest period was the Second Legion Adiutrix or II Adiutrix (meaning the Second Legion, which provides help). The legion that accompanied Hadrian to Britain was the Sixth Legion Victrix or VI Victrix (meaning the victorious Sixth Legion). As these examples show, different legions could have the same number, but be distinguished by their names. The legionary soldiers were all Roman citizens and had a strong sense of loyalty to their own legion.

All legions were stationed in the provinces. Part of their work was, of course, warfare: subduing indigenous peoples, suppressing rebellions, resisting invaders from the beyond the Empire and sometimes battling against other legions during civil wars. But, as recent scholarship has emphasized, we must not focus on the army as simply an instrument of violence.[26] The legionaries had many other functions. Their activities included maintenance of law and order, surveying, engineering, building forts, repairing ships, building roads (or training others to do so) and generally undertaking whatever work was necessary to run the Empire. There was a complex military culture, which included official and unofficial religious practices. The military included many non-combatants. It interacted with local communities around the Empire. These cultural exchanges were part of the process of Romanization discussed in Chapters 9 and 20.

Numerous auxiliaries accompanied the legions. They were soldiers recruited or conscripted from all parts of the Empire. They did not acquire citizenship until they retired. It is a curious but crucial feature of the Roman Empire that subject peoples fought loyally and courageously on the side of their conquerors.[27] The auxiliary soldiers served in cohorts. The auxiliary cavalry served in *alae* (wings). These military units were much smaller than legions and so could be moved around the Empire rapidly to wherever they were needed. In command of an auxiliary unit was a prefect. The officers below him were centurions commanding infantry and decurions commanding cavalry. The auxiliaries brought with them their own native skills: bowmen from Crete, slingers from the Balearic Islands, cavalry from Germany and so forth. One auxiliary cohort whom we will meet in Chapter 8 is the Ninth Cohort of the Batavians. The Batavians were stationed at Vindolanda on the northern frontier of Britain in the late first century. They left behind a rich hoard of tablets. From these we can read about their work and their social lives.

Although no legions were stationed in Rome itself, there was need for a military presence. Augustus established the Praetorian Guard, comprising nine cohorts and a cavalry squadron, to protect the emperor when he was in or around Rome. A detachment of the praetorian guard accompanied the Emperor on his travels. It was the main and most visible source of his executive power. The praetorian guard and its prefects became a major force in imperial politics throughout the Principate. They cheerfully assassinated those who opposed the emperors. They also murdered any emperor whose performance they deemed unsatisfactory.

The Roman army had a strong presence in Britain. Most military units sent to garrison Britain remained here – literally – for centuries.[28] We know with a reasonable degree of accuracy which units served in Britain and where during the Roman occupation.[29] They

---

[26] Haynes (2016).
[27] The British adopted a similar approach after defeating Nepal in the Ghurka War of 1814–1816.
[28] But there was some re-shuffling of the legions in the first century AD.
[29] For comprehensive details of each military unit, see Holder (1982) 104–33.

brought with them their own culture, dialects and religions. They have left behind a rich cache of inscriptions, including dedications to official Roman gods and numerous Celtic or Germanic deities.[30]

In order to keep any army motivated there must be rewards for success, as well as decent pay and conditions for the soldiers. A Roman general who had won a major victory against foreigners could be awarded a 'triumph'. This was a magnificent procession through Rome. Eminent prisoners of war were included in the parade and sometimes publicly executed. From the Roman point of view, these executions added to the noteworthiness of the occasion. An 'ovation' was a victory celebration less lavish than a triumph. The emperor was hailed as 'imperator' if he won a great victory or, more usually, if someone else won such a victory in his name.

Such a comprehensive military force across a huge Empire was expensive. During the first and second centuries AD each legionary soldier earned 900 sesterces[31] per year. Later emperors awarded modest pay rises. The long-suffering auxiliaries always earned less than the legionaries. After successful battles or conquests soldiers were entitled to a share of the booty seized. Happily, no-one had yet invented income tax. So the soldiers had high spending power. This boosted the economy of Britain and other provinces.

After 25 years' service each soldier (if he was lucky enough to be alive) retired. He received a bonus payment and a plot of land. Auxiliaries received an additional benefit, namely the grant of Roman citizenship. Towns established for the settlement of veteran soldiers were known as 'colonies' (*coloniae*). The first such colony in Britain was at Colchester.

The success of an army depends not only on the loyalty of the troops, but also on a proper understanding of military theory and tactics. Fortunately, a record of Roman military theory survives. Publius Flavius Vegetius Renatus, a senior Roman official, wrote a treatise on the art of warfare entitled *Epitome of Military Science*. Vegetius did not approve of modernity (i.e. the late fourth century) and many of his descriptions hark back to earlier years. He produced an entirely practical work, explaining how to build camps, cross rivers, besiege cities, fire catapults and everything else that a soldier or officer might need to understand. This treatise may usefully be compared with *The Art of War*, written by Sun Tzu in China during the fifth century BC. It may also be compared with *On War*, written by von Clausewitz after fighting in the Napoleonic wars and other campaigns. All three books contain a wealth of practical advice. Vegetius, however, does not include any philosophical reflections akin to those of Sun Tzu and von Clausewitz. The Romans took a more practical view of warfare, which was one of their primary instruments of foreign policy.

When not on campaign, the main concern of the army was with practice and training.[32] Soldiers carried out weapons drill, marching and mock battles on the parade ground in front of each fort. The legions usually had amphitheatres near to their fortresses and these were ideal for such exercises. (You can see a good example of an amphitheatre near to a legionary fortress at Caerleon in Wales.) Cavalry units exercised their horses every day, to keep them in good condition. When possible, they used a special parade ground with loose soil (*basilica equestris exercitatoria*). On top of all that, the army had plenty of building work to get on with: forts,

---

[30]See Haynes (2016) 453–8 and Chapter 19.
[31]For a discussion of the value of Roman money in modern terms, see the Online Appendix.
[32]Holder (1982) chapter 6.

fortresses, roads for military use and walls, especially Hadrian's Wall. So, no worries. The soldiers seldom got bored, even in peacetime.

Military training was an arduous affair, even tougher than the modern regime at Sandhurst. In book 1 of his treatise Vegetius describes in daunting detail what lay in store for recruits. They were hardened by prolonged drilling, marching, running, jumping and swimming. Recruits also learnt javelin throwing, shooting arrows, throwing stones from slings and horse riding. Few Roman soldiers would have looked back on their student days with pleasure.

Finally, we come to the navy. This was a necessary element for any hostile power that was planning to invade Britain. Rome was a prosperous Mediterranean city state, whose citizens had possessed trading vessels from an early date. As noted above, during the third century BC Rome became locked in a bitter and long drawn out struggle against Carthage, the greatest maritime nation of its time. A proper navy became essential. So Rome created one. Roman warships were powered by sail, but in battle they used oars. This made them more manoeuvrable for fighting at close quarters and boarding enemy vessels. The Romans put much effort into developing naval strategy. One of their favourite tactics was to attack from the open sea and then hem in enemy ships towards the shore.[33]

The combination of Rome's military strength and naval skills meant that it was well placed to annexe Britain as an outpost of the Empire. It did so in the first century AD.

The following chapters of this book will tell the 'story' of Roman Britain. But before embarking on that story, many readers may wonder how we are able to piece together what happened so long ago.

4. HOW DO WE KNOW WHAT HAPPENED?

There are three principal sources of information about Roman Britain: first, historians who lived at the time of the Roman Empire and took the trouble to record what was going on; second, those few official records that have survived the ravages of time; third, archaeological evidence.

(i) Contemporaneous historians

The contemporaneous historians fall into two broad categories. First, there are senior men (and sadly they are all men) who played a part in the events that they record. They cannot be entirely objective. This is equally true of modern political memoirs.[34] On the other hand, the author has unrivalled access to information. They are likely to record the basic facts from their own perspective accurately, possibly with some diplomatic omissions. Second, there are 'pure' historians, who investigate events and record their findings. Even writers in the latter category have their own agenda. They are building on their own experience and writing for particular

---

[33] Vegetius, *Epitome of Military Science* 4.46.
[34] To take three examples, almost at random, see Harold Wilson (1974); Margaret Thatcher (1993); Tony Blair (2010).

audiences. The ancient authors occasionally mentioned their sources, but generally did not bother with such tedious details. They lived in a carefree age before the footnote was invented.

This book weaves the ancient texts and the principal archaeological evidence now available into a coherent narrative. It is not a detailed textual commentary on the ancient literature.

The first contemporaneous historian on whom we rely, for present purposes, is Gaius Julius Caesar (100–44 BC). Caesar was *par excellence* a man of action, both statesman and warrior. He left a massive imprint on the future Roman Empire and indeed on the modern world. To take three examples: Caesar established the Julio–Claudian dynasty of emperors,[35] though he was never emperor himself. He promoted the foundation of Florence.[36] He established the calendar that we still use,[37] even specifying that in every fourth year February should have 29 days instead of 28. The seventh month of the year is named after him.

Taking Caesar's career briefly, he enrolled as a soldier in his youth. He also practised as an advocate. At the age of 37 he became *pontifex maximus*, the most senior Roman priest. He rose through several official positions to become a consul at the age of 41. In 60 BC he formed an alliance with two other powerful public figures, Pompey and Crassus, to form 'the First Triumvirate'. These three men dominated Roman politics for the next seven years. Between 58 and 51 BC Caesar campaigned in Gaul, bringing the whole of that territory under Roman control. In 55 and 54 BC he invaded Britain. Caesar wrote a history of these events as they unfolded, the *Gallic War*. After his exploits in Gaul and Britain, Caesar returned to fight a civil war in which he was victorious. Between 48 and 44 BC he controlled Rome, variously as dictator or consul. He was assassinated on 15 March 44 BC ('the Ides of March').

Caesar is very much a historian in the first of the two categories discussed above. He had an unrivalled knowledge of the initial Roman invasions of Britain, but we must view his account with caution. Caesar was writing propaganda to serve his own interests, meant to be read by an audience back in Rome.

Strabo (64 BC–AD 24) was an Asiatic Greek, who travelled widely across the Roman Empire, and recorded what he learnt. His historical writings have been lost, but his *Geography* survives. This includes an account of Britain. Strabo, like Caesar, describes the practices of Druids in some detail. He died about twenty years before the conquest of Britain.

Publius Cornelius Tacitus (*c.* AD 56–120) was an orator and public official, who served both as consul and as a provincial governor. But pre-eminently Tacitus was a historian. His shrewd analysis of events, as well as his pithy and caustic style of writing, mark him out as Rome's greatest historian. Tacitus' principal works are the *Annals*, which cover the period AD 14–68, and the *Histories*, which cover the period AD 69–96. He was therefore writing about recent and current affairs. Tacitus had access to many of the key players. His account of what happened can be taken as generally reliable.

It is a matter of regret that the part of the *Annals* which covers Claudius' invasion of Southern Britain in AD 43 has been lost. We are thus thrown back on other historians for an account of this period.

---

[35] The first five Roman emperors could all trace their descent by birth or adoption from Julius Caesar.
[36] Originally known as Julia Augusta Florentia. For an account of the history of Florence from 59 BC to the end of the Renaissance, see Cronin (2001).
[37] Subject to one modification made later by Pope Gregory, viz that three times in every four centuries there should be no leap year.

Tacitus wrote other lesser works, of which the most important for present purposes is *Agricola*. This is a biography of Agricola, who was governor of Britain from AD 77 or 78 to 83 or 84. Agricola was also Tacitus' father-in-law. It is a brave man who publishes books about his wife's family. It may be thought that this laudatory biography, though accurate on the essential facts, is less than objective.

Gaius Suetonius Tranquillus (*c*. AD 70–130) was an author and civil servant. He held numerous public positions, including secretary to the Emperor Hadrian. Hadrian was not an easy man to please. He summarily dismissed Suetonius while they were both touring Britain.

Suetonius is primarily known as a biographer. He wrote *Lives of the Caesars*. This is an account of the lives of all Roman emperors up to and including Domitian. These biographies contain rather more anecdote and rather less hard fact than modern readers would like. Nevertheless, Suetonius provides some helpful material about the Roman campaigns in Britain during the first century AD.

Ptolemy (*c*. AD 100–170) was an Egyptian mathematician and astronomer, who wrote textbooks in Greek. His *Geography* contained maps of the known world. It also included an account of the communities in Britain.

Dio Cassius (*c*. AD 165–235) was a Greek whose family achieved prominence in Rome.[38] His father, Apronianus, was governor of the province of Cilicia.[39] Dio became a senior member of the Roman administration and was in due course appointed to the Senate. He was also a workaholic. In his spare time he wrote *Roman History*, a history of Rome in eighty books. Dio provides the fullest surviving account of Claudius' invasion of Britain in AD 43. His description of events in the later books is based on his own contemporaneous knowledge and questioning of those involved. As senator, he participated in many of the events which he recounts.

The *Historia Augusta* (probably fourth century) is a collection of biographies of Roman emperors, heirs and usurpers during the period AD 117–284. It purports to have been written by six different authors who are referred to as 'Scriptores Historiae Augustae'. But it is more likely to be the work of one author. The *Historia Augusta* is based on a number sources, most of which do not survive. It provides the only continuous account of the emperors in the second and third centuries. Scholars have questioned the accuracy of parts of this work, but we use it because of the paucity of other material for that period.

Herodian (born *c*. AD 178) came to Rome from the Near East. He held several official positions in government. He wrote a history of the Roman Empire in Greek, covering the period AD 180–238. The full title is *History of the Roman Empire after Marcus*. For brevity, this will be referred to as Herodian's *History*. The *History* is unreliable in places. But it becomes more authoritative when dealing with later events, of which Herodian had contemporaneous knowledge.

Sextus Aurelius Victor (*c*. AD 320–390) held several senior official positions in the fourth century. He was a provincial governor and subsequently urban prefect of Rome. He wrote an account of the lives of the Roman emperors from Augustus to Constantius II, entitled *De Caesaribus*. His work is relatively brief, but it comes in useful when dealing with matters that none of the main historians cover.

---

[38] Scott (2018) provides a clear account of Dio's life and work.
[39] Dio, *Roman History* 69.1.3.

Eutropius (*c.* AD 325–395) was a prominent public servant during the fourth century. He served as a senior official[40] under the Emperor Constantius II and later as proconsul of Asia. He wrote a history of Rome from its foundation up to AD 364 entitled *Breviarium ab Urbe Condita*. As the title implies, the work was a short one. The book was hardly challenging for its readers or, one suspects, for its author. Nevertheless, this is helpful in respect of periods that are not covered by any of the major historians.

Ammianus Marcellinus (*c.* AD 330–395) was a Greek from Antioch. He served in the Roman army under successive emperors, before retiring to pursue his second career as a historian. He wrote a history of Rome from AD 96–378, entitled *Res Gestae* and comprising 31 books. Books 1 to 13 have been lost. Books 14 to 31 survive and are of high quality. Ammianus is generally rated as an accurate and reliable historian. His surviving books cover the period AD 353–378. Ammianus participated in some of the major campaigns during that period and he was able to talk to the key players.

The Antonine Itinerary is a document compiled in the third or fourth century, describing routes around the Empire. It provides useful information about Roman roads in Britain.

Zosimus (late fifth century) was a senior official in the Byzantine Empire, who wrote a history of what were (for him) recent times. He was writing in the late fifth century, shortly after the fall of Rome. His work is entitled *Historia Nova*. It is in six books: book 1 outlines the first three centuries of the Roman Empire; books 2 to 6 cover the fourth century and very early fifth century. The narrative breaks off suddenly in 410, possibly because Zosimus died.

Zosimus has come in for much criticism from modern historians, some of which is unfair. Large tracts of his narrative are broadly accurate. Also, he is our most important source for the momentous years AD 395–410, a period during which Britain dropped out of the Empire and a barbarian army sacked Rome. Admittedly, Zosimus' prose style does not match that of Thucydides or Tacitus. But the same comment might be made about some of his critics.

(ii) Official records

The administration of the Roman Empire was a massive bureaucratic enterprise. Most of the records upon which the bureaucrats laboured have, unsurprisingly, been lost. Those which survive are closely scrutinized by historians for any clues as to the 'story' behind them.

The *Laterculus Veronensis* (meaning 'inscribed tile of Verona') is a document listing all the Roman provinces from the time of the Emperors Diocletian and Constantine I. It is so named because it is held in a library in Verona. The existing Verona List is a seventh-century copy derived from earlier versions that have been lost. The original of this list was probably prepared at the beginning of the fourth century.

The *Notitia dignitatum omnium, tam civilium quam militarium* (meaning 'note of all the high offices, both military and civil') is a record of all the important military officers and civilian officials throughout the Empire. The *Notitia* records the titles, but not the names, of the various office-holders together with their areas of responsibility. It sets out the chains of

---

[40] As *magister epistularum* ('master of the letters') he dealt with the Emperor's official correspondence and therefore had first-hand knowledge of events across the Empire.

command and who reported to whom. The document reads as if someone has taken a card index system and copied out the contents. Some of the cards were up to date; some were not; some were lost. The *Notitia* was presumably created as an administrative document, but it may also have served as a piece of imperial propaganda. The *Notitia* is in two parts, one relating to the Eastern Empire and one relating to the Western Empire, including Britain.

The *Notitia* appears to have been progressively compiled and revised throughout the fourth and early fifth century. Thus in respect of each chapter of the *Notitia* there is a lively debate as to which historical period that chapter portrays. The original *Notitia* has been lost, but a copy of it was made in the late eighth century. That too has vanished, but four copies of the eighth-century version survive. Inevitably, the mediaeval scribes who copied and re-copied the *Notitia* made errors, but it is not easy to discern what those errors were.

In short, the *Notitia* is a source of unalloyed pleasure for all concerned. Classical scholars and professional historians write endless articles discussing what individual sections of the *Notitia* might mean, what copying errors could have occurred and which historical period each section relates to. They convene for highly enjoyable seminars to discuss matters further.[41] The correct answers can never be known. This debate will continue indefinitely.

It is currently thought that the Western *Notitia* may have been revised up until AD 428, but the British section may not postdate about AD 390.[42]

A variety of other surviving official records shed light on the story of Roman Britain. Edicts issued by emperors and records of church councils attended by British representatives are examples.

Finally, the panegyrics are a sort of official record. These were speeches of praise declaimed on special occasions. Eleven panegyrics survive, which were delivered to later Roman emperors between 289 and 389.[43] The style is unctuous; much of the content is hyperbole or vacuous praise. Despite those drawbacks, the background facts that they narrate can be taken as accurate.

(iii) Archaeological evidence

Archaeological evidence is scattered across the whole of Britain. Some stands proud for all to see: for example, parts of city walls, Roman monuments or Hadrian's Wall. Most of the important material, however, is buried under ground. It is dug up as and when landowners agree, or when modern development makes excavation possible.

In 1990 the promulgation of Planning Policy Guidance Note 16 ('PPG 16') had a transformative effect. It made the investigation and preservation of archaeological deposits an important consideration in planning decisions. The substance of PPG 16 has been re-enacted in subsequent instruments and is now contained in the National Planning Policy Framework. As a result of PPG 16 there has been a huge amount of developer-led archaeological investigations over the last thirty years, especially in urban areas.[44]

---

[41] See e.g. *Aspects of the Notitia Dignitatum*, Papers presented to the Oxford Conference, December 13–15, 1974: British Archaeological Reports, Supplementary Series 15, 1976. This is a set of extremely interesting and well researched papers on the *Notitia*, including two papers focused on Britain.
[42] Gerrard (2013) 26–7.
[43] The panegyrics are published in Latin and English with commentary in Nixon and Rogers (1994).
[44] Much of this work is summarized in Fulford and Holbrook (2015).

Archaeologists may use geophysics to see what is underground, either as an alternative to physical excavation or as a preliminary stage. The simplest procedure is magnetometry. This involves measuring changes in the ground's magnetic field caused by bits of wall and other structures. They show up as dark areas on the printout; infilled ditches show up as white. Ground penetrating radar ('GPR') is a more precise but more expensive procedure. GPR sends radar impulses into the ground and generates a picture of what lies below. These scientific techniques mean that archaeologists can limit any subsequent excavations to specific areas of interest.

Inscriptions appear on tombstones, altars, monuments or buildings. They contain information about the individuals or events commemorated. Because carving into stone was a slow and wearisome business, the Roman stonemasons used a variety of abbreviations. To add to our difficulties, usually parts of the inscription are missing, so that they are a challenge to decode.[45] Where enough of the inscription survives, it is often possible to date it, for example because of references to an emperor. When an inscription is mentioned in this book, the RIB reference[46] or CIL reference[47] will be given. If the inscription is quoted, the missing letters will be supplied so that the reader is not confronted with lots of square brackets.

Some soldiers who retired after 25 years honourable service were given bronze tablets to commemorate their service. It is convenient to call these tablets diplomas,[48] although their original name is not known. The diplomas contain much useful information. They can often be dated. The original recipients were, and modern historians are, most grateful to the Emperor for this thoughtful gesture.

The Vindolanda tablets are a cache of wooden tablets, recovered from Vindolanda, containing traces of letters, drafts, reports and other documents written by soldiers at around the turn of the first century. These tablets, like those more recently recovered from the Bloomberg site in London, can sometimes be dated. A few actually bear a calendar date.

A curse tablet is a lead sheet with a petition to a god to punish whoever has committed some specified offence, usually theft. Sometimes the author suggests a gruesome punishment for the miscreant.

Coin hoards[49] from the Roman period are still appearing. Coins are particularly valuable, because they often reveal the name of the emperor and much other information. Coin hoards come about because people have either accidentally deposited them or, more usually, deliberately buried them. There are three possible reasons for deliberate burial. The owner may have hidden the coins for safekeeping, with a view to later recovery. Occasionally people buried coins because they were no longer legal tender. Finally, the coins may be a votive offering to the gods. Like many powerful figures, Roman gods welcomed the occasional bung.

Loose coins found on Roman sites are usually the result of accident or coin loss in antiquity. They are of obvious value to archaeology. Metal detectorists have recovered numerous loose coins in recent years and handed them in under the Portable Antiquities Scheme ('PAS'). The

---

[45] Bruun and Edmondson (2015). For a concise guide to interpreting Roman inscriptions, see Rogan (2006).
[46] *Roman Inscriptions of Britain* vols I, II and III, edited by Collingwood, Wright, Tomlin and Hassall.
[47] *Corpus Inscriptionum Latinarum* in 17 volumes is a comprehensive collection of Latin inscriptions from across the Empire.
[48] CIL vol XVI is a collection of military diplomas.
[49] Bland (2018).

Government set up the PAS in 1997 and it has contributed substantially to our knowledge of Roman Britain.

Dendrochronology and other scientific research[50] now supplement traditional archaeology. By taking cores taken from a large number of trees and examining the growth rings it is possible to deduce the annual weather patterns over the last two thousand years and beyond. Scientists have built up a vast data bank from such analyses. By reference to this information it is possible to date wood samples recovered from ancient sites. That tells us when the tree was alive and when it was felled. More generally, scientists are making a significant contribution to our understanding of the ancient world through archaeobotany, zooarchaeology and the study of ancient DNA ('aDNA').

Many items from the Roman era can only linked to specific periods by secondary association, such as coins found in the same place or inscriptions above graves.

Pottery can usually be identified by reference to its material and style. Pottery fragments are a valuable guide for dating by secondary association. Also, pottery finds may reveal trading patterns and routes.

During the first to third centuries AD, Samian ware was mass-produced, good quality tableware manufactured in Italy and Gaul. Like Ikea goods today, Samian ware was exported in bulk and widely used internationally. It can be dated approximately because of its changing styles. Much Samian ware has been found in Britain. Since 2000 English Heritage has funded a project to collate and analyse all these finds.[51]

Other artefacts yield useful information: for example, tiles, weights and measures, jewellery, tools, items of metalwork and so forth.[52]

The precise dates of governors and legionary deployments are the subject of much scholarly controversy. On those matters, this book generally follows Anthony Birley, *The Roman Government of Britain* (2005).

An evolving story

Every generation of historians has a different understanding of Roman Britain.[53] This is principally because new evidence comes to light, which adds to or confounds existing scholarship. Dramatic examples in recent years have been the Vindolanda and Bloomberg tablets. But another factor is also at work, namely academic endeavour. No-one wins fame or fortune by agreeing with everybody else. Each new wave of scholars sets out to reinterpret the evidence and to put their own stamp on the story.

---

[50] See Scheidel (2018).
[51] Steven Willis (2011) has written up the results of the Samian Project.
[52] For a much fuller discussion of all such artefacts, see Allason-Jones (2011).
[53] Millett et al (2016) chapters 1 to 13 demonstrate how our understanding of Roman Britain has continuously evolved.

CHAPTER 2
BRITAIN IN THE IRON AGE

1. Introduction
2. The Iron Age
3. Contact with the Mediterranean world
4. British communities during the late Iron Age
   (i) South-east England
   (ii) Dorset and the Midlands
   (iii) The West Country and Wales
   (iv) The north
5. Rome's perception of Britain in the late Iron Age

1. INTRODUCTION

This chapter is a survey of Britain before the arrival of Rome. Archaeology is our principal source for the period, although two contemporary writers (Caesar and Strabo) provide accounts of Britain in the late Pre-Roman Iron Age ('LPRIA', 150 BC to Roman conquest).

The Celts

The indigenous population whom we will be considering in this chapter was Celtic. The word 'Celts' (in Greek Κελτοί) is a collective name, which the Greeks and Romans gave to all the peoples who occupied central and western Europe to the north of the Alps. They arrived during or before the second millennium BC. In modern usage, the word 'Celtic' has acquired overtones:[1] it is suggestive of particular racial groups or characteristics. There is a lively debate between those who believe in an overall Celtic identity/ethnicity and 'Celtosceptics', who take the opposite view.[2]

In order to sidestep that debate, this book will use the words 'Celts' and 'Celtic' in their original sense. It is a convenient label for everyone who lived in central and western Europe to

---

[1] See Hunter et al. (2015b).
[2] Sims-Williams, 'Celtomania and Celtoscepticism', *Cambrian Medieval Celtic Studies* 36 (1998) 1–35.

the north of the Alps before the Roman annexation. The term 'Britons' means those Celts who happened to be in Britain, due to ancient or recent migration.

There was not a single Celtic language: the Celtic peoples spoke a variety of languages and dialects, although they were all Indo-European.[3] Because of migration, there were common elements in the different languages throughout the Continent. According to an analysis by the Centre for Advanced Welsh and Celtic Studies at the University of Wales, the language of Spain was Hispano-Celtic; the language of Ireland was Goidelic (later Gaelic); the language of Britain was Brittonic and the language of Gaul was Gaulish.[4] According to Tacitus, Brittonic was very similar to Gaulish.[5] Although bilingualism was widespread during the Roman period, very little Celtic writing – either before or after the conquest – survives in Britain.[6] We therefore rely upon indirect evidence for traces of the native dialects spoken in Britain.

The Celtic languages had a core area in western Spain, Brittany, western Britain and Ireland, which were all linked by (somewhat perilous) sea routes. A few Celtic inscriptions have come to light in those regions. Dialects of Celtic origin are still spoken in Scotland, Wales, Ireland and Brittany, and a few Celtic words feature in place names. Towns in Cornwall and Wales often begin with 'Tre', meaning hamlet: for example, Trevarrack, Trevilley, Tredegar and Tregaron. 'Isca' meaning river or water also features in place names such as Usk or Exe.

The Celtic communities were agrarian. Archaeologists have attempted to calculate how much the farmers produced: they have counted animal bones and examined carbonized plant remains. But this is an inexact exercise.[7] All we can say is that the Celts generated sufficient crops and meat to survive. Otherwise many of us would not be here.

Arts and crafts

Celtic artists and craftsmen have left behind some fabulous artefacts:[8] a pair of richly decorated fifth-century BC bronze flagons found at Basse Yutz in France; an ornate fourth-century BC bronze harness piece with complex geometric patterns found at Marne in France; fourth-century BC bronze brooches with the heads of animals or humans found in the Czech Republic; third-century BC gold torc and bracelets found at Waldalgesheim in Germany. This list could go on indefinitely. In 2015 the British Museum put on an exhibition of Celtic artwork, drawn from all parts of Europe.

There was a distinct Celtic style of art. Artefacts across Europe in the pre-Roman period showed several common features: complicated curving and swirling shapes, or patterns that reflected nature. Craftsmen loved depicting animals and birds. Elegant neck rings ('torcs') were popular among the élite.

---

[3] Hunter et al. (2015b) 26–9.
[4] Figure 1 in Research Paper 31 by Gibson and Wodtko (2013) shows the geographical extent of those languages.
[5] *Agricola* 11: 'sermo haud multum diversus'.
[6] Mullen (2016). 'Ricon' the Celtic for king appears on some LPRIA coins; two curse tablets written in Celtic survive from Bath.
[7] Collis (1994) 142–3.
[8] Joy (2015); Hunter and Joy (2015c).

Figure 2.1 Snettisham Hoard. © Wikimedia / Victuallers.

Celtic art emerged in Britain during the third century BC.[9] A third-century iron sword with bronze scabbard has come to light in East Yorkshire. This has fine red inlays and decorated rivets. There is a scrolling decoration down the length of the blade. Anyone being stabbed or beheaded with such a weapon would get a perfect – if brief – view of the exquisite decorations. An early bronze oblong shield, with matching circular patterns, has been recovered from the Thames at Battersea. Perhaps the most famous collection of Celtic artefacts in Britain is the series of hoards found at Snettisham in Norfolk (see Fig. 2.1). These include gold torcs, ingot rings, bracelets, coins, ingots and much other treasure. The Snettisham hoards might have been buried for safekeeping at a time of danger or they might have been votive depositions, buried to appease the gods.[10] They include one elaborate and quite spectacular golden torc.[11] This would surely have placated any deity, however irascible.

Even coins were a form of art. As we shall see in Section 4, money started to circulate in the late Iron Age. This coincided with a sharp decline in the production of other fine art works.[12] The top craftsmen were redirecting their skills to coin production. Making money was more profitable than pure artistic endeavour.

---

[9] Hunter (2015a).
[10] Stead (1991) 447–64.
[11] Hobbs and Jackson (2010) 18–19.
[12] Leins and Farley (2015) 110.

2. THE IRON AGE

Archaeologists divide early human development broadly into three 'ages': Stone Age, Bronze Age and Iron Age. The Iron Age means the historic or pre-historic period when the people of any region mainly used iron, rather than bronze, for the manufacture of implements and weapons. In the Middle East, the Iron Age started in about 1200 BC. In the Celtic regions, the Iron Age came later.

In Britain, the Iron Age started in around 800 BC and continued into the Roman period. Different regions of Britain developed in different ways during those eight centuries. They adopted a variety of funerary practices. This makes any subdivision of the British Iron Age into discrete stages a tricky business. Archaeologists can get cross with each other when they try to sort the matter out. Apparently, at a conference in Cardiff on this sensitive subject, one scholar made 'sceptical comments' and another had an 'outburst'.[13] Readers are advised to tread very carefully if this topic crops up on a social occasion.

Suffice it to say, for present purposes, that most archaeologists divide the British Iron Age into three periods, namely early (800 to 350 BC), middle (350 to 150 BC) and late Pre-Roman Iron Age ('LPRIA', 150 BC to Roman conquest).

Hillforts

In the early Iron Age, Britons fortified suitable hills with massive earthworks and wooden palisades. The earthworks included circuits of ditches and ramparts, sometimes faced with stone. Entrances were cut into the defensive circuits. These fortified hills, now known as hillforts, may have been the residences of powerful chiefs or, perhaps, emerging centres of regional power and economic organization. Alternatively, they may have been the result of a nucleation of scattered populations.[14] Large numbers of hillforts have been identified, especially in southern England, central England and Wales. Many communities were centred on hillforts. Some impressive earthworks survive: Maiden Castle and Hod Hill in Dorset, Uffington in Berkshire, Cleeve Hill in Gloucestershire and Danebury Hill in Hampshire. Most hillforts were abandoned in the late Iron Age, especially in the south-east.

The labour involved in constructing a hillfort would have been immense. In an agrarian society, where all hands were needed to work the land, the groups who created hillforts must have made huge sacrifices. These operations can only have been driven by necessity, although concepts of necessity vary between societies. In the present context, the necessity was at least in part military or defensive. Additionally, there may have been more subtle motives. Making people work together would create a group identity. Hillforts were a method, perhaps the best method, of displaying power and prestige. They would have had wider functions beyond defence. They were an appropriate setting for social or religious ceremonies. Whether hillforts were inhabited as opposed to being centres where people gathered for specific purposes or for shelter during warfare is uncertain.

---

[13] Collis (1994) 127.
[14] Champion (2016) 154–6.

Around 100 BC hillforts went out of fashion. New forms of settlement started to emerge,[15] such as well defended farmsteads. The practice of cremation began. The cremation cemetery at Westhampnett in Sussex dates from the first half of the first century BC. Gold (which had been largely absent since the Bronze Age) reappeared amongst the luxury items used. Specialist production sites emerged, for example at Droitwich and Glastonbury. Along the south coast, trade developed with the Continent. Mediterranean goods began to arrive in quantity. It may be that during this period some of the peoples known to the Romans as Belgae and Atrebates (discussed below) migrated from the Continent to Britain. That migration may have been one of the causes of the instability and social changes which occurred around the turn of the century.

Danebury and Maiden Castle

Anyone who wants to catch up with Iron Age Britain but has only half a day to spare, would do well to visit Danebury hillfort[16] and the nearby Iron Age Museum.[17] The hillfort was created about 500 BC. It reached its final form in around 300 BC, with two formidable circular ramparts. You can still walk round what remains of the ramparts and enjoy some peaceful views of the surrounding woods and fields. The settlement area within the ramparts appears to have been well designed, with a main road running through the middle, clusters of circular houses and large rectangular granaries. All that now remains of those structures are post holes, as identified by excavation. Approximately 4,500 storage pits were dug out, where grain could be held over the winter. In the centre of the settlement some mysterious rectangular buildings once stood. These were probably a religious shrine.

The entrance area, which necessarily cut through the ramparts, was the weakest part of any hillfort. At Danebury there was a cunningly designed entrance on the eastern side with massive earthwork fortifications. The outlines still remain in place. Any invaders would have needed to batter down the huge outer gate and then the inner gate. Between these two gateways there was a narrow passage, along which the invaders had to pass. Many would have perished on the way. The defenders had a vast supply of sling stones with which they bombarded unwelcome visitors. Some 11,000 unused sling stones have been recovered from just one pit near the east gate.

It appears that soon after 100 BC one intrepid band of invaders was successful. The eastern gates were burnt and most of the people who had used the hillfort died or departed. After that cataclysmic event Danebury hillfort, like others in the region, seems to have been abandoned. No more gates were erected.

The remains of numerous dead bodies have been found in pits at Danebury. It by no means follows that those deceased were heroic defenders who met their match around 100 BC. Most of the pits are typical of Iron Age burial practices throughout the site's occupation.

Maiden Castle, just south of Dorchester, is the largest hillfort in Britain (Fig. 2.2). The complex of steep ramparts and ditches, which still surround it, present a challenge for the

---

[15] Creighton (2000) 4.
[16] For a fuller account of this hill fort, see Cunliffe (2011).
[17] 6 Church Close, Andover.

Figure 2.2 Maiden Castle hillfort. © Getty / Heritage Images / Contributor.

modern visitor. They presented an even greater challenge for ancient invaders. This massive hillfort had two well defended entrances, one at the east end and one at the west end. Both entrances involved winding paths between high banks. These enabled the occupants to hurl down rocks onto the heads of unwanted visitors. A collection of Iron Age skeletons from Maiden Castle is on display at the nearby Dorset County Museum. One skeleton has an arrowhead lodged in the spine. We do not know whether this unfortunate warrior was attacking or defending, but either way he suffered a painful death.

Oppida

In late Iron Age Europe, many communities established large, usually lowland, settlements. They had separate areas for specific functions. Caesar first encountered such places in Gaul and called them *oppida*, meaning towns. That name has stuck. Most historians and archaeologists use the term, even though the settlements were not towns in the modern sense. *Oppida* vary greatly across Europe in morphology, scale and function.[18] In France there were very large *oppida*, surrounded by complex ramparts. Elsewhere they were smaller. In Hungary, there were timber-faced ramparts. Some British *oppida* had dyke systems. Caesar used the word *oppida* generally to describe a wide range of urban and proto-urban settlements in France. There is little evidence that any of these settlements formed archaic states.[19]

---

[18] Woolf (1993) 223–34.
[19] Ralston (1988) 786–97.

Comparable centres developed in late Iron Age Britain, although they were not as large or densely populated as their Gallic counterparts. They were communal settlements with defined areas, perhaps for craft activity, occupation or religion. Some Iron Age *oppida*, such as Canterbury and Winchester, were built on the site of previous settlements, but many were not.[20] They were often situated in valley bottoms. Some towns in the south-east seem to have had residential enclosures for their élites. Excavating and mapping these *oppida* is difficult, because many later developments overlie them. Nevertheless, it can be seen that the LPRIA towns varied greatly in both size and character. Silchester, for example, was densely populated, whereas Stanwick covered a vast area and incorporated tracts of countryside within its ramparts. Also, as discussed below, there was a distinct change in settlement patterns during the LPRIA. In this chapter the word 'towns' or '*oppida*' will be used to denote LPRIA urban settlements, without repeating the above explanation.

Iron Age Britain was primarily a subsistence economy. The Britons grew wheat and barley. They stored grain in granaries with raised floors and in deep storage pits, as previously mentioned. They used iron ploughshares and reaping hooks. They also used stone implements, such as quern-stones for grinding and whetstones for sharpening. Many of these Iron Age tools now hang in museums, ready to be gazed at by bored school children.

Throughout the Iron Age, there was contact between the Celtic peoples on both sides of the Channel.[21] There was a shared architectural tradition of building round, rather than rectangular, structures. There were similarities in the styles of artefacts and personal ornament. People both in Britain and mainland Europe practised the ritual deposition of wealth, presumably to appease the gods. There is much evidence of shared cultural traditions, even in regions where there is no sign of goods imported from Europe.

The Celtic communities were in frequent conflict with one another, both in Britain and in mainland Europe. Hence the need for hillforts and town defences. Many of the weapons survive, including spears, javelins and swords. By the first century, Britons were also using chariots as an aid to more efficient warfare.[22] The battles must have been gruesome affairs. One spin-off from internecine warfare was the acquisition of slaves. By the late Iron Age these could be exported to the Continent and sold on the slave market.[23]

3. CONTACT WITH THE MEDITERRANEAN WORLD

From early times there was interchange between the peoples who lived along the Atlantic coasts of Spain, France and the British Isles. By the middle of the first millennium BC, Phoenician sailors were venturing as far north as Britain.[24] Trading routes between Britain and the Continent were well established before the Iron Age.

---

[20]Creighton and Fry (2016) 339.
[21]Champion (2016) 155–62.
[22]Hunter (2015a) describes one such chariot at 97.
[23]Strabo, *Geography* 4.5.2.
[24]Cunliffe (2004) 89–90.

The tin industry

Tin is a mineral resource of the south-west peninsula and the Britons exploited it. Tin, a constituent of bronze, was much in demand during the Bronze Age. There is no archaeological evidence of the extent of tin mining during the Bronze Age or the Iron Age, because later mining operations obliterated what went before. But there is literary evidence (identified below) that from the Iron Age onwards the communities of the south-west peninsula were producing and exporting tin in bulk. Apparently, they mined cassiterite, heated it in furnaces to extract the tin and fashioned the tin into ingots. They sold the ingots to traders who crossed the Channel from Armorica (north-west France).

In recent times, tin ingots from the Iron Age have been found in Devon and Cornwall. These include a large ingot[25] which was buried, no doubt for safekeeping, at Chun Castle. Numerous tin ingots have been dredged up from the seabed of Bigbury Bay. These appear to have come from a trading ship. The vessel probably hit a reef or perhaps set off in bad weather with an over-optimistic skipper.

We know from Herodotus that British tin made its way to Greece. It is possible that from the north coast of Armorica, tin ingots were sold down a line of traders across Europe. There were few major sources of tin in the Mediterranean region.[26] Herodotus, writing in the fifth century, makes just one dismissive reference to Britain:

> I do not know anything about the islands called Cassiterides ('Tin Islands'), from which we get our tin.[27]

The voyage of Pytheas

A couple of centuries later the Greeks became more curious and decided to find out where their tin came from. A scientist and adventurer called Pytheas, who lived in the Greek colony of Massilia (now Marseilles), set off on a famous voyage to the northern Ocean. His travels lasted three years. Pytheas 'discovered' Britain, which he circumnavigated. He also traversed much of the country on foot.[28]

In around 320 BC Pytheas published an account of his exploits in a book called *About the Ocean*. Sadly, *About the Ocean* has been lost. All that survives are some fragments of, or references to, Pytheas' book in the writings of Strabo, Pliny the Elder, Diodorus Siculus[29] and other ancient authors. Piecing together what Pytheas actually wrote, or might have written, is a joyful exercise, which has absorbed many classical scholars for years.[30]

According to Pliny, Pytheas assessed the length of our coastline as 4,875 Roman miles. According to Strabo, Pytheas assessed the length as about 40,000 stades. When these figures are

---

[25] Approximately 20 cm × 17 cm and 6 cm thick.
[26] Broodbank (2013) 69 and 492.
[27] 'οὔτε νήσους οἶδα Κασσιτερίδας ἐούσας, ἐκ τῶν ὁ κασσίτερος ἡμῖν φοιτᾷ': Herodotus, *The Histories* 3.115.1.
[28] For a clear and readable account of Pytheas' voyage, see Cunliffe (2002).
[29] In the mid-first century BC Diodorus Siculus wrote a universal history in 60 books, called *Library*, only part of which survives. It is clear that Diodorus takes much information directly or indirectly from Pytheas, although without express attribution.
[30] Roseman (2005) provides an excellent summary of the available extracts and fragments of Pytheas.

converted to modern kilometres, it can be seen that Pytheas' estimate was surprisingly accurate. This suggests that he was a careful and reliable observer. He also measured the height of the sun at a number of points where he stopped.

Pytheas landed in Cornwall, then called Belerion, and inspected the tin mines. He noted how the natives quarried cassiterite and melted it down to remove impurities. They worked the tin into pieces the size of knuckle-bones and transported them to an island off the coast called Ictis, which was accessible at low tide (probably St Michael's Mount or Mount Batten). Merchants from the Continent came to Ictis to purchase the tin ingots.[31]

Pytheas sailed the length of the south coast and noted that the region at the eastern end was called Kantion (now of course Kent). He sailed up the west coast of Britain to what is now Scotland. He also visited the Orkneys, the Hebrides, the Shetlands and other islands recorded by Pliny. One of these was Thule, described by Pliny as the most distant of all.[32] This lay six days' voyage to the north and was a place with no day in winter and no night in summer. Thule was probably Iceland but might have been Norway. The correct identification of Thule is a matter of much scholarly debate.

Pytheas noted that the inhabitants of our country were called Πρεταυοì (Pretanoi) meaning 'painted people' and that the original name of the country was Albion (because of the white cliffs on the south coast). He called the whole island Πρεττανική νῆσος (Prettanike nesos), meaning island of the painted people. Later authors changed the initial 'P' to a 'B', so that the Greeks came to know this country as Βρεττανική (Brettanike) or Βρεττανία (Brettania). When the Romans emerged as top nation, they adopted the Greek nomenclature. In this way, our island became 'Britannia' and its inhabitants became Britons.

As we shall see in later chapters, the term 'painted people' was re-used in Roman times, but it was applied only to people in Scotland, namely the Picts. 'Picti' is Latin for painted people. In origin, this seems to be a slang name that the Romans applied to strange-looking people in the north.[33]

4. BRITISH COMMUNITIES DURING THE LATE IRON AGE

Names and boundaries

The Celtic peoples[34] who lived in Britain during the Iron Age have not assisted us by writing down any account of themselves or even recording their names. The first systematic description of the peoples who lived in Britain is that provided by Ptolemy.[35] Ptolemy was an Egyptian astronomer and geographer, who lived in the second century AD.[36] In other words, Ptolemy comes onto the scene well after the end of the Iron Age. Despite that unfortunate delay, the

---

[31] Diodorus Siculus, *Library* 5.1–4. It is believed that this passage is based on Pytheas. Pliny's account of British tin on the island of 'Mictis' is hopelessly muddled and of little assistance.
[32] 'Ultima omnium quae memorantur Tyle': *Natural History* 4.104.
[33] Hunter (2007) 3–6.
[34] For further detail, see Cunliffe (2005) and Laycock (2008) chapter 1.
[35] *Geography* 2 is a detailed list of places and their inhabitants.
[36] Berggren and Jones (2000) 3–54. The plate at 128 is a reproduction of Ptolemy's map of Britain.

regions that Ptolemy describes fit reasonably well with the archaeological evidence. The distribution of pottery styles, funerary practices and deposition of coinage broadly coincide with Ptolemy's account of where the various communities lived. It is therefore helpful to use the names allocated by Ptolemy, regardless of whether this is what the inhabitants actually called themselves during the Iron Age.

It used to be conventional to refer to the groupings in different areas of Britain as 'tribes', but we must be cautious about the use of that term.[37] The recorded descriptions of Britain in the late Iron Age come entirely from Roman writers. They were looking at Britain from the outside and through Roman eyes. They were seeking to make sense of a confused situation. Naturally the Romans expected to find bounded groups and kings. That is how they interpreted what they found. The reality was probably much less tidy. Boundaries were fluid and could have shifted rapidly. Different groups would have migrated or intermarried. It is a mistake to think of the various communities as distinct ethnic groups. Each of the so-called 'tribes' contained many sub-groups and separate strands. Leaders would have emerged or been overthrown, sometimes in short order. Power struggles or warfare between neighbouring leaders would have determined the extent of their competing dominions. When the Romans arrived, they fixed the boundaries as they found them for the purpose of creating the *civitas* system (to be discussed later). It is therefore problematic to retroject what the Romans have described back into the Iron Age.

The approximate locations of British communities, as described by Ptolemy and supplemented by Roman historians in the years following the conquest, are shown on Map 2.1. This is a useful working document, provided that it is appreciated that the boundaries were fluid. As previously stated, there is a broad correlation between the literary sources and the archaeological evidence concerning the LPRIA.

Power and wealth

When talking about leaders, Caesar sometimes refers to *reges* meaning kings, and sometimes to *principes*, meaning a broader aristocracy.[38] These would have been the élite groups. They must have used or displayed many of the luxury items that have recently come to light in late Iron Age hoards and graves.

The coinage[39] of western Europe appears to derive from gold staters issued by Philip II of Macedon (359–326 BC). These coins showed the head of Apollo on the obverse and a two-horse chariot on the reverse, since horses were a symbol of wealth and power in the ancient world. The earliest coins minted in Gaul were based on the Macedonian currency. From there regional styles developed. Gallo-Belgic gold coins started to appear in the south-east corner of Britain during the mid-second century BC. Towards the end of the second century the production of coins in Britain began. Horses sometimes featured on coins, denoting kingly authority. Gold coins and gold torcs became the emblems of power and wealth. The élite groups who emerged in late second-century Britain appear to have worn gold torcs and distributed gold coinage.

---

[37] Millett (2007) 138–9.
[38] Creighton (2000) chapter 4.
[39] Creighton (2000) chapter 5.

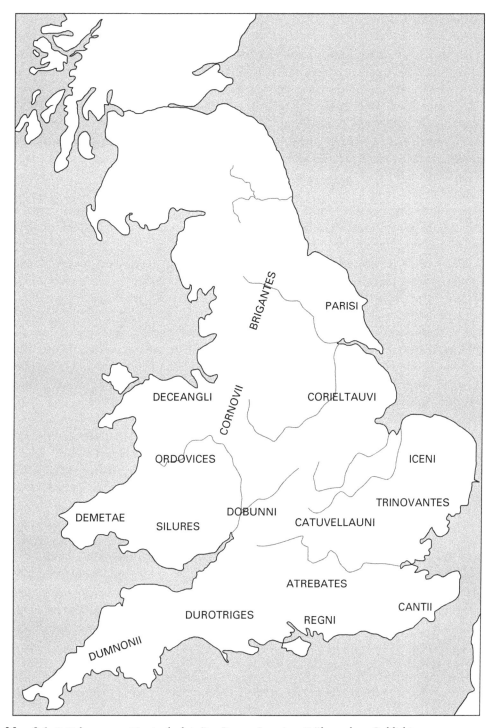

Map 2.1 British communities in the late Pre-Roman Iron Age. © Bloomsbury Publishing.

(i) South-east England

In the Iron Age, as in modern times, south-east England seems to have been the most prosperous part of Britain. Perhaps this is not surprising, as the same geographical factors were in play then as now, namely proximity to the Continent and the convenience of the River Thames as a trading route. Four loose groupings inhabited what is now south-east England: Cantii, Atrebates, Trinovantes and Catuvellauni. Cunliffe describes these four communities as the 'core'.[40] They all minted coins in the LPRIA. Although it is Rome-centric and not universally accepted, Cunliffe's model provides a convenient structure for this account.

The Cantii or the Cantiaci occupied what is now Kent. From early times they had regular contact with Gaul, which lay just across the straits. They progressively adopted continental practices, including cremating the dead and making pottery on wheels. The Cantii started to issue coins in the late second century BC. These were made of bronze with simple patterns, hardly a collector's item.

The Cantii established *oppida* at Rochester and Canterbury. There were no doubt other towns as well. Caesar tells us that in 54 BC Kent was divided into four districts, each with its own king.[41] Apparently, the kings were called Cingetorix, Carvilius, Taximagulus and Segovax. Each probably headed a separate clan or sub-group.

The Atrebates occupied much of what are now Sussex, Hampshire, Surrey, Berkshire and Wiltshire. They were linked to a group of the same name on the other side of the Channel. It is likely that the British Atrebates were an offshoot from the Gallic community, having migrated across the Channel during the late Iron Age. The Atrebates started minting coins in about 70 BC. The Atrebates included two other groups, the Belgae and the Regni.

According to Caesar, the Belgae were one of the three major tribes of Gaul.[42] They occupied what are now Belgium and north-east France. Caesar states that some of the Belgae relocated from Gaul to Britain.[43] This may be correct,[44] although it was probably part of more general population movements rather than a single group migrating en bloc. Possibly the élites had territories on both sides of the Channel. There were similarities of material culture between south-east Britain and the Belgic area of Gaul in the late Iron Age: currency bars and hoards containing iron objects have been found in both areas, as have pedestal urns with horizontal ridges.[45] Tacitus, writing a century after Caesar, makes no reference to the Belgae in his account of Britain. The British Belgae settled in Hampshire and established a town at Winchester.

The Regni were further to the east, probably with their main centre at Fishbourne/Chichester. Late Iron Age dykes defended the area and there was the convenience of Fishbourne harbour. A large quantity of pre-conquest imported material was found during excavations before the new A27 road was built.[46] This included Gallo-Belgic finewares and late Augustan amphorae. The Fishbourne *oppidum* probably included élite residences.

---

[40]Cunliffe (2005) chapter 7.
[41]*Gallic War* 5.22.
[42]'Gallia est omnis divisa in partes tres, quarum unam incolunt Belgae...': *Gallic War* 1.1.
[43]*Gallic War* 5.12.
[44]Cunliffe (2005) 126–7.
[45]Hachmann (1976) 117–32.
[46]Cunliffe et al. (1996) xi–xii, 96–7, 122–8.

In about 25 BC the Atrebates established an unenclosed settlement at Silchester, then known as *Calleva Atrebatum*. '*Calleva*' is a Celtic word meaning 'wooded place'.[47] This indicates that there was no previous settlement there. Some twenty-five years later (while one or two important things were happening in Palestine) the Atrebates built an earth rampart around the perimeter, to create an enclosed *oppidum*. They laid out a road grid, aligned south-east/north-west. The roads did not quite intersect at right angles, which annoys some archaeologists. Lane 3, a major arterial route leading out of the town, intersects with Lane 1 at an angle of 104°.[48] Silchester was accessible from the south coast.

The Roman town of Silchester and the Iron Age remains that lie beneath it have been the subject of successive investigations and excavations over the last two centuries. The most important work is that which Michael Fulford and his colleagues from Reading University have been carrying out since 1974. John Creighton and Robert Fry of Reading University have published a comprehensive review of all the work done at Silchester since the nineteenth century.[49] Chapter 11 draws together their conclusions about the original Iron Age town and provides a clear picture of Silchester life in the late Iron Age. Roman and Gallic tradesmen were doing business there.[50] The town was densely populated. The residents consumed plenty of meat, possibly more than was good for them. Their diet included beef, pork, birds and fowl. The wealthier denizens enjoyed tucking into oysters and imported Mediterranean foods, accompanied of course with fine wines. And the washing up was no problem – slaves did it.

The Trinovantes and Catuvellauni lived to the north of the Thames. The Trinovantes occupied Essex. The Catuvellauni occupied Hertfordshire plus a large swathe of territory to the north and west. Both these communities traded with the Continent, using the Thames and its basin. Like the Cantii they adopted the practice of cremation. They started issuing coins in about 60 BC.

The population of the Trinovantes dropped sharply in the first century BC, for reasons which are not clear.[51] Despite that misfortune, they established a substantial town at *Camulodunon* which meant 'High place of Camulos', the Celtic war god. This was a well-designed *oppidum*, with defined areas for religion, craft activity, occupation and élite residence. The town is now called Colchester and is the seat of Essex University, famed for its excellence in social science. The ancient war god must be furious.

The principal town of the Catuvellauni was originally at Wheathampstead. In about 10 BC they established a new town, *Verlamion*,[52] on the banks of the river Ver.

As discussed in Chapter 4 below, in the LPRIA south-east Britain developed closer links with Rome. Some commentaries suggest that Roman troops may have been stationed at Gosbecks Fort, near Colchester, or at Fishbourne before the Claudian invasion.[53] There is no firm evidence of this. But even if that is correct, modest support for friendly rulers or discreet

---

[47] Fulford (2016) 23.
[48] The road names have been assigned by modern scholars. The original residents would have devised more imaginative names. That would not be difficult.
[49] Creighton and Fry (2016).
[50] Creighton and Fry (2016) 368.
[51] Sealey (2016) 30–55.
[52] *Verlamio* appears on coins minted there. That is probably the locative of *Verlamion*: see Niblett and Thompson (2005) 24.
[53] Creighton (2006) chapter 2 and (2001).

preparations for a future invasion do not mean that Rome controlled south-east Britain before AD 43.

The British élites may have seen interaction with mainland Europe as an opportunity to expand their own power and influence. They developed new alliances and trade routes. They enjoyed Mediterranean produce and displayed Roman luxury items. A mid-first century BC burial at Welwyn Garden City contains Roman silver cups and other high status imports.

(ii) Dorset and the Midlands

Four communities formed a semi-circle around the groupings in the south-east. These were the Durotriges, Dobunni, Iceni and Corieltauvi. Cunliffe describes these four communities as the 'periphery', but their culture was just as rich and diverse as the so-called 'core' communities.[54] They all minted coins in the first century BC.

The Durotriges occupied Dorset and part of Somerset. With their territory running along the south coast, they were well placed for cross-Channel trade. In the first century BC, they had a thriving port first at Hengistbury Head and later at Poole Harbour. Abundant evidence of cross-Channel trade has been found in these areas. Amongst much else, the Durotriges imported amphorae of wine from Italy.

The Durotriges mined silver and lead from the Mendips in pre-Roman times. They may have mined iron ore at sites in Dorset, including Hengistbury Head, or possibly they bought in iron ore. They acquired copper and tin ore from the West Country. The Durotriges operated smelting works. They also developed a pottery industry, using clay from the Poole Harbour area. All in all, the Durotriges ran a thriving export business. Strabo in book 4 of his *Geography* gives an account that fits neatly with the findings of archaeologists.[55] Strabo states that Britain was exporting grain, cattle, gold, silver, iron, hides, slaves and hunting dogs.

The Dobunni[56] were based in Gloucestershire, as well as parts of Somerset, Wiltshire and Oxfordshire. By the late first century they were trading in iron, as evidenced by finds of iron currency bars. They were producing pottery in the Malvern area. There was also long-distance pottery exchange. The Dobunni were generally dispersed and may have lacked any rigid hierarchy. Their key centre was at Bagendon, but even that was small and relatively late. At Worcester, a large Iron Age ditch has been found with a cluster of Celtic coins nearby. The Dubonni may have built a modest enclosed town there, linked to the River Severn.

The Corieltauvi occupied the regions of Warwickshire, Lincolnshire and Leicestershire. They too lacked any major towns. Their territory was dominated by agricultural communities, although there was also some mining and extraction of iron. The main centres of the Corieltauvi were at Leicester and possibly Sleaford.

Between 2000 and 2009 a massive collection of late Iron Age coins came to light at Hallaton in Leicestershire.[57] The Corieltauvi had minted over 4,000 of those coins. The hoards also included a silver-gilt Roman helmet, a silver bowl, ingots, jewellery and other valuables. Some

---

[54]Cunliffe (2005) chapter 8.
[55]*Geography* 4.5.2.
[56]See generally Moore (2007) 79–102.
[57]For a full account, see Score (2011).

of the luxury items are evidence of trade with the Roman Empire or perhaps were diplomatic gifts. The site may have been a religious sanctuary. It was not an *oppidum*.

The Iceni occupied Norfolk and much of Suffolk. It is not known for certain where their main centre was. Their coins were particularly ornate, often depicting horses or boars, but the Iceni's main claim to fame must be their decorative metal work. Many hoards have come to light, containing gold and electrum torcs, arm rings and similar ornaments. The most spectacular hoards were at Snettisham, as noted in Section 1 above. The Iceni seem to have imported fewer luxury goods from the Continent than neighbouring communities. This is unsurprising, given the skill of their own craftsmen.

A mid/late Iron Age centre has come to light at Fison Way, Thetford, which comprises a series of enclosures covering a wide area.[58] This was probably a religious centre. It is typical of significant late Iron Age sites that cannot be classified as *oppida*.

(iii) The West Country and Wales

The Dumnonii occupied the Devon/Cornwall peninsula. They never minted coins. The settlement pattern in the south-west peninsula differed from the rest of Britain. People tended to live in enclosed settlements. In Cornwall, these took the form of small circular enclosures, which are now called rounds. A large late Iron Age nucleated site has been found near the coast at Seaton in south-east Devon, which has some of the features of an *oppidum*.

The coastlines of Cornwall and Devon have rugged headlands jutting out into the sea. From early times the Dumnonii defended the landward sides of such headlands with banks and ditches, creating what are now known as cliff castles. These provided excellent defences for the few people who lived there, but were remote from most of the residential enclosures. So their purpose is uncertain. Cunliffe suggests that they may have served as sacred locations.[59] The Celtic peoples who occupied Armorica built similar cliff castles on their headlands.

As mentioned in Section 3 above, the people of the south-west peninsula were mining and processing tin from the Bronze Age onwards.[60] They developed a successful export trade, although seemingly without the use of money. Tin production remained a staple industry of Cornwall for some three thousand years. Sadly, the tin industry came to an end in 1998, when the last tin mine closed.[61] Tourism, boosted by 'Poldark' films, is now Cornwall's main source of wealth.

The five communities that lived in Wales are marked on Map 2.1. From early times they constructed hillforts inland. They built cliff castles along the coast, similar to those on the south-west peninsula. They did not issue coins or create *oppida*.

(iv) The north

The north of England did not come under Roman control until about AD 75. On one view, therefore, the LPRIA continued in that region until late in the first century AD.

---

[58] Gregory (1991).
[59] Cunliffe (2005) 288–9.
[60] Newman (2016) 18–19.
[61] *Economist*, 20 February 2016, p. 25, 'Cornwall's economy, winter sun'.

The disparate groups that occupied northern England were known to the Romans as Brigantes. That meant that 'the high people', denoting that they were hill dwellers or, possibly, that they were overlords.[62] According to Ptolemy, their territory stretched from sea to sea. Tacitus tersely described them as 'the community of the Brigantes, which is said to be the largest in the province'.[63] The Brigantes were probably a confederation of smaller communities; or perhaps there was a group of communities which the Brigantes dominated. The constituent communities included the Carvetii, whose territory was in the region of the Solway Firth. Possibly there was a community in southern Northumberland with a name like 'Corio', which gave rise to the Roman town name *Coria* (Corbridge). The territory as a whole is sometimes referred to as 'Brigantia'.

In the middle or late Iron Age, people started to enclose the landscape, creating field systems and trackways.[64] The fields were probably used for both arable cultivation and keeping livestock; the trackways provided access to the fields and routes for driving cattle. Being essentially agrarian communities, the people of the north did not mint their own coinage. A few Iron Age and pre-conquest Roman coins have turned up in Yorkshire, presumably brought in by traders.

Stanwick was the principal settlement of the Brigantes. This was a large enclosure (about 750 acres) defended by massive earthworks. It contained an area for habitation with numerous roundhouses and a separate section for craft activity. Much imported pottery has been found at Stanwick, some from southern England and some from the Continent. A hoard of fine metalwork has also been recovered, including a sword, horse fittings and chariot fittings. The Brigantian élite clearly enjoyed wealth and a comfortable lifestyle. For further details of Stanwick, see the Online Appendix.

A major late Iron Age settlement at Scotch Corner came to light during soil stripping for constructing the A1 Motorway in 2014–2015.[65] It is possible that Stanwick and Scotch Corner represented the two ends of a wider Iron Age settlement complex, which flourished before there was a Roman presence in the region.

The territory of the Parisi lay to the north of the Humber estuary. They adopted the practice of burying the dead together with carts or parts of carts. This unusual procedure is known to archaeologists as 'Arras culture', because the first such grave was found at Arras Farm in East Yorkshire. The Parisii in Gaul (who ultimately gave their name to the French capital, Paris) adopted the same method of burial. The similarity of names and burial practices makes it likely that the Parisi in Britain had migrated from France during the Iron Age. Quite why they chose to settle in Yorkshire is unclear. Possibly they had an independent streak and disapproved of southerners.

The communities of Scotland successfully resisted incorporation into the Roman Empire. The details of their habitations, culture and funerary practices are less relevant for present purposes.

---

[62] Ottaway (2013) 52.
[63] 'Brigantium civitatem, quae numerosissima provinciae totius perhibetur': *Agricola*, 17.2.
[64] Ottaway (2013) 52–70.
[65] Fell (2017), 14–21.

5. ROME'S PERCEPTION OF BRITAIN IN THE LATE IRON AGE

To the Romans Britain was a distant land about which little was known. It lay beyond the frontiers of their world. The Romans regarded everyone beyond those frontiers as barbarians and were inclined to exaggerate their strangeness. The accounts that Roman writers gave of foreign peoples often included fictional elements.[66] There are elements of fiction in the descriptions of Britain given by Caesar, Strabo and Pliny.

The poets

The poets saw Rome as the centre of civilization and the more distant countries, especially Britain, as places of mystery and barbarism. Virgil in his Eclogues described Britons as being 'utterly separated from the whole world'.[67] Horace described the Britons as *ultimos*, meaning the most distant people in the world.[68] Even so, he believed that Britain had no business to be independent: it needed to be incorporated into the Roman Empire like everybody else.[69]

Caesar and Strabo

Julius Caesar, unlike the poets, took the trouble to visit Britain. He invaded it, which was Caesar's usual form of visitation. He recorded that much of Britain was densely wooded. It was inhabited by tribes who were in regular conflict with one another. Caesar observed that many of these tribes took their names from their places of origin on the Continent.[70] He added that no-one travelled to Britain without good cause and even visiting traders only knew the coast.

Strabo, in his *Geography*, noted that Britain was an island with much rain and fog. He described the Britons as being taller than the Celts on the Continent and having darker hair. They had powerful chieftains and fought from chariots. 'The forests are their cities.'[71] They cut out circular enclosures in the woods as temporary homes for themselves and their cattle.

Caesar described the indigenous people whom he was about to attack in his *Gallic War*.[72] The men lived in communes, sharing wives. They had long hair but shaved the rest of their bodies. For money they used bronze coins, gold coins and iron rods. They produced their own tin and iron but imported bronze from the Continent. The inhabitants of Kent (*Cantium*) were far more civilized than the others. Finally, the Britons dyed themselves with woad, which produced a blue colour and made them look fearsome in battle. This reference to the Britons painting their bodies was a repetition of what Pytheas had recorded three centuries earlier.

Caesar's statement that the Britons used iron rods as currency sounds surprising. Even in the Iron Age metal bars would hardly be convenient to carry round as small change. Nevertheless, many iron rods of a standard size have been found in the south-east England. A

---

[66] Woolf (2011) chapter 4.
[67] 'penitus toto divisos orbe Britannos': *Eclogues* 1.66.
[68] *Odes* 1.35.29–30.
[69] *Epode* 7.7–8.
[70] *Gallic War* 5.12.
[71] 'πόλεις δ' αὐτῶν εἰσιν οἱ δρυμοί': Strabo, *Geography* 4.5.2.
[72] 5.12–14.

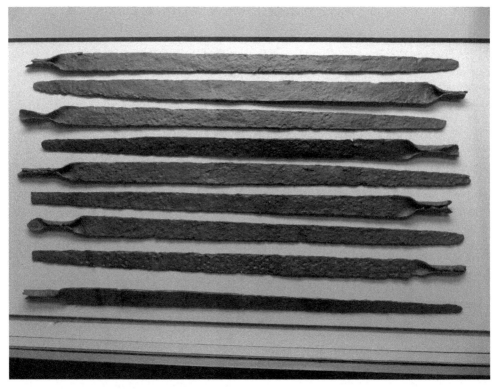

Figure 2.3 Iron currency bars – perhaps not convenient small change. From the Museum of the Iron Age, Andover. © Geoffrey May.

hoard of 21 such bars was found in a pit at Danebury. They each weigh about 450 grams and are long enough to make several small tools, as shown in Fig. 2.3. The most likely explanation for Caesar's comment is that the Britons principally used iron bars for manufacture, but they sometimes bartered them. The ends of the bars were twisted, to demonstrate the good quality and workability of the iron. The thinness of the bars was also a sign of good quality.

Agriculture

Caesar stated that the Britons had farm buildings close together and cultivated the surrounding lands. Their cattle were plentiful. Most of those Britons who lived inland did not sow corn; instead they lived on meat and milk. Tacitus, writing somewhat later, stated that Britain produced abundant crops because of the high rainfall.[73]

Druids

The most prestigious group of people at that time both in Britain and Gaul were the Druids. Three ancient authors have described their practices, namely Caesar, Strabo and Pliny the

---

[73]He also notes that olives and vines cannot grow here because it is too cold: *Agricola* 12.

Elder. According to Caesar, Druids originated in Britain and anyone wishing to study their practices should go to Britain. So, the first overseas students whom Britain took in were trainee Druids.

The Druids presided over religious ceremonies and sacrifices. These sometimes centred on oak trees and mistletoe.[74] The ceremonies often involved human sacrifice. According to Strabo, one favoured procedure was to stick a dagger into the victim's back and then to divine the future from the way in which the subject struggled as he died. For this and other reasons, it was unwise to fall out with the Druids.

The Druids also sat as judges, dealing with criminal offences and civil disputes. Anyone who did not abide by their decisions was banned from sacrifices, denied access to justice and effectively ostracized. Sometimes the Druids even arbitrated between warring tribes. They also provided education for the young. All Druids underwent lengthy training and learnt 'a large number of verses'.[75] Apparently, they believed in immortality of the soul: on death the soul passed from one person to another.

According to Caesar and Strabo, the Druids were held in high esteem. They were exempt from military service and from any liability for taxes. The Chief Druid had authority over them all. As discussed in Chapter 19 below, religion may be viewed as a means of naturalizing power structures. In Iron Age Britain the Druidic system appears to have sustained an élite priestly class and also to have reinforced the authority of the leaders.

Despite the descriptions provided by ancient authors, our knowledge of Druidism as a religion is limited. Caesar, Strabo and Pliny the Elder were all looking at Druidism through Roman eyes. They were reporting what others had told them. Even Caesar did not witness any Druidic ceremonies. Furthermore, these writers were interpreting what they were told against the background of their own religion, which was formalized and complex.

It is reasonable to assume that Druidism, like other primitive religions, was centred on the natural world. Away from the formal ceremonies where victims were butchered, the Britons would have sought out their own ways of propitiating the gods. These seem to have included burying animal parts as offerings to the gods of the earth.[76]

Summary

The accounts of Britain by Roman authors contain some useful material, but must all be viewed with caution. The authors had an agenda, namely the magnification of Rome's achievements. The portrayal of conquered foes as noble warriors (e.g. the statue of the Dying Gaul) adds lustre to Rome's victories. This is part of a long tradition by which classical culture constructs the 'otherness' of the barbarian world.

---

[74] Pliny the Elder, *Natural History* 16.95.
[75] 'Magnum ibi numerum versuum ediscere dicuntur.' Caesar, *Gallic War* 6.14.
[76] Cunliffe (2011) 146–7.

The findings of archaeology tell us more about LPRIA Britain than do the writings of either Caesar or Strabo. It is clear that local craftsmen were producing good quality pottery. They also manufactured fine luxury items, such as gold neck rings. Britons of the mid-first century manufactured chariots to a novel design, which they used in local conflicts and would soon use to resist foreign invasion. They also made fine decorative fitments for their chariots and horses. Caesar was unfair in characterizing Britons generally as barbaric tribesmen, who had little by way of culture.

CHAPTER 3
THE FIRST INVASIONS: JULIUS CAESAR

1. Introduction

2. The Invasion in 55 BC

3. The Invasion in 54 BC

4. Review of Caesar's campaigns in Britain

1. INTRODUCTION

Between 58 and 51 BC Julius Caesar was campaigning in Gaul with spectacular success. He conquered effectively the whole of modern France and Belgium. In the hope of greater glory, he also set his sights upon Britain, which lay only one day's voyage to the north.

Caesar wrote an account of his exploits which he entitled – accurately, if somewhat unimaginatively – *Gallic War*. As Mary Beard points out, we are extremely lucky to have an autobiographical account written by one of Britain's first invaders. Even if that account is biased and culturally loaded, it still deserves to be considered with the utmost care.[1]

Caesar's two invasions of Britain have left little trace, apart from what might possibly be the remains of Caesar's camp at Ebbsfleet. A number of coin hoards were hidden in southern Britain in the mid-first century BC. These may have been a reaction to the Roman invasion,[2] but coin hoards do not tell us the story of what happened. For that we have only Caesar's narrative.

We can assume that Caesar's account was accurate in its essentials. If it were not so, as Caesar well knew, there were plenty of veterans still around who would contradict it. On the other hand, as discussed in Section 4 below, Caesar was clearly set upon presenting his own conduct, his motives and his achievements in the most favourable light possible. This chapter is based upon Caesar's account, but it takes issue with some of the spin that he placed upon events.

In this and later chapters, the term 'Britons' will be used as a convenient shorthand for the indigenous peoples of Britain. In reality, of course, they comprised many disparate and fluid groupings. They were certainly not a unified people.

---

[1] Beard (2013) 205.
[2] Cunliffe (2005) 139–40.

2. THE INVASION IN 55 BC

Preparation

The Romans launched their first attack on Britain in the summer of 55 BC. Caesar states the following reason for the invasion: he 'understood' support for his enemies on the Continent had come from that region.[3] The background to this statement may be that Britons were serving as mercenaries in Gaul. Coinage evidence suggests that there was a significant inflow of money to Britain during this period. Even so, that hardly justified (if justification was intended) an attack upon an inhospitable island beyond the boundary of the Roman Empire. There can be little doubt that Caesar's motives were nakedly political, namely to enhance his reputation as an outstanding general who pushed out the frontiers of the Empire. There was also probably a financial aspect. Caesar needed any booty that he could capture in order to finance his burgeoning political career. In the ancient world, wars of aggression were perfectly normal. The notion that only defence and – *in extremis* – regime change may justify warfare is a modern concept.

As a first step Caesar sent a soldier, Volusenus, in a single warship to reconnoitre the coast.[4] While Volusenus was away, the Romans were gathering their task force for the invasion. The Britons got wind of what was afoot. There must have been much anxious debate within the farms and *oppida* of southern Britain: some communities resolved to stand firm and repel the invaders, while others hastily sent representatives offering to support the Romans. Caesar welcomed these overtures. He sent the representatives back together with a man called Commius. Commius was a protegé of Caesar and a leader of the Atrebates in Gaul. The Atrebates had branches on both sides of the Channel.

Commius duly arrived in Britain as Caesar's ambassador, with clear instructions: to visit the tribes in south-east Britain, to inform them of the forthcoming invasion and to invite their prompt submission to Rome. Unfortunately, the Atrebates in southern Britain did not look kindly upon their Gallic cousins. If Commius was expecting a courteous reception, he was soon disabused of that idea. The Britons threw him into chains and held him as prisoner.

The Roman task force assembled at the 'Itian Port' (in the region of Boulogne). The force comprised the Seventh and Tenth Legions carried on 80 transport ships. A further 18 ships were to follow, carrying cavalry. By the time the task force was ready it was late August, which would allow very little time for effective campaigning, since the soldiers needed to return to Gaul before winter. Nevertheless, Caesar still went ahead. He says that he thought it would be worthwhile to explore the terrain and to see the character of the people, so that he would be better prepared for a full invasion next year.

Invasion

On or around 26 August the Romans set sail and arrived off the coast of Kent 'at about the fourth hour of the day'. The invaders saw their new foes ranged along the cliff tops above them,

---

[3] 'omnibus fere Gallicis bellis hostibus nostris inde sumministrata auxilia intelligebat': Caesar, *Gallic War* 4.20.
[4] Caesar, *Gallic War* 4.21.

ready to hurl down missiles.[5] Whatever may have been the merits of Roman civilization, seemingly the Britons did not wish to be part of it.

A landing in the region of Dover was not practicable. Drawing on the local knowledge gathered by Volusenus, the fleet sailed north-east for about seven kilometres and then ran aground somewhere to the north of Deal, where the beach was flat.

The Britons, who had been following the Roman fleet attentively, were ready to meet the newcomers. They sent forward cavalry and chariots to resist the invasion. They also hurled javelins.

The Roman soldiers started clambering out of their ships, heavily armed and dropping into unknown waters. Then they hesitated. Many must have wondered why they were there at all. Caesar hastily ordered some lighter vessels to row round to the enemy's exposed flank and to pound the shore with slings and arrows. This drove the Britons back a short way.

According to Caesar,[6] the hero of the moment then came forward, namely the standard bearer of the Tenth Legion. He offered up a prayer to the Gods (who could always be counted on to support the Roman cause) and then leapt into the water bearing his standard towards the enemy. At the same time, he called on his comrades to do their duty. The other soldiers duly followed, and the invasion proceeded. Caesar probably embroidered this account of the landing, to emphasize traditional Roman virtues.

There was a period of close fighting in the water. The Britons had the advantage of knowing the beach and the shoreline. The Romans struggled in some disorder and against stiff opposition to reach dry land. Once ashore, the Roman military machine swung into action: the well-disciplined soldiers soon routed the Britons. Luckily for those natives, the Roman cavalry had not yet arrived and so there was no effective pursuit.

The Britons now realized they were in difficulty. They sent representatives to Caesar seeking peace.[7] In addition, they hastily released the unfortunate Commius from his chains and sent him along as part of the delegation. Caesar graciously agreed to forgive the Britons for their 'imprudence' in resisting the Roman invasion, although he required that hostages be provided. Thus forgiven, the Britons peacefully returned to their fields. But not for long.

Three days later there was a violent storm, which smashed into Caesar's ships (some at anchor and some on land) and caused extensive damage.[8] The storm also prevented the arrival of Roman cavalry, which were still attempting to cross from Gaul. The Roman task force was now trapped in Britain, with no means of transport and no provisions for the approaching winter.

The Britons saw their chance. Abandoning their fields, they mustered for war. The Romans meanwhile were primarily focused on repairing the extensive damage to their ships. The Seventh Legion was out collecting corn in what Caesar calls the usual manner (i.e. stealing crops planted by other people), when the Britons attacked. Additional troops came to aid the Seventh Legion, but their position was perilous: the Romans were crowded together while the enemy hurled javelins into their midst.

---

[5] Caesar, *Gallic War* 4.23.
[6] Caesar, *Gallic War* 4.25.
[7] Caesar, *Gallic War* 4.27.
[8] Caesar, *Gallic War* 4.29.

British horsemen and chariots surrounded the legionaries and attacked. The chariots rode rapidly hither and thither, with the Britons leaping off for hand-to-hand fighting and then darting back onto them.[9] This tactic caused confusion amongst the Romans. Caesar ordered a rapid retreat to the safety of the camp.

The Romans once more turned their attention to ship repairs. They also acquired some thirty horsemen whom Commius brought over from Gaul. It is not clear from Caesar's narrative precisely when Commius did this. The Britons, meanwhile, sent messengers to other communities, seeking help. The response was favourable, and resistance fighters congregated in growing numbers.

The scene was set for a final battle. This time the Romans were better prepared and not taken by surprise. In addition to the infantry, they now had the cavalry that Commius had brought over. Although probably outnumbered by the enemy, the Romans prevailed by dint of their superior discipline and training. The Britons fled the battlefield.

Later that day British representatives arrived petitioning for peace. By now it was mid-October. There was a pressing need to return to Gaul before winter. Caesar therefore agreed to the proposed peace, although he demanded an increased number of hostages. The Romans then limped back to Gaul in their damaged vessels.[10]

It is difficult to see that Rome achieved anything useful from this first foray into Britain. The taking of hostages was hardly an assurance of future co-operation. But the picture that Caesar painted in his despatches to the Senate was rather more upbeat. It has generally been the practice of generals, both in ancient and modern warfare, to emphasize the successful aspects of their campaigns.[11] The Senate was delighted with what it understood Caesar to have achieved in Britain. It ordered a public thanksgiving of 20 days.

3. THE INVASION IN 54 BC

A more substantial task force

During the winter of 55 to 54 BC Caesar prepared for a large-scale invasion. He had broader ships constructed with a shallower draught, which would hold more men and be able to sail closer to the shore.

The task force that assembled for the second expedition to Britain was substantially larger and more formidable than the previous one. It comprised five legions, two thousand cavalry and a fleet of about eight hundred ships.[12] As before, they gathered at the Itian Port, but this time in early July.

The armada set sail at sunset on or about the 6 July. They made steady progress through the evening, but during the night the wind dropped and the ships started drifting eastwards. At dawn the British coastline could be seen far off to the west. The soldiers resorted to rowing.

---

[9] Caesar, *Gallic War* 4.33.
[10] 'infirmis navibus': Caesar *Gallic War* 4.36.
[11] See e.g. Max Hastings (2011) for many instances of this in the Second World War.
[12] According to Caesar this included some private ships as well as the purpose-built warships.

The Britons gathered in large numbers along the shoreline, hoping to see off the Roman invaders as they had done before. The fact that they had handed over a few hostages was neither here nor there. They had no intention of giving in. As the armada drew closer, however, the Britons were horrified by the sheer number of ships bearing down upon them. Fighting on the beaches no longer seemed a realistic proposition. They therefore withdrew inland,[13] where they would have the advantage of superior local knowledge.

The task force probably landed on the Ebbsfleet peninsula. This is now about 1 kilometre inland, but two thousand years ago Pegwell Bay lay on the east side and the Wantsum Channel on the west side of the peninsula. In 2017 archaeologists from Leicester University found the remains of a large enclosure there with a defensive ditch around it.[14] The presence of iron weapons, including a Roman javelin (*pilum*), suggests that it was a military base. It can be dated to the first century BC from pottery fragments and radiocarbon dating. This might possibly have been the landing site in 54 BC and the location where Caesar hauled his ships ashore for repair after the storm discussed below.

The task force landed at about midday. This time there was no enemy in sight. Instead the beach lay empty and there were only the sounds of an English summer. After disembarking, Caesar left Quintus Atrius with a detachment of soldiers and cavalry to guard the fleet, while the main army marched inland to attack the Britons.

The British came into view on high ground above a river,[15] drawn up for battle with their usual array of cavalry and chariots. Somewhat optimistically, they bore down on the legions and charged. The Roman cavalry forced them back. The Britons then retreated into the nearby woods, where they established themselves in a makeshift fortress. This was a clearing with all its entrances barred by felled trees, from which the defenders could dart out in small groups to attack the foe.

The forest fortress was not an easy position to attack. So the Seventh Legion adopted a 'tortoise' formation.[16] In other words, the front rank held their shields in front of them and all the other soldiers held shields locked over their heads. The Romans approached inside an impregnable shell. The javelins and other missiles hurled down simply bounced off. This was not good news for the Britons, who abandoned their stronghold and retreated further inland.

Another storm

That night another violent storm struck the Roman fleet at anchor causing mayhem: many vessels crashed into one another.[17] As a result of the storm and the tides nearly all the fleet was washed up on the shore. Some forty ships suffered irreparable damage. The others were badly battered but capable of repair.

Caesar returned to the naval camp and inspected the damage. He set some of the soldiers to work on repairs. He also summoned help from the Continent. After that, he went back to his troops in the field.

---

[13] Caesar, *Gallic War* 5.8.
[14] Fitzpatrick (2018) 26–32.
[15] Probably the Stour.
[16] Caesar, *Gallic War* 5.9.
[17] Caesar, *Gallic War* 5.10.

Correspondence with Rome

Even in the midst of campaigning, Caesar kept his finger on the pulse in Rome and corresponded with important people on the home front. Cicero (the Roman politician, orator and writer) sent a book of his verses for the mighty warrior to peruse between battles. Caesar tactfully replied that the first part was excellent.[18] Cicero's brother, Quintus, was an officer serving under Caesar and he too sent letters home. One of the many remarkable achievements of the Roman Republic was that it established a transport and communication system across Europe at the end of the Iron Age which facilitated such correspondence.

Back in Rome Cicero wrote as follows to his friend Atticus in July 54:

> The result of the war against Britain is eagerly awaited ... But we now know that there is no silver on the island. Nor is there any prospect of booty other than slaves. I don't imagine you will expect any of them to be accomplished in literature or music![19]

This was a dubious piece of stereotyping, which no politician would dare to try now.

In August 54 Cicero wrote to his brother Quintus, who was then probably encamped on some rain-sodden sand dune surveying the wreckage of his fleet. This was a chatty letter with lots of news from Rome. Cicero described debates in the Senate, the current treason trials and a new play which was running. He then comments on the war against Britain:

> I found your letter from Britain delightful. I was fearful of the Ocean and again of the shore-line of the island. Not that I overlooked the other hazards ...[20]

Meanwhile, back in Britain

Cicero's fears for the safety of the Roman army in Britain were well founded. By now the Britons had got their act together: they had put aside their differences and appointed Cassivellaunus as commander-in-chief. Caesar describes Cassivellaunus as the leader of a tribe based to the north of the River Thames (*Tamesis*). That was probably a reference to the Catuvellauni.

There then followed a series of engagements between Cassivellaunus' troops and those of Caesar.[21] Essentially the Britons engaged in guerrilla warfare: they made sporadic attacks on the Romans, achieved some kills and then sped away on their chariots or melted into the dank forests. Eventually, however, there was a larger scale battle and the Britons were driven back.

The Roman army then left their camp and marched north-west, heading for the River Thames. The Britons were ready to meet their foe. They fortified the north bank of the Thames with a line of sharply pointed stakes.[22] As an additional surprise for the Romans, the Britons drove a second line of stakes into the river bank, just out of sight beneath the water line.

Caesar was undeterred. On reaching the Thames, he ordered his cavalry and infantry to cross the river, wading or swimming as necessary. The troops dutifully crossed the river,

---

[18]Cicero, *Letters to his brother Quintus* 2.16.5.
[19]*Letters to Atticus* 4.16.7.
[20]*Letters to his brother Quintus* 2.16.4.
[21]Caesar, *Gallic War* 5.15.
[22]Caesar, *Gallic War* 5.18.

scrambled round the murderous stakes, and mounted the north bank. Whether any of his comrades were impaled upon the concealed stakes was a minor detail to which Caesar does not condescend in his account of the crossing. The Romans, presumably covered in mud, joined battle. The Britons, gleaming blue in their woad,[23] resisted. In what must have been a colourful and desperate struggle the Romans put their opponents to rout.

This proved to be the decisive battle of the campaign. For a time, the Britons continued to wage guerrilla warfare, while the Romans marched through the countryside laying waste fields and burning all properties in their path. By now, however, the Britons were losing heart and beginning to revive their old rivalries. Several groups, starting with the Trinovantes, decided to change sides.[24] They sent deputations to Caesar, who gladly accepted his new allies.

Caesar and his officers were so busy slaughtering people and making new alliances that for several weeks they did not even have time to write home. Their families started to fear the worst. In October 54 Cicero anxiously wrote from Rome to his brother Quintus:

> What worries me greatly is that for more than forty days not only has no letter arrived from you or Caesar, but no gossip has come through from your region. Concerns about the land and the sea in that part of the world are troubling me and I constantly have most unwelcome thoughts.[25]

Cicero need not have worried. Everything was going well in Britain, at least from Rome's point of view.

Cassivellaunus, with his support gradually ebbing away, retreated to a stronghold set amongst woods and marshes. He surrounded this with a trench and wooden rampart. He then awaited the Romans' arrival. Caesar did not delay. His troops attacked and captured the stronghold. As the Britons fled, the Romans killed everyone they caught. In the ancient world killing prisoners was regarded as fair game.

Cassivallaunus made a final and desperate assault on the Roman naval camp, using warriors resident in Kent, but this was unsuccessful. Cassivellaunus then sued for peace. Caesar, for his part, was in no position to impose harsh terms because winter was approaching, and the task force needed to get back to Gaul.

The terms of surrender

In those circumstances, all that Caesar demanded from Cassivellaunus was (a) the surrender of some hostages and (b) a promise to pay annual tribute to Rome.[26] Unsurprisingly, Cassivellaunus agreed. In addition to these feeble terms, Caesar states that he 'forbade' Cassivellaunus from harming the Trinovantes.

---

[23]'Omnes vero se Britanni vitro inficiunt, quod caeruleum efficit colorem, atque hoc horridiores sunt in pugna aspect.' 'The Britons dye themselves with woad, which produces a blue colour and makes them more scary in battle': Caesar, *Gallic War* 5.14.
[24]Laycock (2008) at 48–9 suggests that the Trinovantes may have sided with Caesar from the outset. But it seems improbable that Caesar could either have committed or got away with such a substantial misstatement.
[25]*Letters to his brother Quintus* 3.3.1.
[26]Caesar, *Gallic War* 5.22.

As previously noted, the surrender of hostages was not a guarantee of compliant behaviour. Hostage-taking might, however, have served other purposes. If the hostages were the sons of tribal leaders, they may have received education in Rome and later returned to spread Roman values in their homeland.

There is no evidence that the tribute promised by Cassivellaunus was ever paid and every reason to believe that it was not paid.[27] The Roman troops left the shores of Britain promptly after the peace negotiations. They had no practicable means of enforcing payment. It is quite true (as discussed in the next chapter) that in the century after Caesar's visit Rome's influence over Britain progressively increased, but that is a separate matter. In the years immediately following 54 BC there was no system in place for collecting and remitting annual payments to the Roman treasury. One may ask, on whom did the obligation to pay fall? Was it just the Catuvellauni? How were the funds to be raised? Did the warring communities in Britain club together each year to pool their available coins?

Finally, there were Caesar's stern words about not harming the Trinovantes. Once the great general had passed over the horizon it is risible to imagine that his comments had any impact on the future – no doubt hostile – relations between the Catuvellauni and the Trinovantes. Those two neighbouring groups lived north of the Thames and did not take their orders from Imperial Rome. As we shall see in the next chapter, the Catuvellauni effectively annexed the territory of the Trinovantes.

4. REVIEW OF CAESAR'S CAMPAIGNS IN BRITAIN

Caesar's grand plan

Caesar was a man of many talents, driven by burning ambition. For a summary of his career, see Chapter 1, Section 4. At first sight Caesar's decision to spend almost a quarter of his adult life campaigning in and around Gaul, far removed from Rome, seems an odd one. In fact, this was a shrewd decision, which ultimately paid off. Key factors were Caesar's need for money and for military success.

In the late Roman Republic military success on a grand scale was important for those seeking supreme power and influence.[28] Caesar's chief rival, Pompey,[29] was a highly successful general who had cleared the Mediterranean of pirates and annexed provinces for Rome in both Spain and the Near East. The Gallic campaign provided similar opportunities for Caesar. Caesar seized these opportunities by extending Roman domination as far north as the English Channel. He would no doubt have liked to conquer Britain as well, but this proved impracticable.

Caesar wrote the *Gallic War* as a contemporary account of his own campaigns. This was propaganda, designed to further his political career. The intended audience was the people of the Roman Republic, not twenty-first century historians. Like many modern politicians, Caesar appreciated the benefit of publishing his own version of events in his own words. He adopted

---

[27]For the opposite view, persuasively argued see Creighton (2000).
[28]See Drogula (2015).
[29]Also Caesar's son-in-law and colleague in the First Triumvirate.

The First Invasions: Julius Caesar

Figure 3.1 Julius Caesar. © Wikimedia/FDRMRZUSA (talk | contribs).

an elegant style, always referring to himself as 'Caesar', not 'I'. He wrote in clear and simple Latin. As a result, the *Gallic War* was widely read at the time and is widely read now. It provides much material for GCSE Latin courses.

Overall Caesar's strategy was successful. Having expanded the frontiers of the Empire, he returned to Italy with a huge reputation. He also returned with a loyal and devoted army. After the small matter of a civil war, Caesar eliminated Pompey and enjoyed supreme power in Rome for the last four years of his life.

British campaign

It is in this context that we must consider the British campaign of 55–54 BC. Britain was at the furthest edge of the world. It was a place of mystery, known only through the writings of Pytheas and one or two other geographers. Caesar no doubt calculated that invading and hopefully conquering Britain would give a substantial boost to his reputation. In the event his British campaign was not a success. It rapidly became apparent that Caesar was never going to conquer Britain in the same way that he had conquered Gaul. Such an endeavour would grossly overstretch his resources. On an objective view, the British campaign was a diversion from the serious business of subduing Gaul. It involved massive outlay of resources and achieved nothing of value to Rome in the short term.

In modern times, such a futile military endeavour would give rise to a public inquiry, or more likely a series of public inquiries each with different terms of reference. There would also be an outcry from the families of the soldiers who had died to no useful purpose. In the ancient world, however, the mindset was different.

Although Caesar did not conquer any territory in Britain, he still had the glory of having ventured to such a remote island at the extremity of the known world. He had crossed the 'Ocean', which was symbolic. After leaving Britain Caesar returned to Gaul where he put down rebellions, won some victories and was duly rewarded with another public thanksgiving, this time fully earned. Caesar's lack of success in Britain did no lasting damage to his reputation.

If we look at the long-term consequences of Caesar's British campaign, the picture changes. The invasions of 55–54 BC had the lasting effect of bringing Britain into closer contact with Rome.[30] Furthermore, some thirty years after Caesar's invasions of Britain, Northern Gaul came under effective Roman administration, as discussed in the next chapter. Britain then became a frontier state, facing the Roman Empire. Contacts and exchanges between Britain and the Empire steadily increased. As we shall see in the next chapter, many of the local leaders in Britain became allies of Rome and were handsomely rewarded for their loyalty. This ultimately led to the annexation of Britain as a Roman province in AD 43. Looking back across the sweep of history, we can see that Caesar's invasions of 55 and 54 BC were the first stage of that process.

---

[30]See Creighton (2006).

CHAPTER 4
THE INVASION OF SOUTHERN BRITAIN: THE EMPEROR CLAUDIUS

1. Introduction and Background
2. Relations between Britain and Rome
3. Claudius' invasion in AD 43
4. Consolidation of Roman Control
   (i) South-west England
   (ii) South-east England
   (iii) The Midlands

1. INTRODUCTION AND BACKGROUND

This chapter traces the transition of southern Britain from a collection of fragmented, warring communities all looking towards Rome as the regional superpower to a fully-fledged Roman province.

Some 97 years elapsed between Caesar's brief war against Britain and Claudius' invasion. During this 'inter-war' period local rivalries and conflicts continued much as before, but the context had changed. Rome was now a major player in the game and a potential ally to whom displaced leaders could flee for help. The extent to which Rome influenced, or even controlled, British affairs during the inter-war period is a matter of controversy. Section 2 of this chapter will argue that Britain was not under the control of Rome before AD 43.

Sections 3 and 4 of the chapter will outline the course of the Claudian invasion and its aftermath.

Developments in Gaul

During the 50s Caesar, as governor of *Provincia* (modern Provence), took it upon himself to conquer the whole of Gaul. For the next twenty-five years, the Roman government did very little with this vast new territory. The ruling classes were preoccupied with power struggles, triumvirates and successive civil wars. By 27 BC, however, Augustus was firmly established as Emperor. After visiting the region during that year, he created three new Gallic provinces, namely *Lugdunensis* in the north-east, *Belgica* in the north-west and *Aquitania* further south.[1] The army built a network of roads, which extended up to the Channel ports. The Romans, in conjunction with the indigenous élites, established a 'civitas system' of local government: they identified what they regarded as viable tribal units and declared each one to be a 'civitas'. Each civitas had an urban centre, where the former leaders exercised their power. But they were now answerable to Rome and they had fancy Roman titles, such as 'magistrate' or 'senator'. Modern historians describe those urban centres as 'civitas capitals'. The fact that the Roman Empire stretched right up to the English Channel meant that Britain was now firmly in the sights of Rome.

The volume of trade between Britain and the Empire steadily expanded. Unfortunately, there were also drawbacks: to their dismay, the British traders became liable to pay taxes to the Roman treasury. The imperial authorities in Gaul charged customs duties on all cross-Channel trade. They levied such duties on both exports from Gaul and imports from Britain. These imposts generated healthy returns for the Roman treasury.[2]

Power struggles in Britain

Our principal evidence of what was happening in Britain during this period comes from coinage. The local leaders, most helpfully, started to inscribe their names on coins and sometimes even the towns where the coins were minted. On the basis of the numismatic evidence, supplemented by occasional literary references, it is possible, roughly, to reconstruct the course of events. Nevertheless, a measure of caution is needed. None of the great Roman historians troubled to chronicle what was going on in our insignificant island after Caesar had left. We are therefore dependent on inferences from limited evidence. In his excellent study of pre-Roman British coinage, John Creighton identifies nine phases.[3] By far the strongest Roman influence is in phases 7, 8 and 9. That is between 20 BC and AD 45.

Commius, the former ally of Caesar, fell out with the Romans. He fought alongside two Gallic tribes in revolts against Rome, before eventually returning to Britain. Commius (presumably the same man) then became leader of the Atrebates. He was based at Silchester/*Calleva* and issued coins bearing his name. Commius' coins have been found across the whole territory of the Atrebates, including the areas of the Belgae and the Regni. He was succeeded by another man called Commius, who issued similar coins. Probably the second Commius was, or at least claimed to be, son of the first Commius. Assertions of parentage were a common means of establishing legitimacy in the ancient world. There was no DNA testing to challenge such claims.

The subsequent leaders of the Atrebates appear to have been Tincomarus, Eppilus and Verica, in that order. Eppilus issued coins with the legend 'EPPI COM. F', an abbreviation for 'Eppilus son of Commius', but probably that only meant he was a successor to Commius. The Atrebates were a powerful but querulous group, inclined to overthrow their leaders. Tincomarus was ousted in a coup. He fled to Rome and sought asylum.[4] Some years later, as we shall see, Verica[5] also fled to Rome. Verica was more successful in his plea for help. He precipitated a full-scale invasion of his homeland.

---

[1] See Drinkwater (1983), chapters 1, 5 and 7 for an account of matters summarized in this paragraph.
[2] Strabo, *Geography* 4.5.3.
[3] Creighton (2000) 32, figure 2.3.
[4] Augustus, *Res Gestae Divi Augusti* 32.
[5] Known to the Romans as Bericus.

Addedomaros emerged as leader of the Trinovantes in around 40 BC. He issued coins for about ten years. He was succeeded by Dubnovellaunus, whose coins circulated in the same area. Meanwhile in Kent there seems to have been another king called Dubnovellaunus, who was leader of the Cantii. Augustus states in his autobiography[6] that a British king called Dubnovellaunus fled to him for refuge. Unfortunately, the Emperor does not tell us whether this was the Essex man or the Kent man. Be that as it may, both communities were overshadowed by the growing power of the Catuvellauni.

Other individuals who issued coins in the south-east area included Vosenos, Andoco, Rues and Dias. It is not possible to deduce precisely who ruled whom and when.[7] Any reconstruction of their dynasties would be speculation.

After Caesar's departure the Catuvellauni remained dominant north of the Thames. Curiously however Cassivellaunus, the heroic resistance leader, vanishes from view. In about 20 BC Tasciovanus became leader. Under his rule the Catuvellauni established a new *oppidum* at *Verlamion*/St Albans.[8] This appears to have been a prosperous settlement, with a metal working industry and an élite occupation site at Gorhambury nearby. Fragments of fired clay moulds recovered from the Ver valley show that coins were minted there. There was a burial site at (what is now) King Harry Lane. Grave goods include brooches, metalwork and much imported pottery. The top people in St Albans lived – and died – in some splendour.

Tasciovanus appears to have subdued the Trinovantes, since some of his coins were minted at Colchester/*Camulodunon*. The rise of *Camulodunon* over the next forty years meant that *Verlamion* became of secondary importance. Even so, *Verlamion* continued as a substantial local centre with cross-Channel trading links. A high-status farmstead at Gorhambury was flanked by impressive dykes.

Tasciovanus died in about AD 9. Several individuals issued coins, linking their names to his, including Sego, Ruiis, Dias and Cunobelinus.[9] By far the most prolific coins were those issued by Cunobelinus, who described himself as '*Tasc fil*' meaning the son of Tasciovanus. Once again, the biological link is doubtful: Cunobelinus was claiming dynastic succession from Tasciovanus.

Cunobelinus is the towering figure of pre-Roman Britain. Shakespeare has immortalized him as Cymbeline in the play of that name. Basing himself at Colchester, Cunobelinus ruled for some 33 years, apparently as leader of both the Catuvellauni and the Trinovantes. He minted coins at Colchester and St Albans.

In recent years hundreds of Cunobelinus' coins have been recovered by archaeologists or metal detectorists. Those minted at Colchester (*Camulodunon*) bear the letters 'CAM'. Those minted at St Albans (*Verulamion*) bear the letters 'VER'. Many of these coins have been found south of the Thames. The clear inference is that Cunobelinus extended his control into the territory of the Cantii and the Atrebates. In addition, Dio Cassius tells us that the Catuvellauni 'ruled the Bodunni'.[10] Dio may have been referring to the Dobunni, although the Dobunni were located further to the west. From his power base in Colchester, Cunobelinus ruled over the

---

[6]*Res Gestae Divi Augusti* 32.
[7]Creighton (2000) 74–5.
[8]Niblett and Thompson (2005) chapter 3.
[9]Creighton (2000) 75.
[10]*Roman History* 60.20.2.

most prosperous and wealthy regions of southern Britain. Suetonius described Cunobelinus as 'the king of the Britons'.[11]

In the late first century BC and early first century AD Colchester achieved its peak of prosperity.[12] Trade with the Roman world flourished. Wine arrived from Italy; fish sauce and grape syrup came from Spain. The élite classes dined in style off tableware imported from Gaul. Even after death they kept their comforts: the graves at Lexden cemetery contain many imported luxury items;[13] there were also aristocratic burials involving complex rituals, ditched enclosures and burial mounds.

Cunobelinus had three sons, Adimius, Togodumnus and Caratacus. In about AD 40 Cunobelinus banished Adimius, who fled to Rome. Two years later Cunobelinus died. Togodumnus and Caratacus became joint leaders of the Catuvellauni. Caratacus completed the conquest of the Atrebates, whose leader Verica, like others before him, fled to Rome.

2. RELATIONS BETWEEN BRITAIN AND ROME

As previously noted, by the late first century BC the world had changed: the Empire extended right up to the English Channel. To what extent did Rome dominate Britain during the inter-war period? This is a controversial question.

On any view Roman culture was infusing the south-east of Britain.[14] The Roman alphabet now appeared on British coins; so also did Latin words, such as *rex* (king) and *filius* (son). There was a sophisticated and nuanced use of Latin on some coin legends.[15] Tasciovanus and Tincomarus, copying Augustus, put their portraits on coins. Roman imagery featured on many coins: for example, a boy riding a dolphin (probably Cupid – he liked riding on dolphins) or a pediment with columns. There were maritime images to commemorate Augustus' victory at the battle of Actium. On some coins there was even a star, representing the deified Julius Caesar. At first sight, it may seem odd that any British mint should honour a foreign adventurer, who had smashed up their property and murdered their grandfathers. But the local leaders probably had much to gain with their own people by adopting both the language and the symbolism of the adjacent Empire.

British coins started to depict Roman religious scenes and sacrifices.[16] These coins might have been representations of what was happening in Britain at the time, rather than mere copies of Continental coinage. The Celtic aristocracy could have undertaken Roman-style sacrifices, in addition to their own religious ceremonies. In both the ancient and the modern world, those who conduct religious ritual tend to be members of the élite classes. Religious ceremonial is a way of reinforcing the existing power structure. In the late Iron Age leading Britons may have associated themselves with the authority of Rome, by adopting Roman religious practices. The Hayling Island

---

[11]'Britannorum Regis': *Gaius Caligula* 44.2.
[12]Gascoyne and Radford (2013) chapter 4.
[13]Placed next to the ashes, if the deceased was cremated.
[14]Creighton (2000) chapters 4 and 7; (2006), chapter 1.
[15]Williams (2007) 1–12.
[16]Creighton (2000) 204.

temple (discussed in Chapter 19 below) was a Continental type of structure known in Gaul, which was by then an established province of the Empire.

The more difficult question is how much actual control the Roman government was exercising over British affairs. Some scholars argue that southern Britain had been *de facto* conquered and was part of the Roman orbit.[17] John Creighton develops this argument in his excellent studies of the late Iron Age.[18] He argues that the sons of the British tribal élites were taken as hostages to Rome; there they learnt Roman ways and mastered Latin; they also learnt to take orders from Rome. Creighton argues that Rome supplied gold bullion to friendly kings in Britain; Rome gave Commius suzerainty over much of southern Britain; Rome dealt with questions of succession within the Catuvellauni; after Cunobelinus' death, the question of who should succeed was referred to Rome for decision; Claudius' 'invasion' in AD 43 was simply the annexation of Cunobelinus' territory after his death.

This argument goes too far and cannot be accepted. Admittedly, there is a famous passage in Strabo's *Geography*, which states:

> Some of the British kings have procured Caesar Augustus' favour by sending embassies and paying court to him. They have dedicated offerings on the Capitol Hill. Indeed, they have almost made the whole island Roman property. They submit to paying heavy duties on exports to Gaul and imports from Gaul.[19]

Strabo's assertion that some British leaders have made 'almost the whole island Roman property' is self-evidently an exaggeration. Strabo does not say that Rome has any actual authority over Britain, merely that the various leaders have been trying to curry favour with Augustus. Strabo's discussion of whether it would be worthwhile for Rome to conquer Britain (as to which see below) implies that Rome was not currently controlling British affairs; Rome was simply charging customs duties on trade with Britain.

The only recorded hostage-taking from Britain was during Caesar's invasions of 55 and 54 BC. There is no reason why any prominent Britons should have voluntarily surrendered themselves or their sons to be hostages in Rome after 54 BC. They may well have chosen to visit Rome, as Strabo states, but that is a different matter. Short of undertaking a massive invasion (as happened in AD 43) Rome was in no position to force the Britons to do anything. The three 'client kings' post-AD 43 (to be discussed later in this chapter) only accepted Roman authority because by that time there were four legions and a large number of auxiliaries stationed in Britain. As we shall see, the response of many Britons to Rome's invasion was determined resistance for several years, until they were progressively crushed by military force.

The correct analysis, surely, is that during the late Iron Age there were increasing ties between Britain and the Empire. Some prominent Britons visited Rome and sought to curry favour with the Emperor, as described by Strabo. Some dispossessed British chiefs fled to Rome to seek support for their causes, as described by Augustus. Some Britons visited Rome voluntarily, where they may have chosen to adopt Roman ways, such as language, knowledge, dress and diet. Strabo describes seeing Britons in Rome, but he does not suggest that they were

---

[17] Stevens (1951).
[18] Creighton (2000) and (2001).
[19] *Geography* 4.5.3.

hostages.[20] Trade between Britain and the Empire increased. So also did the cultural exchanges that accompany trade. There was an increase in the importation of Italian luxury goods to Britain. The consumption of Italian wine and the wearing of Roman ornaments was probably a mark of prestige amongst the various élites.

The British local leaders ran their own affairs and fought their own battles over dynastic succession. They were keen to see Rome as an ally and a trading partner. They may have used the symbolism of empire to legitimate their own positions. In short what each was seeking to maintain with Rome was a 'special relationship'. This would provide both protection and a means of coercing their own peoples. Creighton is no doubt correct in saying that Rome cultivated those relationships and sought to maintain friendly kings, where possible.[21] That would explain the luxury items, which seem to have been diplomatic gifts, as noted in Chapter 2 above. It would also explain a possible small military presence.[22] But it is going too far to say that Rome controlled Britain. If that were the case, Claudius would not have needed four legions and numerous auxiliaries to invade Britain; nor would the annexation in the AD 40s have been so hard fought and long drawn out.

Nevertheless, what we can say is this. Although the invasion of AD 43 (to be discussed below) was violent and socially disruptive, there was a trajectory of change that began much earlier and continued after the annnexation.

The Emperor Augustus on several occasions (34, 27 and 26 BC) considered invading Britain, but never actually did so.[23] According to Tacitus, there was a 'long forgetfulness' of Britain; Augustus (the first Roman Emperor) called this 'policy'; Tiberius (the second Roman Emperor) called it 'precedent'.[24]

Contrary to Tacitus, it may be that Rome's foreign policy was driven by neither forgetfulness nor precedent. The decision to leave Britain independent was probably based upon a calculation of naked self-interest. There are, essentially, two reasons for this conclusion.

First, as previously mentioned, Britain was not a threat. The communities could squabble amongst themselves and the 'kings' could murder or banish one another as often as they fancied, without causing the least inconvenience to Rome. Every now and then an ousted British leader would appear at the gates of Rome claiming asylum, but that was hardly a problem. The Emperor could say yes or no, as he saw fit.

Second, the customs duties that Rome levied on cross-Channel trade represented gain without pain. There was no financial or other advantage in incurring the massive expense of invading Britain and incorporating it within the Empire. Strabo pithily summarized the position in book 2 of his *Geography*: 'Although they were able hold Britain, the Romans scorned this idea.'[25] Strabo went on to explain the reasons. First, there was nothing to fear from the Britons, as they could not possibly be a threat to Rome. Second, if Rome conquered Britain and extracted tribute, the cost of maintaining an army there and collecting tribute would far exceed the value of any benefit gained.[26]

---

[20]*Geography* 4.5.2.
[21]Creighton (2006) chapter 1.
[22]Evidenced by chain mail at Lexden and a helmet at Folly Lane.
[23]Dio Cassius, *Roman History* 53.
[24]Tacitus, *Agricola* 13.
[25]'καὶ γὰρ τὴν Βρεττανικὴν ἔχειν δυνάμενοι Ῥωμαῖοι κατεφρόνησαν': *Geography* 2.5.8.
[26]Strabo makes similar points about the futility of annexing Britain in book 4 of his *Geography*.

Another factor in Rome's thinking was, no doubt, the recent disaster in Germany. In AD 9 a Roman army led by Quinctilius Varus suffered a humiliating defeat in the Teutoburgian Forest. Three legions were caught in an ambush and virtually annihilated. Augustus was devastated. The Romans withdrew to the Rhine, which then became the north-west frontier of the Empire. More generally, Rome's policy after this date appears to have been one of retrenchment and consolidation. The objective was to make the existing frontiers secure. Any attempt to take over Britain in the aftermath of Varus' defeat would have been out of the question.

On two occasions Augustus appointed his son-in-law, M. Vipsanius Agrippa, as governor of Gaul. Agrippa introduced a systematic road network[27] centred on Lyon (*Lugdunum*), where the main east–west and north–south roads crossed. One of the roads heading north ran up to Boulogne (*Gesoriacum*). Later governors of Gaul substantially extended Agrippa's basic road system. These extensions included a major highway from Cologne to Boulogne. Some see the construction of roads right up to the Channel as evidence a long-term plan to invade Britain. But this is unlikely, because there were other perfectly good reasons for Rome's road building. First, Rome needed effective communications across the whole region, simply in order to administer the Gallic provinces and gather taxes. Second, the people of Gaul did not take kindly to overseas interference (nor do they now). There were numerous uprisings. Rome needed the ability to move troops rapidly to wherever trouble broke out. Third, the English Channel ('the Ocean') was an extremely effective northern frontier for the Empire. Finally, it would have been directly contrary to government policy to annexe Britain in the years following Varus' defeat. No-one seriously considered invading Britain until Gaius Caligula came onto the scene.

Following the death of Tiberius in AD 37, Gaius Caligula was acclaimed as the third Roman Emperor. He came close to invading Britain in AD 40. Caligula was in Gaul with a substantial army when Adimius, the son of Cunobelinus, defected to the Romans. As previously mentioned, Adimius was banished by his father. According to Suetonius, Caligula drew up his troops on northern shores of Gaul. The Emperor then changed his mind. Instead of invading Britain he commanded the soldiers to fill up their helmets and the folds of their clothes with sea shells as 'spoils of the Ocean'.[28] The Emperor, who apparently believed that he was a god, then returned in triumph to Rome. Suetonius was writing during the reign of Hadrian (under whom he had served as secretary) and was hostile to the later Julio-Claudian Emperors. No doubt Caligula planned and then abandoned an invasion of Britain, but the colourful details are probably fictitious. Suetonius was producing a comical and unflattering account of a 'bad' Emperor.

It may be that Caligula was not quite as mad as Suetonius suggests. Like Nikita Kruschev in 1962,[29] Caligula might have rationally reconsidered his position when he stood on the brink of conflict. The considerations set out above may have persuaded him that annexing Britain was not a good idea. So in AD 40, as in 1940,[30] Britain had a lucky escape when hostile forces massing across the Channel did not invade. In AD 40, however, that good fortune only lasted for three years.

---

[27] Drinkwater (1983) chapter 6. Maps 7 and 8 depict the road system established in Gaul.
[28] 'Spolia Oceani': Suetonius, *Gaius Caligula* 46.
[29] For a concise account of the Cuban missile crisis, see volume 4 of Robert Caro's biography of Lyndon Johnson (2012) 208–23.
[30] Hastings (2011) chapters 3 and 4.

In AD 41, despite his claims to divinity, Caligula was murdered by officers of the Praetorian Guard. Caligula's successor was his uncle Claudius, a man held in general contempt. Apparently, Claudius walked with difficulty and his body was feeble. According to Suetonius, even his mother described him as a 'monster of a man, whom nature had not finished'.[31] Roman matrons did not pull their punches. In an age when physical prowess was prized as the quality of leaders, Claudius began his reign at a huge disadvantage.

Claudius was in a desperate situation. He needed to establish his virility and his suitability for office by a bold stroke at an early stage. In the ancient world military success was the mark of a great leader. Britain was the obvious, possibly the only, country which was readily available for conquest. An additional reason for selecting Britain was that the only previous general to invade the island was Julius Caesar. By going back to Britain Claudius would be establishing a direct link with Caesar. This would help to legitimate Claudius in the Julio-Claudian line. The new Emperor set his sights upon the conquest of Britain.

The decision to annexe Britain as a province was certainly a momentous one: it would involve huge public expenditure, as well as tying up four legions and a significant part of the Roman navy for the foreseeable future. No rational cost benefit analysis could have supported the decision,[32] but such analyses had little place in the ancient world.[33] Anyone who thinks otherwise should try doing long division with Roman numerals. It is reasonable to infer that short-term political expediency was the driving force.

3. CLAUDIUS' INVASION IN AD 43

As previously noted, in AD 42 Verica, the chief of the Atrebates, fled to Rome seeking assistance. Dio says that Verica was overthrown in an uprising.[34] Quite a likely scenario is that a faction of the Atrebates, which supported the Catuvellauni, ousted Verica in a coup and then welcomed in Caratacus. According to Suetonius, Britain was in a state of 'tumult' because of Rome's failure to return some refugees, but that sounds an odd reason for anyone to be in a state of tumult.

Verica's arrival in Rome was opportune. There were welcome indications of continuing strife amongst the British communities, at least some of whom might be willing to support Rome. Verica was not the first displaced Briton to seek help from Rome, but he was markedly more successful than his predecessors. He had the advantage of arriving at just the right time. The Emperor, ostensibly taking up Verica's cause, announced that he would send an army to subdue Britain.

Once the invasion was under way, Verica vanishes without trace. Neither inscriptions nor historical records contain any further reference to him. A small coin has been found at Silchester, depicting Verica in fine regal pose,[35] but this probably predates his flight to Rome.

---

[31]'Mater Antonia portentum eum hominis dictitabat, nec absolutum a natura': *Divus Claudius* 3.2.
[32]Although Britain possessed mineral resources, there is no evidence that the Romans knew their extent or that this was the motivation for the conquest.
[33]The Romans did not have a concept of investment like ours: see Finley (1976) 1.
[34]*Roman History* 60.19.1. Dio calls Verica 'Bericus', but he must be talking about the same person.
[35]See photograph on Reading University website.

There is no suggestion that he was reinstated as leader. The reality, no doubt, is that Verica had served his purpose; the Romans probably forgot about him in their jubilation at gaining another province.

The archaeological evidence throws no light upon the course of the invasion. The relevant parts of Tacitus' *Annals* have been lost. Therefore, in piecing together the momentous events of AD 43 we are dependent upon Dio's account,[36] supplemented by brief references in the other literary sources. Dio was writing over a century after the conquest. He was relying on historians of the late first century (whose works are now lost) but not, apparently, on Tacitus. He probably ran together early Roman victories, which were separated in time.[37] As will be discussed below, part of Dio's account does not stand up to critical analysis.

Aulus Plautius was appointed as commander-in-chief to lead an invasion force of four legions, namely the Second Legion Augusta, the Ninth Legion Hispana, the Fourteenth Legion Gemina and the Twentieth Legion.[38] Auxiliary cohorts accompanied each legion. The auxiliaries brought with them their own native skills: the German troops were of particular value because they could swim fully armed across rivers. It appears from inscriptions that the task force also included detachments from other legions. The total invasion force comprised about 40,000 infantry, together with several hundred cavalry.

Vespasian, the future Roman Emperor, commanded the Second Legion. According to Suetonius, Vespasian secured this appointment through the influence of Narcissus,[39] a former slave who had risen to become a senior member of Claudius' administration.

Since Britain lay beyond the 'Ocean', the Romans had to establish a special fleet. At this stage the 'fleet' was probably an *ad hoc* collection of available ships, although in later years the dedicated fleet which supported the province became known as the British fleet (*classis Britannica*). The first task of the fleet was to transport the invasion force across the Channel, an operation which required about 1,000 transport ships and another 50-100 warships as escorts.[40]

The legions and the auxiliaries duly marched to the north coast of Gaul. Dio tells us that they were reluctant to embark on an expedition 'beyond the inhabited world'.[41] So Claudius sent Narcissus to save the situation. Narcissus addressed the troops, who started chanting 'Yo Saturnalia!' This was a reference to the festival of Saturn, an occasion when slaves would dress up as their masters and celebrate. According to Dio this merriment cheered the soldiers up; they took courage and pressed on with the expedition. It may be that this entire passage is a literary trope, designed to emphasize the character of the leader and to show the military overcoming their fear as brave men. It also accentuated the significance of conquering the 'Ocean'.

The crossing

The Roman task force set off in late April AD 43. They crossed the Channel in three divisions. The crossing of the first division was not a smooth one. Adverse winds drove them off course.

---

[36] *Roman History* 60.19 – 60.23.
[37] Hind (2007) 93–106.
[38] The Twentieth Legion was later given the title Valeria Victrix for its part in suppressing Boudica's rebellion: see Chapter 6 below.
[39] 'Narcissi gratia legatus legionis ... in Britanniam translatus': *Divus Vespasianus* 4.1.
[40] Mason (2010) 78.
[41] 'ἔξω τῆς οἰκουμένης': Dio, *Roman History* 60.19.2.

According to Dio, the superstitious Romans plucked up courage once more, when they saw a streak of lightning flash to the west. That pointed directly to their destination. Happily, it seemed that Jupiter (the top god, who was in charge of thunder and lightning) was on their side.

At least one division landed at Richborough (*Rutupiae*) in Kent. Whether all the divisions landed at Richborough or some landed elsewhere is controversial. The better view is that they all landed at Richborough. See the Online Appendix.

Warfare and diplomacy

According to Dio, the powerful Catuvellauni took the lead in defending the realm. Initially Togodumnus and Caratacus avoided direct confrontation, preferring to conceal their warriors in the nearby forests and swamps. Aulus Plautius stood firm. He eventually forced the Catuvellauni into the open and defeated them in battle.

Dio's account does not fit with the evidence. After the conquest *Verlamion*, the principal stronghold of the Catuvellauni, received the status of *municipium*. This was in the gift of the Emperor and was a reward for loyalty. Furthermore, the Romans did not establish forts in the territory of the Catuvallauni. This is inconsistent with Dio's account of the Catuvellauni leading the opposition to Rome's invasion.

The explanation probably is that two factions emerged within the Catuvallauni, one pro-Roman and one anti-Roman. Caratacus and Togodumnus led the anti-Roman faction. Dio's references to 'the Catuvallauni' are references to the anti-Roman faction. We know from book 4 of the *Gallic War* that a century earlier the Catuvellauni had led the resistance to Caesar's invasion. Dio may have assumed that they were doing the same thing again.

According to Dio, a neighbouring tribe, the 'Bodunni' who were dominated by the Catuvellauni, then hastened to surrender to Rome. Dio may be referring to the Dobunni, although they were located some distance to the west. Alternatively, Dio may have been referring to another group or sub-group which were actually called the 'Bodunni'. Either way, they were people whom Cunobelinus had taken over when he was expanding his empire. They would have strongly resented their subjection to the Catuvallauni and probably saw the Romans as liberators.

Taking up the story from Dio, after defeating the Catuvellauni Aulus Plautius advanced to a river, which was probably the Medway. The Britons set up camp on the other side, believing that they were safe from attack. Not so. The invaders had a detachment of German auxiliaries who were able to swim in full armour over turbulent streams. The Germans duly dived in, crossed the river and attacked the foe. Their initial strategy was to wound or kill the British horses. Without these horses the Britons could not resort to chariot warfare and their cavalry was thrown into disarray. Aulus Plautius then sent Vespasian across the river, together with his brother Sabinus acting as lieutenant, and a posse of soldiers. They joined the fray and cut down many Britons. There was, however, no conclusive result before nightfall.

Next day the fighting resumed. The Roman commander Gnaeus Hosidius Geta narrowly escaped capture. He then went on to defeat the Britons. For his bravery and determination in the face of the enemy Geta was awarded the *ornamenta triumphalia*. This is roughly equivalent to a VC, except that *ornamenta triumphalia* would only be awarded to a general, never to a lowly soldier.

The Britons then withdrew to the Thames. According to Dio they chose a spot close to the mouth of the river, where it formed a lake at high tide. This must have been in the London region. The Britons forded the river with ease because they knew where the firm ground was. The Romans did not have that advantage, but the German contingent once more came to the fore, swimming across the river in full armour. The other troops succeeded in crossing via a bridge further upstream. This enabled the Romans to attack the 'barbarians' from several directions and to kill many of them. The Britons turned and fled across the marshes, no doubt knowing where the ground was safe and where it was treacherous. The Roman invaders gave chase, but lacking that useful local knowledge, some of them sank into the mud and perished.

The principal loss on the British side was Togodumnus, who was killed during the conflict.[42] As a result the Catuvellauni (or at least the anti-Roman faction of the Catuvellauni) and their allies were now under the command of Caratacus alone. The Britons re-grouped and prepared for the next stage of the conflict.

According to Dio, at this point Aulus Plautius became afraid; instead of advancing further, he consolidated his position and sent for Claudius to take command. This passage in the *Roman History* looks like blatant propaganda, which Dio has swallowed gullibly. The notion that a long serving and successful military commander should need to summon a politician with no previous military experience to lead the army into a crucial battle is improbable. The only realistic explanation for Aulus Plautius summoning Claudius at this juncture was that he had been told to do so at the moment when all was going well and a decisive victory was about to be achieved.

The gallant Emperor, as had no doubt been agreed in advance, duly responded to this call to arms. From Rome Claudius sailed down the Tiber to the port of Ostia and thence to Massilia (Marseilles). He travelled overland to the north coast of Gaul and then crossed to Britain. Dio mentions that at the same time reinforcements came from Rome, including elephants, to assist the invading army. This is probably true. Hopefully the elephants had a smooth crossing. They were going to be more use than the Emperor.

After disembarking Claudius hastened northwards to join the army, which was encamped near the Thames. According to Dio,[43] Claudius immediately took command. He led his army across the Thames, engaged the barbarians and defeated them in battle. Claudius captured Colchester (*Camulodunon*), the capital town of the Catuvellauni. 'He then won over more tribes, some by force and others by agreement.'[44] Claudius stripped the conquered Britons of their weapons and handed these over to Aulus Plautius. He was hailed as '*imperator*' several times by his troops, an honour normally only accorded once in any war. Having ordered Aulus Plautius to subdue the remaining districts, Claudius hastened back to Rome.

Claudius was away from Rome for just six months and spent only sixteen days in Britain.[45] It is beyond belief that anyone lacking military experience could achieve such an astonishing series of unbroken victories on unfamiliar terrain against a medley of 'barbarians' in just over a fortnight. This part of Dio's account is an early example of fake news. The reality must be that

---

[42] Hinds (2007) suggests that Togodumnus may have survived and re-emerged as the client king, Togidubnus. This seems unlikely and has no solid foundation.
[43] Dio, *Roman History* 60.21.2–5.
[44] 'κἀκ τούτου συχνοὺς τοὺς μὲν ὁμολογίᾳ τοὺς δὲ καὶ βίᾳ προσαγαγόμενος'.
[45] Dio, *Roman History* 60.23.1; Suetonius, *Divus Claudius* 17.

Aulus Plautius and his team secured the successes that Dio recounts, and that only some of these events can have been squeezed into the few days that Claudius spent on British soil. Dio is no doubt right in saying that the major battle was in the region of Colchester, since that was the Catuvellaunian stronghold. It is clear that the Romans prevailed and that they occupied Colchester from AD 43.

Dio's assertion that Claudius 'won over more tribes, some by force and others by agreement' is significant. The inscription on Claudius' triumphal arch in Rome, erected in AD 51, furnishes more detail (Fig. 4.1). It states that Claudius: 'received the submission of eleven kings of Britain, overthrown without any loss'.[46] The likelihood is that the Romans were exploiting local rivalries. The communities who had been at war with, or oppressed by, the Catuvellauni probably saw the Roman invasion as an opportunity to settle old scores. Hence, they came over to the invaders 'by agreement' (per Dio) and 'without any loss' (per the inscription).

As we shall see, for some time after the annexation, two communities in southern Britain were allowed to retain a measure of independence and to continue under their existing leaders. These were the Atrebates (now including the Belgae and the Regni), and the Iceni. It is a reasonable inference that the Atrebates, the Belgae, the Regni and the Iceni chose to collaborate with Rome at an early date, thereby earning their privileges. Probably the pro-Roman faction of the Catuvellauni also collaborated Rome, thereby earning a privileged status for *Verulamium*.

Figure 4.1 Claudius' triumphal arch in Rome, as sketched in 1756. © Wikimedia/Le antichità Romane.

---

[46]'Reges Britanniai XI devictos sine ulla iactura in deditionem acceperit': CIL vi.920.

Why then does the inscription says eleven kings, not five? The answer lies in the nature of the British communities, each of which comprised many sub-groups. Whether the king of the Dobunni or the 'Bodunni' (as discussed above) falls within the inscription is unclear. According to Dio's narrative, they had surrendered to Rome before Claudius arrived. But such details may not have troubled the author of the inscription, who was manipulating the media for political purposes.

The account of Claudius' British campaign which went into the public domain and which Dio faithfully repeats must have been the product of some skilful spinning by Claudius' officials. Narcissus probably had a hand in the exercise. The Senate decreed that there should be an annual festival to mark the conquest; the Emperor should celebrate a triumph; two triumphal arches should be erected to mark Claudius' achievement, one in Rome and one in Gaul; both the Emperor and his son should receive the title *Britannicus*.

The imperial mints also played their part. They issued a special series of coins to commemorate the conquest. An Alexandrian diobol has been found bearing the inscription ΒΡΕΤΤΑΝΙΚΟΣ ΚΑΙΣΑΡ ('Caesar Brittanicus' in Greek letters).[47] This coin is dated to Claudius' third regnal year, which ended on 29 August 43. Extrapolating backwards from that date, it seems likely that the battle of Colchester took place at about the beginning of August.

The honours heaped upon Claudius during his lifetime continued after death. Like most emperors of the period, he became an immortal god by order of the Senate. Sadly for Claudius, his biographer Suetonius made a more realistic assessment. Suetonius describes Claudius' British campaign as being of little importance (*modicam*). He states that Claudius' only motive was to get the glory of a triumph. He adds for good measure that Claudius was not involved in any battle or bloodshed.[48]

4. CONSOLIDATION OF ROMAN CONTROL

After the first flurry of activity, the Romans embarked upon the long grind of gaining effective control over their new territory. Tacitus states that southern Britain was gradually forced to become a Roman province during the tenure of the first two governors.[49] Aulus Plautius was both commander of the invading army and first governor of the emergent province. He served from AD 43 to 47 before returning to Rome, where he received an ovation. The second governor, Publius Ostorius Scapula (AD 47 to 52) operated a dual policy of political alliances and military suppression.

It is a mistake to think of the Roman 'conquest' as a matter of army units fanning out across Britain and attacking every community that they encountered.[50] Dio aptly described the process when he spoke of 'winning over' (προσαγαγόμενος) communities. The 'conquest' of England and Wales was as much a political process as a military one. Where the Romans could

---

[47]Grainge (2002) 100–1.
[48]'Sine ullo proelio aut sanguine': Suetonius, *Divus Claudius* 17.
[49]'Redactaque paulatim in formam provinciae proxima pars Britanniae': *Agricola*, 14.
[50]Millett (1990) chapter 3.

exploit local rivalries, they did so. If communities submitted, they were treated generously. If they resisted, then they were crushed.

Some leaders on the fringes of the Empire adopted a policy of collaboration. Historians now use the term 'client kings' as a label for those who threw in their lot with Rome. Client kings became allies of Rome and ran their fiefdoms under the patronage of the Empire. Other imperial powers have adopted a similar policy: for example, the Ottoman Empire during the eighteenth century.[51] Client kingdoms were usually temporary arrangements: when a client king died, Rome was likely to annexe his territory, as happened in Judea after the death of King Herod.

There were three client kingdoms in Britain during the early years following the invasion. These were the Brigantes in the north under Queen Cartimandua, the Iceni in the east under Prasutagus and the Atrebates/Regni/Belgae under Togidubnus. These three client kingdoms may be seen as a continuation of the Roman practice of maintaining friendly kings in territories just beyond the frontiers.[52] The big difference, of course, was that post AD 43 southern Britain was part of the Empire. Client kingdoms could now only be temporary enclaves, carved out of a larger province.

As Rome extended its reach across southern Britain, it constructed a network of forts and military roads. The forts can be divided into the following categories: legionary fortresses, vexillation forts,[53] forts for auxiliary soldiers, small forts and supply bases. The majority of all the forts were manned by auxiliaries. The pattern of military bases that were established during the period following the initial invasion gives a fair indication of the course of events.[54] Where communities were compliant, the Roman military presence was reduced although there was still a need to guard supply bases and important routes. Where communities were hostile, a network of forts was established to assert Roman control.

Rome's military operations in Britain required naval support at each stage. Supply depots for the Roman navy were created along the south coast.[55] Ships were used for bringing in supplies and also for transporting troops around the province. Most military bases could be supplied by sea: even Lincoln was established on a navigable river.

(i) South-west England

The Durotriges and the Dumnonii were a widely scattered population, without any major *oppida* or, seemingly, any overall organization. The distribution of forts in the south-west peninsula, as well as the length of their occupation, may indicate that these peoples resisted the Roman takeover. Alternatively, this may simply reflect the exigencies of administering a fragmented society.

Aulus Plautius assigned the task of subduing the south-west of England to the Second Legion Augusta. Vespasian commanded the Second Legion Augusta between AD 43 and 47.

---

[51] Rogan (2009) chapter 2.
[52] Creighton (2006) chapter 1.
[53] A detachment from a legion sent to perform a specific task was a vexillation (*vexillatio*).
[54] Todd (2007) chapter 4.
[55] Todd (2007) 53–4.

According to Suetonius,[56] Vespasian defeated two tribes, which must be the Durotriges and the Dumnonii; he captured twenty towns and also occupied the Isle of Wight.[57] All in all, he had a good war and emerged as a future emperor. As Tacitus put it, 'Tribes were conquered, kings were captured and Vespasian was introduced to destiny'.[58]

The former Iron Age hill forts came in handy for the purpose of establishing military bases. At Hod Hill in Dorset, Roman soldiers constructed their own fort in one corner. Ham Hill in Somerset, Maiden Castle in Dorset and Hembury in Devon all contain evidence of Roman occupation during this period.

In about AD 55 the Second Legion Augusta established a fortress at Exeter.[59] Situated on the banks of the River Exe and close to the coast, it was well placed for receiving supplies by sea. The Exe was navigable up as far as Topsham, where the Romans established a port. The road between the port and the legionary fortress was flanked by military buildings. A grim fortification stood proud on the cliffs above the river. South Devon may now be a haven for holidays and retirement homes, but in Roman times it was more forbidding.

The other forts in the south-west peninsula took their orders from Exeter. The most westerly of these was the auxiliary fort at Nunstallon, which superintended the Land's End region.

(ii) South-east England

As previously stated, the Catuvellauni effectively took over the Trinovantes in the LPRIA. The anti-Roman factions of these two powerful communities were crushed in the first wave of the invasion and Colchester, their joint capital town, fell to the Romans. The Catuvellauni and the Trinovantes chose to accept Rome's domination.

The Twentieth Legion established its fortress at Colchester (*Camulodunum*),[60] where it remained for six years, namely from AD 43 to 49. This involved a massive building operation. The fortress covered 20 hectares, including 22 barrack blocks and other military buildings. A V-shaped ditch and rampart surrounded the perimeter. The fortress stood at the end of a spur of land, with falling ground on three sides, which gave the conquerors a splendid view across their new territory. Little now remains of Rome's first legionary fortress in Britain, apart from a few fragments of one barrack block. These sit ignominiously beneath a shopping mall.[61]

What did the soldiers eat? Archaeologists have carefully analysed faecal remains from the lavatory pits, in order to resolve this issue.[62] Apparently, the soldiers tucked into plenty of ox meat as well as beef, mutton and pork. For pudding, they enjoyed figs, raspberries, grapes and elderberries. Apple crumble hadn't been invented.

The military cemetery was probably next to the road leading west from the fortress. Marcus Favonius Facilis, a centurion of the Twentieth Legion, was buried there. Two of his former slaves set up a magnificent tombstone, which depicts Marcus standing bare headed in full

---

[56] *Vespasian* 4.
[57] Eutropius gives a similar account of Vespasian's exploits: *Breviarium ab Urbe Condita* 7.19.
[58] 'Domitae gentes, capti reges et monstratus fatis Vespaspasianus.' *Agricola* 13.
[59] Holbrook (2015) 96–100.
[60] Gascoyne and Radford (2013) chapter 5.
[61] Wilson (2002) 210.
[62] Gascoyne and Radford (2013) 72.

Figure 4.2 Tombstone of Marcus Favonius Facilis, Colchester. © Flickr/-Ozymandias.

uniform, complete with cloak and dagger (Fig. 4.2). Another tombstone commemorates Longinus, a Thracian cavalryman. He stands in a niche, flanked by a lion and a snake. You can see both these warriors in Colchester Museum.[63]

In AD 49 the Twentieth Legion moved on. The Romans established their first 'colony' for veterans at Colchester on and around the site of the former fortress. Somewhat unwisely, they demolished the existing military defences, to create more land for the colonists. The fortress

---

[63]RIB I, 200 and 201.

roads formed the basic street grid of the new town. The barrack blocks were converted for civilian use; other military structures were partially demolished and re-used. What had been an annexe to the fortress expanded to house a basilica and other public buildings. Retired soldiers were settled there and given land as a reward for past services.

According to Tacitus,[64] the colony was both a bulwark against rebellion and a model town, which set an example of proper civic life to the provincials. This was an admirable pension policy, at least from Rome's point of view. It cost the public treasury nothing; all land required was simply confiscated from the former owners. There was no question of paying compensation. Modern governments, struggling with the massive burden of public sector pensions, may look with envy at the superannuation arrangements of Imperial Rome.

In about AD 54, the Romans built a vast classical-style temple at Colchester. They dedicated this to the divine Emperor Claudius, following his recent death and deification. Priests were duly appointed and the Trinovantes were required to pay for religious observances.[65]

The Trinovantes did not welcome any of these developments. According to Tacitus, those living in the Colchester area were forcibly evicted from their lands and the settlers treated the dispossessed Britons like prisoners or slaves.[66] The Trinovantes also resented the erection of a temple to Claudius on their land and the concomitant obligation to fund religious offerings to the old brute. This account has elements of exaggeration. Archaeology shows that the Romans built their fortress and colony to one side of the Iron Age settlement.[67] It is likely that only a minority of the Trinovantes were evicted.

The Atrebates accepted Roman rule at an early date. Their reward was to retain a measure of independence. Their territory became a client kingdom, ruled by Togidubnus. Tacitus says that 'several states were ruled by King Togidubnus'.[68] The 'several states' must be a reference to the Atrebates, the Regni and the Belgae. Tacitus notes that Togidubnus remained utterly loyal (*fidissimus*) to Rome. He then adds wryly that this was in accordance with the long-established policy of using indigenous kings as 'instruments of servitude'.[69]

Chichester (*Noviomagus Reginorum*) was established as the capital town of Togidubnus' client kingdom. The Romans linked the new town into their road system: Stane Street ran from the east gate of Chichester up to London; another major road led from the north gate to Silchester. The four principal roads of modern Chichester (North Street, South Street, East Street and West Street) still faithfully follow the layout which Togidubnus and the Roman military surveyors devised two thousand years ago.

Togidubnus was the classic example of a client king: he consistently supported the Roman authorities; he acquired Roman citizenship and adopted the additional names Tiberius Claudius. Whether he occupied the luxurious palace at Fishbourne will be discussed in Chapter 18 below. An inscription[70] describing him as a 'Great King of Britain'[71] was placed by a

---

[64]'Camulodunum valida veteranorum manu deducitur in agros captivos, subsidium adversus rebellis et imbuendis sociis ad officia legum': *Annals* 12.32.
[65]Tacitus, *Annals* 14.31.
[66]Tacitus, *Annals* 14.31.
[67]Gascoyne and Radford (2013).
[68]'quaedam civitates Cogidumno regi donatae'.
[69]*Agricola* 14.
[70]RIB 91.
[71]'Regis Magni Britanniae'.

guild of smiths on a temple to Neptune and Minerva in Chichester. The inscription survives, despite being buried under rubble for many centuries. It now hangs on a wall in North Street, still proclaiming Togidubnus to be a 'Great King of Britain'. Sadly, however, the passing shoppers take little notice of the plaque and they appear to be unimpressed by the Great King's status.

There are few signs of any forts standing in the territory of the Atrebates during the first thirty years after the Roman invasion. This is strong evidence that the client kingdom was functioning to the satisfaction of Rome. Probably one or two centurions were posted to the court of Togidubnus. There were also some soldiers stationed by the harbour at Fishbourne, which was a major supply base in the early years after AD 43.

There is a dearth of forts in Kent, which suggests that the Cantiaci[72] also accepted Roman rule from the outset. The only significant military establishments in Kent were the supply base at Richborough and an auxiliary fort at nearby Reculver, but a military presence there was inevitable, since this was a major port. Watling Street, perhaps the most important Roman road in England, ran from Richborough to London and beyond.

(iii) The Midlands

The Iceni, who were based in the Norfolk area, initially adopted a policy of collaboration. As Tacitus puts it, 'they voluntarily became our allies'.[73] Their leader, Prasutagus, became a client king: he continued to issue silver coins in his own name, with a Roman bust on the front above the legend 'SUBRI PRASTO'. But early in the governorship of Ostorius, the Iceni rebelled with some support from neighbouring communities. A Roman army arrived to suppress the rebellion. The Iceni cunningly chose a battlefield surrounded by earthworks with an entrance too narrow for cavalry to negotiate. The Roman cavalry duly dismounted and, together with the infantry, they charged across the embankment. The Britons now found themselves penned in and were overwhelmed. Tacitus reports that the enemy, although defeated, fought with great valour. So also did the Roman soldiers, although only one of them received an honour for his part in the battle. By a strange coincidence or – more likely – by nepotism, that lucky soldier was the governor's son.[74]

After their defeat in AD 47, the Iceni resumed their former policy of collaboration. Prasutagus saw the benefits of peaceful co-operation and stuck firmly to that policy until his death in 60. There is little evidence of forts having been constructed in East Anglia during the 40s and 50s. Whether Prasutagus had quite such a peaceful life on the domestic front may be doubted. His wife was a forceful lady called Boudica, whom we shall meet in Chapter 6.

The Corieltauvi appear to have resisted the invaders, although none of the details are recorded. There is a fairly dense distribution of forts across their territory. The Ninth Legion was responsible for the East Midlands and must have crushed or won over the Corieltauvi.[75] The legion established its fortress on a navigable section of the river Witham at Lincoln in about AD 60.

---

[72]Called Cantii by Ptolemy.
[73]'Societam nostram volentes accesserant': *Annals* 12.31.
[74]Tacitus, *Annals* 12.31.
[75]Jones (2011) chapter 3.

The Fourteenth Legion headed into the West Midlands, a large fertile area watered by the River Severn. The Cornovii did not welcome new arrivals. They probably mustered their forces at the Wrekin hillfort in east Shropshire, which was their principal stronghold.[76] There is evidence of burnt roundhouses within, possibly due to Roman attack. Two javelin heads have been recovered, one from the fort's gate. The Britons may have put up stout resistance, but they could not hold out indefinitely against the Roman military machine. The legionaries established a camp, later a vexillation fort, at Leighton. There was a separate auxiliary fortlet, dated to the conquest period. By the middle of the century, the Fourteenth Legion had brought the whole of the region under Roman control. They set about building a fortress at Wroxeter.

The legionary movements in the West Midlands during the first century are not entirely clear. In part this is because the legions frequently split or sent detachments to different locations – without any regard to the difficulties that they were creating for future historians. Nevertheless, the broad picture seems to be as follows. After leaving Colchester in AD 49, the Twentieth Legion established its fortress first at Kingsholm near Gloucester, then at Usk in AD 58. Although the Dobunni accepted Roman rule at the first opportunity, several early forts have been found in their territory. The Romans may have been protecting supply routes and establishing bases for the future conquest of Wales.

Metchley Roman Fort in Birmingham is a typical example of an auxiliary fort.[77] The original fort, built of earth and timber, was established in about 48 or 49 and occupied an area of some 10.5 acres. The Romans later added a four-acre annexe by extending the two main ditches northwards and building corner towers. The fort stood at the intersection of two major roads, guarding the routes to Wall and Wroxeter. Now, somewhat less glamorously, the remains of the fort sit on a tract of land between Queen Elizabeth II Hospital and the Birmingham Medical School. An earth bank represents the sides of the fort; the Via Decumana, which passed through the centre, is clearly marked.

The extent of Roman control by the middle of the first century

The Fosse Way was a major, well fortified road, which the Romans constructed from Exeter to Lincoln. It used to be said that Fosse Way marked the frontier of the province by the middle of the first century.[78] That, however, is a simplification.[79] First, the vast client kingdom of the Brigantes lay to the north. Although not incorporated into the province, Brigantia was generally loyal to Rome while Queen Cartimandua was in charge. Second, Fosse Way cut across a number of community boundaries. It was the normal Roman practice to deal with communities as coherent entities. It is more accurate to say that Fosse Way and the territories on either side marked the extent of Roman control by the middle of the century. That just happened to be as far as they had got. This was not a significant moment in anybody's mind. The Romans did not pause for breath at this point and no-one told them that it was the middle of the first century.

---

[76] White and Barker (2011) chapter 2.
[77] Webster (1970), 190.
[78] Webster (1960, 1970).
[79] Salway (1993) 73–5; Millett (1990) 55.

CHAPTER 5
BRITAIN IN THE MID-FIRST CENTURY

1. Administration and finances of the emergent province
2. The campaigns against Wales
3. British economy and society in the mid-first century

The focus of this chapter is on the state of Britain after the conquest of southern England and before Boudica's revolt. That was a short but formative period for the fledgling province. Some of the discussion will adopt a wider time frame in order to deal with topics coherently.

1. ADMINISTRATION AND FINANCES OF THE EMERGENT PROVINCE

Governor and first capital

The governor was a man of senatorial rank and a formidable figure. His official title was *legatus Augusti pro praetore*, meaning legate of the Emperor with the rank of pro-praetor. The governor was sometimes a former consul and referred to as '*consularis*'. He was the chief executive of the province, in charge of everything except financial administration: as top general, he commanded the army in Britain; as top judge he had the power of life and death.

In the early years, the governor would have operated from one of the legionary bases. While the Twentieth Legion was based at Colchester, the governor probably had his headquarters there, but he was peripatetic. Each year he spent many months out and about, either campaigning or performing his other duties. Most of the governor's staff went with him.

The first provincial capital,[1] if it could be called such, was at Colchester. The temple of Claudius stood there, as previously discussed. We have little evidence about how people paid their respects to the divine Claudius, but can draw inferences from other imperial cult centres, such as Tarragona in Spain and Lyons (*Lugdunum*) in France.[2] There was probably a provincial council, to which all regions of the emergent province sent representatives. The priest of the imperial cult would have presided over its meetings. A festival and games probably accompanied council meetings, with all costs falling on the local community.

---

[1] Hassall (1996) 19–20.
[2] Gascoyne and Radford (2013) 78.

Financial administration

Financial administration was even more important than worshipping dead emperors. The *procurator provinciae*[3] was the senior official who dealt with financial matters. He was an equestrian, so one notch below the governor in the social hierarchy. As an independent officeholder, he reported directly to the Emperor and was not subject to the governor's jurisdiction. As we shall see, this bifurcation of authority gave rise to substantial problems.

The procurator's first task was to pay the army. With some 40,000 soldiers stationed across the province, that was no easy task. There were four legions at the time of the conquest and three legions in later years, not to mention about sixty auxiliary cohorts. The procurator's second but urgent priority was to create a taxation system on conventional Roman lines and then to organize the collection of taxes.[4] Even in the age of word processors and Excel spreadsheets, these would be formidable tasks. In the first century AD the financial administration of Britannia was highly labour intensive.

The procurator had his own administrative staff, many of whom were freedmen. It is a feature of slave-based societies that sometimes slaves, or former slaves, rise to senior official positions.[5] Narcissus, whom we met in Chapter 4, is a good example of a former slave who enjoyed a fast track career in the civil service. Many of the freedmen who served under the procurator would have possessed considerable administrative and accounting skills.

The procurator required a fixed head office. This was probably located in London from an early date. Tacitus states that Decianus, the procurator in AD 60–61, sent 200 men to defend Colchester during Boudica's rebellion. Therefore, he cannot have been based in Colchester, where the early governors had their headquarters. London was the obvious choice: it was the first proper Roman town in Britain and a major financial centre. Classicianus, a procurator who died in office during the mid-60s, was buried in London and his tombstone is still there, albeit now in the British Museum. Writing tablets with the procurator's official stamp[6] have been found in London. Tiles marked PPBRILON[7] have turned up in the city, which shows that the procurator's remit even extended to tile-making kilns. The modern Treasury would be envious.

London as a financial centre

London was a new town, which developed rapidly on the north bank of the Thames from about AD 47–48. Possibly Gallic traders moved in, seeing a business opportunity. According to Tacitus, London became a major commercial centre in the mid-first century. The recent discovery of wooden writing tablets at the Bloomberg site in Queen Victoria Street amply confirms what Tacitus says. The tablets were small wooden rectangles with waxed surfaces. The wax has vanished, but sometimes messages written in the wax have left scratch marks on the underlying wood.[8] Many of the messages relate to business or financial transactions. Much of

---

[3] Birley (2005) para 1.13 and Hassall (1996) 20.
[4] For details of taxation, see the Online Appendix.
[5] Hazell (2011) 12.
[6] RIB 2443.2: *Proc Aug dederunt Brit Prov*, an abbreviation for 'the imperial procurators of the province of Britain issued this'.
[7] Abbreviation for *Procurator Provinciae Britanniae Londinii*, 'the procurator of Britain at London'.
[8] Tomlin (2016).

the wood used for making the tablets seems to have been recycled from the staves of barrels or casks, which is evidence that London was a trading centre.

Tablet WT44, dated 8 January AD 57,[9] records that Tibullus, the freedman of Venustus, owed 105 denarii to Gratus as the price of goods sold and delivered. That was quite a large sum, the equivalent of six months' pay for a legionary soldier. Hopefully, Tibullus paid up. He certainly had no defence: delivery of the goods was admitted, the contract was in writing and it has survived for two thousand years.

Tablet WT30 also comes from the 50s and apparently refers to London's new forum. The surviving text reads:

> ... because they are boasting through the whole market that you have lent them money. Therefore, I ask you for your own sake not to appear shabby ... you will not thus favour your own affairs.

We will never know the background to this tantalizing snippet. What is significant, however, is that there was a London market in the mid-first century where financial matters were discussed and where reputations could be made or ruined.

Urbanization and the civitas system

The Romans brought with them the concept of the city. Urbanization was a key feature of Roman policy and the growth of cities can be traced across the whole Empire.[10] In the mid-first century Roman style cities and towns started to develop in southern Britain, often on former local centres. Historians put the towns of Roman Britain into neat categories: civitas capital (administrative centre, as discussed below), *municipium* (town with enhanced civic status), *colonia* (veterans' settlement/ model Roman town) and, in the later period, 'small town'. The use of these terms provides a coherent framework, but it is a mistake to think of all towns in each category as being uniform.[11] The high streets of every modern town may look much the same, with the usual chain stores and coffee shops, but people were more imaginative in the ancient world. Romano-British towns varied over space and time. *Coloniae*, in particular, evolved. They may have started as veteran settlements and showcases for the Roman way of doing things, as described by Tacitus. But the veterans married local women; the second and third generations were a fusion of populations. The *coloniae* would soon have lost any special character that they once possessed.

The civitas system was a characteristic feature of Rome's provincial administration. The word *civitas* means a community of citizens. That could be an independent state or a community with some measure of self-governance existing within a state. As Rome extended its reach across Europe, it did not have either the resources or the inclination to micro-manage individual provinces. It therefore promoted *civitates* as separate communities, which would exist within the framework of provinces. The idea was that they would pay their taxes, provide conscripts

---

[9]Expressed as the sixth day before the Ides of January in the consulship of Nero Claudius Caesar Augustus Germanicus for the second time and Lucius Calpurnius Piso.
[10]Woolf (2012) 190–1.
[11]Millett (2001).

to serve as auxiliaries and generally do as they were told by the Roman authorities. Subject to those minor inconveniences, the civitates were free to govern themselves.

In the Mediterranean region, where city states were long established, the existing cities readily evolved into civitates. Northern Europe was different. There were no flourishing city states on the Graeco-Roman model. The Romans therefore found it simplest to take the existing 'tribes' (as they assumed them to be) and characterize these as civitates. The previous informal boundaries were preserved and ratified within the new political order. The Roman authorities promoted this system in Gaul following Caesar's conquest and Gaul seemed to function satisfactorily, apart from the occasional rebellion. They did the same thing again in Britain a century later.

Administrative control passed to pro-Roman aristocrats who governed their traditional territories on Rome's behalf,[12] as explained in Chapter 17 below. The old oligarchies of the Iron Age survived within Roman political structures.[13] These structures reinforced the power and authority of the existing leaders; they in turn acted as tax collectors and were generally loyal to Rome. This relationship of mutual support may be the reason why the civitas system endured.

For the system to work, each civitas had to be centred on a principal town. The provincial authorities and the local élites generally established these civitas capitals either on existing local centres or, where there was no convenient *oppidum*, on military sites after the army had moved on. It is a mistake to think of civitas capitals springing up rapidly as soon as Rome gained control. The process was a gradual one. Religious sanctuaries may have played an important role in the early development of the civitas system.[14] In areas where there was no pre-existing Iron Age polity, it was not easy to operate Roman-style local government. It is likely that centurions, based at local forts, supervised these areas. Before a civitas capital was established at Carlisle, a centurion called Annius Equester was in charge of the region.[15]

During the first century AD, several civitas capitals emerged in southern England (see Table 5.1). This was not a neat and tidy reorganization. Some of the towns in the south-west may have functioned as administrative centres without the full panoply of councillors and magistrates. The Atrebates, the Regni and the Belgae could not become conventional civitates until after the death of Togidubnus. The Iceni did not become a civitas until after the death of the client king, Prasutagus, and his formidable wife, Boudica.

The position concerning the Trinovantes is uncertain. Their existence as a distinct community is well attested.[16] Gosbecks, which principally comprised temples and a theatre, could not have been their administrative centre. Nor could Chelmsford (*Caesaromagus*), which lacked all the usual features of a civitas capital, such as street grids and forum. The most likely scenario is that the Roman authorities in Colchester administered the Essex region. Possibly this was a consequence of the Trinovantes' role in the rebellion.

As we saw in Chapter 4, one faction of the Catuvellauni led the resistance to Rome's invasion in AD 43 and were signally unsuccessful. Subsequently, the pro-Roman faction came to the fore and readily accepted Roman rule. As a result, no forts were located in Catuvellaunian territory[17]

---

[12] Millett (2007) 150.
[13] Millet (1990) chapter 4.
[14] Millett (2007) 158–9.
[15] *Tab Vindol I*, 250.
[16] Rivet and Smith (1979) 476–7.

Table 5.1 First-Century AD Civitas Capitals in Southern England

Community	Capital town	Latin name	Situation
Cantiaci[a]	Canterbury	*Durovernum Cantiacorum*	Iron Age centre
Regni	Chichester	*Noviomagus Reginorum*	Iron Age centre
Belgae	Winchester	*Venta Belgarum*	Iron Age centre
Atrebates	Silchester	*Calleva Atrebatum*	Iron Age centre
Durotriges	Dorchester	*Durnovaria*	Close to Iron Age hillfort
Dumnonii	Exeter	*Isca Dumnoniorum*	Roman fort[b]
Catuvellauni	St Albans	*Verulamium*	Iron Age centre
Dobunni	Cirencester	*Corinium Dobunnorum*	Close to Iron Age centre
Corieltauvi	Leicester	*Ratae Corieltauvorum*	Iron Age centre
Iceni	Caistor[c]	*Venta Icenorum*	Minor Iron Age settlement
Cornovii	Wroxeter	*Viroconium Cornoviorum*	Roman fort

[a] Referred to by Ptolemy as 'Cantii'.
[b] The legionary fortress of the Second Legion Augusta, which left Exeter in about 65.
[c] Caistor St Edmund, near Norwich.

and Verulamium received the status of *municipium* at an early date.[18] Caratacus, the leader of the anti-Roman faction, was appalled by such a supine attitude. He shook the dust of Verulamium from his feet and headed off to Wales, hoping to find to find more sturdy resistance fighters amongst the Silures. He was not disappointed.

Many villas sprang up in south-east England during the period after the conquest. These were well-appointed country residences for the comfort and convenience of well-to-do Britons. They were often built on or close to late Iron Age residences, which suggests continuity of ownership.[19] Most of them were comparatively modest and did not affect agricultural production,[20] but there were exceptions. A major villa was built at Eccles in about AD 55, overlooking the Medway. Seemingly the old nobility was preserving its position, whilst enjoying the Roman lifestyle. The use of baths inside villas shows how deeply the owners were imbued with the new social values. Such villas remained a feature of Roman Britain for four centuries, becoming progressively more luxurious. Some villas, or at least their remains, can still be visited. They make a very pleasant day out, especially if cream teas are available.

The imperial treasury made handsome payments to local leaders, which facilitated the construction of their villas, as well as the purchase of Roman clothing and luxuries. As we shall see in Chapter 6, it subsequently turned out that in the books of the procurator these payments

---

[17] What was once thought to be an auxiliary fort was almost certainly not a military base: Haselgrove and Millett (1997) 294.
[18] Tacitus, *Annals* 14.33.
[19] For example, at Gorehambury near St Albans and Rockbourne in Hampshire
[20] Millett (2007) 151.

were classified as loans rather than gifts. In those early days, however, the well-to-do Britons enjoyed their new wealth. Some also borrowed substantial sums from Seneca, a rich Roman philosopher, in order to increase their spending power.[21]

However pleased the élites may have been with their new status and comforts, the ordinary Britons did not welcome the new regime. As Tacitus explains, the indigenous people regarded both the governor and the procurator as instruments of oppression: 'the governor waged war on them and the procurator plundered their possessions.'[22] As we shall see, this discontent came to a head in the rebellion led by Boudica.

London was not a civitas capital. It was a Roman administrative centre and trading hub, which stood outside the civitas system. Later in the first century, London became the provincial capital, as discussed in chapter 17 below.

The North

In the mid-first century a doughty lady, Cartimandua, ruled the Brigantes, insofar as it was possible for anyone to rule a loosely knit federation of Celtic peoples. She struck an alliance with Rome at the first opportunity and Brigantia became a client kingdom. There appear to have been both pro- and anti-Roman factions within the Brigantes. There was a period when some of them stirred up trouble, but Publius Ostorius Scapula quickly suppressed this: the ring leaders were executed and everyone else was pardoned.[23] After that blip Cartimandua continued her policy of judicious co-operation with Rome, gaining wealth and other rewards in return.[24]

Cartimandua was probably based at Stanwick.[25] The fortifications and earthworks of this massive site were not only to keep out raiders – they were also designed to impress. High-quality glass tableware, brooches and other luxury items found at Stanwick are dated to the mid-first century. An array of Continental imports suggests that Brigantia enjoyed close trading relations with Rome. Some of the luxury items were probably diplomatic gifts.

Most of the Roman forts placed in Brigantia up to the late 70s were around the borders, including the two great legionary fortresses at York (*c.* AD 71) and Chester (*c.* AD 78). The implication is that there was little military activity within Brigantia. This is consistent with its status as a client kingdom. On the other hand, and more ominously, it was normal Roman practice to place forts overlooking territories that they intended to annexe. If the Brigantes were hoping to retain their semi-independent status indefinitely, they would be disappointed.

2. THE CAMPAIGNS AGAINST WALES

Tacitus provides a fairly full account of the campaigns against Wales in the mid-first century, which is consistent with the archaeological evidence. There is no reason to reject Tacitus' account.

---

[21] Dio, *Roman History* 62.2.
[22] Tacitus, *Agricola* 15: 'legatus in sanguinem, procurator in bona saeviret'.
[23] Tacitus, *Annals* 12.32.
[24] Tacitus, *Histories* 3.45.
[25] Haselgrove (2016).

Britain in the Mid-First Century

There were two major Welsh communities, as defined (or perhaps created) by Roman administrators: the Ordovices in mid-Wales and the Silures in south-eastern Wales. There were also two smaller groups, namely the Deceangli in north-west Wales and the Demetae in the south-west. They all remained fiercely independent. Tacitus does not refer to any rulers or kings by name. The inference both from Tacitus and from the archaeological evidence is that the Welsh peoples did not have the same degree of central organization as those in south-east England. They were more widely scattered and less deferential to authority. That may still be so.

Publius Ostorius Scapula arrived in Britain to succeed Aulus Plautius as governor in AD 47. After suppressing the first Iceni revolt in AD 47,[26] Ostorius turned his attention to Wales and attacked the Deceangli. In accordance with normal practice the Romans ravaged their fields and stole everything of value that they could find.[27] The Ordovices and the Silures presented more formidable opposition. Their commander was none other than Caratacus, the Catuvellian leader who had mounted such sturdy but unsuccessful resistance against Aulus Plautius. He now headed a coalition of all who feared what Tacitus delicately describes as 'Roman peace'.

Caratacus chose a battle ground immediately behind a river, with hills and a stone embankment on one side. This terrain favoured the Britons, because it offered a variety of approaches and escape routes. According to Tacitus, Caratacus spurred on his men before battle commenced by recalling how their great grandfathers had seen off Julius Caesar. The Romans attacked, led by Ostorius. In the initial exchange of missiles, they suffered more casualties than the Britons, but then they adopted a 'tortoise' formation with shields locked above heads[28] and so came to close quarters with the enemy. In hand-to-hand fighting the Romans prevailed.

Although the Romans killed everyone they could catch, they spared Caratacus' family who were more useful alive than dead. They captured his wife, daughter and brother. The great resistance leader himself was nowhere to be seen: Caratacus had melted into the Welsh mists before anyone could grab him. He was now the most wanted man in Britain. Caratacus fled north to the Brigantes and sought asylum. Cartimandua was unsympathetic. She coldly handed him over to the Romans (Fig. 5.1). This episode further strengthened her relationship with Rome.[29]

What happened to Caratacus?

Claudius decided to execute Caratacus and his family in Rome as a public relations exercise. According to Tacitus, when invited to utter his last words, Caratacus pointed out that if Rome wanted to rule the world, it was hardly surprising that other nations did not welcome enslavement. If the planned executions went ahead, the defeat of Caratacus would soon be forgotten. But if he was spared, Caratacus would be a constant reminder of Claudius' magnanimity in victory. The Emperor was moved by these words and spared the whole family. This incident affords an early example of the benefits of learning Latin.

---

[26] See Chapter 4, Section 4 (iii).
[27] 'Vastati agri, praedae passim actae': Tacitus, *Annals* 12.32.
[28] As used by Caesar's troops a century earlier: see Chapter 3.
[29] Tacitus, *Histories* 3.45.

The Roman Occupation of Britain and Its Legacy

After their lucky escape, Caratacus and his family settled in Rome. They marvelled at the scale and magnificence of Roman architecture. Then Caratacus posed a highly pertinent question. Why did the Romans, who had such sumptuous possessions, still covet the humble homesteads of Britain?[30]

There was, and is, no rational answer to this question.

Figure 5.1 Cartimandua hands Caratacus over to the Romans. © Chronicle/Alamy Stock Photo.

---

[30]'εἶτα' ἔφη 'ταῦτα καὶ τὰ τοιαῦτα κεκτημένοι τῶν σκηνιδίων ἡμῶν ἐπιθυμεῖτε;' Dio, *Roman History* 61.33.3.

After the defeat of Caratacus the Silures did not give up but continued to harass the Romans with guerrilla warfare. In response, Ostorius took a hard line, advocating genocide: he repeatedly declared that the Silures must be 'completely exterminated'.[31] Tacitus reports that this statement infuriated them. No doubt it did. It is unsurprising that the Silures took exception to that policy.

Over time the Silures began to enjoy some success in their raids on the Roman forces. Heartened by this intelligence, some of the nearby peoples decided to join forces with the Silures. All this was too much for Ostorius. According to Tacitus, the governor was exhausted by the trials and tribulations of the war. In modern parlance, Ostorius was suffering from extreme stress. He died in AD 52. The Silures shed no tears at the news. They re-doubled their attacks on the Roman troops.

There came a time when the Brigantes changed sides and provided support for the Silures. The reason for this dramatic change of policy was, apparently, a marital split: Cartimandua divorced her husband, Venutius; after some internecine strife, Venutius seized power and led one faction into war against the Romans.

After Ostorius' death, Claudius appointed a replacement, Aulus Didius Gallus, who served as the third governor of Britannia from AD 52 to 57. He had some success against the Silures and the Brigantes. According to Tacitus he also established forts in remoter districts.[32]

We now turn to the disposition of Roman troops, so far as we can discern this from archaeological and epigraphic evidence. The pattern of first-century fortresses is consistent with a long-drawn-out campaign against determined Welsh resistance.[33] The Twentieth Legion established an initial base at Kingsholm in AD 48. In the early years of the campaign, vexillation forts[34] appeared in the border region and the south, to house detachments from legions. In about AD 55 the Fourteenth Legion established their fortress at Wroxeter,[35] where they controlled a ford over the River Severn. They were well placed for mounting campaigns against central and northern Wales. They also had good transport links: Watling Street, the main arterial road of the province ran north–south through the centre of the fortress. Tombstone inscriptions record the legion's presence. One of these inscriptions poignantly addresses the reader: 'May the gods prohibit you from the wine-grape and water.'[36] The deceased, Titus Flaminius of the Fourteenth Legion, was rather too fond of the bottle.

In about AD 57 the Twentieth Legion moved forward to Usk, where it established a new fortress as its base for warfare against the Silures. It remained there for some seven years. In AD 65 the Fourteenth Legion was withdrawn from Britain.[37] This triggered a general redeployment. The Twentieth Legion abandoned the conquest fort at Usk and moved north to occupy the now empty fortress at Wroxeter. At the same time the Second Legion Augusta left Exeter and established a new fortress at Gloucester, from where it could watch over the Silures and the Demetae.

---

[31]'Silurum nomen penitus extinguendum.': *Annals* 12.39.
[32]*Agricola* 14.
[33]Birley (2005) 228; Manning (2007) suggests slightly different dates.
[34]A detachment from a legion sent to perform a specific task was a vexillation (*vexillatio*).
[35]White and Barker (2011) chapter 2.
[36]'Di uva vini et aqua prohibent': RIB 292. See also RIB 294.
[37]Dando-Collins (2010) 171.

Many auxiliary forts of the 50s and 60s have been found in the interior of Wales. They are dotted along the principal routes. These forts are stark evidence of a decentralized society, which harassed the Romans with guerrilla warfare. The Romans placed an auxiliary fort at Sudbrook, where there was an Iron Age hillfort that had guarded the Severn Estuary. They probably also established a ferry at Sudbrook to link up with the south-west peninsula.

Whilst Aulus Didius Gallus was battling in Wales and Brigantia, larger events were afoot in Rome. In AD 54 the Emperor Claudius died, probably poisoned by his wife. He was succeeded by his stepson, Nero. As emperor, Nero was not without his faults. He began by murdering his mother; a few years later he ordered Christians to be strapped up and burnt in the evenings.[38] In relation to Britain, however, Nero made a shrewd assessment. The province required a huge military presence and it was separated from the rest of the Empire by the 'Ocean'. Nero seriously considered pulling out of Britain altogether. The only reason why Nero rejected this obviously-sensible course was that he did not wish to detract from Claudius' reputation.[39] Nero derived his authority and his legitimacy from being Claudius' adopted son. Yet again imperial politics triumphed over any rational assessment of Rome's interests.

Quintus Veranius was appointed governor of Britannia in AD 57. He had previously enjoyed a glittering career both as a general and in public life. Everyone, including Veranius himself, expected that he would achieve great things in the turbulent British province. But the gods decided otherwise. He died in AD 58 after conducting some raids against the Silures. Tacitus describes these raids as minor (*modicis*), but that description may be unfair.[40] He may have brought the Silures under effective control, since we know that the following governor (Paullinus) was able to turn his attention to north Wales. Veranius claimed in his will that, if he had lived for another two years, he would have delivered the whole of Britain (i.e. up to the north coast of Scotland) as a province.[41] That was a bold and improbable posthumous boast.

Following the death of Veranius, the governor who had the misfortune to come next was Gaius Suetonius Paullinus, who served from AD 58 to 61. He took the view that capturing the Isle of Anglesey (*Mona*) would be the key to controlling Wales. Anglesey was a centre of Druidism. It was heavily populated and in recent years it had also become a refugee camp.[42] In order to mount an attack on Anglesey, it was first necessary to subdue the Ordovices. Tacitus does not mention this tiresome detail, but the probability is that during AD 58 Paullinus campaigned successfully against the Ordovices. This enabled him to penetrate the territory of the Deceangli and to move against Anglesey in AD 59.[43]

Paullinus duly marched his army to the north coast of Wales and they assembled on the shoreline opposite Anglesey. The Roman infantry set off across the Menai Strait, some swimming and others in flat bottomed boats. A dense crowd of Britons was waiting on the opposite shore. As described by Tacitus,[44] they made a scary spectacle: the women, adorned in black robes and with long dishevelled hair, resembled furies; the Druids stood nearby with hands were raised up to heaven, screaming dreadful curses. The British tactics almost worked.

---

[38] Tacitus, *Annals* 15.44.
[39] 'Ex Britannia deducere exercitum cogitavit,... ne obtrectare parentis gloriae videretur, destitit': Suetonius, *Nero* 18.
[40] *Annals* 14.29.
[41] Tacitus, *Annals* 14.29.
[42] 'receptaculum perfugarum': Tacitus, *Annals* 14.29.
[43] Manning (2007) 68.
[44] *Annals* 14.30.

The superstitious Roman troops wavered and for a time feared to attack before they landed and occupied the island. Neither the Druids nor their gods put up any effective resistance. This colourful passage in the *Annals* probably contain elements of fiction. Tacitus' description of the women in black and the Druids is almost certainly a stereotype, designed to emphasize the 'otherness' of the Britons.

Having gained control of Anglesey, Paullinus stationed a garrison there. He tore down the sacred groves of the Druids and smashed up their altars. Paullinus may have felt some contentment that, at last, the whole of southern Britain seemed to be safely under Roman rule, but that contentment was short lived. As Paullinus strolled around the peaceful woodlands of Anglesey, word reached him of a major rebellion. Queen Boudica was on the march.

3. BRITISH ECONOMY AND SOCIETY IN THE MID-FIRST CENTURY

The notion that foreign settlers should not dispossess indigenous peoples of their property has caused much angst in modern times. This is exemplified by recent litigation in New Zealand and Australia concerning the rights of aboriginal peoples. No such notions troubled the ancient world: it was standard practice to exploit the resources of every country that Rome conquered.

Mining and industry

It was known before the invasion that Britain possessed mineral resources, such as gold, silver, iron and tin. Both Caesar and Strabo recorded this in their descriptions of Britain, but the extent of those resources was not known. Immediately after annexation the Romans set about finding out and expropriating whatever they needed. This exploitation continued for four centuries.

The Mendip Hills were rich in minerals. Britons had been mining here for many years before the conquest. During the 40s, however, there was a rapid change of ownership.[45] The Romans in conjunction with Britons started to excavate lead from the Mendip Hills on a large scale. There were no separate silver ores in Britain, but the lead ores yielded a modest amount of silver.[46] The Roman authorities processed the metals that they excavated. They were principally interested in silver, which they needed for minting denarii. Under the Principate, the imperial government had a monopoly over all bullion mining. Lead was less valuable, but it served as a building material. Lead could also be mixed with copper to make bronze for sesterces. Whereas modern mine owners are meant to restore the environment once they have finished, the Romano-British miners did not bother. The pits and mounds that you can see at Ubley Warren Nature Reserve are the residue of Roman mining operations.

Romans and Britons occupied the former Iron Age site at Charterhouse and established a mining community there, which later acquired both a fort and an amphitheatre. Many luxury goods have been found on this site, including pottery, brooches and figurines. A hoard of Roman coins has also been retrieved. What remains of the Roman town now lies beneath a

---

[45]Fradley (2009) 99–122.
[46]Dungworth (2016) 535.

large field. Anyone who walks from there to the top of the hill can see the amphitheatre, about 100 metres to the left of the radio mast. It is a pleasant pasture for cattle.

Stamped ingots show that legionary soldiers were overseeing the extraction of silver and lead in the Mendips by 49.[47] We cannot, however, infer that the Romans controlled all such mining activity from the fact that a small number of ingots bore official stamps. Once the Roman authorities had extracted most of the silver, they probably let private contractors mine the lead. Archaeological evidence shows that Charterhouse continued as a Romano-British mining centre from the mid-first century until the fourth century.

During the first and second centuries (up to AD 160) lead ingots produced in Roman provinces were stamped to show their place of origin. Those from the Mendips were stamped 'VEB', which was possibly an abbreviation for Ubley. Lead pigs from the Mendips range in weight from 34 kg to 101 kg. Most have been found in the Mendips, but some have appeared further afield including a group of three in London and one in northern France. You can see two of the lead ingots, stamped with Hadrian's name, in Bath Museum.

Both Romans and Britons extracted iron ore from the Kent, Sussex and Surrey Weald, felling oak trees to make charcoal, which was essential fuel for smelting.[48] The *classis Britannica* (British fleet, established in the late first century) became involved in these operations, ensuring that any iron needed for the ships was readily available. Stamped tiles belonging to the *classis Britannica* have been found at mining sites across the Weald. Some commentators describe the fleet as 'controlling' the mining operations, but that is an exaggeration. Iron served a multitude of purposes, such as nails, chisels, hinges, tools, knives, spearheads and all the other comforts of the ancient world. Probably private contractors did most of the mining on the Weald. Only a fraction of the iron produced ended up on Roman ships.

The Britons had been making pots perfectly satisfactorily in the Iron Age, but large-scale production only developed after AD 43. Potteries in Kent and Essex developed a characteristic style now known as 'black burnished ware', although first century potters did not use this term. Because of improved transport links black burnished ware was distributed widely across Britain.[49]

The general state of the province

In Britain, as in other provinces, the Romans embarked upon extensive road building. The initial purpose of the roads was military: they provided quick and easy passage for messengers on horseback and also for the wheeled back-up accompanying the army. They also divided up conquered territories into easily controllable chunks.

One of the first roads that the army built, making use of Iron Age tracks, was Watling Street. It started at Richborough and ran north-west to London, St Albans and Wroxeter. This developed as a key road through the new province. Other roads linked the main sites and towns in Kent. It is uncertain whether the provincial authorities built these other roads or local people did so on their behalf.[50] The emerging road system brought economic benefits.

---

[47] One lead ingot bears the stamp of the Second Legion Augusta and the name of the consul in 49.
[48] Sim (2012) 25–30.
[49] Millett (2007) 167.
[50] Millett (2007) 148.

Despite the expansion of trade and industry, the great majority of Britons continued to live in rural settlements. Britannia in the mid-first century remained primarily an agrarian economy. This is unsurprising. In the ancient world the two principal sources of wealth were agricultural and mineral.

Although it was an agrarian economy, the province was not self-sufficient in food.[51] The substantial army garrisoning Britain needed to be fed. There was a serious problem of transportation: most of the agricultural areas were inland, but the best way to supply Rome's military units was by sea. Therefore, the Roman troops remained dependent on food supplies from the Continent. Many of these supplies came in through the port of London, thus adding to the importance of this new commercial centre.[52]

Richborough (*Rutupiae*),[53] the site of the original Roman landing, remained an important supply base for the army from AD 43 to about AD 85. It remained a primary port of entry into Britain through much of the Roman period.

Join the army and see the world

Fit young Britons were recruited or, more probably conscripted, to serve in the Roman army and generally posted overseas.[54] Tacitus refers to a British cavalry squadron[55] serving in Gaul during AD 69. Diplomas (presented at the end of military service) refer to three British infantry cohorts from which men were discharged during the 80s.[56] Sometimes the diplomas tell us which communities the soldiers came from: a soldier serving in the First British Cohort in Pannonia in AD 105 was a member of the Dobunni; another soldier serving in the same cohort in AD 110 was a member of the Belgae.[57] Two first-century cohorts of Britons (*cohortes Brittonum*) appear in inscriptions overseas. In AD 106 a British cohort received a block grant of Roman citizenship after distinguishing itself in Dacia (now Romania). None of this means that Britain made a major contribution to the Roman Empire.[58] Overall the evidence of Britons serving abroad is meagre. There are no records of any British centurions. Whereas some provinces produced emperors, Britain did not. There was a general lack of Britons in the higher echelons of the Empire.

Tacitus tells us that some of the British recruits served as auxiliaries in Britain.[59] This must have been very much the exception, possibly due to temporary military exigencies. Normal Roman policy in the late first century AD was to recruit troops in newly conquered territories and then move them elsewhere. It was not until the second century (when the province was firmly established) that the army in Britain recruited locally.

---

[51] Millett (1990) 56–7.
[52] Mattingly (2007) 511.
[53] Millett (2007) 141–2; Harris (2002).
[54] Mann and Dobson (1996).
[55] *Histories* 3.41: 'Venere tres cohortes cum ala Britannica'.
[56] *Cohors I Britannica*, CIL xvi.26 and 30; *Cohors I Brittonum*, CIL xvi.31; *Cohors II Brittonum* CIL xiii.12124.
[57] CIL xvi.49.
[58] Mann and Dobson (1996) 51–2.
[59] *Agricola* 32.

CHAPTER 6
BOUDICA'S REBELLION AND ITS AFTERMATH

1. Introduction

2. Background to rebellion: Roman repression and greed

3. Boudica strikes back (AD 60–61)

4. The Romans prevail

5. Aftermath

1. INTRODUCTION

This chapter is an account of the – now celebrated – Boudican rebellion. It was not a unique event, but part of a familiar pattern across the Roman Empire in the early years.

'Native revolt' is a common social movement in the history of imperialism. Stephen Dyson has carried out a study of the subject.[1] On Dyson's analysis, the patterns of revolt were different in the two halves of the Roman Empire.

- In the East, Rome took over ancient civilizations with established city states and recognizable political systems. Revolts, such as the Great Jewish Revolt of AD 66, were attempts to re-establish the cultural and religious norms that the Romans had suppressed.

- In the West, communities were smaller and more fragmented. Rome imposed upon them a complex administrative structure with governors, public officials and taxes. Revolts resulted from the extreme tensions placed on societies in the process of rapid acculturation. They were also expressions of resistance to taxation and the administrative abuse that came with it. Revolts often came after the initial 'conquest' phase, when the Roman government thought that the major problems were over. Such revolts occurred in Spain, Gaul, Sardinia, Britain and elsewhere.

Dyson's analysis is valid so far as it goes, but that is not the complete picture. We cannot simply say that indigenous peoples were resistant to change, implying that they were conservative and backward looking. The more important point is that the local populations wanted to determine

---

[1] Dyson (1975) 138–75.

their own futures and to drive change themselves. They had their own social networks, identity, property rights and ambitions. The demands of the imperial authorities cut across all that.

We have much information about Boudica.[2] Tacitus wrote about her in the *Agricola* and, more extensively, in the *Annals*. Tacitus' father-in-law served as a military tribune during Boudica's rebellion and witnessed her final defeat. The *Annals* provide the only link between Boudica and the Iceni. Dio Cassius, writing a century later, gave an account of the rebellion in book 62 of his *Roman History*. He had access to first-century sources, which are now lost. Tacitus portrays Boudica as a heroic figure, whereas Dio presents her as a monstrous female. Both writers were story tellers, as well as historians: they were seeking to hold the interest of a Roman audience. Their accounts of Boudica's oratory must be fictitious, as no Roman soldier or official heard her speeches. There is also a brief reference to the rebellion in Suetonius' biography of Nero.

In the writings of first- and second-century historians, Boudica reflected a contemporary stereotype.[3] The Romans saw all foreigners as 'barbarians' and expected them to be strange. Writers emphasized their strangeness; in Boudica's case, they exaggerated her savagery and emphasized her 'otherness'. Tacitus and Dio used ethnography to add colour to their stories. They were also suggesting that new conquests had brought new knowledge. This was part of the bigger picture of Roman imperialism.

Dio called the fearsome queen 'Βουδουῖκα'. This has given rise to the popular name 'Boadicea', which appears on her statue by Westminster Bridge (see Fig. 6.1 below). Tacitus called her 'Boudicca'. This chapter will adopt the now conventional spelling 'Boudica'

2. BACKGROUND TO THE REBELLION: ROMAN REPRESSION AND GREED

Both Tacitus and Dio set out their understanding of the background to the great rebellion. Essentially, they describe two causes: first, a general cause, namely Roman oppression and continuing resentment amongst the Britons; second, a specific cause, namely abuses against Boudica and her daughters, who were the 'first family' of the Iceni. Ancient writers may have exaggerated the first cause,[4] but both factors were present.

General discontent

The Roman authorities required their new subjects to pay taxes and annual tribute. Taxation in the provinces principally took the form of poll tax and duties on trade. The Britons had to pay their taxes in either cash or kind, for example grain.[5] According to Dio,[6] the Romans demanded taxes in respect of death, but this is doubtful. Dio may have been referring to the Roman habit of grabbing some people's estates after death. That happened in the case of Boudica's husband

---

[2]Hingley and Unwin (2005) chapter 2.
[3]Woolf (2011).
[4]Gambash (2012) 1–15.
[5]For a fuller account of the Roman taxation system, see the Online Appendix.
[6]*Roman History* 62.3.4.

and so would have been particularly topical in any account of the Boudican revolt. It does not mean that there was any general regime of inheritance tax. That was probably impractical in first-century Britain.

Official Roman policy was that taxation in the provinces should be set at moderate levels, which subjects could afford to pay. The Emperor's guidance on tax policy had been sensible and pithy: 'The good shepherd should shear his flock, not skin it.'[7] Unfortunately, not all administrators in Britain followed that advice. In a famous, but probably fictitious speech to the Gauls, Cerialis (a commander whom we shall meet later in this chapter) justified Roman fiscal policy as follows: 'No peace without arms; no arms without pay; no pay without taxes.'[8] No modern budget speech is as clear or concise as that.

The precise mechanism by which taxes and tribute were collected in Britain is not known. Where possible, the procurator and his team carried out this formidable task with the co-operation of the local élites. Whether the procurator also used *publicani*, we do not know (see the Online Appendix). According to both Tacitus and Dio, the Britons deeply resented the new taxes: they felt that they were paying out large sums and getting little back in return. The welfare state had not yet been invented.

In addition to taxation, there was debt. Well-to-do Britons had received cash payments from the Emperor Claudius to encourage their loyalty to Rome. It now turned out that these were not gifts at all: they were loans and, apparently, had been so all along. The procurator, Decianus Catus, demanded repayment and enforced his demands with vigour.[9] The philosopher Seneca was also dabbling in finance: he loaned 40 million sesterces to Britons at high rates of interest and subsequently called in the loans, using strong measures to enforce repayment.[10] Britain was caught in a debt crisis because of over-spending and imprudent lending by bankers. This gave rise to widespread social unrest. That may have been a novel problem then. It is not so now.

Trigger events

In AD 60, Prasutagus, king of the Iceni tribe, died leaving a widow, Boudica, and two daughters. He bequeathed his kingdom jointly to his daughters and to the Emperor Nero. According to Tacitus, Prasutagus' motive was to protect the Iceni from a Roman attack after his death. The fact that he had no son was probably a factor in his decision. In practice, it was quite common for 'friendly kings' on the frontiers of the Empire to bequeath their domains to the Roman Emperor.[11] The Romans took Prasutagus' death and bequest as an opportunity to move in and seize whatever property they fancied. According to Tacitus, they flogged Boudica, raped her daughters and treated the whole family as slaves. A major rebellion was the immediate consequence.

The outrages perpetrated on Boudica's family reflect the abuses of the early stages of imperial annexation. The debts owed by the ruling families were more advanced problems. This

---

[7] 'boni pastoris esse tondere pecus, non deglubere': Suetonius, *Tiberius* 32.
[8] 'Neque quies gentium sine armis neque arma sine stipendiis neque stipendia sine tributis haberi queunt': Tacitus, *Histories* 4, 74.
[9] Dio, *Roman History*, 62.2.1.
[10] 'βιαίως ἐσέπρασσεν': Dio, *Roman History* 62.2.1.
[11] King Herod, who died in about 4 BC, bequeathed Judaea to Augustus.

combination of causes reflected the rapid pace of events in southern Britain, which compressed massive social changes into the space of twenty years.[12]

3. BOUDICA STRIKES BACK (AD 60–61)

In either AD 60 or 61, Boudica asserted her claim to the throne of her late husband and set about seeking revenge. No contemporary artist painted Boudica's portrait or carved her statue. Luckily, however, Dio provides a graphic description, although his first-century sources probably contained hearsay rather than any eye-witness description. Apparently, she was a tall lady of terrifying appearance, with a mass of dishevelled golden hair, which hung down to her hips. Boudica dressed the part of a warrior queen. She generally wore a multi-coloured tunic fastened with a brooch and a large golden torc around her neck. She brandished a long spear. The queen had a fierce glare and her voice was harsh. One fears that during his lifetime poor king Prasutagus may have been henpecked.

Boudica began by making fiery speeches, rallying the Iceni and others to her cause. She secured the support of the Trinovantes, who had strong grievances as noted in Chapter 4.[13] According to Dio, Boudica recruited an army of 120,000 men for her campaign. It is likely that in each of the emerging civitates there were pro- and anti-Roman factions. Some people were doing well from the Roman occupation and others were losing out. Anti-Roman factions dominated the Iceni and the Trinovantes. They took a leading role in the rebellion. By contrast, the leaders of the Catuvellauni were already enjoying the perks of the civitas system: pro-Roman factions were in control. Likewise, we know from Tacitus that the client kingdom of the Atrebates, the Belgae and the Regni remained staunchly loyal to Rome.[14] Nevertheless it is highly probable that disaffected Britons from all those regions flocked to the banner of Boudica.

At least eleven coin hoards from this period have come to light in Essex,[15] including denarii (none later than Nero) and coins minted by the Iceni. There are also six metalwork hoards. Such hoards may have been linked to the rebellion, but that is not certain. East Anglia had a long tradition of burying hoards for religious purposes. The Iceni may simply have been making offerings to the gods of the earth.

In AD 60/61 the governor Paullinus was campaigning in Wales. He had with him the Fourteenth and Twentieth Legions and many auxiliary cohorts. This was a golden opportunity, which Boudica seized. Her army set off, marching south towards the hated Roman colony at Colchester. On the way, she captured several forts and killed any occupants who did not escape in time. Colchester had no surrounding earthworks and only a small garrison to protect it. Far outnumbered by the approaching Britons, the veterans and soldiers sent a message to the procurator seeking help. The procurator, Catus Decianus, was grudging in his response. Like

---

[12] Dyson (1975) 167–9.
[13] Laycock (2008) at 74–7 argues that the Trinovantes were Boudica's target rather than her allies. This is ingenious but unconvincing. His inferences from the archaeology are tenuous and contrary to (a) contemporaneous historians and (b) the inherent probabilities.
[14] *Agricola* 14.
[15] Hingley and Unwin (2005) 98–100.

many accountants, he kept a closer eye on costs than the requirements of military strategy. Decianus sent just two hundred men.[16] According to Tacitus, they were not properly armed.

Boudica arrived at Colchester and attacked. Having routed the opposition, she set fire to the Roman settlement and ravaged the surrounding farmland. Some Roman soldiers, together with veterans and their wives took refuge in the great temple. The Britons set about besieging this edifice without regard to religious niceties. Sadly, the divine Claudius, despite the sacrifices and offerings that he had enjoyed over recent years, did not come to the rescue. After a siege of two days the Britons took the temple by storm and massacred everyone who was cowering inside.

The Ninth Legion was then based in the East Midlands, under the command of Quintus Petillius Cerialis. The legion hastily marched southwards, to provide relief for Colchester. Boudica attacked the approaching legion and massacred the infantry. The cavalry escaped. They galloped back to the safety of their fortress. It might be thought that this unfortunate episode would blight Cerialis' career. Not so. Like Winston Churchill after Gallipoli, Cerialis was later to make a comeback. We shall meet him again in Chapter 7 as the governor of Britannia.

The procurator Decianus was probably based in London,[17] surrounded by his books, tablets and accounts. After the fall of Colchester, he found himself uncomfortably close to the enemy action. Decianus did not wait to see how events would unfold: instead he fled from London to the coast and caught the next available boat to Gaul. Decianus was in considerable disgrace. In the eyes of many, his financial mismanagement and greed had played a major part in stirring up the rebellion.

In the meantime, the provincial governor, Paullinus, was hastening back from Wales with his troops. On reaching London, he concluded it would be impossible to defend the city, so he withdrew taking many of the city's inhabitants with him. This must have seemed like a sign of weakness to Boudica. It certainly underlined the seriousness of the predicament in which the Roman authorities were placed.

The queen did not delay. Boudica soon arrived and occupied the city. The rebels seized all valuable property that they could find and massacred the inhabitants. The Britons showed no more tenderness towards their enemies than the Romans did when they were on top. According to Tacitus, the rebels cut the throats of some whom they caught. They hanged, burned or crucified others. By now Queen Boudica was thoroughly enjoying herself.

The British army then marched northwards to St Albans. They captured the city, seized all valuable property and killed everyone in sight. By this stage, according to Tacitus, the Britons had killed approximately 70,000 Romans and collaborators.[18] The collaborators to whom Tacitus refers ('*sociorum*') would have included the élite of the Catuvellauni and other Britons who were benefiting from the civitas system. It went without saying that all prisoners had to be killed. Boudica liked to do this in the most painful way possible, to maximize the entertainment value for her troops. According to Dio, female prisoners of high rank were accorded special treatment. They were hung up naked. Their breasts were cut off and sewed to their mouths, so that the victims seemed to be eating their own breasts. The prisoners were then cut down and

---

[16] Tacitus, *Annals* 14.32.
[17] There is no direct evidence of this. It is a matter of inference, as explained in Chapter 5, section 1.
[18] *Annals* 14.33.

impaled upon sharp skewers pushed lengthwise through their entire bodies. While this was going on the audience would be banqueting or making sacrifices to their gods.

Tacitus and Dio were probably exaggerating Boudica's barbarity. Roman writers regularly portrayed the savagery of foreigners as a literary device. Their readers and listeners expected this. On the other hand, even in modern times rebellions against the established order may involve extreme barbarity. Recent events in Syria and Iraq, such as ISIS beheadings, graphically show how rebel leaders may treat their victims.

Probably the figure of 70,000 deaths was also an exaggeration. It is unlikely that the rebel army killed anything like that number of 'Romans and collaborators'. As we shall see, after the rebellion London rapidly revived as a major trading and administrative centre. This suggests that most of the entrepreneurs who had built London up during the 50s must have made their escape before Boudica arrived. They returned soon after the rebellion and carried on much the same as before.

Marrying up the findings of archaeology with the writings of contemporaneous historians is never easy. Nevertheless, there is evidence of extensive burning in the cities that Boudica attacked. In Colchester[19] the destructive layer varies in depth from a few centimetres to half a metre. Burnt assemblages include items from pottery shops, a burnt bed, lamp moulds, pieces of molten metal and glass, collapsed wall plaster and many household items. Some of the clay that was incorporated into the early timber buildings has survived, because it was fired. If there had been no major fire, the clay would have disintegrated long ago. The burnt layer also includes two keys and a bronze dice-shaker with two dice. Occasionally the lower parts of walls have survived up to a height of about 0.6 of a metre. Apart from that minor omission, the rebels seem to have done a thorough job in razing the hated colony to the ground. Parts of human skulls and bones have been found in the fortress ditch, but linking these with the Boudican massacre is tenuous at best.

The head of an equestrian bronze statue of Claudius has been recovered from the river Alde in Suffolk. This might have been loot from Colchester. Britons tended to regard the heads of statues as sacred. So, throwing Claudius' head into the river could have been ritual deposition, rather than mockery of a hated Emperor.

Verulamium[20] was still a small town, so there was less to burn down. Even so, the damage was severe. Timber buildings in insulae XIV and XVII were destroyed by fire. The bathhouse in insula XIX suffered extensive damage. The workshops by Watling Street were burnt down and took some time to rebuild.

Curiously both Dio and Suetonius refer to two cities, not three, being destroyed in the revolt.[21] They were probably unaware how rapidly the new town of London had developed. A layer of burnt debris covers the site of early Roman London. It can be dated to Boudica's rebellion from coins and pottery fragments. The burnt layer is typically 30–60 centimetres thick, including the remains of grain and other foodstuffs. A burnt shop at 1 Poultry contains charred spices and small spoons. Many of the structures lacking fire debris are next to buildings that were obviously burnt. The inference is that in those areas the fire debris was cleared away more effectively. The left hand and forearm of a gilt-bronze statue was recovered from 20–30

---

[19]Gascoyne and Radford (2013) 96–7; Hingley and Unwin (2005) chapter 3.
[20]Niblett (2001) 67–8; Niblett and Thompson (2005) 149–50.
[21]Wallace (2014) chapter 4; Hingley and Unwin (2005) 53 and 88–9.

Gresham Street in 2001. This appears to have been discarded in a quarry pit, which was backfilled between AD 60 and 70. The original statue would have been slightly larger than life and may have portrayed an emperor or a god. It seems quite possible that this statue was deliberately broken up when Boudica sacked London.[22]

4. THE ROMANS PREVAIL

Having abandoned London to its fate, Paullinus set about gathering reinforcements: from the Fourteenth and Twentieth Legions he assembled a force of about ten thousand men, including auxiliaries. An army of this size would be heavily outnumbered, but Paullinus felt ready to engage the fearsome queen. What the Romans lacked in numbers they made up for in discipline, training and experience.

Boudica and her army marched northwards to the Midlands, where the Roman force was gathering. The scene was set for the final battle. The stakes were high: if Boudica could win another crushing victory, she was on her way to liberating the entire province from Roman rule. Both Tacitus and Dio provide accounts of the battle. Unfortunately, the two accounts are inconsistent and neither historian tells us where the battle took place. Tacitus' account is more reliable, for obvious reasons.

Paullinus drew up his troops in a valley with woods behind them and open country ahead. The Britons could only approach from the front, with no cover for ambushes. Paullinus placed his heavily armed soldiers in the centre with lighter armed auxiliaries at the side and cavalry on the wings. The British army arrived, much larger than the foe and more widely dispersed. According to Dio, the Britons at this stage numbered 230,000, although that figure appears improbably high. Boudica herself rode majestically on a chariot, so that she was visible to her troops and could issue orders.

According to Tacitus (whose father-in-law was present) the Britons even brought their wives to watch the fun. These ladies were given ringside seats in carts drawn up around the edge of the battlefield.

Boudica's speech

Both Tacitus and Dio attribute to Boudica a stirring speech before the battle. By all accounts Boudica was a good orator. She may possibly have addressed her troops, or at least those who were within earshot, but it is highly unlikely that she said anything remotely like either Tacitus' or Dio's version. No Roman heard the speech and the Britons would not have been taking notes. According to Tacitus Boudica said that, although a woman, she was descended from great men. She was fighting as an ordinary person to avenge the disgraceful conduct of the Romans. She poured scorn on the enemy for their cruelty and their cowardice. She was confident that the gods would give victory to the Britons. She finished, as she had begun, by emphasizing her courage, despite being a woman.

---

[22]Bayley et al., (2009) 151–62.

Tacitus' account of Boudica's speech has delighted many British readers over the last two millennia. It may not be too much to say that this powerful (though imaginary) speech has affected the way that some British people see themselves. There are echoes of that speech in the fiery address that Queen Elizabeth I delivered to her troops at Tilbury in 1588, as they prepared to face the Spanish Armada. She declared:

> I know that I have the body of a weak and feeble woman, but I have the heart and stomach of a king, and of a king of England too, and think foul scorn that Parma or Spain or any prince of Europe should dare to invade the borders of my realm.

A nineteenth century statue of Boudica, as warrior queen, stands in London on the Thames Embankment. Whether or not historically accurate, this statue vividly reflects the image of Boudica as emblazoned in English culture (Fig. 6.1).

Figure 6.1 Statue of Boudica by Westminster Bridge. © Flickr/Paul Walter.

Paullinus also addressed his troops. He emphasized the superior skill and discipline of the Roman militia, as compared with the disorderly rabble on the other side. Tacitus' account of that speech is more likely to be accurate, as his father-in-law heard it.

Once the oratory was complete, the battle began. The Romans waited until the enemy came within range and then hurled their javelins. The swarm of javelins threw the Britons into disarray. At this point the Roman soldiers advanced in wedge formation, with the auxiliaries attacking on both wings. The Britons gave ground. Finally, the Roman cavalry charged. The Britons, unable to resist, turned and fled. Unfortunately, flight was difficult because of the carts that were blocking their exit routes. The Romans seized this opportunity to kill everyone they could. They massacred many British soldiers. With even greater ease they slaughtered the unarmed lady spectators who were sitting in their carts. This was a war in which chivalry had no part to play on either side. Finally, and perhaps with excessive zeal, the Romans killed all the British horses as well.

Tacitus proudly records that this was a glorious victory, comparable to Rome's great triumphs of the past.[23] Roman casualties were light, with only 400 dead and slightly more wounded. On the other side almost 80,000 Britons were killed, which represented a large part of the army.

Boudica had no intention of falling into enemy hands or of being paraded through the streets of Rome. Still less would she emulate Caratacus and beg for the Emperor's mercy. The mighty Queen committed suicide by taking poison. According to Dio the Britons mourned Boudica greatly and gave her a lavish funeral.

Tacitus, Dio and Suetonius all describe the rebellion as a terrible disaster. Although 'native revolts' were common in the early years after conquest, as Dyson demonstrates, the Boudican revolt was particularly devastating both for Rome and for Britain.[24] The process of subjugation produced severe social and economic tensions in Britain. Key elements were (i) Rome's demand for taxation, which forced communities to develop a monetary economy, (ii) the long-term dangers of growing debt, (iii) abuses of power by Roman officials and (iv) Rome's total disregard for the aspirations of the indigenous peoples. Most revolts in the West were the product of rapid and imposed changes, Roman excess and opportunity. In Britain the absence of Paullinus (who was in Wales with much of the occupying army) provided the opportunity.

5. AFTERMATH

Paullinus secured further troops from Germany, comprising legionary soldiers, auxiliaries and cavalry. With his enlarged army he attacked those communities or regions that had been in rebellion. The Britons not only faced attacks from Paullinus' army, but also their harvest failed because few crops had been planted during the rebellion.

Leaving aside revenge attacks, there seem to have been no serious military campaigns in Britain during the years following Boudica's rebellion. Tacitus' account of the period focuses on

---

[23] 'Clara et antiquis victoriis par ea die laus parta:' *Annals* 14.37.
[24] Dyson (1975) 170–3.

other issues. It is almost as if 'project Britannia' has ground to a halt. Rome may still have hoped to bring the whole of Britain under Roman control, but during the 60s it did nothing towards achieving that goal. Such control as Rome had secured over the Welsh peoples appears to have weakened. This is the natural inference from the fact that both the Silures and the Ordovices were invaded in the 70s. It is likely that Roman policy during the 60s was to concentrate on consolidating southern England and stabilizing the civitas administration. Many of Rome's initiatives appear to have been directed to pacifying the province and healing divisions.[25] Given the extent of the recent unrest and devastation, that was probably a wise course.

Following the departure of Decianus in disgrace, there was a vacancy to be filled. Gaius Julius Alpinus Classicianus was sent to Britain as the next procurator.[26] He favoured a policy of reconciliation, rather than revenge. He restored the finances and the civil administration of the province, all of which had been shattered by the rebellion. We know from Classicianus' tombstone that his wife was Pacata, the daughter of Julius Indus. Indus was chief of the Gallic Treveri and had helped to crush a rebellion against Tiberius. It is quite likely that Classicianus was also a Trever.[27] Nero's choice of a provincial from Gaul to serve as procurator was a shrewd move. It was probably part of a policy to assuage the fractured province.

Classicianus and Paullinus were as different as chalk and cheese: Classicianus was financially prudent and a wise administrator; Paullinus was a brutal general, who had no qualms about slaughtering or starving the people he was governing. The governor and the new procurator heartily loathed one another. A breakdown in the relationship between the head of government and the chief finance minister always makes administration difficult, as both Margaret Thatcher and Tony Blair confirm in their memoirs.[28] The feud between Paullinus and Classicianus encouraged the Britons to continue their resistance to Rome. Meanwhile Classicianus sent urgent despatches to the Emperor, recommending that a new governor be appointed.

Nero decided to set up an independent inquiry into the British situation.[29] Commissioning such inquiries is a time-honoured procedure for kicking problems into the long grass, where with luck they will remain until the fuss has subsided. In this instance Polyclitus, a former slave but now a senior member of Nero's administration, was despatched to Britain with instructions to investigate and report. Polyclitus duly arrived with a large entourage of officials and scribes. This caused much consternation to the Roman army (or at least the senior officers) and much merriment amongst the Britons. The Britons thought it absurd that the Roman army should be deferring to a former slave.[30]

In due course Polyclitus submitted an anodyne report to the authorities and returned to Rome. However bland the official report may have been, Paullinus' days as governor were numbered: soon afterwards a few ships were lost from the fleet and Paullinus was removed from office. His brutality was making any reconciliation with the British communities impossible. This was an intelligent move by Nero and his advisers.

---

[25] See Gambash's analysis of the events of the 60s: (2012) 1–15.
[26] Tacitus, *Annals* 14.38.
[27] Gambash (2012) 1–15.
[28] Blair (2010) chapter 20; Thatcher (1993) chapter 24.
[29] Tacitus, *Annals* 14.39.
[30] Tacitus, *Annals* 14.39.

The next governor was Publius Petronius Turpilianus, who was a nephew of Aulus Plautius, the first governor.[31] That may be why he got the job. Turpilianus served from AD 61 to 63. In that short period he maintained a low profile, so far as possible avoiding any armed conflicts with the Britons. Tacitus acidly observed that Turpilianus called his inactivity 'an honourable peace'.[32] Despite that observation, Turpilianus' policy may have been sensible in the circumstances. The province needed time to recover from a widespread rebellion with much loss of life.

Classicianus, the procurator, died in about AD 65 and was buried in London. His wife commissioned a fine tombstone for him, one part of which was found in 1852. Another part was found in 1935.[33] As reconstituted, the inscription reads:

> To the spirits of the departed and of Gaius Julius Alpinus Classicianus, son of Gaius, of the Fabian voting tribe ... procurator of the province of Britain; Julia Pacata Indiana, his wife, set this up.[34]

This is the earliest surviving inscription relating to any high Roman official in Britain. Its particular interest lies in the fact that it can be married up with a passage in Tacitus' *Annals*.[35] It is rare to find such a direct link between archaeological discoveries and the literary sources.

Marcus Trebellius Maximus was appointed governor in AD 63 and served for six years. According to Tacitus, Trebellius was somewhat lazy[36] and had no military experience. Happily, however, he kept the province under control by diplomacy.[37] According to Tacitus the barbarians (i.e. the Britons) learnt to indulge in pleasant vices, which distracted them from warfare.[38]

Was Trebellius really a 'lazy' governor? Tacitus was one of the 'great' historians and he was writing about events in his own lifetime. But even Tacitus had his own agenda. He had firm views about 'good' and 'bad' governors and emperors. Also, it was important to Tacitus' narrative to downplay the qualities of governors during the 60s, in order to emphasize the achievements of Agricola, who took over a few years later. Perhaps readers should not judge Trebellius too harshly. In the aftermath of the rebellion, it may have been helpful to have a governor who was not hyperactive.

Archaeological evidence indicates a period of rebuilding in southern Britain during the decades following Boudica's rebellion.[39] The Romans rebuilt their colony at Colchester,[40] largely following the previous street grid. Learning from bitter experience, they built a substantial wall around it between AD 65 and 80. The wall was 2.8 kilometres long and 2.4 metres thick, rising

---

[31] Birley (2005) 51.
[32] 'honestum pacis nomen segni otio imposuit.' *Annals* 14.39.
[33] For the story of these discoveries, see Higgins (2013) 54–5.
[34] 'Dis Manibus G. Iul. G. F. Fab. Alpini Classiciani ... Proc. Provinc Britanniae Iulia Indi. Filia Pacata Indiana, Uxor F': RIB 12.
[35] 14.38.
[36] 'segnior': *Agricola* 16.
[37] *Agricola* 16.
[38] 'Didicere iam barbari quoque ignoscere vitiis blandientibus': *Agricola* 16.
[39] For an account of the rebuilding of London, see chapter 17.
[40] Gascoyne and Radford (2013) 99–107 and 113.

to a height of at least 6 metres. This was the first town wall in Roman Britain. It enclosed a large area to the north, to allow for future expansion. The re-building of Claudius' temple came later. Such delay is hardly surprising: during Boudica's onslaught the divine Emperor had not lifted a finger to help the colonists, even those who sought shelter in his temple. You can still see the temple foundations, which lie beneath the city museum.

The stylus tablets[41] recently recovered from the Bloomberg site in London reveal just how quickly normal life in the province resumed. Those tablets include routine correspondence, legal disputes and business letters both before and after the rebellion. Tablet WT45, dated 21 October AD 62, is the most important example (Fig. 6.2). It records that Gaius Valerius Proculus will transport twenty loads of provisions from St Albans to London for Marcus Rennius Venustus at a price of quarter of a denarius per load. The real point of interest is that Proculus and Venustus were doing routine business only a year or two after the Boudican rebellion; and that routine business concerned transportation between two towns that Boudica had destroyed. This tablet also helps to resolve the long running debate about dating. It strongly suggests that the revolt began in AD 60, not 61. Like Venustus, we are much indebted to Proculus for his help.

Four legions were required for the original annexation of southern Britain, but Nero hoped that three legions would suffice for the day-to-day business of running the province. Accordingly, in about AD 66 he recalled the Fourteenth Legion to serve in Pannonia.[42] This led to a general redeployment of the legions, as explained in Chapter 5. The permanent army stationed in Britain now comprised the Second, Ninth and Twentieth Legions plus auxiliaries.

Figure 6.2 Bloomberg tablet WT45. © Museum of London.

---

[41]Deciphered and translated in Tomlin (2016).
[42]See Birley (2005) 228 and Dando-Collins (2010) 171.

This reduction in the size of the occupying army suggests that the project of annexing the whole of Britain was temporarily on hold.

In AD 68 the Roman Senate declared Nero a public enemy because of his maladministration and abuse of office. To avoid being murdered or executed, Nero took his own life. He was the last emperor in the Julio-Claudian dynasty. A bitter civil war followed in 69 ('the year of the four emperors') when Galba, Otto, Vitellius and Vespasian each became Emperor in quick succession. Vespasian was the survivor. He was a veteran of the conquest of Britain and served as Emperor for ten years.

Now that there was no major campaign afoot, the legions in Britain became bored and restless.[43] They had no opportunity for mass slaughter or seizing booty. The soldiers did not welcome this state of affairs and mutiny was in the air.[44] To make matters worse, Trebellius had gained a reputation for meanness and greed. He was unpopular with the army.

Roscius Coelius, the legate commanding the Twentieth Legion, was a particularly strong critic of the governor. He chose this moment to speak out,[45] accusing the governor of robbing the legions and leaving them poor. Trebellius in turn accused Coelius of inciting mutiny and undermining discipline. Tensions between politicians and military commanders are not, of course, uncommon,[46] but the degree of hostility between Trebellius and Coelius made working together effectively impossible. Trebellius was in an increasingly difficult position. There was no doubt whose side the military were on. Both the legions and the auxiliaries were openly insulting the governor. In those circumstances Trebellius took to his heels. He headed off to join Vitellius, who had recently been proclaimed Emperor.[47]

Following Trebellius' unseemly exit, there was a hiatus before the next governor arrived. During this period, the legates of the three legions jointly administered the province. Strictly speaking they were of equal authority, but in practice Coelius was pre-eminent. Coelius was respected by his two colleagues because he had had the courage to take effective action against Trebellius.

Vitellius' career as Emperor was neither long nor distinguished. He did, however, make two decisions affecting Britain: he appointed Vettius Bolanus to take over as governor and he ordered the Fourteenth Legion to return. Apparently the Fourteenth Legion had been getting above themselves,[48] so Vitellius decided that another spell in Britain would do them good.

The Fourteenth Legion duly returned to Britain, but their stay here was brief and ineffectual. Within a matter of months Vespasian replaced Vitellius as Emperor. Vespasian ordered the legion back to the Continent, this time to serve on the Rhine.[49] The Fourteenth Legion had now been sent to Britain twice and recalled to the Continent twice. On each occasion the crossing entailed a massive operation for the Roman navy. Below decks on the triremes there may have been some dark mutterings about Emperors who could not make up their minds.

---

[43] Tacitus, *Agricola* 16.
[44] Tacitus, *Agricola* 16.
[45] Tacitus, *Histories* 1.60.
[46] See e.g. Roberts (2008).
[47] Tacitus, *Histories* 1.60.
[48] Tacitus, *Histories* 2.66.
[49] Dando-Collins (2010) 171.

In AD 69 Vettius Bolanus duly arrived as the new governor, possibly travelling with the Fourteenth Legion. He served for two years and, according to Tacitus, did so with no great distinction. Apparently 'he did not trouble the Britons with discipline'.[50] His tenure was marked by inaction against the enemy and disorder in the camp. Unlike his predecessor, Bolanus did not incur the hatred of the army: the soldiers regarded their new governor with some affection, but they did not respect his authority.

Up in the north, there was conflict between Cartimandua and Venutius, her estranged husband. Each headed different factions of the northern communities. After leaving Venutius, the queen cohabited with Vellocatus, who had been Venutius' arms bearer. This only added to Venutius' humiliation and bitterness. The marital rift reflected the wider divisions within the Brigantian confederacy. The queen and her supporters were firmly committed to collaboration with Rome. They were probably based at Stanwick.[51] Venutius and his team stood for British independence and resistance to the occupying forces. They may have been based at Scotch Corner.[52] Venutius believed that the turmoil caused by the events of AD 69 presented a good opportunity. Rallying many of the Brigantes to his cause, as well as other groups, he waged civil war against Cartimandua. According to Tacitus, Venutius was motivated by hatred of Rome, but even more by bitterness towards his ex-wife.[53] No-one who has dealt with matrimonial litigation would find that difficult to believe.

In the resulting conflict, as her support ebbed away, Cartimandua became isolated. She sent a plea to the Romans for help. The Romans sent a task force, which succeeded in rescuing Cartimandua, but they enjoyed no other success against Venutius' army. The limited nature of Rome's intervention on this occasion is further evidence of the change of policy identified above. As Tacitus observed, 'the kingship was left to Venutius, the war to us'.[54] The client kingdom of Brigantia was no more. Another round of warfare lay ahead, this time on the northern frontier.

Bolanus cannot have been sorry when his short tour of duty in Britain came to an end.

---

[50] Tacitus, *Agricola* 16.
[51] Haselgrove (2016) chapter 28.
[52] A major late Iron Age site came to light there in 2014–2015: see Fell 2017, 14–21.
[53] *Histories* 3.45.
[54] 'Regnum Venutio, bellum nobis relictum' *Histories* 3.45.

CHAPTER 7
THE FLAVIAN PERIOD

1. Introduction
2. Improving the infrastructure and administration of the provimce
3. Cerialis' campaign against the Brigantes
4. Campaigns in Wales : Frontinus and Agricola
5. Agricola's campaigns in the north
6. The period after Agricola
    (i) From Domitian to Trajan
    (ii) Consolidation of the province and rebuilding the legionary fortresses in stone

1. INTRODUCTION

The Flavian period (AD 69–96) was when Rome consolidated its grip on the province. Tacitus is our most authoritative source for this period, but there is need for a health warning. Historians, like the politicians they write about, often have their own personal agenda. Tacitus, although he was one of the 'great' historians, certainly did. He classified Vespasian as a 'good' emperor and all his appointees as 'good' provincial governors. He tells us that 'when Vespasian took over running Britain and the rest of the world, generals became great, armies became excellent and the enemies' hopes were crushed'.[1] Some commentators regard Tacitus as so biased as to be unreliable, especially in his biography of Agricola.[2] This chapter takes the opposite line. Tacitus was writing about events in his own lifetime and is likely to have stated the basic facts correctly. If he had done otherwise, his book would have lost all credibility. Nevertheless, where possible, Tacitus slanted his account to show both Vespasian and Agricola in a favourable light.

---

[1] 'Sed ubi cum cetero orbe Vespasianus et Britanniam reciperavit, magni duces, egregii exercitus, minuta hostium spes': *Agricola* 17.
[2] Forder (2019) *passim*, especially 20.

The Flavian period

By the end of AD 69 Titus Flavius Vespasianus, 'Vespasian', had emerged as Emperor. He reigned for ten years and was followed by his sons, Titus (79 to 81) then Domitian (81–96). These three Emperors are known as the Flavian Emperors, because they all had the family name Flavius.

As Emperor, Vespasian held supreme legislative, judicial and executive power. He hired and fired provincial governors and gave them their orders. In effect, he was ruler of the world. Many modern heads of state, obliged to run to Parliament or Congress every time they want to start a war, may look with envy at Vespasian's freedom of action.

Vespasian came to power after several years of misrule and a civil war. His central theme was restoration.[3] To that end, he sponsored major building projects in Rome and the provinces. These included rebuilding the Temple of Jupiter on the Capitoline Hill, which had recently been destroyed. Vespasian was also seeking to erase the memory of Nero. He built a vast amphitheatre in the grounds of what had been Nero's palace (the *domus aurea*). The amphitheatre is still there. We call it the Colosseum.

Although Vespasian never visited Britain during his reign, he took a keen interest in the province. This was where he had made his name as a young man, commanding the Second Legion Augusta during the invasion of AD 43. He had come to know some of the leading Britons, in particular Togidubnus, with whom he probably kept in touch for many years.[4] Vespasian must have been devastated by the news of Boudica's rebellion.

As previously noted, following the great rebellion there had been a change of approach: Rome's project of annexing the whole of Britain was temporarily put on hold. Under Vespasian, there was another change of direction. The establishment of Britain as an effective and stable province once more became a central objective. In practice this required:

(i) improving the infrastructure and administration of the province;
(ii) subduing the Brigantes, who were no longer functioning as a client kingdom;
(iii) completing the annexation of Wales, a task which earlier governors had begun before Boudica's rebellion;
(iv) invading Scotland.

It is not suggested that Vespasian sat down and wrote out those four tasks in a 'to do' list. That was simply what the governors found that they had to do, when they were trying to sort out Britain. It was not an official change of policy. In our world, governments are forever announcing and pursuing new policies. Things were different in the Roman world: government was usually reactive, not proactive. The Emperor's daily work (unless he happened to be mad) was corresponding with provincial governors, appointing new governors, issuing edicts, quelling rebellions, administering justice and so forth.[5] Individual emperors also had their own interests. In relation to Britain, Vespasian was trying to distance himself from Nero (a 'bad' Emperor, who let the province go to ruin) and align himself with Claudius (a 'good' Emperor) who had overseen the conquest. That mirrored what Vespasian was doing in Rome.

---

[3] Shotter (2004) 1–8.
[4] See Chapter 18.
[5] Millar (1992) chapter 5.

Vespasian appointed three governors:

- Quintus Petillius Cerialis from 71 to 74
- Sextus Julius Frontinus from 74 to 77
- Gnaius Julius Agricola from 77 to 84.[6]

Vespasian selected these governors with care:[7] Cerialis and Agricola had specialist knowledge of Britain; Frontinus was a skilled administrator and engineer. The length of Agricola's term was exceptional, since appointments were usually for much shorter periods.

2. IMPROVING THE INFRASTRUCTURE AND ADMINISTRATION OF THE PROVINCE

During the late first century, there was an upsurge of new public buildings in the recently established civitas capitals. In Silchester a timber amphitheatre and basilica appeared. The laying out of the street grid was completed. At Canterbury, there was major redevelopment. At Verulamium,[8] a new forum and basilica were constructed. Streets were restored. Houses and shops that Boudica had burnt down were rebuilt. A substantial bath building was constructed. Fragments survive, probably from AD 79, of an inscription dedicating Verulamium's forum and adjacent buildings to the Emperor.[9]

Rome was making a determined effort to place its stamp on the province. Completing the Temple of Claudius at Colchester was part of that project, as was the construction of a monumental arch at Richborough. During the 80s the Romans built a large quadrifrons arch,[10] which straddled Watling Street and marked the formal entrance to Britain. The arch stood about 25 metres high, overlooking the harbour and dominating the skyline. It was clad in white Carrara marble imported from Italy. Bronze statues, possibly depicting a sea battle with Roman gods in attendance, were arrayed on top. This monumental structure commemorated the conquest of Britain. It also made a statement about the military and cultural dominance of Rome. The arch was the first thing that travellers would see on arrival in Britain. Modern visitors may be less impressed: all that remain are the foundations and a few bits of rubble.

London

In London there was a massive building programme during the Flavian period.[11] This included new public baths, forum and basilica, as described in Chapter 17. There was also a major

---

[6] It is uncertain whether Agricola succeeded Frontinus in 77 or 78. This chapter follows Birley (2005) in taking the earlier date.
[7] Birley (1961).
[8] Niblett et al., (2006) 53–188.
[9] RIB 3123.
[10] Illustrated in Millett (2007) at 142.
[11] Hingley (2018) chapter 5.

development just to the east of Walbrook stream.[12] The Roman authorities and entrepreneurs developed a substantial port on the north bank of the Thames.[13] This involved terracing the slopes leading down to the river, the lowest terrace standing about 2 metres above flood level. Along the waterfront ran a line of huge squared oak posts, forming a timber quay about 620 metres long, dated by dendrochronology to AD 70–90. There was also a complex area of quays and jetties around the mouth of the Walbrook stream. The remains of warehouses from the Flavian period have been found set back from the line of timber quays, including a large stone building, approximately 16 metres square, which stood next to the bridge approach road.

The stylus tablets recovered from the Bloomberg site provide insights into everyday life in first-century London. Some pre-date the Boudican rebellion (as discussed in Chapter 5), but most come from the Flavian period. The authors were all men – generally businessmen or soldiers. Tablet WT14 is an instruction to give something to Junius, a cooper, who lives 'opposite the house of Catullus'. WT 31 is a plea 'by bread and salt'[14] for the repayment of 36 denarii. WT12 is a letter to Tertius, the brewer. He is probably the same brewer called Tertius who is referred to in one of the Carlisle tablets. The inference is that Tertius' brewing business extended from London to Carlisle.[15] WT50 is a written acknowledgement by a slave called Florentinus that his master has received two payments from a farm. WT55 is an acknowledgement by Atticus of a debt to Rogatus, the slave of Narcissus. There is a line through the text, to show that the debt has been cancelled.

Tablet WT51 is part of a judgment in ongoing litigation between Litugenus and Magunus. This was probably a dispute between businessmen, like countless other cases that have been resolved in London over the last two thousand years. The tablet is dated 22 October AD 76. The trial was fixed for 9 November. The full text has vanished, but it appears to have been the judge's decision on a preliminary point of law. By deciding such questions at the outset, the judge would have shortened and focused the trial: both Litugenus and Magunus benefited from sensible case management.

London flourished as a trading centre.[16] Probably most merchants were selling provisions to the army. There were no bulk supply contracts organized by the government – in those carefree days Whitehall was still virgin woodland. It is likely that individual military units made their own arrangements with private contractors. The Bloomberg tablets evidence regular contact between London and other regional centres. WT39 talks about something being sent to Julius Suavis at a fort in the region of the Iceni. A man in Wroxeter wrote WT23 and despatched it to the son of Gessinus in London. WT59 was a letter to Attius in Rochester.

As previously noted, the procurator had been based in London from an early date. At some point in the second half of the first century the governor established his headquarters in London. The governor was peripatetic for much of the year, either campaigning or touring the province in his judicial capacity. He would have taken a retinue of officials with him but must have left his 'administrative tail' in London. So, from the late first century onwards, London may fairly be called the capital of the province.[17]

---

[12]Bryan et al. (2017) 30–5.
[13]Milne (1985).
[14]Bread and salt were seen as the minimum to support life: Pliny, *Natural History* 31.41.
[15]Tomlin (2016) 82.
[16]Millett (2016) 1697.
[17]Hassall (1996).

There is evidence of legionary soldiers and auxiliaries (detached from their regiments) serving in London during the Flavian period. They probably formed the governor's bodyguard when he was in London. Three of the Bloomberg tablets (WT 33, 48 and 55) record the presence of auxiliary units, namely the Nervii, the Vangiones and the Lingones. These may have been reinforcements brought over from Gaul to help restore order after the great rebellion. A bronze diploma granting Roman citizenship and marriage rights to an auxiliary soldier has been found at Watling Court, just to the north of Cannon Street.[18] It was lying amongst the remains of a town house burnt down in the early second century, so is probably dated about AD 100.

The overall picture that emerges is that London was a thriving new town. It had recovered rapidly from Boudica's intervention. The population was a mixed trading and military community, with many cavalry units. Most of the authors of the Bloomberg tablets were provincials, but they used good Latin. London, rather than any of the ancient Iron Age centres, was the obvious place to locate Rome's seat of provincial government.

Role of the provincial governor

The governor combined the roles of prime minister, head of the armed forces and lord chief justice. So naturally he needed a back office (*officium*) to help him.[19] The head of this office was the *princeps praetorii*, a legionary centurion on secondment. That was a senior government post, roughly equivalent to Cabinet Secretary. One incumbent was Vivus Marcianius, a centurion seconded from the Second Legion Augusta. His tombstone[20] shows an important looking man in a tunic, holding a centurion's staff in his right hand and a scroll in his left hand. His feet are angled as if he is walking casually. Part of the face is missing, but Marcianus is looking to the left. He is probably strolling round the office, checking up on people. Officers known as *beneficiarii* performed special duties for the governor. They had a status just below that of centurion, apparently gained through patronage.[21] Not much scope for social mobility there. Altars are dotted around the country recording their names.[22]

There was a registry (*tabularium*) headed by a clerk of equestrian rank (*scriba*). The governor had secretaries, shorthand writers, administrative officers and accountants. Sometimes veteran soldiers helped in the office.[23] In all there were about 40 officials with clerical duties.[24] The figure of a late first-century legionary soldier has been recovered from a London wall, carrying tablets and a scroll in one hand.[25] He was probably serving on the governor's staff: he does not look as bossy or important as Vivus Marcianus.

Each legion provided *speculatores* to serve on the governor's staff.[26] They were military policemen, whose role included executing prisoners under sentence of death. Hopefully, the *scriba* kept reasonably accurate records of who had, and who hadn't, been sentenced to death.

---

[18] Frere et al. (1983) 344–5.
[19] Birley (2005) para 1.1.2 and Hassall (1996).
[20] RIB 17.
[21] Hassall (1996) 22.
[22] RIB 88, 235, 602, 1030, 1031, 1085, 1225, 1599.
[23] WT 20 is a letter to one such veteran.
[24] Jones (1949) 38–55.
[25] Perring (2011) figure 16.
[26] The tombstone of one *speculator* has been found in London: RIB 19.

Torturers (*quaestionarii*) assisted with the interviewing of witnesses and suspects. Individuals brought in for questioning may well have been reluctant to make admissions without some 'encouragement'. No record survives of the conviction rate, but it was probably high. The governor needed a team of muscular bodyguards (*singulares*) to protect him. The Bloomberg tablets (at WT56) refer to one called Rusticus: possibly this was a nickname, because he looked like a peasant – the age of political correctness had not yet arrived.

The governor's groom, obviously, looked after the horses. One of the grooms was Veldedeius. He had a brother called Chrauttius, who was serving on the northern frontier. A chatty letter between the two brothers survives.[27] They shared happy memories of military service together. Apparently, they had a sister, Thuttena, living in London. In the letter Chrauttius asks Veldedeius to pass on his love to their sister. This scrawled tablet is a touching reminder that the governor's officials had their own family lives and domestic affairs to think about.

The governor spent much of the year travelling around the province, either campaigning or performing his other duties. He probably stayed at the *principia* of forts. It is unlikely that he had a sumptuous official residence in London: governors generally came to Britain on relatively short terms of duty and spent most of their time away from London anyway. During the early Flavian period it is likely that when he was in London the governor stayed in the newly built fort on the city's eastern hill,[28] although later that fort fell into disuse. The quest by some archaeologists to find the grandest London house and identify that as 'the governor's palace' is probably chimerical.

3. CERIALIS' CAMPAIGN AGAINST THE BRIGANTES

As commander of the Ninth Legion, Quintus Petillius Cerialis had tried to relieve Colchester during the Boudican rebellion and been defeated. He subsequently redeemed himself by siding with Vespasian during the power struggle of AD 69 and then marrying the Emperor's daughter.[29] In 71 Cerialis returned to the province as governor.

Cerialis brought with him the Second Legion Adiutrix, which he based at Lincoln.[30] This was a new legion, which Vespasian had recently created. Now, somewhat confusingly, there were two Second Legions in Britain: the Second Legion Augusta with their fortress at Gloucester and the Second Legion Adiutrix in Lincoln. Tombstones have been found at Lincoln of two soldiers who died during this period, namely Lucius Licinius Saliga and Titus Valerius Pudens.[31] Both belonged to the Second Legion Adiutrix. Saliga died at the age of 20. He must have enlisted as a teenager and died a few years later on his first overseas posting. Pudens died in AD 76 at the age of 30. Almost the whole of his tombstone survives. It is adorned with two fishes and a trident on the top. The bottom line tells us that Pudens' heir 'set this up at his own

---

[27] *Tab Vindol* II, 310.
[28] Dunwoodie et al. (2015).
[29] Birley (2005) 65.
[30] Birley (2005) 228.
[31] RIB 253 and 258.

expense'. The heir must have spent a substantial sum from his inheritance on this splendid memorial.

The most urgent task facing Cerialis was to deal with the Brigantes. As previously noted, Venutius headed the anti-Roman faction within the Brigantes and that faction was now in the ascendant. Cerialis headed north, taking with him his old legion, the Ninth. He based the Ninth Legion at York (*Eburacum*), where it established a new fortress.[32] Cerialis established a modest-sized wooden fort at Carlisle[33] in AD 72 or 73. Archaeologists have recovered fragments of ink writing tablets from the drain. Sadly, the few legible letters on those early tablets are insufficient to decipher. The tablets from the drain can all be dated to the 70s.

Agricola, the future governor of the province, commanded the Twentieth Legion. He marched his troops north to meet up with Cerialis, probably somewhere in Yorkshire. According to Tacitus, Cerialis frequently entrusted the command of a large part of the army to Agricola.[34] The details of the campaign against the Brigantes are difficult to discern. Traces of marching camps have been found, which suggest that Cerialis headed to Carlisle. According to Pliny the Elder, Cerialis' campaigning extended as far north as the Caledonian Forest, i.e. Scotland.[35] Tacitus states that Agricola invaded the territory of the Brigantes, striking terror into their hearts.[36] Many battles were fought and 'sometimes they were not without bloodshed'.[37] This was Tacitus' jocular way of saying that lots of people were killed. In the end Cerialis subdued 'a large part' of the Brigantes. At this point Venutius vanishes from history, probably because he was killed. Cerialis did not go on to establish a network of forts across Brigantia. In late 73 or early 74 he was recalled to Rome.

Following Cerialis' campaign, the ancient Iron Age settlement at Stanwick fell into disuse. The massive earthworks and fortifications no longer served any purpose. The emerging network of Roman roads avoided Stanwick altogether.[38] A substantial Roman settlement developed over the Iron Age field system at Scotch Corner.[39] It first came to light during soil stripping for constructing the A1(M) Motorway in 2014–2015. In Roman times, as now, Scotch Corner was a major road junction. That was where a trans-Pennine road ('Margary 82') intersected with Dere Street, running north–south. The Roman settlement may have started as a military base, but as the conquest of Brigantia evolved Scotch Corner became a prosperous civilian community, serving both passing traffic and the local area. Many luxury items have been found on the site. These include the toga-clad torso of a figurine carved from a block of amber, rare imported ceramics and a clear glass bowl. There is even a miniature sword with iron blade, copper-alloy scabbard and bone hilt. Perhaps that was a Christmas[40] present for a child; or it may have been a votive offering.

---

[32] Birley (2005) 67 and 228.
[33] Tomlin (1998) 31–84.
[34] *Agricola* 8.
[35] *Natural History* 4.102.
[36] *Agricola* 17.
[37] 'multa proelia, et aliquando non incruenta'.
[38] Haselgrove (2016) 489.
[39] Fell 2017, 14–21.
[40] Romans and Romano-Britons exchanged gifts at the Saturnalia in late December.

4. CAMPAIGNS IN WALES: FRONTINUS AND AGRICOLA

Sextus Julius Frontinus took over as governor in AD 74. He was a man of wide talents and much practical common sense. He had served as consul before coming to Britain and in later life became Rome's water czar (*curator aquarum*). He was the author of a well regarded book on Rome's aqueducts and other technical works. In short, he had a wider range of skills than many who have held, or now hold, high office in this country.

Frontinus' main task was the re-conquest of Wales. Tacitus describes Frontinus as a great man (*vir magnus*). Unfortunately, he only devotes one sentence to telling us what the great man did. Apparently Frontinus campaigned against the Silures, 'a powerful and warlike tribe'.[41] He defeated them in numerous battles. This involved overcoming 'both the strength of the enemy and the physical difficulties of the terrain'.[42]

Frontinus assembled a massive military force for the campaign.[43] The Second Legion Adiutrix transferred from Lincoln to Chester (*Deva*). The Second Legion Augusta moved to Caerleon (*Isca*), where it was destined to remain for three centuries. The legion built its first fortress there with earth, clay and timber ramparts. Dendrochronology indicates a construction date of about AD 74.[44] The Twentieth Legion was already well placed at Wroxeter. Several Flavian forts have been identified along the south coast of Wales. It is probable that Frontinus used the fleet to support his operations. The great general probably followed the route of the future M4 motorway[45] for part of the way, as he penetrated the territory of the Silures. This would have given him access to the hinterland up the valleys. If ships were providing back up, there was little that the warlike Silures could do to cut off the supply route.

The precise course of Frontinus' campaign cannot now be deduced. His troops probably established a marching camp at Y Pigwn. The ramparts of two legionary camps still survive on desolate high ground at Y Pigwn in an area of rugged beauty. This site is well worth a visit, provided you are prepared for a long walk and don't mind getting lost. You will see that the second camp is built on top of the first, but at a slightly different angle. The first camp may date back to the campaigns of Ostorius. If so, Frontinus probably established the second camp 25 years later.

Frontinus served as governor from AD 74 to 77. He succeeded in crushing the Silures and also presumably the Demetae, but at a cost. Three out of the four legions and many of the auxiliary forces in Britain were tied up for three years in one remote part of the province. Elsewhere trouble was brewing. The Ordovices and the Deceangli were in open rebellion. Brigantia was no longer a client kingdom and, despite Cerialis' campaign, remained unwilling to accept Roman rule.

We now come to Agricola. Gnaeus Julius Agricola was born in AD 40. He twice served in Britain before becoming governor: first, as a military tribune during Boudica's revolt and, second, as legate of the Twentieth Legion under Cerialis. He was governor of Aquitania from

---

[41]'validamque et pugnacem Silurum gentem': *Agricola* 17.
[42]'virtutem hostium locorum quoque difficultates': *Agricola* 17.
[43]Birley (2005) 227–8.
[44]Davies (2007) 91–111.
[45]The section of M4 between Pyle and Briton Ferry follows the line of the Roman South Wales road.

AD 73 to 75 and then returned to Rome to serve as consul in 76. In 77 he was despatched to Britain as the next governor.

Because of the recent concentration on South Wales there were uprisings in many other parts of the province, as both Tacitus and Dio record. The corroboration of Dio is important, since it might otherwise be suspected that Tacitus was fabricating the problems that his father-in-law faced. Dio states pithily that war had broken out in Britain and Agricola overran the whole of the enemies' territories there.[46] It is clear that there was unrest in Britain at this time, but both Tacitus and Dio may have been exaggerating the scale of the problem. As we shall see in later chapters, references to 'trouble in Britain', whenever a new emperor or governor came onto the scene, became almost a literary convention amongst historians. Tacitus says that the uprisings in AD 77 were triggered by an event in mid-Wales shortly before Agricola arrived. The Ordovices had annihilated a unit of Roman cavalry and this had stirred up the whole province.[47]

Even allowing for elements of hagiography in Tacitus' account of his revered father-in-law, it may be that Agricola's arrival coincided with a 'critical juncture' in the history of Britannia.[48] The age of client kings was ending. Thirty years after the so-called conquest, despite intense military and financial investment, less than half of Britain was under direct Roman rule. The native populations of Wales, Brigantia and East Anglia had all put up repeated resistance. If Britain was ever to become a viable province, it needed someone who would not only complete the conquest, but also establish 'strong and stable government'. It may have been for this reason that Agricola was appointed to serve for twice the normal term of office.

Agricola arrived late in the summer.[49] Taking detachments from the legions and several auxiliary units, the new governor marched against the Ordovices in West Wales. The Ordovices sought the safety of the higher ground, but to no avail. The Romans massacred most of them. Agricola then headed north to the shoreline opposite Anglesey. He selected a detachment of German auxiliaries who were capable of swimming fully armed and sent them across the Menai Strait. This attack caught the islanders unawares, as they had been looking out for a fleet of ships. The island surrendered and once more fell under Roman control, this time permanently.

Recent experience indicated that a firm military presence was essential to keep Wales under control. Accordingly, two legions established their long-term bases effectively on each side of Wales.[50] The Second Legion Augusta constructed a fortress at Caerleon and this remained its base for the next three centuries. The Second Legion Adiutrix built a fortress at Chester. The Chester fortress, being close to Brigantia, also had a role in the planned conquest of the north. This massive fortress, for which construction work started in AD 74, may have been intended as an imposing display of Rome's strength.[51] In the mid-80s the Second Legion Adiutrix was

---

[46]'πολέμου αὖθις ἐν τῇ Βρεττανίᾳ γενομένου τά τε τῶν ἐκεῖ πολεμίων Γναῖος Ἰούλιος Ἀγρικόλας πάντα κατέδραμε': *Roman History* 66.20.1.
[47]*Agricola*, 18.
[48]See the analysis of critical junctures in Acemoglou and Robinson (2012) chapter 4.
[49]This paragraph and subsequent paragraphs concerning Agricola's governorship of Britain are based upon the detailed account given in Tacitus' biography of Agricola.
[50]Birley (2005) 227–8.
[51]Shotter (2004) 1–8.

withdrawn from Britain. At that stage, the Twentieth Legion transferred to Chester, where it was to remain for two hundred years. Thus, two legions guarded Wales on a long-term basis: the Second Legion Augusta watched over the Silures and the Demetae; the Twentieth Legion watched over the Ordovices and the Deceangli.

A network of auxiliary forts was constructed across Wales for the purpose of controlling the population.[52] These forts were on average 17 to 20 kilometres apart, often in valleys or on important routes. The largest such fort was at Caernarfon on the north coast and appears to have housed a milliary cohort (an auxiliary cohort of double strength). In addition, some of the Iron Age hillforts have evidence of use during the Roman period.

Although the Welsh peoples were doughty warriors, they were not quite so skilled at local government. They did not have any recognizable *oppida*; none of the Welsh communities had developed any central organization akin to that elsewhere in Britain. The Romans probably established a system of military government, headed by the two legionary legates at Caerleon and Chester. Individual centurions would have administered local areas, based at nearby forts. The procurator's officials collected taxes, probably without assistance from local élites.

5. AGRICOLA'S CAMPAIGNS IN THE NORTH

Having made his mark militarily, Agricola turned to his civil duties. According to Tacitus,[53] Agricola was scrupulously fair both in the administration of the province and in the despatch of judicial business. Those convicted of lesser offences were treated mercifully. Agricola put an end to abuses of the tax system and only required Britons to pay the proper level of tribute. He appointed officials and magistrates on merit, not based on his personal feelings or private recommendations. Seemingly, Agricola was a model whom our own Judicial Appointments Commission would do well to follow. Unfortunately, this section of the biography seems too good to be true. It is probably a literary topos.

Accurate information is an essential tool of imperial administration. Britain undertook the Great Trigonometry Survey of India during the nineteenth century. That took fifty years. George Everest completed the project and had the bright idea of naming the highest mountain after himself. Agricola did not have fifty years to spare or feel the need to rename any mountains. He did, however, need reliable maps; he was not even sure whether Britain was an island.[54] Accordingly, Agricola began his second year here (AD 78) by sending out soldiers to survey the rivers and estuaries across Britain.[55]

While the surveyors were at work, Agricola adopted a policy of sudden raids against troublesome areas. He established a network of forts at strategic locations, taking hostages where necessary. By the end of 78 Agricola had brought the whole territory of the Brigantes under effective Roman rule. The Roman province of Britannia now extended as far north as a line drawn between the Tyne and Solway Firth.

---

[52]Davies (2007) 93–7.
[53]*Agricola* 19.
[54]Dio, *Roman History* 66.20.1.
[55]*Agricola* 20.

In AD 79 Agricola turned his attention to Scotland. He attacked the indigenous communities, ravaged their possessions and established a network of forts. A garrison was stationed in each fort and given sufficient provisions to last for twelve months. By this means Agricola extended the Roman conquest as far north as the estuary of the River Tay (*Tanaus*). Since this was Rome's first incursion into Scotland, there was no co-ordinated resistance.[56]

In AD 79 Vespasian died and his son Titus succeeded as Emperor. Titus had previously served as a military tribune in Britain[57] and, like his father, took a close interest in the province. According to Dio, Titus was given the title *imperator* for the fifteenth time as a result of Agricola's achievements.[58]

In AD 80 Agricola concentrated on consolidating the territories he had gained, rather than pushing further north. He established forts on the estuaries of the Clyde and the Forth[59] and brought everywhere south of that line under Roman control. Tacitus observed that at this point the two seas on the east and west side of Britain are separated by only a short distance; 'this could have formed a natural frontier for the province of Britannia, if only the valour of the army and the glory of the name of Rome had allowed it.'[60] Despite the logic of Tacitus' comment, as later history showed, this line never became established as the permanent northern frontier of the province.

In about AD 80 the army set about road building in the north. They built one road from Carlisle, leading up the western side of southern Scotland, and another from Corbridge up the eastern side. A large fort at Newstead was directly linked into the road system. These were serious infrastructure works, which evidenced a firm intention to extend the province up to the Clyde/Forth line.

In AD 81 the Romans campaigned in western Scotland defeating previously unknown communities. Tacitus gives us little detail of these operations, save that Agricola was in the first boat to cross the Clyde.[61] The question of invading Ireland arose. An Irish chieftain had recently been driven out following a coup and sought the protection of Rome. Agricola believed that he could subdue the whole island with a single legion and some auxiliaries.[62] This belief was wildly optimistic. In the event Agricola thought better of his plan and he left Ireland in peace. Subsequent history suggests that he was wise to do so.

In September 81 Titus died and was succeeded by his brother Domitian. Domitian reigned as Emperor from 81 until his death in 96. By all accounts he was a disaster: wasteful of public money, incompetent as a general and cruelly vindictive.[63] According to Suetonius, Domitian put many senators to death.[64] Again we must be cautious of stereotypes. Tacitus (like Suetonius) classified Domitian as a 'bad' Emperor and constructed the whole of his narrative from that perspective.

---

[56] That is what Tacitus implies: see *Agricola* 22.
[57] Suetonius, *Divus Titus* 4.
[58] 'ὁ μὲν Τίτος αὐτοκράτωρ τὸ πεντεκαιδέκατον ἐπεκλήθη': *Roman History* 66.20.3.
[59] Traces of these forts still survive, including one at Camelon.
[60] 'si virtus exercituum et Romani nominis gloria pateretur, inventus in ipsa Britannia terminus.' *Agricola* 23.
[61] The river is not specified, but there are indications that it was the Clyde.
[62] Tacitus often heard his father-in-law saying that he could have achieved this: *Agricola* 24.
[63] Dio, *Roman History* 67.
[64] *Domitianus* 10.

Agricola remained in post as governor of Britain, even though his relations with the new Emperor were chilly. In AD 82 he campaigned on the east side of Scotland, attacking those who lived to the north of the Forth. He established a line of forts running northwards towards Aberdeen, to guard his supply route. The fleet operated in tandem with the army. The unfortunate denizens of northern Scotland, who had been minding their own business since the Bronze Age, suddenly found themselves assailed by the infantry, cavalry and warships of the Empire. Unsurprisingly, the Romans won a series of victories. They were fired up with success and, according to Tacitus, exultant.

The communities of the Scottish Highlands (*Caledonia*) hastily set about organizing resistance. The force that they assembled was large, but not as large as reported. Tacitus comments that this is usually the case when the enemy is unknown. Tacitus' shrewd comment about the tendency of generals and military planners to over-estimate the size of the opposition was echoed by von Clausewitz eighteen hundred years later in his famous treatise on military strategy.[65]

The Caledonians[66] started to storm the Roman forts. They had some success. There was earnest debate within the governor's camp as to whether this was a campaign too far and whether, perhaps, they should retreat behind the Clyde/Forth frontier.[67] It was pointed out that the enemy were about to attack in several divisions and with far superior numbers. Agricola disagreed. He divided his army into three sections, so that they could proceed separately, and set off once more heading northwards.

The Caledonians now saw their chance. They identified the Ninth Legion as the weakest of the three Roman units and prepared for a surprise attack. Under cover of night, they swooped on the Roman camp. After overpowering and killing the guards they set upon the sleeping soldiers. A general melée followed, in which the attackers had an obvious advantage. Fortunately, from the Roman point of view, help was at hand. Agricola, whose unit was only a few miles away, sent a rapid response force of cavalry and infantry. This force attacked the flanks of the Caledonian army, as the short summer night was ending. The Caledonians panicked and Roman morale was restored.[68] There was particularly fierce fighting in the narrow gateway of the legionary camp. Eventually the Caledonians lost heart and gave up. Most of them escaped unscathed, melting into the marshes and the forests, where pursuit was impracticable.

The night time battle put an end to the debate within the Roman camp: everyone now favoured pressing on towards the north. Their ambition was to conquer the whole of Scotland – an impossible goal, which Rome was never going to achieve. For the time being, however, that became the objective of Agricola's expedition.[69] It is not clear how far north the Romans marched before the campaigning season ended. The remnants of some of Agricola's forts have been found in a line extending northwards from the River Tay. These guarded the Roman supply route. They generally stood at the ends of glens, from where marauders were likely to issue. The most important military building project was a massive legionary fortress at Inchtutil,

---

[65] Von Clausewitz (1832/2008), *On War*, book 1, chapter 1, section 18.
[66] The term 'Caledonians' is used in this chapter as a collective term for the Highland communities resisting Agricola's advance. These are not the same as the 'Caledonians' whom we will meet in Chapter 12, although there must be overlap.
[67] *Agricola* 25.
[68] 'Romanis rediit animus': *Agricola* 26.
[69] Tacitus, *Agricola* 27.

which stood on raised ground overlooking the north bank of the River Tay. Work started in AD 82 and continued for several years, but was never completed. The legionary legate at the fortress became the senior officer to whom all the fort commanders in the region would report.

In the meantime, the Caledonian communities were re-grouping. They were not prepared to submit to the boundless ambitions of Rome. Tacitus characterizes the Scottish attitude as arrogance (*adrogantia*), but that may be uncharitable. It is hardly surprising that the Caledonians wished to resist being massacred or conquered by an Italian senator who had no business to be there.

One contingent of the Roman army was far from happy. This was a cohort of Usipi, conscripted in Germany and sent to fight in Britain. They decided to mutiny, which Tacitus describes as a 'great and memorable crime'.[70] The Germans murdered their commanding officers, stole three ships and put out to sea. Unfortunately, their talents did not include navigation. The Germans were carried wherever the winds and the currents took them.[71] They travelled northwards, then around the top of Scotland and down the treacherous west coast. Their journey was ghastly: when they landed to gather food and water, they had to battle against the natives; occasionally they resorted to cannibalism, eating the weakest of their number. Eventually they circumnavigated Britain. The Germans were treated as pirates and, when captured, sold into slavery. Ultimately some of them fell into Roman hands. The miscreants provided vital information that Agricola needed: they confirmed that Britain was an island.

In AD 83 Agricola suffered a devastating personal loss: his young son died. There was no question of compassionate leave. It was the Roman tradition to take such bereavements unflinchingly and to get on with the business of conquest. As Tacitus pithily observed, Agricola sought solace for his grief by making war.[72] Agricola set off for Scotland once more, this time hoping to have a full-scale battle. The fleet went ahead. Their task was to launch coastal raids and spread general panic. This they dutifully did. The army followed. Agricola's destination was *Mons Graupius*, where a massive Scottish army had assembled. This was to be the setting for the final and decisive battle between Agricola and the Caledonian peoples.

Where is *Mons Graupius*? There is a veritable wealth of literature arguing the case for different locations. One suggestion is Strathearn,[73] but this has come under lively attack.[74] Another suggestion is Moncrieffe Hill at Perth.[75] Anyone stuck for a PhD topic could do worse than pitch into this fray. The true answer, incidentally, is that no-one knows where the battle happened. The most we can say is that a line of Roman marching camps,[76] some attributable to Agricola, has been traced running up the east coast of Scotland. *Mons Graupius* must be one of the mountains well to the north of Edinburgh.

---

[70] 'magnum ac memorabile facinus': *Agricola* 28.
[71] 'που τό τε κῦμα καὶ ὁ ἄνεμος αὐτοὺς ἔφερε': Dio, *Roman History* 66.20.2. Interestingly Dio devotes just half a sentence to Agricola's seven years campaigning, but a whole paragraph to the exploits of the German rebels and their discovery that Britain was an island.
[72] 'in luctu bellum inter remedia erat.' *Agricola* 29.
[73] Fraser (2005).
[74] Campbell (2015) 407–10.
[75] Forder (2019) 221–36.
[76] Forder (2019) 122.

The Roman invasion had incentivized the highland communities to come together and confront the common enemy. According to Tacitus, the Scottish army numbered some 30,000 men. A chieftain called Calgacus was the overall commander.

> ### Calgacus' speech
>
> Tacitus attributes to Calgacus a long and eloquent pre-battle speech. This speech, like that attributed to Boudica twenty years earlier, must be a work of fiction.
>
> In the imaginary speech Calgacus begins by extolling the freedom of Scotland and stating that his troops must win this battle to avoid slavery. He then delivers a savage attack on the Romans for their insatiable greed and cruelty; they bestride the world stealing whatever they can and killing all who oppose them. He utters the immortal and much quoted line:
>
> > 'They make a desert and they call it peace.'
> > ('ubi solitudinem faciunt, pacem appellant': *Agricola* 30).
>
> Calgacus warns the Scots what lies in store if they are conquered: their goods and chattels will be seized to pay tribute; their grain and produce will be requisitioned to feed the occupying army; their future will be one of slavery. Finally, Calgacus mocks the opposing army and is particularly scathing about the Britons who are fighting as auxiliaries on the Roman side.
>
> Calgacus' speech is not only a fine piece of prose. It also has a universal quality: it expresses the perceptions and feelings of freedom fighters generally. A similar speech could be attributed to Indian leaders in the Great Rebellion (or First Indian War of Independence) of 1857 or to Taliban leaders after the American occupation of Afghanistan in 2001. Calgacus' speech embodies an idea which, in every age, has galvanized nationalist groups and inspired supreme acts of sacrifice or brutality.

Tacitus also sets out Agricola's speech in full. This passage may be substantially accurate. After all Tacitus had unrestricted access to the general and every reason to record this oration accurately. Agricola began by reminding the soldiers of their great victories in recent years, both against 'the enemy' (i.e. everyone in their way) and against the forces of nature. He pointed out that retreat was not an option for the Romans, who were campaigning in unfamiliar terrain. He poured scorn on the assembled Scots as the most cowardly[77] of the Britons: in the previous year they had attacked a single legion by night and then run away. Now was the Roman army's chance for a glorious and total victory.

The Roman troops were roused for battle. Agricola drew up 8,000 auxiliary infantry in the centre, with 3,000 cavalry on the wings. The legionaries (all of whom were Roman citizens) were drawn up in front of a palisade, from where they could provide reinforcements if necessary. In this way, Agricola hoped to win a victory without any loss of Roman life – an

---

[77] Tacitus' word 'fugacissimi' means most inclined to flee. There is no elegant way of translating this.

admirable plan which may not have thrilled the auxiliaries. The Caledonians were on higher ground, sloping downwards. Because of the lie of the land, the whole Scottish army could be seen, rank upon rank stretching back up the hillside. Their war chariots were noisily manoeuvring, as they prepared to slice up the opposition.

The battle began at long range.[78] The Romans hurled their javelins, the Scots threw their spears in reply. Hand-to-hand fighting followed. Here the auxiliaries had an advantage, because the Scots' swords were too long and their shields too short for effective close combat. The Batavi and the Tungri, two cohorts of auxiliaries, gained the upper hand. They were striking the enemy with the bosses of their shields and stabbing them in the face. The Scots began to retreat up the hillside. Other cohorts of auxiliaries joined the charge, killing their opponents or sometimes leaving them injured on the ground. Meanwhile the Roman cavalry routed the Scottish chariots, then turned to assist the infantry battle. Here the cavalry found themselves in difficulty because of the close ranks of the enemy and the unevenness of the ground. Other Caledonians who had not yet joined the battle now descended from nearby hilltops and surrounded the flanks of the Roman army. Agricola sent in four squadrons of cavalry, which he had previously held back, to deal with the final wave of barbarians. Ultimately, the Roman army prevailed.

The Caledonians turned to flee. The Romans concentrated on capturing as many as they could, which was easiest on open ground. Everyone whom they captured was duly killed. Some Scots despaired: they threw down their arms and offered themselves up for slaughter. This was all good sport for the Roman army, who liked nothing better than an opportunity for mass murder. By the end of the day, the battlefield was a sea of bloodstained corpses and abandoned weapons. As darkness fell, many Scots made their escape to safety. The Roman army was jubilant,[79] no doubt high on adrenalin. They celebrated wildly and exulted in the plunder which they had stolen. In the distance could be heard the wailing and crying of Scottish folk as they dragged away their wounded survivors.

Tacitus states that on the Scottish side, some ten thousand men died in the battle. On the Roman side, casualties were low: there were just three hundred and sixty dead, including Aulus Atticus who had valiantly charged into the enemy line. The Scottish resistance was now crushed. The Caledonians were not re-grouping to fight another day. Instead they abandoned their homesteads, sometimes killing their own families[80] because all seemed lost. Tacitus describes the scene on the day after the battle in stark terms: dismal silence across the vast landscape, deserted hillsides and the smoking wrecks of people's homes.[81] Even now, two thousand years later, it is difficult not to condemn the savagery of Rome's unprovoked attack on Scotland.

Agricola had no time for sentiment. His first step was to take hostages from the defeated foes. He then returned to the important task of gathering geographical information. He ordered the commander of the fleet to circumnavigate Britain. This exercise confirmed the account previously given by the German mutineers, namely that Britain was an island.[82] In the meantime

---

[78] Tacitus, *Agricola* 36.
[79] Tacitus, *Agricola* 38.
[80] This is credible. There were similar scenes in Germany at the end of the Second World War. Goebbels and many others killed their own families.
[81] 'vastum ubique silentium, deserti colles, fumantia procul tecta': *Agricola* 38.
[82] Dio, *Roman History* 66.20.2; Tacitus, *Agricola* 38.

Agricola marched southwards, returning to the centre of the province that he had now governed for just over six years. His tour of duty was coming to an end.

In about AD 83 the major internal buildings of the fort at Carlisle were rebuilt and enlarged.[83] Agricola may have ordered those works as part of his project to consolidate Rome's grip on the province. One of the governor's bodyguards was present during this period and carelessly dropped a writing tablet addressed to himself.[84]

Agricola returned to Rome in the spring of AD 84 with some misgivings. Domitian was not a sympathetic emperor and Agricola was not his favourite governor. The Emperor felt obliged to honour Agricola and duly did so, but beneath the surface there was jealousy and hatred. Agricola kept a low profile: he lived quietly with his family in Rome, taking the opportunity to regale his son-in-law, Tacitus, with tales of his exploits in Britain. It was Agricola's good fortune that he had given his daughter in marriage to the top historian of the age. Other retired generals who yearn for a favourable press might like to follow this example. When eventually Agricola died, there was a rumour that he had been poisoned on the orders of Domitian.[85] Tacitus was unsure whether this rumour was correct.

6. THE PERIOD AFTER AGRICOLA

(i) From Domitian to Trajan

For the three decades following Agricola's departure from the province, we have no surviving account of events in Britain, merely a few snippets. Sadly, the later books of Tacitus' *Histories* have been lost. This period coincides roughly with the reigns of Domitian, Nerva and Trajan. Dio in his magisterial survey of Roman History deals with that period in books 67 and 68, but he does not trouble to recount what happened in Britain.

Tacitus states that Agricola handed over a peaceful and safe province[86] to his successor but omits to tell us who that successor was. Suetonius provides a clue, because he says that Sallustius Lucullus was governor of Britain during the reign of Domitian. Although there is some debate about dates, it seems likely that Lucullus was Agricola's immediate successor. He probably served from AD 84 to 87.[87] Lucullus had previously been proconsul of Baetica and, according to Pliny the Elder, had made a study of octopuses.[88] This was no doubt excellent preparation for his posting to Britain.

Suetonius records that Lucullus invented a new form of lance. This was probably for the purpose of warfare against the Britons. He unwisely named these weapons after himself, calling them 'Luculleas'. Domitian took exception to such impertinence by a mere provincial

---

[83]Tomlin (1998) 31–84.
[84]*Tabulae Luguvalienses* (hereafter, *Tab Luguval*) 44.
[85]Tacitus *Agricola* 43; Dio, *Roman History* 66.20.3.
[86]'provinciam quietam tutamque': *Agricola* 40.
[87]Birley (2005) 95–9. These dates are a deduction from limited evidence, as is the identification of 'our' Lucullus with the Lucullus who had served in Baetica.
[88]*Natural History* 9.89–93.

governor and imposed the usual punishment for anyone who offended him, namely immediate execution.[89] Poor Lucullus was less fortunate than Mikhail Kalashnikov.

Two inscriptions in Britain feature the name Lucullus, both found in Chichester. One is a stone with a dedication by Lucullus, the son of Amminus.[90] The other is an altar (now lost) with an inscribed dedication by Sallustius Lucullus, the imperial legate, to the god Jupiter. These inscriptions have prompted the delightful theory that Lucullus was the grandson of Cunobelinus, who had come back to rule over his native land as Roman governor.[91] Sadly, the link between Amminus in the first inscription and Cunobelinus is far-fetched. The second inscription is probably a hoax.[92] Lucullus may have been an expert on octopus behaviour, but he was not a grandson of the great Iron Age King.

When the provincial governor was too busy to discharge his judicial functions personally, he appointed a lawyer, known as *iuridicus*, to take on this role.[93] The first recorded *iuridici* in Britain were appointed during the Flavian period. Gaius Salvius Liberalis served between AD 78 and 81 or possibly between 81 and 83. Lucius Javolenus Priscus served between AD 84 and 86. Both men were jurists of high repute, particularly Javolenus.[94] Many of Javolenus' opinions are cited in Justinian's *Digest*.

It is always a pleasure to see lawyers arriving. But why did such eminent and expensive jurists travel to the remote province of Britain at this particular time? A possible explanation is that good lawyers were needed to deal with the dissolution of the last surviving client kingdom.

As we know from Tacitus,[95] Togidubnus was a loyal client king who, for many years, ruled over 'several civitates'. Those civitates must have included the Regni, who were a community around Chichester. It is generally assumed that the Atrebates and the Belgae were also part of Togidubnus' domain, but this is less certain. We do not know the precise territory that he controlled or what form that control took. Togidubnus probably died in the 80s, the last of the client kings. Rome would have been anxious to avoid the chaos that had followed the dissolution of the other two client kingdoms in Britain. The domain of Togidubnus lay in the heart of south-east Britain, close to the provincial capital and close to major ports. Accordingly, able lawyers were needed in order to ensure an orderly transfer of power when the aged king died.[96] The governor and his legal team seem to have been successful. Togidubnus' lands in the Hampshire/Sussex area were safely absorbed into the Roman province, becoming conventional civitates. Silchester was the administrative capital of the Atrebates; Winchester the administrative capital of the Belgae; Chichester the administrative capital of the Regni.

In modern Britain, contentious probate is big business for lawyers. With property values rising and serial marriages increasingly common, there is often much to argue about when a loved one dies. The first recorded probate litigation was in about AD 83. Seius Saturninus, a helmsman of the *classis Britannica* (the British fleet) died leaving his estate to Valerius Maximus

---

[89] Suetonius *Domitianus* 10.
[90] RIB 90.
[91] Russell (2006). The argument is that Amminus was Adimius, who had been banished by his father King Cunobelinus.
[92] Magilton (2013) 85–92.
[93] Birley (2005) 268–72.
[94] Nicholas (1987) 29.
[95] *Agricola* 14: 'quaedam civitates Cogidumno regi donatae'.
[96] Magilton (2013) 85–92 at 88.

(a captain in the fleet) to hold on trust until Seius' son became sixteen and then to hand it over to him. The son died before attaining sixteen. There was a dispute between the boy's maternal uncle and Maximus as to who should have Seius' estate. Javolenus dealt with the matter as iuridicus. He ruled in favour of the uncle.[97] Any modern judge would come to the same conclusion.

There have been many references in this and earlier chapters to a Roman fleet supporting operations and supplying military bases in Britain. At some point in the late first century it became established as the *classis Britannica*, which was one of several fleets constituting the imperial navy.[98] The commanding officer of the fleet was known as the prefect (*praefectus*). He was a relatively junior military officer.[99] Self-evidently, the *classis Britannica* was established by the early 80s, when Javolenus was serving in Britain. As discussed in Chapter 10 below, the fleet probably had its main base in Boulogne, but anchored in various harbours around Britain as necessary.

In book 1 of his *Histories* Tacitus briefly summarizes the period of history that he is going to narrate in the later books. As the later books relating to Britain have been lost, this brief summary is all that we have to go on. Tacitus states that Britain was 'subdued and at once let go'.[100] This is a perplexing comment, since the Romans did not abandon Britain. They stayed here for another three centuries. The statement 'at once let go' must be a reference to Scotland, not the whole of Britain. Possibly what Tacitus was conveying by that pithy phrase was that (i) the Romans unwisely withdrew from Scotland after Agricola's departure, (ii) Britain without Scotland was not a viable province, or at least not easy to defend. If that is what Tacitus meant, he had quite a good point, as we shall see in later chapters. The question whether Scotland should be united with, or severed from, the rest of Britain is one that has continued to exercise policy makers over the last two thousand years. It is still a matter of intense debate.

The Roman withdrawal from Scotland took place in stages, in part because of events overseas. In AD 85 the Dacians invaded the eastern frontier of the Empire. Rome became embroiled in a long running war in the Danube region. It could no longer spare four legions to serve in Britain. In about AD 87 Domitian recalled the Second Legion Adiutrix from Britain to serve in the Dacian wars.[101] He also probably recalled some auxiliary units. The consequence of the troop reduction was immediate and dramatic. Lucullus and his successors did not have enough resources to hold the conquered territories to the north of the Forth. Accordingly, Rome withdrew to the Clyde/Forth frontier.

The forts that Agricola had constructed up the east coast to the north of Edinburgh, at huge cost, were all abandoned within six years. The latest coins found in forts north of the Forth are bronze dupondii and asses of Domitian. They are in mint or nearly mint condition. Other sites reveal that the supply of bronze coinage to Britain was low in the period AD 81–85, high in the period 86–87 and low in the period 88–96. It is a reasonable inference that Rome abandoned the forts north of the Forth in AD 86 or 87.[102]

---

[97] Justinian, *Digest* 36.1.48.
[98] Mason (2010) chapter 3.
[99] Birley (2005) 298.
[100] 'perdomita Britannia, et statim omissa': *Histories* 1.2.
[101] Birley (2005) 228.
[102] Hobley (1989) 69–74.

The fortress at Inchtutil, which had been built as a legionary base, was abandoned in about AD 87. Some of the construction work was still incomplete. Almost as soon as they had been built, the massive fortifications were left to gather moss and crumble. Excavations in the mid-twentieth century have revealed the complete layout of the fortress. Curiously, Inchtutil is the only fortress anywhere in the Empire whose entire ground plan is preserved.[103] The Inchtutil fortress was originally built in timber and then rebuilt in masonry. It is possible to infer the original size of the fortress from the ground plan and other evidence. It has been estimated that some 2.7 million man hours were spent in its construction.[104] The main timbers would have weighed 17,170 tonnes; external cladding: 1,170 tonnes; wall and other stone: 25,200 tonnes. Approximately 741,000 tiles would have been used for roofing. The Romans left behind some 700,000 nails and ten tonnes of other iron objects, carefully buried on the site.[105] The Inchtutil fortress was the ultimate white elephant.

Following their withdrawal to the Clyde/Forth frontier the army made a determined effort to retain control over southern Scotland. They rebuilt the fort at Newstead on a grand scale. It now spread over 5.78 hectares and the ramparts were thickened to nearly 14 metres. Building works at Newstead fell into two distinct phases. Two coins of AD 86 in mint or nearly mint condition have turned up in the phase 1 ditch. A coin of AD 87 has been found in the phase 2 ditch. It seems clear that the military rebuilt the Newstead fort at the same time as they abandoned the far north.[106] In south-west Scotland, the Romans greatly enlarged the fort at Dalswinton, which probably housed both legionary infantry and auxiliary cavalry.[107] The army also constructed a network of less grandiose forts across the lowlands.

In September 96 Domitian was murdered.[108] This marked the end of the Flavian dynasty.[109] The next Emperor appointed was essentially a stopgap: he was Nerva Cocceius, an elderly senator in poor health, who only survived for two years. According to Dio, Nerva ruled well. However, he had no impact on the distant province of Britain. It appears from a diploma[110] that one Nepos served as governor during Nerva's reign.

Nerva died in AD 98, having adopted Marcus Ulpius Nerva Trajan as his successor. Trajan was a Spaniard and a former governor of Germany. He reigned from 98 to 117, reportedly as a good and conscientious emperor.[111] He undertook major infrastructure improvements in Italy and fought two wars against the Dacians, from which Rome emerged victorious. All Trajan's military campaigns were far removed from Britain and from the subject matter of this book.

Little is recorded about the governors of Britain who served under Trajan.[112] We know from a diploma that the first was Titus Avidus Quietus. The next was Lucius Neratius Marcellus. Marcellus is mentioned in a draft letter[113] prepared by Flavius Cerialis, who was commander of

---

[103] Jones (2013) 272.
[104] Wilson (2002) 598.
[105] Jones (2013) 273.
[106] Hobley (1989) 69–74.
[107] Hanson et al. (2019) 317.
[108] Suetonius, *Domitianus* 17.
[109] Being Vespasian and his two sons, Titus and Domitian.
[110] CIL xvi.43.
[111] Dio, *Roman History* 68.
[112] Birley (2005) 100–14.
[113] *Tab Vindol* II, 225.

the fort at Vindolanda between 101 and 105. Cerialis refers to Marcellus in suitably deferential terms as 'that most distinguished man, my governor'.[114] Sucking up to the top man has always been a wise career move.

Marcellus also gets a mention in one of Pliny's letters.[115] Pliny was a leading lawyer and avid letter writer who lived in the late first and early second century. In about 103 Pliny wrote to Suetonius (the famous biographer of the Caesars) about the position of military tribune in Britain, which was waiting to be filled. Pliny's letter refers to the fact that he had previously spoken to Neratius Marcellus and obtained this position for Suetonius. Now Suetonius wants the position transferred to his relative Caesennius Silvanus. Pliny says that he will be happy to oblige. The letter is interesting in two ways. First, it shows the considerable influence that Pliny from his office in Rome was able to exercise over the affairs of Britain. Secondly, Pliny's letter shows that the appointments system in Rome was hardly meritocratic. It all depended on who you knew and what strings they could pull. Surprisingly, this seems to be quite an effective way to run an empire. The British Empire operated on this basis with striking success. So did the Han and Tang dynasties of China, which controlled a large proportion of the world population.[116]

Turning to more mundane matters, we have a record of twenty-one lances that went missing from one of the auxiliary units stationed near Carlisle during the period AD 103–105. A writing tablet[117] survives, setting out the names of the errant soldiers and the types of lance that each had lost. The only other governor whom we know about was Marcus Atilius Bradua,[118] who served towards the end of Trajan's reign. The *Historia Augusta* states that serious rebellions were developing,[119] but that might be a literary flourish in order to boost Hadrian's achievements.

During Domitian's reign the Roman authorities made a determined effort to fortify and control southern Scotland but, at some point, they put that policy into reverse. The forts in lowland Scotland were abandoned and burnt to the ground. It is possible that Scottish peoples mounted an attack and burnt down the forts, but more likely that the Romans set fire to their own forts when they departed. The reasons for the retreat are unknown, but possibly the withdrawal of yet more auxiliary troops to serve in the Dacian wars was the catalyst. The Romans withdrew to the Tyne/Solway line. Pottery finds in southern Scotland suggest that this retreat occurred soon after 100. The Stanegate Road, running from Corbridge to Carlisle, now effectively marked the northern frontier of the province.[120]

Corbridge (*Coria*) originally comprised a succession of forts. A Roman town and military centre developed on this site in the first century. Following the Roman withdrawal from Scotland, Corbridge grew in importance. It became one of the frontier towns, at least until the construction of Hadrian's Wall a quarter of a century later. Dere Street, the main Roman road running north from York, crossed the Stanegate Road at this point. The town became a useful base and supply depot for periodic incursions into Scotland.

---

[114]'clarissimum virum consularem meum'.
[115]*Letters* 3.8.
[116]Fairbank (1994) 83–4.
[117]*Tab Luguval* 16.
[118]An inscription found in Greece reveals that he was governor of Britain.
[119]*Hadrian* 5.1.
[120]Hodgson (2000) 11–22.

(ii) Consolidation of the province and rebuilding the legionary fortresses in stone

Archaeological evidence suggests that the late first century was a period of consolidation. Having retreated to the Tyne/Solway line, Rome had no intention of withdrawing any further. To the south of that line new forts were constructed. There were major public works in the civitas capitals. The three legionary fortresses were rebuilt, using stone rather than timber. The army established two new colonies at Lincoln and Gloucester.

Colchester was, of course, the first colony in Britain. Around AD 100 it acquired a monumental arch by the Balkerne Gate (Fig. 7.1), a large theatre and an adjacent temple complex. These confirmed Colchester's special status.[121] The town already possessed the famous (some would say infamous) temple to Claudius. Colchester probably served as the 'religious capital' of Britain throughout the first and second centuries.[122] The provincial council continued to meet there and to ensure that all due homage was paid to the divine Claudius. This is a matter of inference from religious practice in other provinces.[123]

The late first century and the early second century were the great age of town building across Roman Britain, as discussed in Chapter 17 below. But who did the work? Much of what

Figure 7.1 Colchester, Balkerne Gate. © Flickr/Carole Raddato.

---

[121]Gascoyne and Radford (2013) 104.
[122]Hassall (1996) 20.
[123]Tarragona (*Tarraco*) served as religious capital in Spain. A huge circus was built there, as well as an additional forum. Lyon (*Lugdunum*) served as a religious capital in Gaul.

we call 'Roman' was built by indigenous peoples.[124] They were copying building design and lifestyles that had spread across Europe since the Augustan age. In Britain, Roman engineers and architects provided some of the expertise, but the occupying army did not have the manpower to build a dozen new cities in the late first century. Once the Romans were here, there must have been a strong impetus amongst the local élites to exploit the situation. They could put their own people to work building baths, temples, basilicas and so forth with the assistance of expert Gallic stonemasons.[125]

More importantly, who paid for it all? Mostly, wealthy Britons. As previously noted, the local élites who threw in their lot with Rome did very well for themselves. They sat as magistrates and held grand public offices. They collected taxes and no doubt held back some cash for themselves before accounting to the procurator. By financing public works, the local aristocrats further enhanced their standing with the imperial authorities. Many commemorative inscriptions record who paid for public buildings.[126] This was a vital aspect of munificence. Probably the claims in inscriptions are broadly correct: the purpose would be undermined, if everyone knew that the benefactor was exaggerating.

Scholars have counted up the commemorative inscriptions all over Europe. Apparently, the numbers of such inscriptions in Britain are close to the average in the Gallic and German provinces.[127] There are 77 public works attested on inscriptions in Britain. Of these, 37 are in the south and 40 are in the north. They are mostly on sacred structures, such as temples or altars. Some are on milestones, civic buildings and other secular constructions. In 59 instances, the benefactors are individuals. One individual was particularly generous: Marcus Ulpius Ianuarius made a gift of a theatre proscenium at Brough-on-Humber.[128] Fourteen of the benefactors are corporate bodies or groups. In six instances, the named benefactor is the Emperor or the legate.

Urban development was not simply a matter of building basilicas, baths, forums and temples. Infrastructure works, such as drainage and water supply, were equally important, though less glamorous. At Verulamium, the Roman engineers designed pipes and possibly an aqueduct to bring fresh water from the river Ver into the town.[129] Some bits of the timber pipes still survive. There was also an ingenious network of gullies and channels to catch rainwater.

Villa-building continued, sometimes even in the militarized northern half of Britain. A stone villa was built at Holme House, near Piercebridge in the late first century.[130] Pottery and vessel glass shows that it was occupied from then until the mid-second century. The Holme House villa boasted painted walls, mosaic floors, glazing and a bathhouse. Such a luxurious residence was something of an oddity in the north.

The Second Legion Augusta rebuilt its fortress at Caerleon in stone around the turn of the century. A fine commemorative slab records the construction date of one section. The marble for the slab appears to have been imported from Tuscany, indicating that no expense was spared. The text states that the legion constructed the relevant building when Trajan was consul

---

[124]Millett (2007) 137.
[125]See Chapter 9.
[126]Fagan (1996) 91–2.
[127]Blagg (1990) 13–31. Britain and Gaul have a larger proportion of dedications by corporate bodies. Britain and Germany, being frontier provinces, have a larger proportion of military benefactors.
[128]RIB 707.
[129]Niblett and Thompson (2005) 86–90.
[130]Cool and Mason (2008) 295–6. This may have been the second most northerly villa in Britain.

for the third time, which was AD 100.[131] The slab now hangs in the Legionary Museum at Caerleon. You will see that the third 'I' of "COS III" (meaning third consulship) is out of line. It slopes down to the right. The original stonemason obviously carved his inscription during Trajan's second consulship. But delays are a common feature of building work. By the time the structure was ready to receive its commemorative slab, Trajan had become consul yet again. So a local technician in Caerleon had to add an extra 'I'. The technician made a hash of it and probably received a flogging.

Modern Caerleon is a small town, so that many parts of the fortress are still visible. The fortress baths are – most conveniently – right next to a car park. The cold bath (*frigidarium*) is well preserved. So also is a long rectangular swimming pool (*natatio*) which lay immediately in front of the bathhouse. Parts of the fortress wall still stand. The remains of one barrack block are on display in an area of parkland. In all there were six groups of barrack blocks, with workshops, granaries, stores and similar buildings in between. As usual, the headquarters building (*principia*) was in the centre of the fortress, with the legate's residence (*praetorium*) next door.[132] The latrine block stood in the north-west corner and the foundations are still there. You can see the main drain that ran under the lavatory seats. Just in front is a small gutter in which the soldiers washed their sponges after use, before passing them on. These arrangements would not meet modern hygiene standards. To make matters worse, the lavatory block stood right next to a line of cooking ovens and the kitchen. Despite those imperfections, the legionary soldiers seem to have survived. They stayed there for over two hundred years.

In around 90 the Second Legion Augusta built an amphitheatre on the south-west side of the fortress. Following excavations in 1926, it is now one of the best preserved amphitheatres in Britain.[133] It had a seating capacity of about 6,000. This amphitheatre would have had many uses in addition to the usual games, gladiatorial contests and fights between wild animals. The army could have used it for military training and weapon demonstrations. Also, if the entire legion needed to assemble for a speech by the legate, the amphitheatre would have been the ideal place (Fig. 7.2).

Less remains to be seen of the fortress at Chester. This is because both mediaeval and modern town planners have chosen to build a city on top of it. Nevertheless, an inscribed stone slab[134] survives in Chester, which records the rebuilding of the legionary fortress in stone during Trajan's reign. The precise date is unclear but was about 102. This new fortress was massive, even by the standard of legionary fortresses. It included all the usual offices, namely headquarters building (*principia*), legate's residence (*praetorium*), barrack blocks, granaries, baths and senior officers' residences. There were twenty-two interval towers built along the fortress walls, spaced approximately 54 metres apart. Their walls were approximately 1.2 metres thick.[135] There was also a multi-purpose amphitheatre, similar to that at Caerleon, but much less of the Chester amphitheatre survives.[136] The mediaeval walls around Chester incorporate Roman fortress walls on the north and east side.

---

[131] RIB 330.
[132] For the layout of the fortress, see Knight (2010) 17.
[133] Wilmott (2010) 143–50.
[134] RIB 464.
[135] Mason (2012) chapter 9.
[136] Mason (2012) 113–5; Wilmott (2010) 135–43.

Figure 7.2 Caerleon amphitheatre. © Rob Farrow (cc-by-sa/2.0).

The Ninth Legion built their stone fortress at York around the turn of the century. York, unlike Caerleon and Chester, was more than just a fortress with a civilian settlement attached. It was the principal military base in the north of Britain. A stone tablet,[137] which once stood above the fortress gate, can now be seen in Yorkshire Museum. It proudly proclaims:

> The Emperor Caesar Nerva Trajan Augustus, son of the deified Nerva, conqueror of Germany, conqueror of Dacia, pontifex maximus, in his twelfth year of tribunician power, six times acclaimed imperator, five times consul, father of his country, built this gate by the agency of the Ninth Legion Hispana.

That dates the tablet to AD 107–108. It is one of the final records of the Ninth Legion in Britain, the more poignant because we do not know for certain what happened to the legion afterwards. It was probably recalled to the Continent, for service in Lower Germany.[138]

Auxiliary units were based in forts at strategic locations around the province.[139] Many were ranged along the northern frontier. Once auxiliary units were established here, they usually recruited locally. Auxiliary soldiers gained Roman citizenship on retirement. Their sons usually signed up for the army.

---

[137] RIB 665.
[138] Birley (2005) 228–9.
[139] Mann and Dobson (1996) 43.

CHAPTER 8
LIFE ON THE NORTHERN FRONTIER

1. Introduction
2. Vindolanda: The forts and the tablets
3. The First Cohort of the Tungrians (AD 85–92)
4. The Ninth Cohort of the Batavians (AD 92–105)
5. The First Cohort of the Tungrians (AD 105–128)
6. The picture that emerges from the Vindolanda tablets

1. INTRODUCTION

Evidence emerging in recent years shows that literacy was widespread in Roman Britain. The army has left a vast number of inscriptions in stone.[1] The Bloomberg tablets, discussed in earlier chapters, provide examples of businessmen corresponding. The curse tablets discussed in the Chapter 19 are notes written by ordinary people to deities, venting their grievances.

The tablets discussed in this chapter add significantly to that body of evidence. They are documents written by auxiliary soldiers and their families at Vindolanda. It is a reasonable inference that a vast number of similar tablets once existed at other forts but have been lost. The subject matter of these tablets is revealing. They relate to military matters, army purchases, domestic matters, leisure pursuits and even literary education. We shall see examples of children copying out lines of Virgil, presumably because they were going to read (and hopefully enjoy) good Latin literature in later life.

2. VINDOLANDA: THE FORTS AND THE TABLETS

The Romans constructed a wooden fort at Vindolanda on the Stanegate Road, as part of their project to bring northern Britain under effective control. Between AD 85 and 128 there were five successive wooden forts on this site. The fourth and fifth forts were larger than the earlier

---

[1] See generally Tomlin (2018).

ones and projected further to the south. Eventually the last wooden fort was demolished to make way for a bigger and grander stone fort. That dates from the second century.[2] The remnants of the early wooden forts remained buried beneath the stone fort until the late twentieth century.

The *principia* was the headquarters of the fort and the administrative hub. Official correspondence and military reports were created or filed in this building. The *praetorium* was the residential complex where the commanding officer and his household lived. Many personal letters were sent to or from the *praetorium*.

The remains of the five wooden forts sit roughly on top of one another and have now become an archaeologists' paradise. Their approximate dates are:

- First wooden fort   AD 85–92
- Second wooden fort   AD 92–97
- Third wooden fort   AD 97–105
- Fourth wooden fort   AD 105–120
- Fifth wooden fort   AD 120–128.

Robin Birley directed the excavations at Vindolanda. He has provided a full account of the five wooden forts, as well as the story of their excavation.[3]

The soldiers who garrisoned forts along the northern frontier were auxiliaries drawn from all quarters of the Empire. At Vindolanda there were three sets of occupants:

- Between AD 85 and 92:   The First Cohort of the Tungrians;
- Between AD 92 and 105:   The Ninth Cohort of the Batavians;
- Between AD 105 and 128:   The First Cohort of the Tungrians again.

Both the Tungrians and the Batavians were Germanic tribes. They were conscripted into military service for their conquerors in the normal Roman manner. The First Cohort of the Tungrians was an infantry unit. They moved out in AD 92 to make way for the Ninth Cohort of the Batavians, who comprised both cavalry and infantry. In AD 105 the Batavians were re-deployed to fight in the Dacian wars and the Tungrians moved back in. In AD 128 the last wooden fort at Vindolanda was abandoned. The First Cohort of the Tungrians probably moved up to occupy the newly constructed fort at Housesteads on Hadrian's Wall.

In 1973 archaeologists discovered the first of several valuable caches of documents amongst the remains of the wooden forts at Vindolanda. These documents were in two forms, wax tablets and leaf tablets.[4]

- The wax tablets were pieces of wood hollowed out and filled with wax. The author could then write on the wax using a stylus. The wax has now disappeared, but the words etched into the wood beneath can sometimes still be discerned.

---

[2] Hodgson (2009a) 117–18.
[3] Birley (2009).
[4] For a fuller account of these remarkable documents, see Bowman (2003).

- The leaf tablets were very thin leaves of wood, usually about the size of a postcard. They were often folded, so that the writing was on the inside and thus protected. The writing on these tablets was in ink.[5]

There were about 180 wax tablets and 1,450 leaf tablets. During the twenty-first century further fragments of tablets have emerged from excavations at Vindolanda, but their content is less exciting than the early discoveries.[6]

The tablets were deposited in layers of bracken and straw flooring inside the buildings and on the streets outside. Some seem to have been thrown out as rubbish; others were thrown onto fires, but not completely burnt. The water and the anaerobic environment at the deep levels where the tablets lay buried have preserved them to a considerable extent. Unsurprisingly, many words on the tablets are missing or incomplete. The decipherment of the Vindolanda tablets has been a massive exercise of collaborative scholarship.

The tablets are stored in the British Museum. A team of scholars is engaged upon publishing the texts of the tablets in successive volumes. At the same time, they are making the tablets available online: see Vindolanda Tablets Online[7] and Vindolanda Tablets Online II.[8] This is a remarkable facility. At the click of a mouse, anyone can now browse the personal letters and military reports of the forces that were stationed here almost 2,000 years ago. Unfortunately for the Tungrians and the Batavians, they do not have the benefit of data protection.

There is an excellent museum at Vindolanda, which tells the story of the forts and the tablets graphically. A visit to this museum is strongly recommended.

3. THE FIRST COHORT OF THE TUNGRIANS (AD 85–92)

A modest number of tablets has been recovered from the first wooden fort. Several refer to Julius Verecundus, who commanded the First Cohort of the Tungrians. Tablet 154, recovered from an inner ditch of the fort, is a strength report which appears to read as follows:[9]

18 May, net number of the First Cohort of the Tungrians, of which the commander is the prefect Iulius Verecundus, 752 including 6 centurions.

The following are absent:

- 46 men serving as guards of the governor at the office of Ferox in Corbridge, including 2 centurions
- 1 centurion at London
- 6 men outside the province, including 1 centurion

---

[5] A mixture of carbon, gum and water.
[6] See Bowman, Thomas and Tomlin (2010, 2011, 2019).
[7] vindolanda.csad.ox.ac.uk/.
[8] http://vindolanda.csad.ox.ac.uk/TVII-291. Volumes I to IV of the Vindolanda tablets are also available on romaninscriptionsofbritain.org.
[9] *Tab Vindol* II, 154.

- 9 men set out to Gaul, including 1 centurion
- 11 men at York to collect pay
- 1 man ...
- 45 men ...
- ...

Total absentees, including 5 centurions   456

Remainder present, including 1 centurion   296

Of these:

- 15 men are sick
- 6 men are wounded
- 10 men are suffering from inflammation of the eyes

Total 31 men.

The remainder are fit for active service: 265 men, including 1 centurion.

The 'governor' Ferox, who was at Corbridge (*Coria*), was probably the legate of the Ninth Legion, stationed at York. Alternatively, Ferox may have been the provincial governor. Either way, he was a senior Roman official visiting Corbridge, a frontier town. No doubt Julius Secundus was ordered to send a detachment of 46 men to provide a guard for the occasion. It is striking that two centurions (out of a total of six) were included in the group. The army recognized the importance of protecting its top brass.

A total of 31 men were unfit for service. That represents 4 per cent of the total cohort, which was not an unreasonable proportion. The six wounded soldiers may have come by their injuries in armed conflict with raiders from the north. Or perhaps they were injured by their colleagues in over-enthusiastic weapons training. Death or injury from friendly fire has always been a feature of army life. The 25 men who were ill had probably succumbed to local infections.

Tablet 154 seems to have been an internal document. It would have been held on file and the contents used to prepare a fuller report for despatch upwards to the military headquarters in York. The Roman army, both the legions and the auxiliary troops, must have produced many thousands of similar strength reports. Tablet 154 is the only strength report that survives in Britain. More specifically, it is the only strength report relating to an auxiliary infantry cohort that survives from the entire Roman Empire. Significantly, the strength report reveals that 60 per cent of the cohort were absent from their home base. This illustrates the mobility of the auxiliary troops and the frequency with which detachments were redeployed to other locations or other duties.

4. THE NINTH COHORT OF THE BATAVIANS (AD 92–105)

The Ninth Cohort of the Batavians occupied the second and third wooden forts on the Vindolanda site. They left behind a rich hoard of tablets. It is not always possible to distinguish between the two phases of their occupation, although the majority of the tablets seem to derive from the third fort.

One letter that definitely comes from the second wooden fort relates to grain supply.[10] This letter to a resident of the fort says that some Britons will be delivering a cartload of grain. The Britons are entitled to be paid carriage money of one denarius each, of which half has been paid in advance. The letter is interesting for two reasons: first, it refers to the Britons and not many tablets deign to do that; second, it shows that the occupying forces were paying the Britons for their work.

At an early stage of their occupation the Batavians constructed a bathhouse. This has recently been excavated and contains all the usual offices, including furnaces, air vents, hot baths, cold baths and lavatories. A duty roster[11] has been found, which refers to the building of the bathhouse. It lists various tasks upon which soldiers were engaged on the 25 April of an unknown year. These tasks included shoemaking, leadwork, plasterwork, something to do with wagons and so forth. Eighteen men were engaged as 'builders for the bathhouse'.[12] Since the Batavians had been uprooted from Germany and sent to the north of Britain, they can hardly be blamed for seeking a little luxury.

When the Batavians were ordered to leave Vindolanda, their departure was a hurried one. They did not bother to tidy up their rubbish. They threw unwanted correspondence and records onto a large bonfire (or group of bonfires) and hastened away to do battle in Dacia. The Batavians' bonfire, like some modern bonfires, was not a success: the flames died down before everything had been burnt. The remnants of the bonfire became buried beneath later layers of occupation. It was not until 1993 that archaeologists dug down to find the bonfire site. The debris from that site and the other rubbish that the Batavians left behind contained a large number of tablets.

Many tablets from the third wooden fort refer to Flavius Cerialis, who was prefect of the Ninth Cohort of the Batavians between 101 and 105.[13] He lived in the *praetorium* together with his wife, Sulpicia Lepidina, and their children.

Flavius Cerialis might have been a king within the Batavian community. According to Tacitus' *Germania*, the Batavians retained some of their privileges after being incorporated into the Empire. These included being commanded by their own nobles. In one letter[14] Cerialis is expressly addressed as 'king': a decurion called Masclus begins his letter: 'Masclus to Cerialis his king greeting.'[15] The letter goes on to seek instructions and to request some beer for Masclus' men. Presumably they were on an assignment away from Vindolanda. It is possible that the opening words of the letter are merely a courtesy; alternatively, they may be an acknowledgement of Cerialis' royal standing.[16]

Many *renuntia* have been found: these are the daily returns of duty officers, reporting on the state of their men and equipment. There are numerous lists of names and requests for leave. These are all ephemeral documents, which in other circumstances would not have survived.

---

[10] *Tab Vindol* II, 649.
[11] *Tab Vindol* II, 155.
[12] 'structures ad balneum xviii'.
[13] Birley (2009) chapter 7.
[14] *Tab Vindol* III, 628.
[15] 'Masclus Ceriali regi suo salutem'.
[16] Cuff (2011) 145–56.

Tablet 164 is a tantalizing fragment of a document, which describes the Britons.[17] This may have been a report or perhaps it was a memo from a departing officer for the assistance of his successor. The fragment says that the Britons do not wear armour; they have many cavalry and the cavalry do not use swords. The text then continues: 'nec residunt Brittunculi ut iaculos mittant'. This means 'nor do the wretched little Britons mount in order to throw javelins'. The dismissive term *Brittunculi* indicates the author's contempt for the indigenous people. This may reflect the general attitude of the troops towards the native population, although that must have mellowed as they intermarried with local women.

It is also worth noting that the author of tablet 164 makes correct use of the subjunctive following *ut*. The writer was a Germanic tribesman conscripted to serve in Britain, but he had learnt to speak and write good Latin. Perhaps that was another reason for his feeling of superiority over the natives.

It is a longstanding military tradition that top officers like to live in comfort, attended by batmen and other staff. They also enjoy elegant dinner parties. Cerialis subscribed to that tradition. A notebook[18] containing the domestic accounts of the *praetorium* has been recovered from the bonfire site. A reference to the fifth consulship of Trajan and other clues suggest that it covers the period April 102 to July 104. The notebook describes the food and drink consumed, chicken being a popular dish. Sometimes the guests are named – often commanding officers from nearby forts. On one occasion a legionary legate, possibly the officer commanding the Ninth Legion, dined with Cerialis. On another occasion the governor of Britain himself was a guest: he stopped off for lunch at Vindolanda, presumably when he was touring the northern frontier.

Aelius Brocchus was another commanding officer, although we do not know where he was stationed. Brocchus and Cerialis corresponded with each other about both social and military matters. Apparently hunting was a popular pastime. Brocchus' wife, Claudia Severa, was a friend of Cerialis' wife, Sulpicia Lepidina. The wives, like the husbands, wrote letters to each other. All this correspondence gives us a glimpse of army social life two millennia ago. Life on the frontier seems to have been quite congenial, at least for those who were on top.

Brocchus starts one letter[19] to Cerialis with the comment that the Saturnalia has now passed. The Saturnalia was a major Roman festival in December, during which everyone honoured Saturn with much merriment and celebration. It was similar to our Christmas. In the second paragraph, Brocchus invites Cerialis and Lepidina to come and stay for a few days over New Year. At the end he adds 'my Severa greets you',[20] in much the same way that a modern correspondent may throw in 'Jane sends her love' – probably without troubling to consult his wife.

Severa's birthday fell on 11 September. In one of the surviving letters[21] Severa invites Lepidina to her birthday party: 'Sister, I warmly invite you to come to my birthday celebration, so that you make the day more enjoyable for us.'[22] Severa goes on to send greetings from her

---

[17] *Tab Vindol* II 164.
[18] *Tab Vindol* III, 581. Only parts of each line are preserved.
[19] *Tab Vindol* III, 622.
[20] 'Severa mea vos salutat'.
[21] *Tab Vindol* II, 291.
[22] 'soror ad diem sollemnem natalem meum rogo libenter facias ut venias ad nos iucundiorem mihi.'

husband and her young son to Cerialis. The whole letter is in most affectionate terms. Also, like other correspondents, she uses good grammatical Latin, including the subjunctive when appropriate. The letter appears to have been written by a scribe, although composed by Severa.[23] A note at the end is in a different hand, probably that of Severa.

Another jovial occasion was Lepidina's birthday party. Seemingly Cerialis organized the event and invited the guests. Come the day unfortunately one of the guests, Clodius Super, could not make it. Super sent a gracious letter of apology, parts of which survive.[24] Writing to Cerialis as the host, Super explained that if it had been possible he would have attended 'as you wanted'.[25] It seems that birthday parties, but mercifully not surprise parties, were a regular feature of life on the northern frontier.

The poems of Virgil were often used when teaching people in the provinces to write Latin. Papyri containing lines of Virgil, probably examples of writing practice, have been found at Masada and in Egypt. The works of Virgil were available at Vindolanda and no doubt other forts as well. Apparently, Cerialis' children were required to copy out passages from the great poet as part of their education. One of the tablets recovered[26] contains parts of line 473 of *Aeneid* book 9; another tablet[27] contains parts of line 125 of *Georgics* book 1, referring to the golden age. Whether Cerialis' children enjoyed Virgil any more than modern GCSE students may be doubted.

Before sending important letters Cerialis used to prepare drafts. Some of these drafts survive in what we can now recognize as Cerialis' handwriting. The most interesting one[28] is the text of a letter to Crispinus, who appears to have been a senior official in London: he may have been a senator or legionary legate. Cerialis addressed Crispinus in unctuous terms and was obviously seeking to curry favour. Also, most helpfully for modern scholars, he identified the governor as Marcellus. We know that Neratius Marcellus was serving as governor of Britain in 103.

Requests for references are the bane of life for anyone who holds a senior or middling position. No doubt Cerialis received many such requests. One[29] survives. It is a request that Cerialis should support the application of Brigionus for appointment to an official position at Carlisle (*Luguvallum*). Apparently, this appointment was in the gift of Annius Equester, the centurion in charge of the region. Carlisle had not yet attained the status of civitas capital, so it was still under military administration. It seems that Annius Equester was the top man, at least when Brigionus was job-hunting.

Interestingly, Carlisle has also yielded up a small number of ink-written tablets from the late first and early second century.[30] These are not as chatty as the Vindolanda tablets. One of the Carlisle tablets tells us that there was an issue of barley and wheat to a 500-strong cavalry regiment.

---

[23] Bowman (2003), p. 90.
[24] *Tab Vindol* III, 629.
[25] 'sicut volueras'.
[26] *Tab Vindol* II, 118.
[27] *Tab Vindol* IV, 854. See further Bowman et al. (2010).
[28] *Tab Vindol* II, 225.
[29] *Tab Vindol* I, 250.
[30] Tomlin (1998).

5. THE FIRST COHORT OF THE TUNGRIANS (AD 105–128)

The First Cohort of the Tungrians returned in AD 105. They built and occupied the fourth wooden fort at Vindolanda. Thankfully, they did not trouble to sweep away the debris from the Batavians' bonfire; they simply built on top.

In about AD 120 the Tungrians demolished their existing quarters and built a fifth wooden fort on the site. This was the last and largest of the wooden forts at Vindolanda. It probably housed some legionary soldiers, as well as the Tungrians. During the 120s a large number of legionary soldiers were engaged upon building Hadrian's Wall. Extra accommodation for the wall-builders had to be found wherever possible.

A modest number of tablets survive from the fourth wooden fort, but nothing like the rich hoard from earlier periods. Even fewer tablets survive from the fifth fort. The remnants of the fifth fort are at a higher level and generally do not lie in anaerobic conditions. The tablets from these two periods provide a snapshot of ordinary life in Vindolanda, rather than the doings of top people in the *praetorium*.

Tablet 180[31] is an account of wheat deliveries, probably made by a civilian contractor. It is a useful document, but hardly brimming with human interest. The reverse side, however, is more revealing: a foreign merchant got hold of the tablet and wrote a petition on the back.[32] It appears that he had been beaten and his goods had been poured down the drain. The merchant addresses his petition to an important person, including the words 'I implore your majesty'.[33] He begs the recipient to prevent any further beatings, asserting that he is an innocent man from overseas. He says that he could not complain to the prefect, who was ill, and the centurions took no notice.

The background story to the merchant's letter is a matter of speculation. It is possible that he tried to sell poor quality foodstuffs to the fort; that the soldiers rejected his produce and then flogged him. Why they were proposing to flog him again is unclear. Perhaps trading standards officers were unduly severe in those times. One also wonders who the addressee was. It has been suggested that 'your majesty' could mean the Emperor, Hadrian.[34] Hadrian probably called in at Vindolanda during his tour of Britain. But it is unlikely that the Emperor was there at exactly the time of this incident or that he would have been bothered about such trivial matters as traders being beaten.

A letter[35] recovered from one room of the fort was addressed to a soldier and states: 'I have sent you socks from Sattua, two pairs of sandals and two pairs of underpants, two pairs of sandals …' [next words missing, but presumably they state a different source from the previous sandals]. Possibly a mother wrote this letter to her son, worrying that he might get cold up there in Northumberland, which was not an unreasonable fear. On the other hand, the letter goes on to send greetings to named soldiers. It is more likely that the writer was a former colleague who had served at Vindolanda and was now fulfilling a request for clothes.

---

[31] *Tab Vindol* II, 180.
[32] *Tab Vindol* II, 344.
[33] 'tuam maiestatem imploro'.
[34] Birley (2009) 94.
[35] *Tab Vindol* II, 346.

A statement of account[36] survives, identifying the consular year, which can be dated to AD 111. The account relates to the purchase and delivery of supplies, including boot nails, salt, Celtic beer and pork. Some of the prices are legible – the price of the boot nails was 2 asses. The account also states that three men had collected the goods, namely Audax, Gracilis and Similis. Many similar statements of account survive from Vindolanda, often showing prices, but on none of the others is it possible to discern the year. Probably there were thousands of documents like this. They reflect not only proper book keeping, but also careful control of military expenditure. The UK Ministry of Defence might benefit from perusal of the Vindolanda tablets.

A fragment[37] recovered from a barrack room appears to contain on both sides an attempt to write out the opening line of book 1 of Virgil's *Aeneid*. The whole of that line reads: 'arma virumque cano, Troiae qui primus ab oris'.[38]

In view of the location of this tablet, it may be evidence that someone was teaching the soldiers to write. The first sentence of the *Aeneid* would be familiar to most Romans, in the same way that most Englishmen would recognize the first sentence of Jane Austen's *Pride and Prejudice*.[39] So this would be a good passage to choose for adult education.

Figure 8.1 Vindolanda tablet (*Tab Vindol* II 343, two complete diptychs) referring to 'bad roads'. © Wikimedia (BM).

---

[36] *Tab Vindol* II, 186.
[37] *Tab Vindol* II, 452.
[38] 'I sing of arms and the man, who first from the shores of Troy …'.
[39] 'It is a truth universally acknowledged, that a single man in possession of a good fortune must be in want of a wife.'

The longest letter[40] recovered contains 45 lines of text written by Octavius to Candidus. Probably both men were centurions. Apparently, Octavius needed a large cash sum, 500 denarii, for the purchase of equipment. Probably the equipment was related to wall building, which was the dominant activity in the later years of Vindolanda. Octavius had already paid a deposit of 500 denarii and did not want to lose that. He explains that he has not collected certain hides from Catterick, because he did not wish to travel there 'while the roads are bad' (Fig. 8.1).[41] These grumbles about bad roads and potholes have a modern feel.

6. THE PICTURE THAT EMERGES FROM THE VINDOLANDA TABLETS

A variety of military records have emerged, one of the most informative being the strength report of the First Cohort of the Tungrians. It is helpful to stand back and consider the entire cache of *renuntia*, accounts, official correspondence, requests for leave and other routine documents collectively. These fragmentary tablets bear witness to the huge bureaucracy that supported the functioning of the Roman army. It is now clear that written communications were central to the effective operation of both the legions and the auxiliary units.

It is also clear that there was a high level of literacy amongst the officers at auxiliary forts and possibly also amongst the soldiers. These men may have been conscripts from conquered nations, but they had espoused the language and culture[42] of the Romans. Indeed, the auxiliaries saw themselves as Romans, even though they did not formally attain citizenship until retirement.

Cerialis and his household were all well educated. So were the centurions, soldiers, slaves and others who wrote letters or official documents. The proper use of Latin grammar has already been noted. The tablets with quotations from Virgil, which appear to have been writing exercises, give us a fleeting glimpse of classroom life in Northumberland nineteen hundred years ago.

Virgil had a special place amongst classical authors. In his majestic poem, *The Aeneid*, Virgil recounted the mythical story of Rome's foundation. He cleverly included divine prophecies of Rome's future glory and its destiny to rule the world. The whole poem became an encomium of Rome and an endorsement of its world domination. Reading Virgil must have been thoroughly heartening for centurions and soldiers as they went about their daily business of conquering territories and grabbing local resources. *The Aeneid* reassured them that what the Romans were doing was a Good Thing and anyway it was all planned by the gods. The writings of Virgil were powerful propaganda. They were also ideal material for educating young men destined to run the Empire.

Seemingly the soldiers at Vindolanda did not lead monastic or celibate lives. Ladies' ornaments have been recovered from all layers of the wooden forts. There is abundant evidence of women and children having been present. Discarded material from a cobbler's shop in the first wooden fort has survived, including some children's shoes.

---

[40] *Tab Vindol* II, 343.
[41] 'dum viae male sunt'.
[42] As to which, see Chapter 9.

The correspondence gathered from Cerialis' living quarters gives us an intriguing glimpse of social life at Vindolanda and the surrounding forts. The senior officers and their wives had a good time: birthday parties and New Year gatherings were jovial affairs. The hidden message underlying all this jollity is that at the turn of the century the northern communities were firmly under control and, for the most part, life on the frontier was peaceful. The officers and their families had ample time for leisure activities[43] and social gatherings.

It is a reasonable inference from Tablet 649 (the letter about delivering grain) that the Roman army was paying the Britons for their services. By the end of the first century the presence of the Roman army must have been boosting the local economy. At this stage the province of Britannia was far from self-sufficient. Although the Britons were probably paying their taxes, they were also in effect receiving overseas aid. Rome was using both economic incentives and military force to keep Britain pacified and compliant.

---

[43] See e.g. *Tab Vindol* III, 593 about hunting nets.

CHAPTER 9
THE ROMANIZATION OF BRITAIN IN THE FIRST CENTURY

1. Introduction

2. Tacitus' account of Romanization in the first century

3. Haverfield follows Tacitus

4. The meaning of Romanization

5. How was Britain similar to other provinces in its infrastructure and organization during the first century?

1. INTRODUCTION

This chapter will seek to rehabilitate the much-maligned concept of Romanization and will discuss how Britain was Romanized in the first century. We will return to the topic more broadly in Chapter 20.

Any tourist who trails around Europe, looking at the remains of Roman temples, villas, baths, mosaics, forts, town walls, basilicas and amphitheatres would be tempted to say: 'Gosh, Rome made its mark in much the same way everywhere. It seems that Britain and the whole of western Europe were "Romanized" – if there is such a word'. At the level of generality, our imaginary tourist would be right. The Roman army and the Roman authorities controlled most of Western Europe. Across the Empire the layout of towns and cities followed common principles, although the pattern seems to have been Hellenistic in origin. Latin was the official language of Western Europe.

But that simple summary does not present the full picture. Within the uniform general framework, there were huge variations between different regions and different social groups. There were also huge variations over time. Importantly, there were interchanges of practices, habits and religions between the separate provinces under Roman control.[1]

There is also another factor at work, namely academic endeavour. It is patently obvious that, at the general level discussed above, the whole of Europe west of the Rhine acquired Roman features. But no-one makes their name by stating the obvious. In recent years scholars have been vying with one another to debunk the idea of Romanization. In 2006 David Mattingly

---
[1] Reece (1988) 9–11.

wrote an excellent account of Roman Britain, entitled *An Imperial Possession, Britain in the Roman Empire*, in which he roundly condemned the concept of Romanization. He wrote that it meant everything and nothing; only the intellectually lazy had recourse to it.[2] Four years later, Miles Russell and Stuart Laycock pitched in. They published a splendid book called *UnRoman Britain*, which emphasized how little Rome really influenced us, despite the minor matter of running the country for nearly four centuries. There are many similar publications, all dedicated to debunking Romanization and creating new ways of looking at things.

There are, however, still some powerful voices who argue against this trend. M.J. Versluys argues that the general consensus to do away with Romanization has stifled much useful discussion.[3] Post-colonial scholarship should enrich the study of Romanization. The main structuring principle should be globalization, rather than simply examining how provinces responded to Rome.

The whole issue of Romanization is, therefore, controversial. There are two separate questions. First, what do we mean by 'Romanization'? Second, to what extent and how were the various communities in Britain Romanized during the first century? Before addressing either of these questions we should consider what Tacitus said on the topic.

2. TACITUS' ACCOUNT OF ROMANIZATION IN THE FIRST CENTURY

Tacitus describes the process of Romanizing the Britons during the first century in a famous and much quoted passage.[4] The passage begins with a candid statement of Rome's objective. The intention was 'that the scattered and uncivilised natives, hitherto accustomed to warfare, should instead come to appreciate the pleasures of leisure and peace'.[5]

Tacitus gives most of the credit for this operation to his father-in-law, even though in reality the process must have taken many decades. According to Tacitus, in the winter of AD 78–79 Agricola turned his attention to the task of winning hearts and minds. He promoted the construction of houses, temples, forums and other public buildings. Apparently, Agricola did this by privately encouraging individuals and 'publicly assisting communities'.[6]

What did Tacitus mean by 'publicly assisting communities'?

From the first century onwards a mass of Roman-style buildings sprang up across the province. These included a range of public buildings, such as basilicas, temples, amphitheatres and baths, as well as private villas for the élites. Either Roman officials or experts from other provinces must have played a part in these construction projects. Otherwise there would not have been such a similarity of style between public buildings in Britain and on the Continent. It has been

---

[2]See Mattingly (2006) xii, 14–17 and *passim*.
[3]Versluys (2014), 1–20.
[4]*Agricola* 21.
[5]'ut homines dispersi ac rudes eoque in bella faciles quieti et otio per voluptates adsuescerent.'
[6]'adiuvare publice'.

suggested that the assistance to which Tacitus was referring may have been tax breaks, rather than military architects or stonemasons actually doing the work.[7] There is good sense in the suggestion that Rome's assistance may have been financial.

Before his untimely death in 2000, Thomas Blagg carried out an in-depth analysis of Roman architectural ornament in Britain.[8] He divided column capitals into three groups – composite, Corinthian and foliate. He carried out a similar categorization of column bases and the columns themselves. He then compared the architecture in towns with military architecture in Britain and with urban architecture on the Continent. This led to the following conclusions:

(i) The forums and basilicas of the Flavian period preceded, and were much more elaborate than, the stone forts and principia built by the army.

(ii) The army started building in stone towards the end of the Flavian period. The forms of architectural ornament on military buildings were different from those established in the civitas capitals of southern Britain.

(iii) The designs of public buildings in major British towns of the first and second century had much in common with the designs of public buildings in Gaul. They were probably the work of designers and stonemasons who came over from Gaul. The Corinthian column capitals at Cirencester and Verulamium are strikingly similar to those in north-east Gaul.

(iv) Probably, therefore, the legionary architects and stonemasons were not involved in the design or construction of civic buildings.

(v) The impetus for creating fine Roman-style civic buildings came from the civitates themselves and from those who governed them. The Roman authorities probably assisted by remission of taxes and by encouraging Gallic builders to come over here and do the work.

(vi) The one exception is the quadrifrons arch at Richborough, which was highly elaborate. It was making a statement about the power of Rome. This was the direct concern of the imperial administration.

The temple of Sulis Minerva at Bath (discussed in Chapter 17 below) is an example of high-quality Gallic stonework.

Although they gained assistance from Gallic stonemasons, self-evidently it was the indigenous Britons who actually built the monumental structures and the civic buildings, which started to appear across Britain in the first century AD. The one exception may be Fishbourne palace, discussed in Chapter 18 below. That was so magnificent and so out of character with other first-century villas in Britain, that immigrant labour may well have been used.

Tacitus gives a somewhat garbled account of public building projects, compressing everything into the six years of Agricola's governance. According to Tacitus, Agricola praised the energetic and rebuked the indolent; rivalry for Agricola's compliments took the place of compulsion. Here surely the great historian is exaggerating. It is not credible that Agricola became an omniscient and omnipresent clerk of works. The most that the provincial governors

---

[7] Blagg (1980) 27–42.
[8] Thomas Blagg, *Roman Architectural Ornament in Britain*, BAR British Series 329 (2002).

(including Agricola) could do, and probably did do, was to provide incentives and some form of financial assistance.

Gaining the support of the indigenous élites

As Tacitus acknowledges, any occupying army needs to win the support of the pre-existing élites. The Americans' failure in this regard was one of the causes of the problems that they faced in Iraq after 2003.[9] The Roman occupying army did not make that mistake. Tacitus tells us that Agricola was impressed by the natural abilities of the British and thought they were cleverer than the Gallic people.[10] (Such racist comments were acceptable in those times.) He set up a training programme for the sons of chieftains, who received 'a liberal education'.[11] The syllabus is not recorded, but it would have involved learning many lines of Virgil (a favourite with Roman schoolmasters) and regular athletics.[12] There were probably periodic floggings, since corporal punishment was widely practised in Roman schools.[13] The public school system had arrived in Britain, reserved for the ruling classes.

As a result of these endeavours, according to Tacitus, Roman culture began to take hold amongst community leaders. It became fashionable for the élites to converse in Latin. According to Tacitus, they even tried to master rhetoric.[14] Probably they studied Cicero, the famous orator who had been so scathing about the British a few years earlier. Roman styles of clothing also became fashionable: wealthy Britons started wearing togas. A good quality toga was an expensive purchase. Happily, in those days the fashions did not change every year.

According to Tacitus the Britons were gradually drawn into alluring vices: they came to enjoy the pleasures of 'colonnades, baths and elegant dinner parties'. Tacitus conjures up the image of swarthy tribesmen abandoning their warlike ways and instead meeting up to discuss philosophy or enjoy formal dinners. Having created this charming image, Tacitus returns to his natural cynicism. He remarks that all these developments were forms of slavery, which the simple natives called culture.[15]

Tacitus' final sardonic comment epitomizes Roman imperialism. The secret of Rome's success was that, so far as possible, it absorbed defeated nations into its own (evolving) way of life, starting with their ruling classes. Ultimately, as we shall see, the entire population of Britain were destined to become Roman citizens. To say that Romanization is 'meaningless' or that it didn't happen misses the point. Romanization (a concept which we will explore further) was the key to Roman imperialism.

Even so, there are difficulties with Tacitus' analysis. In particular, the Britons who started wearing togas, speaking Latin and enjoying fine wines in sumptuous villas were very much in the minority. Most of them lived in the south east of England. The general population did not 'go Roman'; they continued, so far as they could, the way of life and the

---

[9]Rogan (2009) 489.
[10]'ingenia Britannorum studiis Gallorum anteferre'.
[11]'liberalibus artibus erudire'.
[12]Quintilian, *Institutio Oratoria* 1.11.15.
[13]Criticized by Quintilian at *Institutio Oratoria* 1.3.13.
[14]'eloquentiam concupiscerent'.
[15]'Idque apud imperitos humanitas vocabatur, cum pars servitutis esset.' *Agricola* 21.

practices that they had developed in the Iron Age. Even those few who actually visited Rome probably hybridized what they saw.

Conclusion

The process that Tacitus describes so graphically applied only to the urban élites, not to the vast majority of the population who lived and worked in the countryside. But that was enough for Rome's purposes: it made Britain a governable province. The public building projects which, according to Tacitus, the imperial government encouraged (temples, basilicas etc) bore the imprint of other provinces. The indigenous élites consciously chose to develop public buildings and private residences in styles that were similar to those prevailing on the Continent.

3. HAVERFIELD FOLLOWS TACITUS

Francis Haverfield (a professor of ancient history at Oxford in the early twentieth century) wrote an influential book about how provinces within the Empire were transformed.[16] He accepted Tacitus' model.

Every historian is the product of their own age. Haverfield lived when the British Empire was at its zenith and he belonged to what might be called the Rudyard Kipling school of thought.[17] He regarded imperialism as an excellent institution. In relation to British foreign policy, he observed: 'We know well enough the rule of civilised white men over uncivilised Africans.'[18] Such comments (now unacceptable) reveal the standpoint from which he was writing.

Haverfield was a strong admirer of the Roman system of government. In chapter 6 he noted that colonies for veteran soldiers in Britain adopted the Roman institutions, including pairs of magistrates. He thoroughly approved of the decision to structure civitas capitals in the same way. Haverfield concluded: 'The greatest work of the imperial age must be sought in its provincial administration.'[19] In Haverfield's view, the Roman conquest of Western Europe was beneficial, because the indigenous peoples had the intelligence and ability to accept Rome's culture. The Romans brought with them substantial architectural, artistic, artefactual and administrative skills. They also possessed a refined language and extensive literature of high quality. The Romans shared all these assets with those native populations who were lucky enough to be conquered. Happily, Britain was part of that Empire.

There are obvious difficulties with Haverfield's analysis: he treated Roman culture as essentially static and monolithic; he regarded the cultural exchange that followed conquest as a one-way process. Haverfield accepted too readily the views of Tacitus and Virgil about the benefits of Roman imperialism.

---

[16] Haverfield (1912).
[17] As epitomized in Kipling's poem *The White Man's Burden*.
[18] Haverfield (1912) 12.
[19] Haverfield (1912) 9.

Having rejected that analysis, we must now tackle the two questions identified earlier, namely (i) what Romanization actually means and (ii) the extent to which Britain was Romanized in the first century AD.

4. THE MEANING OF ROMANIZATION

'Romanization' is generally taken to mean the adoption of Roman building styles, Roman political systems and Roman culture. But Roman building styles changed over time. So did Roman systems of governance and Roman religions. '*Romanitas*' was a continuously evolving concept.

Roman culture was not uniform across the Empire – there were significant differences between the eastern and western halves. In the east, Greek was the dominant language and many local coinages predominated until the third century. In the west, Latin was the universal language of those in authority and Roman coinage was universal. Increasingly non-Italians were recruited into the legions, to serve in all parts of the Empire. The auxiliary troops who made up a large part of the army were, by definition, not Italian. Most soldiers intermarried with the local populations and after retirement usually settled in the countries where they had served. By the second century even the emperors did not need to be Italian. Furthermore, traders regularly circulated between provinces, for example bringing wine and foodstuffs from the Mediterranean or Samian ware from Gaul. The provinces of the Empire, including Britain, became teeming cosmopolitan communities.[20]

Some commentators suggest that, because of the absence of Latin and the continuity of Greek social structures, the eastern provinces were not really Romanized at all, but that goes too far. Even the eastern provinces adopted Roman institutions, such as *collegia* or professional associations.[21] It was merely that the impact of Romanization was different in the east.

Despite the variations identified above, there were significant common elements of Roman culture, which were imposed upon Britain and other provinces. In essence, these were:

- Deference to the Emperor and the imperial cult
- Circulation of coinage with the Emperor's portrait
- Progressive extension of Roman citizenship
- The Latin language (mainly in western provinces)
- Roman law
- Urbanization and the development of Roman-style towns
- Public buildings, such as baths and amphitheatres
- Infrastructure works such as roads and aqueducts
- Local administrative systems based on the Roman model

---

[20]Hanson (1994); Higgins (2013) 171–2.
[21]Eckhardt (2016) 147–71.

- Worship of Roman gods, usually combined with the indigenous or chthonic gods of the individual provinces.

The Haverfield model treats Romanization as a one-way operation, by which civilized Romans bestowed their culture on uncivilized natives. That is not correct. First, the Celtic peoples were not uncivilized. Second, the provinces acquired by Rome had a massive impact on Rome and on each other. There was a merging of cultures and a merging of religions. Some scholars call the process creolization, not Romanization.

As J. Hill points out,[22] there was no simple 'Roman' or 'non-Roman' identity in the Western Empire. Identity has a psychological basis, reflecting how people see themselves and each other. People's identities are not fixed: they are affected by age, gender, social position and region; so liable to change over time. Take an auxiliary soldier of Gallic ethnicity, whose family had served on the Rhine frontier for two generations. It must be debatable whether he saw himself as Gallic or Roman, or perhaps even Germanic. Institutions exist at the private level (e.g. marriage) and at the public level (e.g. the institutions of civitas government). The imposition of Roman government had a profound effect on the institutions of the provinces.[23]

Romanization as an ongoing process

Romanization was a process whereby the evolving cultures of Rome became blended with the cultures of the provinces that it annexed. This impacted differently on each section of society and each region within the Empire. Whether deliberately (as Tacitus maintains) or incidentally, the process of Romanization enabled the Roman government to maintain long-term control over the Empire. Rome's domination and the imperial transport system also had the effect of facilitating cultural exchanges between provinces. This is an important aspect of Romanization, which is often overlooked.

5. HOW WAS BRITAIN SIMILAR TO OTHER PROVINCES IN ITS INFRASTRUCURE AND ORGANIZATION DURING THE FIRST CENTURY?

We must now review the state of Britain at the end of the first century. London was the provincial capital, controlled by Roman officials and administered on Roman lines. Colchester, Lincoln and Gloucester were now established as colonies (*coloniae*) to accommodate veteran soldiers: these three colonies were high status towns, whose inhabitants were Roman citizens. There were established civitas capitals at Canterbury, Chichester, Winchester, Silchester, Exeter, Wroxeter, St Albans, Cirencester, Leicester, Caistor St Edmund and Dorchester.

The occupying army

The fortresses for the three legions based in Britain were at Caerleon, Chester and York. The Second Legion Augusta was based at Caerleon; the Ninth Legion Hispana at York; the Twentieth

---

[22] Hill (2001).
[23] Gardner (2013) 1–25.

Legion Valeria Victrix at Chester. This remained the position for many years to come, save that in about 122 the Sixth Legion Victrix replaced the Ninth Legion at York.

A network of auxiliary forts was spread out across the province. The function of the military based at these forts was to maintain order and to support the civil administration, including the collection of taxes. In areas where there was no civitas capital the army was responsible for civil administration and, presumably, collected taxes directly.

The legions and auxiliary units were highly versatile.[24] They brought with them a wide range of skills, both military and civilian. Once the annexation of Britannia was complete, the role of the Roman armed forces changed. They still undertook regular training and exercises, but they were no longer primarily engaged upon warfare. Instead their other functions and skills came to the fore. Roman soldiers acted as builders, designers, administrators and industrialists. Under specialist military engineers they built bridges, roads, siege-works, walls, baths[25] and aqueducts, so far as these were necessary for their own operations and comfort. As discussed earlier in this chapter, however, the army was not the only show in town. Much of the impetus for public building projects seems to have come from the local population. Gallic stonemasons and designers did some of the work. The army concentrated on construction projects that had a military purpose. They built bases ranging from temporary overnight camps to stone forts. They controlled some of the quarries and mines, although much of this work was entrusted to private contractors as discussed below. They manufactured weapons and military equipment. They set up potteries, when local suppliers did not meet their needs. They even manufactured and worked glass, as confirmed by finds at Coppergate in York.[26] Roman soldiers also acted as provincial policemen. They were a protective occupying force, whose main purpose was to preserve the interests of the state and its élites.

Road system

There was a network of roads linking all the important towns of the province,[27] with the principal roads radiating from London. Most were originally constructed by the army to facilitate control of the province. Military engineers carefully planned the layout of the road system, after surveying the ground to find the most practicable routes.[28] So far as possible the roads followed straight alignments, but sometimes they wiggled because of following rivers or Iron Age trackways. The quality of the roads varied. Many were little more than a pair of ditches with gravel in between. A few were closer to the idealized Roman design. That involved an embankment (*agger*) at the base built from earth or stony material. Large stones placed on top of the *agger* formed the foundation of the road. The top surface of the best roads comprised gravel, small stones, flint or chippings. These were bedded in and cambered to assist drainage.

As time went on the network grew and the function of the roads changed. In addition to their military use, they also became the infrastructure for commerce and the general economic

---

[24] James (2001).
[25] As recorded in *Tab Vindol* II, 155.
[26] Cool et al. (1999) 147–62: the discovery of semi-reacted batch materials suggests that, unlike other producers, the soldiers were manufacturing glass from raw materials.
[27] Margary (1973) chapter 1.
[28] Davies (1998) 1–16.

life of the province. The civitas authorities commissioned the building of additional roads, primarily for trade and communications. In the south-east, local trackways linked into the roads. These facilitated transport between London and iron working sites on the Weald or corn growing districts on the South Downs. At Bignor, a short track linked the productive farmland into Stane Street.

Anyone seeking a full description of the road network in Roman Britain should turn to Ivan Margary's magisterial 550-page work, *Roman Roads in Britain*,[29] or the Antonine Itinerary.[30] In summary, however, the following were major roads:

- Watling Street ran from Richborough in Kent (then a major port) through London and St Albans to Wroxeter.
- A substantial road ran north-east from London through Chelmsford and Colchester.
- Fosse Way ran from Exeter to Lincoln, passing through Cirencester and Bath. Stane Street ran from London to Chichester.
- A network of roads linking Silchester, Winchester, Bath and other major centres ran from London to the port at Bristol (*Portus Abonae*).[31]
- A major road from London to Exeter ran through Silchester and Dorchester.
- A major road ran from Silchester through Cirencester, Gloucester and Caerwent to Carmarthen.
- Ermine Street ran from London to York.
- Dere Street ran from York to Corbridge and then further north into Scotland.
- Stanegate Road ran east/west, passing through Corbridge and Carlisle.

Most of the Roman towns and roads created in the first century are still in use today, although heavily overlain by medieval and modern construction. The suffix 'chester', which appears in many town names, is a corruption of the Latin word *castra*, meaning military camp. Some towns, such as Chester or Colchester, really do stand on or close to the site of a military camp, but often the suffix 'chester' simply denotes a town that had Roman walls: for example, Chichester, Winchester or Silchester.

Mining operations and construction

Britain was a hugely expensive province to run. The Romans therefore needed to extract as much as possible of the available minerals.[32] They asserted, with supreme insouciance, that all minerals within the province were the property of the Emperor. In practice, the Roman authorities were principally interested in bullion, which they needed in large quantities for minting coinage. The Emperor graciously allowed private contractors to undertake most of the other mining operations, on condition that those contractors paid royalties to the imperial treasury. The procurator and his officials dealt with the contractual and financial arrangements.

---

[29] Margary (1973); for a shorter account, see Davies (2011).
[30] Rivet and Smith (1979) chapter 4.
[31] The fragmentary remains suggest that the port was at Sea Mills where the river Trim joins the Avon.
[32] Mattingly (2006) chapter 16.

Where there was a public interest at stake, the Roman authorities would themselves take control. The *classis Britannica* may have controlled part of the mining and processing of iron ore on the Weald; alternatively, the fleet may simply have bought in the iron that it needed from private contractors.

A ready supply of metals was vital for the functioning of the Empire. Metals were used for the manufacture of armaments and other military equipment, as well as for building projects. Metals also had an economic function. The imperial mints used gold, silver, copper and brass to manufacture coinage. Modern economists might call that 'quantitative easing', but the Roman government had no such scruples. They had to maintain the coin supply and pay the army.

By the end of the first century, mines were established at key sites across the province. Either the Roman authorities or private contractors were extracting copper at Anglesey and at Llanymynech in north Wales; gold at Dolaucothi in South Wales;[33] iron ore at sites in the East Midlands, the Forest of Dean and the Weald; lead at many sites across England and Wales; and (probably) tin in Cornwall. Forts generally stood close to mines that yielded gold, silver (as a bye-product of lead) or copper. The Romans were less bothered about lead, which was plentiful and could easily be bought.

Gold mine

The quartz within the rocks at Dolaucothi contains gold dust, which the Roman authorities set about mining. They dug opencast pits and cut mineshafts into the hillside along the seams of quartz. You can still walk through these workings, but a guide is necessary if you want to find your way out again. Following the main tourist route, as you clamber back up towards the daylight of Ogofau Pit, you will be using a flight of steps that Roman engineers (or perhaps their slaves) cut into the rock two thousand years ago.

To extract gold, you must crush the quartz and then wash the fragments in running water. Gold dust sinks to the bottom. The Romans followed this procedure, which needed a plentiful supply of water. They cut a series of leats and ponds into the hillside at Dolaucothi, which can still be traced. The remains of a water-wheel and wooden panning cradle from their operations are now in the National Museum of Wales.

It is estimated [see Annels and Burnham (2013) at p. 59] that the Roman miners removed about 500,000 tonnes of rock from the main Ogofau pit. That may have yielded some 830 kilograms of gold. They would also have extracted gold from the mineshafts and the other opencast pits, but probably not as much as from the main pit. In total it is unlikely that the Romans obtained more than 1,500 kilograms of gold from the entire enterprise. The fact that Britain boasted one gold mine yielding such modest returns does not suggest that the province was somehow paying its way or was a source of wealth for Rome.

---

[33]Brewer (2010) 27–8; Annels and Burnham (2013).

Figure 9.1 Dolaucothi, gold mine. © Wikimedia/Nilfanion.

The construction boom in first-century Britain meant that demand for lead was steadily increasing: lead was used for aqueducts, as flashings for roofs and for manufacturing pipes or tanks. The lead mines in the Mendips could not meet all these needs. By the end of the century additional lead mines were operating in the Peak District, the Pennines and North Wales. The Romans were particularly interested in the silver that they could recover from these locations. Many lead pigs from the Mendips and Derbyshire bear the inscription 'EX ARG'.[34] That may mean all the silver had been extracted. Once metals had been mined and processed, if they were not seized by the provincial authorities, they could be traded like any other goods. One of the Vindolanda tablets records that a man called Ascanius had bought 90 pounds (29 kilograms) of iron for 32 denarii.[35]

By the end of the first century there was a network of roads, towns and industrial centres. It is reasonable to assume that there was a well-developed local economy, with a fairly stable currency and an established market for commodity trading.

Another consequence of the construction boom was a huge demand for tiles:[36] they were needed for forts, public buildings, villas and town houses. Private contractors undertook most of the manufacture, supplying both local communities and the army. If there was a shortage, the legions undertook some of the manufacture, but military production represented a small proportion of the total. Workmen made the tiles by throwing wet clay into a four-sided mould and punching the clay to ensure that the mould was completely filled. They then dried and fired

---

[34] Gardiner (2001), 11–13: on UCL's website.
[35] Bray (2010) 175–85.
[36] Warry (2010) 127–47.

the clay tiles. It was a simple matter to stamp tiles during manufacture, in order to show their origin. Some tiles bear the stamp of individual legions or the *classis Britannica*. In recent years archaeologists have recovered over two thousand stamped legionary tiles, which provide evidence of the movements of legions or detachments from the legions.

An enterprising kiln owner in Sussex designed and manufactured a new form of box tile,[37] which was a hollowed-out voussoir. It could be used in vaults and improved the central heating arrangements. These tiles were used in the walls of the fortress baths at Caerleon and Exeter, as well as the Huggin Hill baths in London. Some of the tiles are still in use. They are built into the wall of St Peter's Church, Westhampnett.

Cultural exchange

By the end of the first century, Rome had left an indelible mark upon this country. It had established what was then and is now our capital city, as well as other major towns. It had created the beginnings of our present road system. It had also generated a massive expansion of mining operations, construction works, trade and industry.

The effects of imperialism are two-way. Both conqueror and conquered are permanently changed. As the Roman Empire took shape, the provinces had a profound impact upon Rome. Britons were becoming Romanized and Rome was becoming 'provincialized'.[38]

Equally important were transactions between provinces, which bypassed Rome altogether. The common currency, road network and established sea-routes of the Empire (to which both London and Richborough were linked in) facilitated trade between Britain and all the western provinces.[39] This led to continuous cultural exchange. So did the presence here of auxiliaries from around the Empire. Altars in Britain dedicated to Germanic gods are evidence of that process. Works done by Gallic stonemasons on monumental buildings at Cirencester, Verulamium, Bath and elsewhere are further examples of cultural exchange. Pottery styles in Britain and Gaul were converging. Britain was becoming more Gaulish, Spanish, Rhinelandish and Danubian.[40]

We will look again at the issue of Romanization in Chapter 20. However, it is fair to note that at this early stage, only sixty years after the conquest, the process of Romanization was already well advanced in Britain. As Versluys points out, this may be seen as a form of globalization.[41] It principally affected urban dwellers, rather than those living in the countryside. Also, there was still a sharp divide between soldiers and civilians, as we saw from the Vindolanda tablets.[42]

---

[37]Lancaster (2012) 419–40.
[38]Reece (1988) 11.
[39]Scheidel et al. (2007) 663–5.
[40]Reece (1988) 9.
[41]Versluys (2014), 1–20.
[42]Especially *Tab Vindol* II, 164.

CHAPTER 10
THE EMPEROR HADRIAN VISITS BRITAIN

1. Introduction
2. Britain during the early years of Hadrian's reign
3. Hadrian's visit to Britain in AD 122
4. Hadrian's Wall
   (i) The frontiers of the Roman Empire
   (ii) The construction of Hadrian's Wall
   (iii) What was the purpose of the wall?
   (iv) What was the effect of the wall?
5. Britain in the years following Hadrian's visit
   (i) Urban development
   (ii) Salt industry and the Fens
   (iii) The fleet and the establishment of a new port at Dover

1. INTRODUCTION

We now come to a towering figure, who has left a permanent mark on Britain: Publius Aelius Hadrianus. Hadrian was the subject of a major exhibition at the British Museum in 2008 and is still the focus of much ongoing scholarship.[1] For further details about Hadrian,[2] see the Online Appendix.

This chapter will examine events in Britain during Hadrian's reign, so far as we can reconstruct them from fragmentary sources. The contemporary writers give us little assistance about this period.

---

[1] Opper (2013) draws the recent research together.
[2] For more details of Hadrian's life, see Birley (1997). The principal ancient texts are *Historia Augusta, Hadrian* and Dio, *Roman History* 69.

2. BRITAIN DURING THE EARLY YEARS OF HADRIAN'S REIGN

According to Dio, Hadrian brought to an end a number of wars that were ongoing at the start of his reign.[3] Dio does not tell us where the wars were happening or how serious they were, but it is likely that one was in Britain. The *Historia Augusta* states that 'the Britons could not be kept under Roman rule'.[4] This sentence may well be an exaggeration. As we shall see time and again in later chapters, 'trouble in Britain' was a common theme for historians writing about the accessions of emperors. This was a convenient literary device to show the new Emperor taking control. Despite that reservation, there was probably some degree of unrest in Britain. Otherwise, Hadrian might have been content to maintain Stanegate as the northern frontier. As it was, he required the construction of a substantial frontier wall.

Probably the Brigantes, who were not yet absorbed into the civitas system, were involved in the unrest but unfortunately the rebel leaders on this occasion (unlike Boudica half a century earlier) had no-one to record their exploits. All we know is that they failed. Hadrian appointed Quintus Pompeius Falco, an experienced general who had been decorated in the Dacian wars, as governor. Serving from AD 118 to 122, Falco rapidly brought the province back under control.

In AD 119 the Romans issued a new set of coins, to mark their victory and the restoration of peace in Britain. The fact that there was a new coinage issue does not mean that the conflict had been especially noteworthy, or terribly fierce. Coins were an excellent form of propaganda. Most people handling money would not have known what was going on in distant provinces. Like modern newspaper readers, they would be inclined to believe what they read.

The coins minted in AD 119 had a picture of Britannia on the back. This was the first time that Britannia appeared on any coinage. She was portrayed as a seated female warrior holding a shield and some sort of stick, which may have been a javelin (Fig. 10.1).

The Britannia image

The first known image of Britannia as a female representation of Britain appears on a mid-first century AD marble relief at Aphrodisias in modern Turkey. That relief shows the Emperor Claudius conquering Britannia, who is lying beneath him.

The coins minted in AD 119 started a trend. Throughout the second and third centuries, Britannia often featured on the backs of coins. This was an enduring image. In 1672 Britannia once again started to appear on the backs of coins circulating in Britain. During the eighteenth and nineteenth centuries the motif became increasingly popular. The first coins showing Britannia holding a trident and seated above the waves were minted in 1797. In this majestic pose she symbolized Britain's naval superiority under admirals such as Nelson and Collingwood. Ironically, the image that once represented Britain's subjection to Rome mutated to become the symbol of Britain's imperial power. At the time of writing, Britannia still appears on the back of 50 pence coins. She is seated with a shield at her side and is duly carrying a trident. Finally, despite some criticism, a lusty rendition of "Rule Britannia" continues to enliven each Last Night of the Proms.

---

[3] *Roman History* 69.5.
[4] 'Britanni teneri sub Romana dicione non poterant': *Hadrian* 5.1.

The Emperor Hadrian Visits Britain

Figure 10.1 First coins showing Britannia, *c.* AD 119. © Wikimedia/Narwhal2.

One tantalizing piece of evidence, which may date from the period of Falco's governorship, is a bronze head of Hadrian retrieved from the Thames in 1834 and now in the British Museum.[5] The head appears to have been forcibly wrenched from a statue of the Emperor and thrown into the river. We do not know when or why this happened. One possibility is that the statue was erected at the start of Hadrian's reign (always a good move when there is a new Emperor) and destroyed during the unrest that Falco suppressed. Another possibility is that the statue was built during or after Hadrian's visit to Britain and destroyed much later, for example in AD 409 when Britain rejected Roman rule.

Whichever theory is correct, the violent destruction of Hadrian's statue is evidence of British resentment of Roman rule. Destroying the statue of a deposed ruler is a traditional way of expressing popular hatred. A recent example is the toppling of Saddam Hussain's statue in Baghdad in April 2003. In the ancient world religious sensitivities intervened. It is significant that the iconoclasts who smashed Hadrian's statue did not melt down and re-use the head. Throwing it into the Thames may have been a symbolic act or a form of ritual deposition.[6]

3. HADRIAN'S VISIT TO BRITAIN IN AD 122

As part of his first grand tour, Hadrian came to Britain in AD 122. There are many problems with reconciling the evidence about Hadrian's visit. What follows is the conventional interpretation.

Aulus Platorius Nepos, who was a longstanding friend of Hadrian, accompanied the Emperor and replaced Falco as governor of the province. Nepos brought with him the Sixth Legion Victrix from Lower Germany.

The Emperor arrived in early July with his retinue. He began with a formal ceremony, probably held in London. On 17 July Hadrian conferred citizenship and the right to marry on a group of veterans who had recently retired from auxiliary units serving in Britain. The diploma received by one of those soldiers, Gemellus, has survived.[7] Unusually, it refers to two

---

[5] Birley (1997) plate 13.
[6] See the discussion of ritual deposition of statue heads in Chapter 19 below.
[7] CIL xvi. 69.

governors: Falco, who granted the soldiers an honourable discharge, and Nepos, the new governor of the province. The discharge of the soldiers may have been deferred to await Hadrian's arrival.[8]

After leaving London, Hadrian headed north. He stationed the Sixth Legion Victrix in the fortress at York, which had formerly been the base of the Ninth Legion Hispana. He either ordered or approved the construction of a bridge over the River Tyne. This was duly named *Pons Aelii*, meaning the bridge of Aelius (Hadrian's middle name). Hadrian and the army dedicated two matching altars there, one to Neptune and the other to Oceanus.[9] This was a tactful choice of deities, since the troops in northern Britain depended heavily on supply by sea. At the same time as dedicating the altars the Emperor probably made sacrifices to both gods.

Like much else that Hadrian did, the bridge that he founded near the mouth of the Tyne has left a lasting legacy. A fort was later constructed next to the bridge and a settlement grew up around the fort. The whole of this development was known as *Pons Aelii*. It did not acquire its modern name for another nine centuries. In 1080 the Normans built a castle on the Hadrianic site. Unsurprisingly that castle was new when it was built. So *Pons Aelii* gained the name Newcastle.

Hadrian's visit to Britain was a brief episode in the Emperor's towering career. It receives only scant attention in the surviving historical works. Dio describes the more interesting parts of the Emperor's grand tours but says nothing about what he accomplished in Britain. The *Historia Augusta* is marginally more helpful. Chapter 11 of the Life of Hadrian includes the following passage:

> Hadrian set off for Britain, in which he corrected many things and was the first to build a wall eighty miles long, which would separate the Romans from the barbarians.[10]

Chapter 12 adds the statement that after Hadrian had 'sorted out matters in Britain',[11] he crossed to Gaul. Unfortunately, the author does not trouble to mention what were the many things requiring 'correction' or what Hadrian did to 'sort matters out'.

Hadrian returned to Gaul at some point before the winter. It is clear from the epigraphic evidence that he visited Wroxeter and ordered a substantial expansion of that town. We can safely assume that the Emperor inspected the three main legionary fortresses and all the major cities, issuing instructions as he passed.

While Hadrian was in Britain[12] an incident concerning his wife, Sabina, came to light. Suetonius, the Emperor's private secretary, along with the prefect of the Praetorian Guard and other senior officials were behaving towards Sabina with undue familiarity. Apparently, Sabina did not rebuff them. Hadrian summarily dismissed all the officials involved. Possibly he had other motives as well. Suetonius was the famous author and biographer, whose work is relied

---

[8] Birley (2013) 132.
[9] RIB 1319 and 1320.
[10] 'Britanniam petiit, in qua multa correxit murumque per octaginta milia passuum primus duxit, qui barbaros Romanosque divideret.' *Hadrian* 11.2.
[11] 'Compositis in Britannia rebus': *Hadrian* 12.1.
[12] The dating of this incident is inferred from where it appears in the *Historia Augusta*. See also Birley (2005) 121.

on in earlier chapters of this book. Being an independent thinker, Suetonius may have ventured to disagree with some of the Emperor's less intelligent decisions.

The Suetonius incident brought the discord between the Emperor and his wife to a head. Hadrian was not, of course, either the first or the last head of state to be plagued by matrimonial problems while he was trying to deal with public affairs. Other examples from the Tudor period or modern times may spring to mind. According to the *Historia Augusta*[13] Hadrian often said that he would have divorced Sabina at the same time as dismissing Suetonius, if only he had been a private citizen. Apparently, Hadrian was disenchanted with his wife because she was 'moody and bad tempered'.[14]

Poor Sabina had good reason to be moody and bad tempered. With all due respect to the great Emperor, he must have been insufferable to live with. He quarrelled with most of his friends.[15] He was absolute ruler of almost the entire known world and seldom seemed to let up. He had dragged his wife away from the comforts of Rome on a seemingly endless tour of military outposts. It is hardly surprising that Sabina was grumpy with her husband.

The Emperor's main concerns, however, were not related to his marriage. He was set upon creating monuments across the Empire, which would overshadow the achievements of his predecessors – and hopefully those of his successors as well. The most famous of all the projects which Hadrian initiated in Britain was, of course, the wall that bears his name. This massive edifice stretched from coast to coast across the north of England. It is to that we must now turn.

4. HADRIAN'S WALL

Hadrian ordered the construction of a wall along the northern frontier of the province, running from the North Sea to the Solway Firth. He probably did this when he was here in AD 122. He would have wanted to be on site, when taking such a far-reaching decision. Also, there is evidence that the Sixth Legion, which accompanied Hadrian to Britain, was involved in building the first section of the wall. But there is a possible alternative scenario. This is that wall-building began shortly before AD 122 and that the decisions that Hadrian took while he was in Britain concerned re-locating the forts and constructing the Vallum (as discussed below).[16] On this analysis, a detachment of the Sixth Legion would have come to Britain in advance and helped to get work under way before AD 122. Two fragments of an inscription[17] found in Jarrow church often feature in the debate. They appear to be part of an official announcement about building the wall.[18] But the Jarrow inscription is so incomplete that it gives little assistance in dating the commencement of work.

Hadrian's Wall gives rise to many issues. These include: how does the wall fit with other frontiers of the Empire? How and why it was built? What useful purpose did it serve? Many

---

[13] *Hadrian* 11.3.
[14] 'uxorem . . . morosam at asperam': *Historia Augusta, Hadrian* 11.3.
[15] *Historia Augusta, Hadrian* 15.2.
[16] Graafstal (2018) presents a forceful argument for this interpretation.
[17] RIB 1051 a and b.
[18] Graafstal (2018) at 92–7.

scholars have grappled with these questions. Hadrian probably never gave them a moment's thought, as he moved on to other and grander projects.

In order to consider Hadrian's Wall in its proper context, we must begin by looking at the frontiers of the Roman Empire more generally.

(i) The frontiers of the Roman Empire[19]

Should there be any frontiers at all? This is logically the first question and it is not a frivolous one. The notion that Rome had a right, indeed a destiny, to rule the entire world was deeply ingrained in the Roman psyche.[20] Augustus in his autobiography, the *Res gestae*, spoke of bringing the whole world under Roman rule.[21] In Virgil's *Aeneid* (which had the status of religious text as well as epic poem) Jupiter states that he has given 'power without limit' to Rome.[22] It was hardly surprising that the Romans held this comforting belief. For a thousand years they had won every significant war. They had expanded from being a small Italian town to gaining sovereignty over most of the known world. Fortified by their history and their religion, the Romans were inclined to see all frontiers (other than oceans or mountains) as either temporary arrangements or symbols of failure.

In the second century Rome controlled an Empire that embraced Western Europe, Turkey, the Near East and North Africa. There was therefore a need to identify which territories were within the Empire and which territories were not yet included. Roman generals regarded themselves as free to campaign beyond the frontiers and they frequently did so. But for an efficient system of administration, the borders had to be clearly demarcated.

The frontiers themselves were defined in a variety of ways. Some geographical features were in roughly the right place and the Roman government cheerfully used them. The Atlantic Ocean was certainly in the right place. That constituted the western boundary of the Roman Empire.

Rome's dominions in the south comprised Egypt (*Aegyptus*) and a relatively narrow strip of land which ran along the north coast of Africa from Egypt to what is now Morocco. These were the provinces of Cyrene, Tripolitania, Numidia and Mauretania. Once again there were natural features in roughly the right place. The Sahara Desert and the Atlas Mountains marked the limits of Rome's control, but these did not form a complete and continuous frontier. In Tripolitania the Romans built some short lengths of mortared walls and some earthen banks with ditches in front, to define their southern frontier. They also maintained forts and fortlets in strategic locations along the southern boundary of Egypt between the Nile and the Red Sea. The African frontier was never a serious problem for Rome. No hostile tribes from the deserts or from the hinterland of Africa posed a threat to the Empire.

The eastern frontier was always going to be a problem. Wherever Rome drew the line, there were hordes of Germanic peoples, Goths, Parthians and others who were eager to encroach upon the Empire. Ultimately, they would bring about the fall of Rome.

---

[19]See Breeze (2011).
[20]Mann (1974) 508–33.
[21]'orbem terrarum imperio populi Romani subiecit': preamble to *Res gestae Divi Augusti*.
[22]'Imperium sine fine dedi': *Aeneid* 1, 279.

It is helpful to discuss the eastern frontier in two parts, namely that to the south of the Black Sea and that to the north-west of the Black Sea. To the south of the Black Sea natural features were available to form a frontier. These were the River Euphrates, together with mountains to the north and deserts to the south. To the north-west of the Black Sea two mighty rivers marked the eastern frontier, namely the Rhine and the Danube. The Rhine flowed into the North Sea and the Danube into the Black Sea. Between the rising of the Rhine and the rising of the Danube there were no natural features to mark the boundary. During Trajan's reign a line of towers and small forts was built between the head-waters of the two rivers. Hadrian visited the region during his first grand tour and ordered the construction of a wooden palisade. Parts of the timbers from this sturdy palisade survive. They come from trees felled in AD 119/120.[23]

Under Augustus and Tiberius the northern boundary of the Empire was not a problem. The English Channel and the North Sea provided an ideal, indeed impregnable, frontier. It was also a very lucrative frontier, since the Romans charged customs duties on all trade between Britain and the Continent.[24] The Channel provided a good communication line. Roman troops and supplies could move by sea to wherever they were needed along the coast.

All that changed under Claudius. Rome now acquired a new and turbulent province, namely Britain. There was no way that the Scottish peoples would willingly accept Roman rule. Nor did they ever do so. Thus, Rome faced the entirely self-inflicted problem of deciding where to locate, and how to defend, the new northern frontier of its Empire. The chosen solution was to build Hadrian's Wall. This was the most substantial and expensive frontier of the Empire.

(ii) The construction of Hadrian's Wall

As set out above, the *Historia Augusta* states that Hadrian 'was the first to build a wall eighty miles long, which would separate the Romans from the barbarians'. This laconic statement hardly does justice to the massive engineering operation that the Roman army undertook. Nevertheless, factually the statement was correct. The wall as originally constructed ran from Newcastle in the east to Bowness-on-Solway in the west. It was 120 kilometres long. The wall was later extended eastwards to Wallsend and westwards along the Cumbrian coast. The wall marked the northern frontier of Britannia and of the Empire.

The statement in *Historia Augusta* that Hadrian was 'the first' to build this wall embodies an important truth. Although the original wall was built at Hadrian's behest, it was subject to extensive remodelling and rebuilding under later emperors.

The route of the wall is shown on Map 10.1. Stanegate Road had been the northern frontier (*limes*) under Trajan. Hadrian's Wall was built slightly to the north of the Trajanic *limes*. This route was carefully chosen. The distance between the east and west coasts is narrowest at this point. Furthermore, part of the route passes along the top of a rocky outcrop. This natural feature of the land made the wall an even more formidable barrier.

The construction operation began in, if not before, AD 122. It continued for some years after Hadrian had moved on. Highly skilled engineers, architects, surveyors, stonemasons and

---

[23]'Frankfurt am Main'. Supplement to *Archaeological Journal* 171 (2014) 6–8. Under Antoninus Pius the southern section of the palisade was moved forwards about 30 km.
[24]See Chapter 4 above.

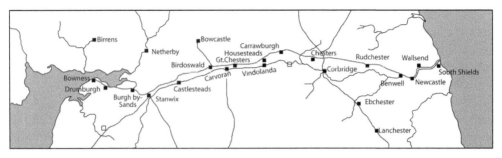

Map 10.1 Hadrian's Wall and Stanegate Road. © Bloomsbury Publishing.

other craftsmen were involved, as well as manual labourers. Detachments from all three legions stationed in Britain, namely the Second, Sixth and Twentieth Legions, took part in the project. Some auxiliary units, as well as slave labour, assisted. A detachment from the fleet, the *classis Britannica*, also undertook part of the work. Anyone visiting the wall now, some 1,900 years post-construction, will be struck by the sheer scale of the operation. Hadrian's Wall is stark evidence of the skills and versatility of the Roman armed forces. It is also the largest surviving monument of the Roman Empire.[25]

Whatever the merits or demerits of Hadrian's Wall, one undeniable fact was that it kept everyone busy for a long time. That was a good thing. Unemployed soldiers can be dangerous. The wall-building operation also stimulated the economy of northern Britain and generated much spin-off work. As John Maynard Keynes observed eighteen hundred years later, 'public works even of doubtful utility may pay for themselves over and over again'.[26]

The wall itself was not a uniform structure. The eastern end was built of stone. The western end was originally built of turf, but a stone wall was soon substituted for the turf. For reasons that are no longer apparent, some sections of the stone wall were broad, and some were narrow. The broad sections were about 3 metres wide. The narrow sections were about 2.5 metres wide. The original height of the wall appears to have been about 4 to 5 metres.[27]

The central section of the wall stood on tall crags, which made any fortification to the north both impossible and unnecessary. Along the rest of the wall, however, a ditch was dug on the north side.[28] The ditch was V-shaped. It was about 8.4 metres wide at the top and about 2.7 metres deep. The gap between the wall and the ditch, known as the 'berm', was about 6 metres wide. The spoil thrown up from digging the ditch was piled on the north side to create a mound.

At various points in the eastern part of the wall, pits have been found in the berm.[29] Each pit held wooden stakes, pointing upwards and sharpened at their tips. All this meant that anyone attacking from the north would have to clamber over the mound, scramble down and up the sides of the ditch and then sprint across the berm. If they had the good fortune to reach the berm alive, they were still at risk of being impaled on the stakes.

---

[25]Goldsworthy (2018) 16.
[26]Keynes, *The General Theory of Employment, Interest and Money* (1936), chapter 10.
[27]All measurements and evidence concerning the dimensions of the stone wall are set out and tabulated at 53–7 of Breeze (2006a).
[28]Breeze (2006a) 62–3.
[29]Breeze (2011) 64–5.

To ensure the even stationing of soldiers and to accommodate them, a series of forts and turrets was built along the whole length of the wall. The earliest and most numerous fortlets were milecastles. These small structures stood at regular intervals along the length of the wall, on average one Roman mile (1.48 kilometres) apart. Each milecastle had gateways to the north and the south. The gateways enabled Roman soldiers to pass through the wall, so that they could patrol the territory beyond. There is no evidence of soldiers patrolling on top of the wall.[30]

In each stretch of wall between milecastles there were two turrets or watchtowers. They were about 6 metres square and built of stone. There is little evidence of roofing slates having been used. This suggests that the turrets were simply covered with thatch or other organic material.[31] The weather in Cumbria and Northumberland can be pretty wet and miserable, even in the summer. Life would not have been pleasant for the soldiers on turret duty.

The soldiers who manned the wall were auxiliaries. Initially they all remained living in the forts previously established along Stanegate Road, for example at Corbridge and Vindolanda. Soon, however, it was decided that the soldiers who manned the wall should be garrisoned there. Accordingly, another substantial construction operation was put in hand.

Nineteen primary forts and six secondary forts were built along the line of the wall.[32] Some (like the milecastles) but not all were astride the wall. The *via principalis* ran across the width of each fort with elaborate gates at both ends. The usual buildings stood inside. These included barracks, granaries, hospital, stores, stables, *principia* and *praetorium*. The uniformity of the forts suggests that the *architectus* or *agrimensor* in charge at each location was working from a manual, setting out the size and disposition of the internal buildings.

On average the forts were 11.6 kilometres apart. That is half a day's marching for a Roman soldier or a day's walking for the modern rambler. Fine examples of these forts can still be seen at Chesters, Housesteads and Birdoswald.

After the forts had been built, a wide flat-bottomed ditch was excavated on the south side of the wall along its entire length except between Newcastle and Wallsend. The ditch was about 6 metres wide at the top. It was 3 metres deep, with steeply sloping sides. The excavated material was placed on both sides to form two continuous mounds, each about 9 metres from the ditch. The Venerable Bede (an Anglo-Saxon historian writing soon after AD 700) called this entire earthwork the '*Vallum*', which is Latin for rampart.[33] It seems a bit odd to call a ditch a rampart. But Bede is highly regarded – indeed he is a saint – so everyone has followed suit.

Two main roads crossed the Vallum and then passed through the wall, heading northwards. Access roads led up to the forts. In each instance, there was a causeway across the Vallum, with a gate in the middle. These arrangements emphasized the tight security at the frontier forts.

And finally – what did people call Hadrian's Wall? Until this century the name was a mystery. That changed in 2003 when a metal detectorist discovered a vessel that is now called the 'Staffordshire Moorlands Pan'.[34] An inscription round the side helpfully lists all forts at the

---

[30] Mann (1990) 51–4.
[31] Breeze (2006a) 71.
[32] Taylor (2000).
[33] *Ecclesiastical History of the English People* 1.12.
[34] Hodgson (2009a), chapter 2.

western end of Hadrian's Wall. Even more helpfully it refers to the wall as *vallum Aelium*. So now we know. Everyone called it the 'Aelian Rampart'.

That completes a brief factual summary of what the wall was. We now come to the more difficult question of identifying its purpose.

(iii) What was the purpose of the wall?

The precise functions of the wall are a matter of keen debate amongst scholars. Most agree that one purpose was the prevention of raiding. The main controversy relates to its wider role, in particular, whether its primary purpose was defence.[35]

Given the scant literary references, our principal source must be the wall itself. It formed a continuous and almost impregnable barrier. It accommodated large numbers of auxiliary soldiers. It was linked into a network of forts that stretched across the north of England, all subject to control from York. The Brigantes were effectively pacified by the end of the first century. Most (but not all) communities further north were hostile to Rome. Against that background, it is suggested that seven separate purposes of the wall can be discerned: demarcation; prevention of raiding; military base; border control; revenue protection; bulwark against invasion and architectural display. How well the wall served those purposes will be considered shortly.

As to demarcation, the construction of the wall brought to an end a difficult situation in which boundaries were fluid and ill-defined. From then on everyone in northern Britain knew what formed part of the formal Roman Empire and what (at least for the time being) did not. The wall emphatically did not mark the limit of Rome's territorial ambitions. Hadrian's Wall performed essentially the same function as the other frontiers discussed above, such as the wooden palisade in Germany.

The second function was prevention of raiding. The raiding of nearby territories was a perfectly normal pastime of Iron Age peoples. Many of the Iron Age defences discussed in Chapter 2 were a bulwark against repeated attacks by raiding parties. The arrival of the Romans would have changed all that, at least in the areas under Roman control. The Iron Age communities now became respectable civitates with town councils and magistrates. But the Roman conquest would not have ended raiding between the lowland Scottish peoples and the Brigantes. The Stanegate Road did not form an impregnable barrier. Up until AD 122 brigands could still slip through by night. There can be little doubt that Hadrian's Wall was intended to and did stop petty raiding.

Third, as is obvious from the forts described above, the wall served as a vast military base. Although the wall marked the boundary of the province, it did not operate like a modern frontier between hostile states, for example that between North and South Korea. The Romans were not confined to 'their' side of the wall. They patrolled territory and maintained forts in the regions north of the wall to such extent as was necessary to protect their interests. The wall was essentially a base, which the Romans used for operations both to the north and to the south. As discussed below, the wall was less than ideal for this purpose.

---

[35]Breeze (2014) 106–7.

The fourth function was border control. The wall and the area on either side formed a militarized zone with tight security, as described above. Civilian and other access was strictly forbidden, except at authorized crossing points. The Roman military controlled who entered and who left the province. The army stationed along Hadrian's Wall constituted, in effect, the first border agency in Britain. It was rather more effective than some of its successors.

The fifth function was revenue protection. Rome had always asserted the right to levy import and export taxes (*portoria*) on goods entering or leaving the Empire.[36] The turrets and milecastles on Hadrian's Wall were extremely useful for revenue protection. Any trader moving between Britannia and Scotland had to pass through one of those fortifications. If he did not pay the taxes due, the border guards could seize his goods.

The wall was also, self-evidently, a bulwark against invasion. It was designed to be a formidable barrier. The total width of this barrier from the mound and ditch on the north side to the Vallum and mound on the south side was over 100 metres. The elaborate arrangement of the ditch, the berm, the pits and the sharpened stakes set inside the pits placed fearsome obstacles in the path of any invaders from the north. While the invaders were negotiating those hazards, the Roman guards would have had ample opportunity to hurl down javelins and other missiles. No-one can deny that the wall was an excellent bulwark against full frontal invasion from the north. But that leaves open the question just how useful such a formidable bulwark was in that location. We shall return to this question shortly.

Finally, there is architectural display. Hadrian was deeply interested in architecture. One of his driving ambitions was to build monuments across the Empire, by which he would be remembered. Hadrian's Wall was far more elaborate than it needed to be for any of the purposes mentioned above. The structure contained many architectural features.[37] The gates of the milecastles were intricately designed and crafted. They had towers and guard chambers on each side. The *principia* of the forts along the wall also contained much intricate detailing. It is hard to resist the conclusion that a large part of the purpose of Hadrian's Wall was architectural display. This display was achieved both in matters of detail and by the sheer scale of the enterprise. The towering wall, with its line of turrets and milecastles stretching out of sight in both directions, was making a dramatic statement about the might of Rome.

(iv) What was the effect of the wall?

The principal question is whether the wall was a success from a military point of view. The answer must be no.[38]

Hadrian's Wall was a magnificent piece of engineering and it served other purposes as indicated above, but militarily it was of little use. This was essentially for five reasons. First, the regular spacing of forts, milecastles and turrets along the wall at fixed intervals (probably dictated by Hadrian) was a triumph of rigidity over operational considerations.[39] From a military point of view flexibility was needed. This is illustrated by the very different arrangements

---

[36] Strabo *Geography*, 4.5.3.
[37] Taylor (2000) 27–76.
[38] Mann (1990).
[39] Breeze and Dobson (2000) 81.

that were made on the Antonine Wall (the subject of the next chapter) and by later modifications to Hadrian's Wall. Second, Rome had not given up hope of conquering Scotland. Indeed, it would make periodic attempts to do so over the next two hundred years. The wall would be an obstacle in the path of Roman armies heading north. Third, although the Romans maintained Hadrian's Wall for three hundred years, they abandoned most of the turrets about half a century after building them. Because of the other fortifications, the turrets were of little utility. Fourth, Hadrian's Wall was not sensibly designed for the purpose of serving as a military base. The soldiers billeted there were divided between nineteen primary forts, six secondary forts and numerous milecastles. Fifth, the military defence of Britain did not depend upon Hadrian's Wall. The Roman army performed best in the open field. If any serious attack was looming, the commanders would deploy their troops in open country well north of Hadrian's Wall, where their manoeuvrability would really count. Save in rare and exceptional circumstances, the Roman army would not allow any sizeable enemy force to get anywhere near the wall.

A more important question to consider is the impact of the wall on the local population. This must have been disastrous. Some landowners were evicted to make way for the construction project. An even bigger problem was that the wall cut across the territory of the various Brigantian peoples. The construction of the wall must have split communities. Dedications to Brigantia have been found on both sides of the wall. The Goddess of the North would have been furious about this unnecessary barrier. There is evidence that one farm was actually sandwiched between the wall and the Vallum,[40] like the lonely farmhouse that now sits between two carriageways of the M62 motorway.

Figure 10.2 Hadrian's Wall at Greenhead Lough. © Wikimedia/Velella.

---

[40]Shotter (1996) 121.

The Romans expected populations to be static. But they were not. Hadrian's Wall interfered with the normal seasonal movements of people, such as bringing sheep down from the uplands for the winter. More generally population groups were not tied to the same region from one decade to the next. Before the Roman intervention, groups could migrate to wherever they chose. The Wall put a stop to that. Furthermore, local traders could only cross the frontier if the military gave permission. The border guards should have levied taxes, but probably they took bribes. All of this must have been devastating for the local populace. The one redeeming feature was that Hadrian's Wall put an end to cross-border raiding by the lowland tribes. That must have come as a relief for the Brigantes, or at least for the majority who lived on the southern side.

Nowadays Hadrian's Wall is more popular. It generates revenue for local businesses. A footpath runs along the entire route of the wall. The views are stunning, except during fog or rain – which seem to be frequent. An excellent guide for the use of walkers is published by National Trail Guides. In planning any walk along Hadrian's Wall, it is wise to allow time for stopping to look at forts, milecastles and monuments. Such breaks make the walk more like a holiday and less like an ordeal.

5. BRITAIN IN THE YEARS FOLLOWING HADRIAN'S VISIT

Having reorganized Britannia to his satisfaction, Hadrian moved on to deal with the rest of his Empire. Wherever the Emperor went, he left a mountain of work to be done: there was certainly plenty for Britain to be getting on with. Having set sail for Gaul in AD 122, Hadrian never returned to our shores. This must have been a relief for those who were trying to run the province.

Nepos continued as provincial governor until AD 126 or 127. It was his duty to ensure that all the Emperor's instructions were carried out. At the top of his to-do list was, of course, wall-building and he made substantial progress with that project over the next four years.[41] Hadrian had every reason to be grateful. But he was not. For reasons we do not know, Nepos fell out of favour with the Emperor. Hadrian was suspicious of all his friends and he ended up quarrelling with most of them.[42] Nepos had in the past been a particularly close friend, but apparently Hadrian came to detest him.[43]

The construction of Hadrian's Wall had far-reaching consequences. Stanegate Road was no longer the northern frontier. Most of the forts along that road were abandoned, although those at Carlisle, Vindolanda and Corbridge continued to be occupied.[44] Both Corbridge and Carlisle went on to become major regional centres. Carlisle was close to the western end of the wall and ultimately became the civitas capital of the Carvetii.

Coinage and pottery finds suggest that a garrison town grew up around the Corbridge fort in the early second century.[45] It stood at a point of strategic importance, namely where Dere

---

[41] Frere (1991) 120.
[42] *Historia Augusta*, *Hadrian* 15.2.
[43] 'in summa detestatione habuit Platorem Nepotem': *Historia Augusta*, *Hadrian* 23.4.
[44] Hodgson (2009a) 15.
[45] Cool and Mason (2008) 298–300.

Street crossed Stanegate Road. Much of Roman Corbridge can still be seen today. It is about three miles to the south of Hadrian's Wall and well worth a visit. The museum contains the 'Corbridge Hoard', a collection of artefacts belonging to a second century Roman soldier.

Although no longer a frontier, Stanegate Road remained a major thoroughfare and determined the settlement pattern of the region. The Romano-British builders were kept busy and their labours still serve a useful purpose. If you visit Hexham Abbey, you will see that all the stonework in the chapel and antechapel of the crypt is Roman. Some of the inscriptions are still legible, providing a diversion for anyone whose mind wanders from the sermon.

We know little about the subsequent governors who were posted to Britain during Hadrian's reign. There are some names in inscriptions and diplomas, but there is no recorded history of what they did and when. Trebius Germanus replaced Nepos in AD 126 or 127.[46] Sextus Julius Severus served as governor between about 130 and 133, but Dio records that he was redeployed to deal with Rome's war against the Jews.[47] Publius Mummius Sisenna probably took over the province between AD 133 and 136.[48]

Archaeological evidence suggests that there was a general revival of the province in the early second century. Extensive construction projects and engineering works were put in hand and, for the first time, architectural ornament in stone started to appear in the north.[49] Rome provided funding for the infrastructure works. It is ironic that in those times regional development grants were flowing from southern Europe to the north.

Many commentators describe the developments in the early second century as a 'Hadrianic revival'.[50] Martin Millett is cautious about using this term,[51] which arises from a tendency to link archaeological findings with known historical events. No doubt that caution is wise. Nevertheless, Hadrian's visit must have been the stimulus for at least some of the major building works of that period, not least because he ordered them to be done.

In considering the revival of the province during this period, it may be helpful to look separately at urban development, the growth of the salt industry and the construction of a new port at Dover.

(i) Urban development

In the 120s there was a burst of building activity in London, which was unparalleled in scale and ambition during any other period or in any other Romano-British town.[52] A massive new forum was constructed, which required adjustments to the surrounding street plan. The amphitheatre was remodelled in stone.[53] A large official building appeared on the south bank of the Thames, fitted out with all modern facilities and fine wall paintings. A colonnade was

---

[46] Birley (2013) 134.
[47] *Roman History* 69.13.2.
[48] Birley (2005) 133–4.
[49] Blagg (2002) 187.
[50] E.g. Wacher (1995).
[51] Millett (1990) 120–1.
[52] Perring (2015) 20–43 and the town plan at figure 6; Hingley (2018) chapter 7.
[53] Bateman et al. (2008).

constructed to create a covered walkway along the approach road to London Bridge, which emphasized the monumental character of London's main through road. A temple and bathhouse were built just behind the road.

The city expanded to the north. To allow for expansion, the town planners filled in the ditch that had marked the Flavian northern boundary. This probably left the city undefended until the great wall-building project of the late second century, but there were plenty of soldiers on hand to provide protection: during the 120s the Romans built a substantial masonry fort at Cripplegate. This housed soldiers who had been detached from their legions to serve on the governor's staff.

During this period London was a prosperous city. It has been estimated that the population was about 26,000.[54] We gain a glimpse of London life from a writing tablet unearthed at 1 Poultry in 1996.[55] This records the sale of a slave girl, Fortunata, for 600 denarii. She is warranted to be healthy and not to run away. The purchaser, Vegetus, was himself a slave, but a very senior one working in the procurator's office.

Another city that had major expansion was Wroxeter (*Viroconium*), the civitas capital of the Cornovii (Fig. 10.3). Hadrian had decided that the city should be doubled in size by introducing new settlers and this necessitated a massive rebuilding operation. The civic authorities created a large new forum, together with basilica. They also constructed new public baths on a grand scale.[56] These developments gave a boost to the local economy. In return for the Emperor's

Figure 10.3 Wroxeter. © Wikimedia/HARTLEPOOLMARINA2014.

---

[54]Perring (2015) 32.
[55]Tomlin (2003) 41–51.
[56]The construction of the baths started in about 120 but continued into the reign of Antoninus Pius: Gaffney and White (2007) 178.

munificence, the Cornovii erected an engraved slab over the entrance to the forum: 'To the Emperor Caesar Trajanus Hadrianus Augustus … [then follows a long list of Hadrian's accomplishments] the civitas of the Cornovii erected this'[57] This slab was the Roman equivalent of a thank you letter, but more permanent. The slab remains on display for all to see (now in the Shrewsbury Museum), expressing the town's gratitude for Hadrian's generosity nineteen hundred years ago.

Leicester received monumental architecture at about the same time as Wroxeter. Thomas Blagg, who made a study of evolving architectural styles, has identified striking similarities between Wroxeter, Leicester and Trier.[58] It is likely that, during Hadrian's reign, a group of stonemasons came over from north-east Gaul, specifically to work at Wroxeter and Leicester.

As part of the early second-century revival, the provincial government brought more communities within the civitas system. The Brigantes or some sections of them became a civitas with their capital town at Aldborough (*Isurium Brigantum*). It is also possible that the Parisi became a civitas with their capital at Brough-on-Humber (*Petuaria Parisorum*), but this is uncertain.[59]

In Wales, the Silures became a civitas with their capital at Caerwent (*Venta Silurum*). The Demetae became a civitas with their capital at Carmarthen (*Moridunum Demetarum*). The unfortunate Deceangli never achieved civitas status. Nor did the Ordovices, although the eastern part of their territory may have merged with that of the Cornovii and so come within the jurisdiction of Wroxeter. As regular civitas government developed in Wales, auxiliary forts fell into disuse.[60] During the second century, the Roman army progressively abandoned forts at Beulah, Caer Gai, Neath, Pen-y-gaer, Tomen-y-mur, Trawscoed, Usk, Abergavenny, Llandovery, Caerphilly and Coelbren.

We now turn to an important industry, which substantially expanded during the Hadrianic period.

(ii) Salt industry and the Fens

Salt is a vital part of the human diet, but harmful in excessive quantities. It can also be used to preserve foodstuffs. The Roman Empire treated it as a precious commodity. The road system facilitated the salt industry, making both trade and transportation easier.

The Iceni had been extracting salt from the Fens in East Anglia since the Iron Age. They captured sea water in channels or tanks at high tide and then heated the water till it evaporated, leaving salt. In the early second century the Romans or Romano-Britons substantially expanded the salt industry in the Fens. They probably butchered cattle there and salted the meat before sending it off to the army by sea or by waterways.[61] Any modern dietician would be horrified by the salt content of the meals served up to Roman soldiers.

The salt and butchery industry in East Anglia needed a proper infrastructure. The Romano-Britons undertook a major Fenland redevelopment. They constructed roads, canals and an

---

[57] RIB 288.
[58] Blagg (2002) 187.
[59] Wacher (1995) 394–400.
[60] Nash-Williams and Garrett (1969) 22–7.
[61] Malin (2005) 128.

extensive drainage scheme. Settlers moved onto the land reclaimed by drainage. In about AD 125 a new community emerged at Stonea. This was laid out in the usual style, with a grid of streets running in straight lines across each other. One view is that Stonea became an administrative centre for the local salt industry.[62] Alternatively, it may have grown up as a religious sanctuary. Stonea had a substantial temple complex. We do not know which deity was in residence, but presumably it was a god or goddess who took a keen interest in salt production.

The principal town linked to the Fenland development was *Durobrivae*, close to modern Peterborough. This was established in the early second century at the junction between Ermine Street and the Fen Causeway. Ermine Street, which ran from London to Lincoln, was one of the main thoroughfares of the province, originally built by and for the army. The other roads which radiated out from *Durobrivae* were principally trading routes. They were used for transporting pottery, salt, iron ore and other goods intended for market.[63] The Fens and East Anglia appear to have been a highly prosperous region in the second century. One theory is that the whole of the Fens was an imperial estate,[64] but modern scholars tend to reject that view.[65] Private enterprise, rather than public ownership, probably drove the local economy. In 2008 the remains of a large villa came to light at *Durobrivae*. The occupants of this villa may have been successful entrepreneurs.

Another substantial salt production operation developed in the Severn estuary. Whether this was an initiative of the Roman authorities or an independent enterprise of Romano-Britons is difficult to say – by the second century the Roman occupation had lasted for a hundred years and there had been much mingling of cultures, not to mention intermarriage.

(iii) The fleet and the establishment of a new port at Dover

The British Fleet (*classis Britannica*) established a new port at Dover (*Dubris*) in the early second century.[66] This replaced Richborough as the main supply base. At Dover they established a substantial fort above the harbour.[67] It included granaries and barrack blocks but – unusually – no headquarters building.

It seems likely that the principal base of the *classis Britannica* was not in Britain at all, but at Boulogne (*Bononia* or *Gestoriacum*).[68] The fort there was much larger than the fort at Dover and it included a headquarters building. Numerous inscriptions recording the presence of commanding officers of the fleet have been found at Boulogne. If this analysis is correct, then the fleet was a mobile force using different harbours around Britain, with a substantial port at Dover and its main base at Boulogne. Ceramic tiles with the stamp of the *classis Britannica* (RIB 2481) have been recovered from Lympne, Richborough and Dover. The importance of Dover was its location. It was opposite Boulogne and had a convenient harbour.

---

[62]Malin (2005) 126.
[63]Fincham (2004).
[64]Rome established a substantial network of state-owned lands and estates across the Empire: Kehoe (2018) 34.
[65]Frere (1991) 267–8; Fincham (2004) 44–5; Malin (2005) 125.
[66]Mason (2010) 109.
[67]Philp (1981).
[68]Millett (2007) 175–9.

The fleet had many functions. It suppressed piracy. It secured a safe Channel crossing for the supply of the army. All the major military centres in Britain were accessible by sea; they were either on the coast or next to navigable rivers. The fleet must have played a vital role in supplying such bases by sea. The fleet was also useful for moving soldiers around the province, when the need arose.

During the second century a flourishing civilian settlement developed around the port at Dover.[69] Its main function was probably to serve the needs of the fleet. There is little evidence of large-scale cross-Channel trade in everyday commodities. The town included an elaborate house with painted plaster, which is still there.[70] This may have been a lodging house for important travellers on official business (*mansio*).[71] It is now known as 'the painted house' and is open to the public.

To assist navigation of the ships into the new port, the Roman military built two stone octagonal lighthouses on the headlands at either side of the mouth of the River Dour. The lighthouse on the eastern side still stands. At 13 metres high, it is the tallest surviving Roman building in Britain. Incongruously, the lighthouse is now squashed up against the Church of St Mary in the grounds of Dover Castle.

As so often, the Romans chose their location wisely. Dover has continued to serve as a major port for almost two thousand years. Cross-channel ferries still enter the harbour directly beneath the Roman lighthouse.

---

[69] Millett (2007) 169.
[70] Philp (1989).
[71] Whenever the remains of a large and well appointed town house are found, there tends to be speculation whether it was a *mansio*. We can never know for certain. But having regard to the location of Dover's 'painted house', the case for identifying it as a *mansio* may be a little stronger.

CHAPTER 11
BRITAIN IN THE SECOND CENTURY

1. Introduction

2. The reign of Antoninus Pius (AD 138–161)
   (i) The war
   (ii) The wall
   (iii) Abandonment of the Antonine Wall and return to Hadrian's Wall

3. Taking stock: Was Britannia paying its way?

4. The reign of Marcus Aurelius (AD 161–180)

5. The reign of Commodus (AD 180–192)

1. INTRODUCTION

The second century was the key period of urban prosperity in Roman Britain.[1] Villa-building was gathering pace in the countryside around towns. There was substantial investment in public buildings. This was the time when the major components of many Romano-British towns appeared: forum-basilica, public baths, theatre, amphitheatre, *mansio*, temples and so forth. Silchester is a good example of this general pattern. The first phase of urban construction at Silchester was in the latter part of the first century, when the amphitheatre, baths and forum-basilica were constructed, principally with the use of wood. The masonry forum-basilica was built in the period AD 125–150. Masonry town houses appeared at about the same time.

This chapter will focus on three Emperors who held sway in the second century and their impact upon Britain. The principal impact was the construction of a new coast-to-coast wall under Antoninus and its later abandonment. We will also look at the general state of the province in this period.

2. THE REIGN OF ANTONINUS PIUS (AD 138–161)

Antoninus was the adopted son and designated successor of Hadrian. He ruled from AD 138 to 161 and was a highly regarded Emperor, on whom the Senate conferred the title *Pius*. It is

---
[1] Fulford (2012) 257–8.

not easy for any national leader to please everyone. But Antoninus seemingly achieved that feat – according to Dio, he was agreed by all to be noble and good;[2] the *Historia Augusta* and Eutropius[3] make similar comments.

Unlike Hadrian, Antoninus was not a keen traveller. He never set foot in Britain. Nevertheless, the province underwent major upheavals during his reign: Antoninus took the momentous decision to move the northern frontier up to the Clyde/Forth line.

The *Historia Augusta* deals with these events extremely tersely, as follows: 'He defeated the Britons through his legate Lollius Urbicus; after the barbarians had been driven back a second wall was built of turf.'[4] Unfortunately Dio cannot assist, because almost all of book 70 of his *Roman History* has been lost.

(i) The war

It appears from inscriptions that Quintus Lollius Urbicus was governor of Britain from AD 138 to 142. The *Historia Augusta* tells us that he defeated the Britons but does not reveal where or why the conflict arose. The war may not have been terribly serious. As noted in the previous chapter, 'trouble in Britain' at the start of each Emperor's reign seems to have become a literary convention for second century historians.

It is clear that the war took place in Scotland: there is evidence of forts in the north of Britain being rebuilt during this period. A fine dedication slab at the High Rochester fort, about 20 miles north of Hadrian's Wall, commemorates rebuilding works by the First Cohort of the Lingones, a Gallic auxiliary unit.[5] The inscription says that they did this under Lollis Urbicus, 'the Emperor's propraetorian legate'. This and similar restoration works in the north were clearly part of a military operation.

Why did the war start and why did it lead to the construction of a new wall?

These two questions are linked, and we must address them together. There are several theories. One possible cause was the wrath of the Brigantian communities,[6] who must have resented Hadrian's Wall cutting through their territory. It disrupted their established way of life and restricted population movements. As a 'good' Emperor, Antoninus Pius may have appreciated the need to end this state of affairs. There could be no question of retreating southwards, so the next obvious location for a wall was between the Forth and the Clyde, where the distance from coast to coast was only 37 miles. That would have given rise to a new imperative, namely the need to invade lowland Scotland.

This theory gains some traction from a passing comment by Pausanias, a second-century Greek travel writer. Pausanias states that Antoninus deprived the Brigantes in Britain of most

---

[2]'ὁ γὰρ Ἀντωνῖνος ὁμολογεῖται παρὰ πάντων καλός τε καὶ ἀγαθὸς γενέσθαι': *Roman History* 70.2.3. The *Historia Augusta* paints a similarly favourable picture of Antoninus Pius.
[3]*Breviarium ab Urbe Condita* at 8.8.
[4]'Britannos per Lollium Urbicum vicit legatum alio muro caespiticio summotis barbaris ducto': *Antoninus Pius* 5.4.
[5]RIB 1276.
[6]Laycock (2008) 89.

of their land because they had begun aggression on the district of Genunia.[7] We do not know where 'Genunia' was, but possibly Pausanias was referring to the territory of the Votadini, an Eastern Lowland community traditionally loyal to Rome. The problem with this analysis is that only a modest proportion of the Brigantes lived to the north of the Wall. There were not enough of them to cause real trouble, unless they joined forces with other Lowland Scottish communities. Some scholars argue that this passage has been corrupted and that Pausanias was really referring to the Brigantii in Raetia, not the Brigantes in Britain.[8]

An alternative explanation for the conflict might simply be that the lowland communities were making trouble and needed to be brought under permanent control. A third possibility is that Hadrian was a hard act follow. Antoninus wanted to make his mark on the Empire by extending one of its frontiers. It was not practicable to move the Rhine/Danube frontier eastwards. As to the southern and western frontiers, not even the Roman Emperor could move the Atlantic Ocean or the Sahara Desert. Therefore, the only option was to invade Scotland and advance the northern frontier.

A fourth possible explanation is that Hadrian's Wall was proving unsatisfactory. As previously discussed, the design of Hadrian's Wall had serious shortcomings. Design defects have a nasty habit of coming to light when it is too late to put them right. The Roman army probably discovered the shortcomings in their first wall at an early stage. They may have decided to try again and get it right next time. For obvious reasons, this operation could not start during Hadrian's lifetime. A logical place to build their next wall would be where the isthmus was narrowest, namely on the Clyde/Forth line, but that would necessitate conquering lowland Scotland. In other words, this was a war initiated by Rome for its own purposes.

It is suggested that there was probably a combination of causes. Each of the above factors may have played a part.

Ending of the war

Whatever the reason for the war may have been, there is no doubt about its outcome. The *Historia Augusta* tells us that the Romans won and that they gained control of all territory up to the Clyde/Forth line. Two diplomas issued on 1 August 142 record that Antoninus had been hailed as 'Imperator' for the second time.[9] Also the Imperial mint produced special coins to mark the victory in northern Britain: they show Britannia seated with her chin on one hand, looking thoughtful. Presumably Britannia is reflecting on her defeat and on the need to behave better in future. The words 'IMPERATOR II' appear on the back. That is a reference to the acclamation which Antoninus received after the victory.

To modern eyes, it seems strange that the head of state should receive honours for somebody else's bravery, but this was quite acceptable in the ancient world. The anonymous author of a later panegyric explained Antoninus' acclamation in this way: 'When Fronto ... was praising Antoninus for having completed the war in Britain, even though he had remained at his palace

---

[7] Pausanias, *Periegesis* viii, 43.
[8] Rivet and Smith (1979) 47 and Birley (2005) 147.
[9] Breeze (2006), chapter 2.

in Rome and had delegated the command of the war to others, he averred that the Emperor, like the helmsman of a warship, deserved the glory of the whole voyage.'[10]

The gods had also played their part in the conquest. The Romans acknowledged this by building a stone temple on the banks of the river Carron. It was shaped like a beehive and probably dedicated to Victory.[11] She was certainly the relevant goddess. The temple survived in excellent condition until the eighteenth century. It was one of Scotland's most famous monuments, known as 'Arthur's Oven' or 'Arthur's O'on' because of its shape. Sadly in 1743 the landowner demolished the temple and re-used the stone to build a dam.[12] All that we have now are a few sketches of the structure.

(ii) The wall

The new wall ran from the Firth of Forth in the East to the Clyde in the west. In other words, it was in the same region as the line of forts that Agricola had established in AD 80. The route of the wall took advantage of the landscape. For much of its length, the wall ran along the southern side of the Midland Valley of Scotland, looking down on the River Carron and the River Kelvin.[13] There was a natural trough in front of the wall, which was probably very boggy then as it is now. The surveyors who planned the route of the wall appear to have used long-distance alignments.[14]

Once again the Roman engineers, stonemasons and foot soldiers set to work. Detachments from all three legions stationed in Britain, namely the Second, Sixth and Twentieth Legions, took part in the operation. That was about 8,000 legionary soldiers. Also, several auxiliary cohorts were assigned to wall-building. The older soldiers would have remembered, with a few sighs, doing precisely the same thing twenty years previously at Hadrian's behest. Some of them must have complained that if every Emperor wanted a new wall, army life would be no fun at all. In inscriptions the Romans called the wall '*vallum*' and described the construction work as '*opus valli*'.

Despite the annoyance of starting a new building project, the soldiers seem to have taken pride in their work. Perhaps they were the younger ones who had not built a coast-to-coast wall before. They commemorated their work in a set of distance slabs, placed at the end of each section of wall. These slabs were ornately carved and included both text and illustrations.[15] For example, one depicts a winged, naked lady languidly seated beneath a pediment. She holds a huge feather in one hand. Her other hand rests elegantly on a roundel. The inscription states: 'For the Emperor Caesar Titus Aelius Hadrianus Antoninus Augustus Pius, father of his country, a detachment of the Twentieth Legion Valeria Victrix built this for a distance of 4,411

---

[10]'Fronto ... cum belli in Britannia confecti laudem Antonino principi daret, quamvis ille in ipso Urbis palatio residens gerendi eius mandasset auspicium, veluti longae navis gubernaculis praesidentem totius velificationis et cursus gloriam meruisse testatus est.' *Panegyrici Latini* 8 (5), 14.2.
[11]Breeze (2006) chapter 4.
[12]Higgins (2013) 148–51.
[13]See the Ordnance Survey map of Roman Britain.
[14]Poulter (2018) 113–46.
[15]Breeze (2006) chapter 5.

Figure 11.1 The Bridgeness slab, a distance slab in Antonine Wall. © Wikimedia/George MacDonald.

feet.'[16] Another distance slab (known as the Bridgeness slab) erected by the Second Legion Augusta, shows on the left of the inscription a victorious cavalryman trampling and spearing naked Britons; on the right a religious ceremony (Fig. 11.1).

The Antonine Wall differed from Hadrian's Wall in important respects,[17] probably with good reason. They constructed the wall out of turf blocks placed on top of a stone base, about 4.4 metres wide. The reason for using turf may have been to improve drainage, which had been a problem on Hadrian's Wall. The Antonine Wall included drainage holes. Archaeologists have counted up to 20 turf lines. This suggests that the total height of the turf rampart was at least 3 metres.

As before, the troops dug a ditch in front of the wall. They threw the spoil onto the north side, to create a wide mound. The ditch alone was a substantial obstacle for any assailants. Along the central section it was about 12 metres wide and 4 metres deep. Elsewhere the ditch was about 6 metres wide. Collectively the turf rampart, the ditch and the mound formed a formidable defence. There was no vallum.

The army established a line of forts and fortlets along the length of the wall, each just visible to its neighbours. This meant that in good weather signals could pass rapidly down the line. It appears to have been an ingenious alarm system.[18] Unlike at Hadrian's Wall, the forts did not straddle the wall. Instead they stood behind it. Also they were built to a new design, usually with turf ramparts, stone main buildings and timber barracks. Some had annexes attached. Most of the forts were large enough to accommodate an entire auxiliary unit. The forts were placed at strategic locations, not at fixed intervals as on Hadrian's Wall.

The turf wall constituted the new northern frontier of the province and indeed of the Empire. It was 60 kilometres long. Map 11.1 shows the province as it was after the construction of the Antonine Wall.

Once the new wall and forts were established, approximately 6,000 to 7,000 troops were stationed there to maintain the frontier.[19] This was essentially the same as the garrison on Hadrian's Wall, but the Antonine Wall was half the length and functioned more satisfactorily as a military base.

---

[16]RIB 2208.
[17]Breeze (2011) 71–6; Breeze (2006) 71–80; Breeze and Dobson (2000) 89–109.
[18]Poulter (2018) 129–38.
[19]Moorhead and Stuttard (2012) 139.

The Roman Occupation of Britain and Its Legacy

Map 11.1 Britain in the mid-second century. © Bloomsbury Publishing.

Good communications were essential. The Romans extended their road system northwards up to the Antonine Wall and constructed a new east–west road, running along the length of the wall on the south side.

Redeployment of the occupying army

The establishment of a new frontier, garrisoned by several thousand soldiers, was a massive logistical exercise. Detachments from legions and auxiliary units in the south were sent up to man the forts along the Antonine Wall. The procurator's office in London had to arrange for payment. Even that was no simple task. Two inscriptions found near Edinburgh record the presence of a procurator called Quintus Lusius Sabianus. He was probably in Scotland to pay the troops.[20]

The Antonine Wall, like Hadrian's Wall before it, did not denote the limit of Rome's influence. Roman troops patrolled the regions beyond the frontier. Near the east coast, they established four forts to the north of the Wall, along the line of the road that Agricola had constructed a century earlier. These were at Camelon, Ardoch, Strageath and Bertha.[21]

Territory to the south of the Antonine Wall now formed part of the province Britannia and was subject to military administration. In the period following AD 143 the troops built a network of new forts across southern Scotland.[22] As in the Flavian period, the Romans placed very few forts in the territory of the Votadini, who were traditionally friendly to Rome.

The new stone fort at Newstead played a key role in controlling the region. It housed two cohorts of the Twentieth Legion, as well as a cohort of auxiliary cavalry. Gaius Arrius Domitianus, a centurion of the Twentieth Legion posted to Newstead, enjoyed much good fortune in hunting and on the battlefield. No less than three altars survive recording his gratitude to the gods.[23]

Most of the forts that Rome established across the lowlands were of modest size and no more than fortlets. There may be two reasons for this:

i. Whereas during the first century the army had placed substantial forts close to existing centres of power, they were now adopting a different approach. There were less centralized power structures in the Scottish Lowlands. The Roman strategy was to control the landscape rather than people. Numerous small forts appeared at river crossings, valleys, the exits of mountain passes and other strategic locations.

ii. The army was probably overstretched. During the same period, they abandoned several of their forts in the Pennines.

Hadrian's Wall no longer served as a defensive barrier along the northern frontier of Britannia. Instead it straddled the province at a most inconvenient location: an obstacle in the way of troops who were heading northwards or southwards. To reduce this problem, gates were removed from all entrances of the milecastles. Also, the Vallum was filled in at points where

---

[20] Birley (2005) 310–11.
[21] Breeze (2006) chapter 6.
[22] Frere (1991) chapter 7.
[23] RIB 2122, 2123, 2124.

soldiers would need to cross. Soil from the mounds on each side of the Vallum was used for this purpose, so that a clear passage was created. These adaptations would, incidentally, have resolved some of the grievances of the Brigantes.

(iii) Abandonment of the Antonine Wall and return to Hadrian's Wall

Towards the end of Antoninus' reign the Romans abandoned their new turf wall. They demolished the buildings inside the forts but left the wall and the ditch largely intact. They buried some of the distance slabs in pits, to prevent defacement. The army retreated back to the Tyne/Solway line. Archaeological evidence suggests that the abandonment started in about AD 158[24] and was completed within three years: there were no inscriptions on the wall after the reign of Antoninus Pius, who died in 161.

The whole episode raises difficult questions. First, why did the Romans abandon their new wall so soon after building it? There are no literary references to the abandonment or indeed to anything that happened on the wall after its construction. It is clear that during the 150s there were fierce struggles in northern Britain, but we do not know the details. The most likely inference is that the occupying army simply lacked the resources to control this additional segment of the province.

The second question is whether there was one U turn or three U turns. There is lively debate amongst scholars about whether (a) the Romans returned to the Antonine Wall after abandoning it and then abandoned it for a second time or (b) they just abandoned it once. This question is so fraught that Sheppard Frere (a giant of Romano-British history, who died in 2015) has supported both points of view at different times. Part of the problem is that there is archaeological evidence that the forts on the Antonine Wall were repaired after they had been abandoned. Also, there was a coin issue in AD 154–155, which shows Britannia subdued. Some argue that this relates to a successful war against the Brigantes and that the army had been temporarily recalled from the Antonine Wall to fight that war.

The most likely reconstruction[25] of events seems to be as follows. The coin issue in AD 154–155 relates to a war in southern Scotland, not Brigantia.[26] So there was no need to recall troops from the Antonine Wall at that stage. After 155 hostilities in the lowlands continued, the root cause being that the occupying army in Britain was overstretched. By AD 158 the Roman authorities decided that it was simply not practical to maintain a frontier as far north as the Clyde/Forth line: hence the decision to retreat to Hadrian's Wall. It was not feasible to abandon the Antonine Wall instantaneously. Therefore, some of the forts were occupied or re-occupied during the transitional period. The transition might have lasted for two or three years, while Hadrian's Wall was being reinstated. In other words, the Romans only abandoned the Antonine Wall once, but the process may have taken a little time. Possibly some of the forts on the Antonine Wall were mothballed or used as outposts for a period.

---

[24]Breeze (2006) chapter 9.
[25]Hodgson (2009) 185–93.
[26]The evidence for war in Brigantia is slender, resting mainly on the repair of a fort at Brough-on-Noe in the mid-150s: RIB 1322.

The re-establishment of Hadrian's Wall as the northern frontier was another substantial operation. The alterations so recently made all had to be reversed. Areas where the Vallum had been filled in were dug out again and gates were re-fitted to the milecastles. In an effort to help us with the dates, some soldiers of the Sixth Legion have left an inscription stating that they did their rebuilding work during the consulship of Tertullus and Sacerdos,[27] i.e. in AD 158.

Gnaeus Julius Verus arrived as governor of Britain in about AD 158. He brought with him reinforcements for all three legions stationed in Britain. They were probably needed to replace casualties sustained during the recent war. Inscriptions reveal that Verus oversaw rebuilding works along Hadrian's Wall and the re-establishment of the old frontier.

Gaius Calpurnius Agricola was governor during the 160s. All the inscriptions from his period indicate that Hadrian's Wall was the frontier. Inscriptions left by auxiliary cohorts are to the same effect. The First Cohort of the Vardullians were at Castle Cary in AD 155, where they erected a splendidly ornate altar to Neptune.[28] By the 160s they were back at Corbridge, where they made a rather less ornate dedication 'to the discipline of the Emperors'.[29] Other inscriptions show that the First Cohort of the Tungrians had returned from the Antonine Wall to Housesteads by the mid 160s.

As before, the army continued to patrol territory to the north of Hadrian's Wall. They maintained forts beyond the wall for that purpose: on the east side at Birrens, Netherby and Bewcastle; on the west side at Newstead, High Rochester and Risingham. They abandoned Newstead and Birrens in about 180.[30]

At some point in the second century the Romans constructed a road between Hadrian's Wall and the Vallum, probably after retreating from the Antonine Wall.[31] Historians now call this the Military Way. We have no idea what the Romans called it, if indeed they called it anything. The Military Way was about 6 metres wide and cambered up to 46 cm high. It was formed of large stones surfaced with gravel.[32] The road tends to meander rather than proceed at a fixed distance from the wall. Sometimes it lies on top of the north mound of the Vallum. If you walk the length of Hadrian's Wall, you can see some sections of the Military Way as a raised track covered with earth and grass.

Assessment

It must be said that Antoninus Pius, for all his piety, did not make life easy for the legions stationed in Britain or for the officials who administered the province. The construction of a substantial wall across Britain from one coast to the other was a huge engineering operation, especially before the age of mechanical equipment. The idea of building one wall across the country, then abandoning it, then building another wall across the country, then abandoning the second wall and finally going back to the first wall must have seemed absurd to the troops on the ground. In the privacy of their milecastles they probably made some harsh comments about the quality of decision-making by distant bureaucrats in Rome.

---

[27] RIB 1389.
[28] RIB 2149.
[29] 'disciplinae Augustorum': RIB 1128.
[30] Bidwell (2007) 36.
[31] Southern (2011) 189.
[32] Breeze (2006) 89.

Antoninus must have hoped that the new wall would be one of the great monuments of his reign. In a sense, those hopes have been fulfilled. Despite the tiresome detail that Rome abandoned it almost immediately, the Antonine Wall has dominated the landscape for many centuries and left its imprint on the social history of the middle ages.[33] Today, two millennia later, parts of the wall are still standing, and they remain the subject of scholarly debate.

3. TAKING STOCK: WAS BRITANNIA PAYING ITS WAY?

By the end of Antoninus' reign Britannia had been under Roman control for just over a century. This is therefore an appropriate moment to pause and consider whether the province was paying its way.

More troops were required to garrison Britain than any other province. The Roman army in Britain comprised about 55,000 men: that was 10–12 per cent of the total Roman army defending about 4 per cent of the Empire.[34] All the soldiers required to be housed, fed and paid. Although it is not possible to put a figure on this, by the middle of the second century Britannia had emerged as the most expensive province to maintain.

Throughout the first and second centuries the agricultural produce of Britain was probably insufficient to support the occupying forces. Alternatively, even if the agricultural yield was sufficient, there were substantial difficulties in transporting the produce to where it was needed. The army was dispersed across numerous fortresses, forts and fortlets around the province. Therefore, foodstuffs were imported from the Continent and distributed from London.[35] Most of the major roads in the province fanned out from London. It is also possible that the grain stored at South Shields (another major supply centre) came directly from the Continent.

The location and defence of the northern frontier was a perennial problem, because the Romans never managed to extend their control to the north coast of Scotland. It was always necessary to create an artificial line across northern Britain and then to defend that line at enormous expense. No other frontier of the Empire required the construction of a stone wall of such length.

Although the Romans exploited the mineral resources of Britannia and squeezed what taxes they could from the inhabitants, the province could not pay its way. The historian Appian, writing in about AD 150, comments:

> Crossing the Northern Ocean to Britain, a continent in itself, they [the Romans] took possession of the better and larger part, not caring for the remainder. Indeed, the part they do hold is not of much use to them.[36]

The economy of the Roman Empire is a huge subject, far beyond the purview of this book. A study has recently been undertaken of the Gross Domestic Product in the mid-second century,

---

[33] Maldonado (2015) 225–45.
[34] Mattingly (2006) 166.
[35] Fulford (2007) 314–16.
[36] Preface to Appian's *History of Rome* 5.

when the Empire reached its demographic peak.[37] It is estimated that the population generated a total income roughly equivalent to 50 million tons of wheat or 20 billion sesterces per year. The state and local government probably captured about 5 per cent of this. The top 1.5 per cent of households probably controlled about one fifth of the total income. The vast majority of the population lived close to subsistence level, but cumulatively generated more than half of the overall output. Although this analysis does not address the impact of individual provinces, there can be little doubt that Britain was consuming more of the GDP than it contributed.

4. THE REIGN OF MARCUS AURELIUS (AD 161–180)

In fixing the long term future of the Empire, Hadrian had designated two successors for Antoninus Pius, namely Lucius Verus and Marcus Aurelius. They were, effectively, an heir and a spare. This was just as well. Although the two men duly became joint Emperors in AD 161, Lucius Verus died in 169. Marcus Aurelius then continued as sole Emperor until his death in 180.

Marcus Aurelius was first and foremost a philosopher. His most famous work is *Meditations*, a book that reflects his Stoic philosophy and sets out his considered views on ethical issues. By all accounts Marcus Aurelius was a man of exemplary character and high moral standards.[38]

Sadly, the constant wars that pressed in on the Empire during the 160s and 170s left Marcus Aurelius with little leisure for the pursuit of philosophy. The Emperor was diligent in discharging the full range of his duties, both military and civil. Whenever he had some respite from warfare, Marcus presided over courts. He was scrupulously fair in his despatch of judicial business, though perhaps somewhat lax in case management. Apparently, he allowed barristers an inordinate amount of time for their speeches; he conducted preliminary inquiries at great length, and he might spend twelve days trying a single case. This would include sitting at night.[39]

The first governor of Britain whom Marcus Aurelius appointed was Marcus Statius Priscus. He arrived in the summer of 161 and served for about a year. Inscriptions record his presence here as governor but shed no light on what he did. Statius Priscus was a highly effective general. In 162 he was recalled to deal with a crisis in the East, where he won a major victory. Although that may have been good news for the Empire, such rapid changes of government were not good for Britain, where trouble was brewing once more.

Unrest in Britain

Apparently one of the conflicts that broke out at the start of Marcus' reign was a war in Britain. Dio tells us nothing about this war. The *Historia Augusta* provides the briefest snippet of information, namely the following: 'War was about to break out in Britain...and Calpurnius Agricola was sent against the Britons.'[40] As noted in Chapter 10, we have to treat with caution

---

[37] Scheidel and Friezen (2009) 61–91.
[38] Dio, *Roman History* 71 and 72; *Historia Augusta, Marcus Antoninus Philosophus*.
[39] Dio, *Roman History* 72.6.1.
[40] 'Imminebat etiam Britannicum bellum ... et adversus Britannos quidem Calpurnius Agricola missus est': *Historia Augusta, Marcus Antoninus Philosophus* 8.7.

the recurrent statements about 'trouble in Britain' at the start of each new Emperor's reign. No doubt there was some unrest in the early 160s, but it may not have been unduly serious.

We know from inscriptions that Sextus Calpurnius Agricola served as governor between about AD 162 and 168. A dedication slab[41] found at Corbridge, dated AD 163–164, confirms his presence. No details are available of the 'war' mentioned in *Historia Augusta*, but it is tolerably clear that Calpurnius Agricola suppressed whatever insurrection was breaking out. That is the natural inference from the passage quoted above.

Throughout Marcus Aurelius' reign the north of Britain remained a turbulent region. The number of functioning forts in Brigantia south of Hadrian's Wall increased to 33. Approximately 18,500 auxiliaries were required to man those forts.[42] In AD 175 Aurelius sent 5,500 Sarmatian cavalry to Britain as reinforcements. They probably all went to the north. There is archaeological evidence that some of them were at Chesters fort on Hadrian's Wall.

Construction of city and town defences

The construction of walls around cities and towns began earlier in Britain than elsewhere in the Empire. In the late second century such defences started to appear in various forms. Stone walls were built around London and Colchester. An earth rampart was built around Silchester (to be replaced a century later by a stone wall). Earth defences were constructed around St Albans with stone gateways inset. Similar defences sprang up around small towns such as Towcester, which stood on Watling Street. The fact that Britain erected such defences early on is yet another indication that this was an expensive high-maintenance province.

Towards the end of the century, a stone wall was built around London. The London Wall was about 2 metres thick and 6 metres high with a ditch in front and a bank behind.[43] The wall was constructed of Kentish ragstone and was about 5 kilometres long. It required the transportation of some 85,000 tons of stone from Kent. The fortification of London was a massive engineering operation.

The London Wall, like much else of that period, was built to last. The wall served as London's defence for over a thousand years. Parts of the wall can still be seen in the Barbican area, around Tower Hill and at the Museum of London. One section of the wall has been found in the basement of the Old Bailey. It lies immediately beneath the side wall of the former Newgate Prison. If any readers have the misfortune to be detained at that court, they will have an excellent opportunity to study the Roman wall. It is on the right shortly before you enter the condemned cell.

Why did British towns build these expensive defences at such an early date? This is an interesting question, which many historians have pondered. The cost and effort of constructing the defences was huge. One view is that there was serious violence in the late second century, which necessitated such elaborate fortifications. Laycock[44] argues that the Brigantes may have been mounting raids on central and southern England. He cites various traces of fire damage and the distribution of unretrieved coin hoards as supporting evidence. That evidence is not convincing. Periodic fires were a fact of life in the ancient world. So were unretrieved coin hoards in a society where people did not have access to banks.

---

[41] RIB 1149.
[42] Frere (1991) 145–7.
[43] Hobbs and Jackson (2010) 100–11.
[44] Laycock (2008) 93–106.

There is an alternative explanation. As noted elsewhere, the second century was a time of prosperity in Britain. Urbanism was flourishing. The civic authorities were erecting fine public buildings, not to mention some delightful villas just outside town. This was not a period when central and southern England faced any imminent threat of attack. It is therefore suggested that, although the wall builders had an eye on defence against future attack, they were also making a statement. The masonry walls and earthen ramparts of the late second century may be seen as a form of civic display. Also, these fortifications, like Hadrian's Wall a few decades earlier, were a good way of keeping people busy. Both the occupying army and the civilian population must have been heavily involved in the enterprise. As noted above, Britain had a high concentration of troops – much higher than any other province. It was important to keep the soldiers occupied. If left idle, their thoughts may turn to mutiny.

5. THE REIGN OF COMMODUS (AD 180–192)

Marcus Aurelius designated his son, Commodus, as successor and the Senate duly ratified that appointment. According to both Dio and the *Historia Augusta*, Commodus did not inherit any of his father's good qualities.[45] Spurning philosophy, he pursued the pleasures of this world with vigour. Commodus kept bad company. He gambled and spent extravagantly. Dio had firm views about both 'good' and 'bad' emperors[46] and he was writing with an agenda. We cannot therefore accept his description of Commodus uncritically. If Commodus was as obviously unsuitable as Dio says, it is surprising that he secured appointment. There was no longer any established principle of hereditary succession. That approach had lapsed a century earlier when Domitian was assassinated.

By all accounts, Commodus was a disappointment as Emperor. Dio, who was a senator during this period, describes how Commodus took to chariot racing and gladiatorial combat against disabled opponents. On days when the Emperor was fighting, all senators were expected to attend the amphitheatre and applaud his performance.

Ulpius Marcellus was governor of Britain during the early years of Commodus' reign. This eccentric general had iron self-discipline. He was a model of rectitude, but not altogether easy to deal with. Marcellus ensured that his food was stale in order to avoid the temptation of over-eating. In fact, he ate very little. He also slept very little, possibly due to hunger. The general was determined that his officers should have a similarly arduous lifestyle.[47]

Marcellus, for all his peculiarities, was an able general. He ruthlessly defeated invaders from the north. He re-established control over Hadrian's Wall and the surrounding territory. A dedication slab found at Carlisle records one of Rome's victories during this campaign. The Augusta cavalry regiment slaughtered a large band of barbarians ('*barbarorum multitudine*'). They thank Hercules for protecting them while they did so.[48]

---

[45] Dio *Roman History* 73; *Historia Augusta, Commodus Antoninus*.
[46] Scott (2018).
[47] Dio, *Roman History* 73.8.4.
[48] RIB 946.

Following his success in Britain Marcellus returned to Rome, where he narrowly escaped execution.[49] Commodus took full credit for Marcellus' defeat of the Britons. He received the title 'Britannicus'. Those seeking to flatter the Emperor regularly made use of this title.[50]

Meanwhile, there was disaffection amongst the troops in Britain. The first sign of mutiny came when the legions in Britain proclaimed Priscus, one of their officers, as Emperor. Priscus was no fool. According to Dio, he quickly rejected the offer, stating: 'I am no more an emperor than you are soldiers.'[51] Dio then adds a curious story about the British garrison sending a delegation to Italy to speak to the Emperor.

According to the *Historia Augusta*,[52] Commodus appreciated that there were real problems in Britain. He decided to call on the services of Helvius Pertinax. Pertinax was an energetic and capable commander, who had previously served as a tribune in Britain. Unfortunately, Commodus had quarrelled with him. The Emperor now sent a letter to Pertinax, making amends and asking him to take over as governor of Britain. Pertinax agreed to the proposal. In AD 185 he set off for Britain as its newly appointed governor.

When Pertinax arrived, he found a highly volatile situation. One legion mutinied and almost succeeded in killing him. Pertinax held his nerve. He succeeded in suppressing the mutiny amongst the troops and bringing the province back under control. In order to prevent any further mutiny, he imposed harsh discipline on the army. Although Pertinax had accomplished his mission, he was hardly a popular figure in Britain, either amongst the legions or amongst the Britons. He was far from happy in this distant outpost of the Empire. In AD 187 Pertinax applied to be relieved early of his governorship and that request was granted.

It is necessary to read this section of the *Historia Augusta* with caution. Provinces with large garrisons were a threat to the Emperor, since the governors might use the forces at their disposal to usurp his position. Sometimes ambitious generals were sent to distant provinces to keep them out of the way. Sometimes ambitious governors were recalled early to prevent a usurpation. In the power politics of imperial Rome things were not always as they seemed. Commodus may have had an ulterior motive for sending Pertinax to Britain or he may have had an ulterior motive for recalling Pertinax early. The so-called 'mutiny' may have been one unit of the army in revolt against the Emperor.

What lies behind the story of Pertinax's 'harsh discipline'? Pertinax may well have been positioning himself for the top job and lining up the frontier army in Britain to support him. If that was his ambition, then as we shall see, he was successful.

Commodus reigned as Emperor until December 192, when he was assassinated by the prefect of the Praetorian Guard. If Commodus' conduct was as bad as Dio and the *Historia Augusta* suggest, he was lucky to survive for so long.

It is not known who had the dubious fortune of taking over as governor after Pertinax. By AD 192, however, when Commodus was murdered, the governor of Britain was one Decimus Clodius Albinus. Like Pertinax, Albinus was aiming for higher things.

---

[49] Dio, *Roman History* 73.8.6.
[50] *Historia Augusta*, *Commodus Antoninus* 8.4.
[51] Dio, *Roman History* 73.9.2.
[52] The *Historia Augusta* is our principal source for these events. Dio merely confirms in *Roman History* 74.4.1 that Pertinax quelled 'that great revolt' ('τὴν μεγάλην ἐκείνην στάσιν') in Britain.

CHAPTER 12
THE EMPEROR SEVERUS ARRIVES AND STAYS

1. The Civil War (AD 193–197)

2. The reign of Severus (AD 197–211): A turning point for the Roman Empire

3. Britain during Severus' reign

4. Severus campaigns in Scotland

This chapter spans a period of just eighteen years. That short period marked a turning point for the Roman Empire. It was also a time when Britain moved to the centre of the world stage and became the hub of imperial administration.

After a brief account of the civil war, this chapter will look at the state of the Empire and of Britain in the early second century. It will then review Severus' campaigns in Scotland. Contrary to the view of many scholars, it will be argued that the Emperor was seriously attempting to bring the whole of Scotland within the province Britannia.

1. THE CIVIL WAR (AD 193–197)

Five years of turbulence followed the assassination of Commodus before Septimius Severus emerged as the sole ruler of the Roman Empire. Britain played an important part in the upheavals. Both Dio (as a senator) and Herodian (as a young man and future civil servant) lived through these events and describe them in their respective histories.[1]

In January 193 the immediate challenge was to find a new emperor. The choice fell on Pertinax, who was by then an elderly and respected senator. As previously noted, Pertinax may have been playing his cards carefully with an eye to getting the top job: he had proved his worth in Britain and then secured an early return to Rome. He gained the support of both the Praetorian Guard and the Senate. Pertinax impressed Dio by treating the Senate with respect; he impressed Herodian by making substantial improvements to the administration of Rome and the Empire.[2] But the Praetorian Guard soon turned against the new Emperor, apparently because of the firm discipline that he imposed. In March 193 a group of soldiers from the

---

[1] This and the following paragraphs are based principally on Dio, *Roman History*, books 73 to 76 and Herodian, *History*, books 2 and 3.
[2] *History* 2.4.2.

Praetorian Guard confronted Pertinax and killed him. According to Herodian, Pertinax[3] retained his sense of humour, commenting on the irony that his murderers were the very people who were meant to protect him.

You might think that after those events the role of Emperor would look less attractive and there would be few applicants. Not so. Two candidates were desperate for the position namely Sulpicianus, the prefect of the city, and Didus Julianus, an ex-consul. Julianus prevailed by promising to pay each soldier 25,000 sesterces. His manner of appointment hardly inspired confidence. Nor did his performance, once installed. Julianus is reported to have been an idle and incompetent administrator, who was unpopular with the general public from the start. He very soon became unpopular with the Praetorian Guard as well, because he could not pay the promised donative. The Senate hated Julianus from the start. In these circumstances, the new Emperor had no prospect of surviving for long and everyone turned their attention to the more interesting question of succession.

There were three serious candidates. Each was a provincial governor with an army to back him. They were Decimus Clodius Albinus, the governor of Britain; Pescennius Niger, the governor of Syria; and Septimius Severus, the governor of Pannonia. In each of those three provinces the legions proclaimed their own commander as Emperor. Civil war was inevitable.

Severus was the wiliest of the three contenders.[4] He despatched a letter to Britain appointing Albinus as his Caesar, i.e. Co-Emperor but junior to Severus. Poor Albinus was completely taken in. He remained in his province, believing that if all went well, he and Severus would soon share imperial power without the need for any further effort on his part. Having despatched that artful letter, Severus headed for Rome with his legions from Pannonia. The Senate, astute as ever to protect their own backs, could see where power now resided. As Dio neatly puts it: 'We sentenced Julianus to death and we declared Severus to be Emperor.'[5] For good measure the Senate also passed a decree making Pertinax a god. Severus arrived at Rome and was duly heralded as Emperor. He stayed just long enough to pass death sentences on those responsible for Pertinax's murder and to organize the deification ceremony.

There then followed a bloody civil war between the legions loyal to Severus and those loyal to Niger. The Senate decided to keep a low profile[6] until it knew which side was winning. In AD 194 Severus defeated Niger, who fled to Antioch where he died.[7] The Senate duly confirmed Severus as Emperor.

Albinus followed the course of events with considerable satisfaction. He was now not only governor of Britain, but also a Caesar. He started minting coins which showed his new imperial status. Unfortunately for Albinus, this was not destined to last. Severus, as he had no doubt always intended, soon fell out with him and declared war. In AD 196 Severus set off with his legions, seeking a full-scale battle against the governor of Britain. Albinus hastily marshalled an army and embarked for Gaul.[8] We do not know how many troops Albinus took with him to Gaul, but there would have been considerable logistical difficulties in transporting too many

---

[3]Herodian, *History* 2.5.6.
[4]'τῶν ... τριῶν ἡγεμόνων ... δεινότατος': Dio, *Roman History* 74.15.1.
[5]'τοῦ τε Ἰουλιανοῦ θάνατον κατεψηφισάμεθα καὶ τὸν Σεουῆρον αὐτοκράτορα ὠνομάσαμεν': *Roman History* 74.17.4.
[6]Dio, *Roman History* 76.4.2.
[7]Herodian, *History* 3.4.6.
[8]Herodian, *History* 3.7.1.

people across the Channel at short notice. Possibly Albinus took a single legion, alternatively detachments from all three legions, together with some auxiliaries. We should not assume (as some historians do) that Albinus would have left strings of forts sitting empty across Britain. It was normal practice to leave 'care and maintenance' detachments in charge of forts when most of the garrison was absent. Garrisons frequently left their forts to go on campaign, not just during a civil war. Many forts primarily functioned as winter quarters.

Once in Gaul, Albinus augmented his army by recruiting any troops who were sympathetic to his cause. He initially defeated a detachment led by Virius Lupus, one of Severus' commanders, but this early streak of luck did not hold. The final and decisive encounter took place near Lyon (*Lugdunum*), then a large and prosperous city. The battle was bitter and drawn out, with great heroism on both sides. Albinus' army included many Britons, now serving as auxiliaries alongside the Roman legions. Herodian reports that the Britons fought with considerable courage and 'enthusiasm for slaughter'.[9] Victory, however, fell to Severus, who had the larger army. Albinus lost his life: according to Dio, he committed suicide; according to Herodian, he was taken prisoner and executed.

2. THE REIGN OF SEVERUS (197–211): A TURNING POINT FOR THE ROMAN EMPIRE

Severus became undisputed Emperor in AD 197 and held power until he died fourteen years later. He made major changes to the structure of the imperial government. In particular, he gave the army a dominant role, which was unsurprising as he owed his position to military success. He raised the salary of legionary soldiers from 1,200 to 1,800 sesterces per year and allowed the soldiers to marry, thus legitimating what had long been an informal practice. Severus generally recruited his officials from the equestrian order, rather than from those of senatorial rank. As a result, the Senate declined in power.

In retrospect we can see that this period marked a turning point. For two centuries Rome had been strengthening its grip upon Europe, the Middle East and North Africa; local communities had been absorbing and adapting Roman systems of civic administration. Amphitheatres, baths, basilicas, fountains, magistrates and senates were to be found everywhere from the Straits of Gibraltar to Carlisle. Mediterranean-style architecture and the Roman model of urbanism were universal. After, or perhaps even during, the reign of Severus things began to change. Esmonde Cleary demonstrates in his excellent archaeological study[10] that after the end of the second century the Roman Empire started to lose vitality. There was a reorganization of cultural values and economic expression; major public building projects became rarer; there was less civic activity by élites in the West. Even the number of inscriptions started to drop, as fewer people bothered to record their doings.

Major shifts of history such as that described by Esmonde Cleary are not evident at the time they happen. Only historians, who have the luxury of looking back over several centuries, can

---

[9] 'ἀνδρείᾳ τε καὶ θυμῷ φονικῷ': *History* 3.7.2.
[10] Cleary (2013b), in particular chapters 3 and 10.

identify how individual events fit into the wider pattern. When Severus proudly put on his purple robe, he had no notion that he would be ushering in a period of gradual decline.

3. BRITAIN DURING SEVERUS' REIGN

Back in Britain people were not worrying about the broad sweep of history. The province had become more turbulent during the civil war, because part of the occupying army was re-deployed to Gaul.[11] Severus appointed Virius Lupus (the commander whom Albinus had previously defeated) as governor of Britain from AD 197 to 200. Lupus faced two immediate tasks: to restore the strength of the garrison and to make urgent infrastructure repairs in the north.

By this stage the Roman army across most provinces was recruiting locally for both legions and auxiliary units.[12] The distinction between 'citizen legions' and 'non-citizen auxilia' had become blurred.

The troops garrisoning Britain were much depleted by the recent civil war, having been on the losing side. Lupus probably resorted to vigorous recruitment or conscription in Britain. There is epigraphic evidence of a British *frumentarius* (someone dealing with the corn supply) in the Sixth Legion Victrix, who may have been recruited at about this time.[13] Several additional auxiliary units were redeployed to Britain during Severus' reign. By AD 210 approximately 55,000 troops were stationed in Britain, which may have represented about 3.5 per cent of the total Romano-British population.[14]

There was much repair work to be done. Archaeology reveals extensive building operations during this period, especially in the Pennine region.[15] But a note of caution is needed: we cannot assume that all the damage was caused while Albinus and his army were in France or that all repair works were done soon afterwards. Pottery dating now becomes less reliable, because Samian ware of the early third century remained in use for long periods, as did the coinage issued by Severus. The various infrastructure repairs may have continued well beyond Severus' reign.

One building operation at the beginning of the century was the construction of a new stone bridge, to replace an earlier timber structure, at Piercebridge (*Morbium*?) where Dere Street crossed the Tees. The foundations were huge close-fitting stone blocks, held together with iron tie-bars. The river has changed course since AD 200. You can now see the foundations of the bridge in the grounds of the George Hotel: they are in remarkably good condition, but after eighteen centuries the iron looks rusty. The site where Roman troops once marched over the Tees is now a popular venue for wedding receptions.

Whatever the problems in the north, they do not seem to have disturbed the pleasant rhythm of life further south. At Verulamium, the late second century and early third century

---

[11] E.g. garrisons at Bainbridge, South Shields and Bowes had been reduced in size: see Bidwell (2012) 69.
[12] Mann and Dobson (1996) 44–6.
[13] Mann and Dobson (1996) 50–1.
[14] Pearson (2010) 91.
[15] Major repairs to the fort at *Segudunum* included the installation of a cistern: Bidwell (2018) 73–4.

The Emperor Severus Arrives and Stays

were a period of general confidence and lavish construction.[16] Cellars started to appear in town houses and in the nearby villas at Gorhambury and Park Street. The new cellars, a rare luxury in Britain, would have been used for storing produce. They were also probably a talking point at dinner parties.

Threat from Scotland

Dio records that the Scottish peoples were preparing to invade. They were formed into two large confederacies, the Maeatae and the Caledonians:[17] the Maeatae lived 'next to the wall which cuts Britain in half'; the Caledonians were further to the north. Dio states that all these barbarians inhabited wild and barren mountains; they were 'very fond of plundering'; they were immensely tough, being able to endure hunger, cold and all manner of hardship. On any view, they were well suited to Scottish independence. According to Dio, the tribesmen plunged into swamps and remained there for many days with only their heads above water. Quite why they did this and what they achieved as a result is not clear. Apparently, they lived as savages and fought with the utmost savagery.

With due respect to Dio, it is unlikely that the Scottish peoples were as wild as that. The Romans stereotyped everyone beyond the frontiers of the Empire as barbarians and therefore uncivilized; it became a literary convention for Roman writers to characterize foreign nations and their barbarity in extravagant terms.[18]

There is good evidence that the name 'Caledonian' was used by some of the peoples in Scotland to describe themselves from the Iron Age onwards:[19] variants appear in ancient place names; 'Caledonians' were one of the tribes identified by Ptolemy; Pliny the Elder referred to the 'Caledonian Forest'. In an inscription at Colchester the creator described himself as the grandson of Vepogenus, a Caledonian.[20] When Severus was in power the term 'Caledonians' probably related to a loosely linked group of communities in the eastern part of the highlands. The name 'Maeatae' first occurs in Dio's account of events in the early third century. Having regard to where Severus campaigned, 'Maeatae' is probably a reference to the peoples who occupied the northern lowlands, the Antonine Wall area and Fife.

Dio records that the Caledonians did not abide by promises that they had made; instead they prepared to assist the Maeatae in making war against the Romans.[21] There must have been some previous treaty between the provincial governor and the Caledonians, but we are not told what that treaty was. After the depletion of his troops, Lupus lacked the resources to resist a major invasion; therefore, he had purchased peace for a 'large sum'.[22] Large silver coin hoards of that period have been found in the territory of the Caledonians and the Maeatae.[23] Some of those hoards are still there, but now sitting in glass cases at the Scottish National Museum. If Dio is to be believed, the outlay achieved nothing more than a few years' respite.

---

[16] Frere (1981).
[17] *Roman History* 77.12.
[18] Woolf (2011) 93–115.
[19] Hunter (2007) 3–9.
[20] 'nepos Vepogeni Caledo': RIB, 191.
[21] *Roman History* 76.5.4. The numbering of paragraphs in this section of Dio is uncertain and confused.
[22] 'μεγάλων χρημάτων': Dio, *Roman History* 76.5.4.
[23] Hodgson (2014) 34.

There was nothing exceptional about using 'gifts' to maintain peace along the frontier. Rome usually made payments to communities in the hinterland, rather than those located in the frontier region: this was a shrewd policy, based on the adage 'my enemy's enemy is my friend'. The Romans appear to have adopted that approach in Scotland, since many of the coin hoards have turned up a long way to the north of the war zone.[24]

In AD 208 Severus took the momentous decision to head north and establish his headquarters in Britain. According to Dio, he did not anticipate ever returning to Rome,[25] but this assessment is dubious. Britain was hardly an easy place from which to administer the Empire on a long-term basis. It is more likely the Severus came here to conduct a long-term campaign. Such campaigns by emperors were not uncommon. They did not signify an intention to abandon Rome.

According to both Dio and Herodian, part of Severus' motivation was to encourage a more responsible attitude on the part of his two sons, Antoninus (better known as Caracalla) and Geta, who were living idly in Rome; there was huge enmity between them. It is credible that this was part of Severus' thinking.

According to Herodian,[26] the governor of Britain wrote to Severus, stating that people were rebelling and devastating the countryside; he asked the Emperor either to send more troops or to come in person. Herodian does not name the governor, but inscriptions suggest that it was a senator called Alfenus Senecio. Historians now question whether the governor really wrote in those terms: such letters can be a literary device in texts on Roman Britain.[27]

If there really was such a letter, one wonders whose idea it was. Was this a genuine request from the governor (which seems most unlikely) or did Severus ask him to send it? Indeed, did Severus or his courtiers draft the letter? The answer, sadly, is that we do not know. The most that can be said is this. First, there was probably some unrest in the north of Britain, although the extent of that unrest is uncertain. As previously noted, 'war in Britain' and its suppression were a leitmotif in much historical writing of the period. Second, for whatever reason, Severus decided to give the province his personal attention.

In AD 208 Severus travelled to Britain with his entire retinue of officials, his wife (Julia Domna) and their two sons. Severus had already elevated Caracalla (aged 20) to the rank of Augustus. Geta (aged 19) did not have long to wait, as he was promoted to that rank in the autumn of 209. For three years Britain became the administrative centre of the entire Roman Empire. This had never happened before and would never happen again.

Severus made the journey to Britain swiftly, even though he had to be carried on a litter for much of the way.[28] On arrival, he held a general review of the troops. Word of the Emperor's arrival soon reached Scotland. According to Herodian the Maeatae and the Caledonians hastily despatched an embassy to London, expressing regret for their recent actions and offering to discuss peace terms. Severus would have none of this. He sent the embassy away with a few harsh words. There is no reason to doubt Herodian's account. The Emperor had not travelled all the way to Britain just to sign a peace treaty. He wanted a proper military campaign, hopefully including a massacre or two. He also hoped to earn the title Britannicus.

---

[24]Hunter (2007) e.g. at 30.
[25]Dio, *Roman History* 77.11.1.
[26]*History* 3.14.1.
[27]For example, Aulus Plautius' supposed letter asking Claudius to come to Britain in AD 43.
[28]Herodian, *History* 3.14.3.

4. SEVERUS CAMPAIGNS IN SCOTLAND

Severus travelled north to York (*Eboracum*), which he made his headquarters and the base for his planned military campaign. The Emperor's family, as well as his administrative and clerical staff, required permanent accommodation. There was no question of building a luxurious palace or laying out ornamental gardens for their enjoyment. It was normal practice for emperors to take over existing accommodation when they were campaigning. Severus' retinue probably occupied the *praetorium* of the legionary fortress.[29] The unfortunate legate and his family would have had to decamp.

The *Historia Augusta* records that Severus 'built a wall across Britannia from one shore of the Ocean to the other and that this was the greatest glory of his reign'.[30] This sentence cannot be read literally, because the *Historia Augusta* has previously told us that the wall in question was built by someone else, namely Hadrian. The sentence can only mean that Severus organized restoration or repair works to Hadrian's Wall. But even this interpretation calls for caution. Restoring the infrastructure or monumental buildings was the mark of a 'good' Emperor. There was therefore a tendency to exaggerate the scope of restoration works undertaken.[31] It may well be that the restorative works which Severus ordered to Hadrian's Wall were quite modest.

The fort at South Shields[32] stood close to the mouth of the Tyne, so was well placed to receive and despatch supplies by sea. The army converted the fort into a major supply depot by extending its curtilage and adding substantial granaries. The increased capacity was linked to the planned campaign in Scotland: the troops heading north would always remain close to the coast, so that they could receive provisions by sea. Recent excavations have banished earlier doubts about the date of the conversion works at South Shields. Lead sealings have been found at foundation level marked 'AUGG' and, in one case, 'AUGGG'. 'AUGG' refers to Severus and Caracalla as co-Emperors. So those sealings must be dated before the autumn of 209. 'AUGGG' refers to Severus, Caracalla and Geta as co-Emperors. That sealing must be dated between autumn 209 and February 211. A separate lead sealing indicates that the Fifth Cohort of the Gauls were garrisoning the fort during the period of the conversion works. Severus decided to take his elder son, Caracalla, with him on campaign in AD 209.[33] This just left the minor question of who would run the Roman Empire while Severus was away. The Emperor decided that this task could safely be delegated to his younger son, Geta, then aged nineteen. Severus duly summoned the boy and told him to take charge of the Empire; a council of elders, composed of Severus' friends, would be available to give advice. This must have been quite a challenge. At an age when young men nowadays may be starting university or a gap year, Geta was being asked to govern the whole of Europe, North Africa and the Middle East. He was required to do so from a remote island in the north at a time when communications were slow.

---

[29]Bidwell (2006) discusses this issue at 32.
[30]'Britanniam, quod maximum eius imperii decus est, muro per transversam insulam ducto utrimque ad finem Oceani munivit.' *Historia Augusta*, *Severus* 18.2. Eutropius makes a similar comment at *Breviarium ab Urbe Condita* 8.19.
[31]Thomas and Witschel, 'Constructing reconstruction: claim and reality of Roman rebuilding inscriptions from the Latin West', *Papers of the British School at Rome* 60 (1992) 135–78.
[32]Hodgson (2009a) 62–8.
[33]Herodian, *History* 3.14.9.

It is worth pausing to consider what 'running the Empire' entailed.[34] Descriptions of the Emperor at work survive from a number of sources, including a famous letter from Fronto to Marcus Aurelius.[35] Much of the Emperor's work took the form of face-to-face-contact – receiving messengers, embassies and delegations. His paperwork, or perhaps tablet work, included answering letters from provincial governors and responding to petitions (*libelli*). The Emperor issued edicts, which had the force of law, sealed with his imperial signet ring to confirm their authenticity.[36] In general the Emperor's work tended to be reactive, but his decisions were far-reaching. This was a daunting task for young Geta.

Dio tells us that Severus' military objective was to bring the whole of Scotland under Roman control.[37] Francis Haverfield doubts that Dio was right, since there would be little point in restoring Hadrian's Wall if Rome was going to annexe the whole of Scotland. Other scholars have pitched into the debate with vigour, usually agreeing with Haverfield. In a well-researched article Nick Hodgson maintains that the Severan campaign was an instance of the 'management of neighbouring peoples through aggressive and far-reaching war and the establishment of a powerful advance fort near the source of the trouble'.[38] Hodgson therefore rejects Dio's statement.

Contrary to the views of Haverfield, Hodgson and others, it is suggested that Dio's statement should be accepted for six reasons:

(i) Severus was near the end of his reign and wanted to finish in a blaze of glory. What better way to do so than by completing the conquest of Britain? This had been unfinished business since the first century. There would also be a substantial benefit in terms of dynastic propaganda, if Severus and his sons achieved a victory that had eluded all previous emperors.

(ii) If Britannia was going to become a secure Roman province, the objective of subduing the troublesome top bit of the island was entirely rational. So long as Scotland remained independent, hostile peoples north of the border would be a constant threat.

(iii) Hodgson is right to point out that Rome had a long running policy of dealing with societies beyond the imperial frontier by means of silver-coin subsidies, present-giving, hostage exchange, treaties and periodic wars.[39] That was obviously necessary along the eastern frontier of the Empire. Wherever Rome drew the line there would be barbarian hordes beyond. But in the north the position was different. Scotland was a defined area, with no warlike peoples on the other side. There was just the 'Ocean'. Rome had conquered, by area, some two thirds of Britain. It must have tempting to conquer the rest. Then there would be no need for all that bribery, present-giving, hostage-taking, treaty-making and periodic warfare.

(iv) If Rome had conquered Scotland, it would have adopted its usual policy of turning its enemies into friends. That had worked everywhere else in Europe, give or take a few rebellions. There was no reason why it should not work in Scotland.

---

[34]Millar (1992) chapter 5.
[35]Fronto, *Ad M, Antoninum de eloquentia* 2, 7.
[36]Pliny, *Natural History* xxxvii, 4.
[37]'ὁ δ᾽ οὖν Σεουῆρος πᾶσαν αὐτὴν καταστρέψασθαι ἐθελήσας ἐσέβαλεν ἐς τὴν Καληδονίαν': Dio, *Roman History* 77.13.1.
[38]Hodgson (2014) 45.
[39]Hodgson (2014) 35.

(v) The very fact that the Roman Emperor established himself in Britain for a period of years indicates that there was a serious military purpose. If Severus' only objective was border control, he could have left that to the governor.

(vi) The restoration of Hadrian's Wall is not inconsistent with that objective. Severus did not want to count his chickens before they were hatched. He had to secure the existing province, before setting out to extend it.

There were two major campaigns between AD 208 and 211, but the accounts given by Herodian, Dio and the *Historia Augusta* are confused. In his excellent article previously mentioned, Hodgson has reconstructed the sequence of events from all available literary and archaeological evidence as follows:

(i) In the summer of 209 Severus and Caracalla launched a campaign against Caledonia and achieved some successes. In the winter of 209–10 the enemy came to terms and ceded territory,[40] whereupon Severus and his two sons each took the title *Britannicus maximus*. Coins were minted to celebrate their victory. One of these coins refers to a bridge of boats, which might be a reference to crossing the River Tay at Carpow.

(ii) There was then a revolt by the Maeatae. In the summer of 210 Caracalla marched against them. The Caledonians joined the revolt.[41] In the winter of 210–11 Severus was preparing to lead another assault on Scotland, but his plans were thwarted when he died.

According to both Herodian and Dio, Severus' troops were engaged in numerous skirmishes but they fought no major battle. The artful opponents avoided a full encounter by devious means: one of their tactics was to drive a mass of sheep and cattle in front of them; another tactic was to mount lightning strikes on the Roman army and then melt back into the forests and marshes. The invading army had more of a battle with the elements than with the enemy. Scotland presented a difficult terrain for soldiers who had no accurate maps or local knowledge. The one advantage that the Romans enjoyed was their engineering skill. They used that skill to fell trees, fill swamps, bridge rivers and even to remove some natural obstacles in their path.[42] All these engineering works en route must have slowed down the army's progress.

Pottery and coinage finds indicate that during these campaigns the Romans were occupying two major forts on the coast – one at Carpow on the Firth of Tay, the other at Cramond on the Firth of Forth. Severus probably founded the fort at Carpow.[43] At Cramond there was an existing Antonine fort, which Severus extended. This became the key point for seaborne access to central Scotland. A well preserved altar at Cramond bears the inscription: 'To Jupiter the best and greatest, the Fifth Cohort of the Gauls, under the command of Lucius Minthonius Tertullus, the prefect, gladly, willingly and deservedly fulfilled its vow.'[44] This is the same auxiliary cohort whom we met at South Shields a few paragraphs ago. Possibly the whole cohort moved

---

[40]*Historia Augusta, Severus* 19 and 22; Dio, *Roman History* 77.13.
[41]Dio, *Roman History* 77.15.2.
[42]Dio, *Roman History* 77.13.1.
[43]See further Keppie (2019) 265–83.
[44]RIB 2134.

northwards to garrison the crucial fort at Cramond. Alternatively, the cohort may have divided, with the lucky ones staying at South Shields and the others moving to Cramond.

Many Roman marching camps survive in Scotland, but it is not easy to identify which are referable to Agricola, which to Severus and which to other generals.[45] It is quite likely that a line of 165-acre camps running up Dere Street to Cramond are Severan. It is also likely that a line of 130-acre camps stretching north from the Forth to the Mounth are attributable to Severus. The inference is that when the army reached Cramond it split into two groups of smaller size.

Caracalla did not share his father's enthusiasm for campaigning in Scotland. The only way out that he could see was to kill his father, then assume the role of Emperor and put an end to the Scottish wars. Both Dio and Herodian are agreed that Caracalla tried to murder his father, but they disagree about his method. According to Dio, Caracalla tried to persuade Severus' doctors to kill him under the guise of medical treatment. The doctors refused. Herodian's account is more colourful, but less credible. One day as Caracalla and Severus were riding together through the highlands, they were some way ahead of the rest of the army and were seeking an opportunity for a skirmish with the Caledonians. Caracalla drew his sword and prepared to stab his father in the back, but others were riding close enough to see what was happening. They cried out in alarm. Severus turned round in time to see the raised sword and Caracalla desisted. Severus made no immediate comment about his son's unhelpful behaviour, but waited until they were back at their base. He then summoned Caracalla and two senior officers. Placing a sword on the table in front of them, Severus stated that if Caracalla wished to kill him, he should do so there and then. The young man was duly shamed and left the sword untouched.

In the end, the Scottish campaigns were not a success. Severus never established a new northern frontier. The well-defined northern frontier of Britannia remained where it had been before, namely along the line of Hadrian's Wall. Indeed, Severus consolidated that frontier by carrying out repair works to the great wall, as previously discussed.

Events in York and Severus' death

While Severus was busy campaigning in Scotland his wife, Julia Domna, lived in greater comfort at York. Dio gives us a glimpse of her social life. Apparently, a Caledonian lady was teasing Julia about Severus' laws banning adultery. She said: 'We satisfy our natural needs much better than you Roman women! We consort openly with the finest men. You are secretly taken to bed by the worst of men!'[46] This vignette, which has survived almost by chance, gives us a picture of Julia and the other ladies in York having jolly hen parties while their husbands were away at the war.

Severus' health deteriorated during the winter of 210–11. He hoped to recuperate in the comfort of his quarters at York, but his decline was irreversible. The biggest weight on his mind was the conflict between his two sons, which had been the tragedy of his life. In early February

---

[45] Hodgson (2014) 38–41.
[46] 'πολλῷ ἄμεινον ἡμεῖς τὰ τῆς φύσεως ἀναγκαῖα ἀποπληροῦμεν ὑμῶν τῶν Ῥωμαϊκῶν· ἡμεῖς γὰρ φανερῶς τοῖς ἀρίστοις ὁμιλοῦμεν, ὑμεῖς δὲ λάθρᾳ ὑπὸ τῶν κακίστων μοιχεύεσθε.' *Roman History* 77.16.5.

211, Severus summoned them to his bedside and delivered his final fatherly advice: 'Live together in peace. Enrich the soldiers and scorn everybody else.'[47] On the 4 February 211 the Emperor died, apparently with some help from Caracalla. He cannot have been optimistic that the boys would heed his advice.

Severus was cremated at York. His two sons subsequently organized a magnificent state funeral for him in Rome, before placing the ashes in Hadrian's mausoleum.

---

[47]'ὁμονοεῖτε, τοὺς στρατιώτας πλουτίζετε, τῶν ἄλλων πάντων καταφρονεῖτε': Dio, *Roman History* 77.15.2.

CHAPTER 13
THE THIRD CENTURY

1. Reign of Caracalla (AD 211–217)
2. The mid-third century (AD 217–284)
3. The Tetrarchy
4. The shore forts
5. The usurpation of Carausius and Allectus

This chapter will cover a period when Britain diminished in importance and came under attack from the sea. The chapter will support the view that all the third-century shore forts were all built for a similar purpose, namely as defences against seaborne attacks, even though the construction period spanned a hundred years. We will also review the career of two rebel emperors, who set themselves up in Britain.

1. THE REIGN OF CARACALLA (AD 211–217)

After the death of Severus his two sons became joint Emperors, but Caracalla was the dominant partner. As Dio observed, 'nominally he ruled with his brother, but in reality he ruled alone'.[1] Even that degree of supremacy was not enough for Caracalla, who was intent upon eliminating his younger brother. His immediate priority, however, was to get away from Britain, where he believed the imperial court had already spent more than enough time. He sent Geta and their mother back to Italy ahead of him.

Caracalla concluded peace treaties with the Scottish communities. According to Herodian,[2] the essence of those treaties was that the Romans would abstain from further campaigns in Scotland in exchange for guarantees of non-aggression on the part of the Maeatae and the Caledonians. According to Dio,[3] the Romans withdrew from the parts of Scotland that they had recently conquered and abandoned the forts which Severus had established there.

---

[1] 'λόγῳ μὲν γὰρ μετὰ τοῦ ἀδελφοῦ, τῷ δὲ δὴ ἔργῳ μόνος εὐθὺς ἦρξε': Dio, *Roman History* 78.1.1.
[2] *History* 3.15.6.
[3] *Roman History* 78.1.1.

The archaeology tells a different story from Dio's account.[4] An inscription at Carpow refers to a single Emperor, which indicates continuing Roman presence as far north as the Tay after the murder of Geta in AD 212. Pottery finds at Cramond on the Firth of Forth reveal continued Roman occupation through the early part of the third century. The Fifth Cohort of the Gauls may not have returned from Cramond to South Shields until some date between AD 222 and 235. Looking at all the evidence, the most likely inference is that a Roman 'peace keeping' force remained in the key forts to police Caracalla's treaties for several years.

Caracalla hastened back to Rome as soon as practicable. The enmity between the two Emperors was intense, despite their mother's efforts to effect a reconciliation. Caracalla struck at the first opportunity: he arranged for some centurions to stab Geta to death. Immediately afterwards, while the corpse was still bleeding and warm, Caracalla announced to the world that he had had a lucky escape; Geta had been plotting a bloody coup, which was only foiled at the last moment.[5]

Now sole Emperor, Caracalla took prompt steps to obliterate all traces of Geta: Coins bearing his image were melted down and references to Geta in inscriptions were chiselled out.[6] Loyal workmen across the Empire duly set to work, but some were less than diligent. On one dedication slab,[7] now in the crypt of Hexham Abbey, the stonemason has done a poor job. Both Caracalla and Geta are named and given credit for building a granary.

It will be recalled that on his deathbed Severus gave two pieces of advice to his sons. The first was to live together in peace; the second was to enrich the soldiers and scorn everybody else. Although Caracalla ignored the first bit, he certainly took to heart the second piece of advice. Following his accession as sole Emperor, Caracalla raised the soldiers' pay; he also gave them a generous donation,[8] which he funded by raiding temples and treasuries. Caracalla was not the first leading politician to consolidate his position by giving away other people's money, nor the last.

In AD 212 Caracalla issued an edict, *Constitutio Antoniniana*, conferring Roman citizenship on all free inhabitants of the Empire. When news of this edict reached our shores, the Britons discovered that they had all become Roman citizens. Although the privileges of citizenship were no doubt welcome, they came with a price tag. Dio explains that the Emperor's motives for this reform were financial.[9] Citizens were liable to pay taxes from which aliens were exempt.

Herodian states that Severus set the affairs of Britain in order and divided the province into two.[10] It is generally thought that Herodian's timing is not correct. It is more likely that the division of Britain occurred in the reign of Caracalla. Southern Britain became *Britannia Superior*, because it was closer to Rome; northern Britain became *Britannia Inferior*, being further away from Rome. Each of the two provinces had its own administration. The governor of *Britannia Superior* was usually of consular status and based in London. The governor of *Britannia Inferior* was the legate commanding the Sixth Legion, so based in York.

The division of Britain into two separate provinces was a part of a broader pattern of dispersal. The old notion of separate legions and auxiliary cohorts each housed at their own

---

[4]Breeze (1996) 96.
[5]Dio, *Roman History* 78.2 and Herodian *History* 4.4.
[6]Tomlin (2018) 177.
[7]RIB 1151.
[8]Dio, *Roman History* 78.10.4 and Herodian *History* 4.4.7.
[9]Dio, *Roman History* 78.9.5.
[10]*History* 3.8.2.

base was breaking down. Increasingly detachments of soldiers were being stationed at distant outposts or forts, as we saw in the Vindolanda tablets.[11] That practice increased in the second and third centuries. By the third century there was a general policy of reducing the number of legions under the command of any one governor. The division of Britain into two provinces reduced the military strength of both governors. There would never again be a governor of Britain powerful enough to challenge the Emperor. The lesson of Albinus had been learnt.

Whatever settlements Caracalla negotiated with the Maeatae and the Caledonians seem to have been effective.[12] The third century was a period of relative peace on the northern front. There was abundant trade between Britannia and Scotland. Roman finds on non-Roman sites across Scotland tend to be denser in the south than in the north and denser in the east than in the west.

Coin hoards and other treasures recovered from Scotland imply that Rome was still 'buying' peace. As previously noted, Rome tended to target its diplomatic gifts on people in the hinterland, rather than those just behind the frontiers of the Empire. The gifts took many forms. Bags of silver coins were common, although these could hardly have been legal tender amongst the mountains and swamps of Scotland. The recipients probably treated them as bullion. The trappings of fine dining made excellent presents. Some are now on display at the National Museum of Scotland. A sparkling example is the Helmsdale Hoard – a collection of elegant serving bowls and wine strainers, which would grace any modern wedding list.

Despite striking peace treaties with Scotland and paying occasional bribes, Rome for the time being maintained a formidable military presence on its northern frontier. In the early third century the Sixth Legion rebuilt the timber fort at Carlisle in stone. The importance of this location was emphasized by the fact that detachments from the Second and Twentieth Legions, rather than auxiliaries, manned the fort.[13] Detachments of the Second Legion and either the Sixth or Twentieth Legion were placed at Corbridge,[14] so that legionary soldiers were stationed at both ends of Hadrian's Wall. The permanent stationing of legionary detachments at Carlisle and Corbridge is part of the pattern of dispersal discussed above. It was more useful to put legionary soldiers in areas that needed guarding, rather than to coop them all up in massive fortresses.

The South Shields fort remained in occupation after the Severan campaigns, but doubt has been expressed as to as to whether the occupants were soldiers or civilians.[15] It is most unlikely that the Roman authorities would have allowed a civilian settlement to develop on a potentially important military site. It is far more likely that they mothballed the fort, which would have required only a small military presence. The few remaining soldiers at South Shields may well have brought in civilian contractors to assist with care and maintenance.

After serving in the Severan campaigns the bulk of the Twentieth Legion returned to its base at Chester and undertook a major reconstruction of the fortress.[16] They demolished and rebuilt everything that stood within the perimeter wall. The new buildings included barracks, baths, granaries, hospital and *principia*. Some of the bricks and tiles used were stamped 'ANTO',

---

[11] E.g. *Tab Vindol* II, 154.
[12] Hunter (2007) 10–32.
[13] Hodgson (2009a) 147.
[14] Hodgson (2009a) 32.
[15] Jones (1981) 400.
[16] Strickland (1981) 417–28; Mason (2012) chapter 11.

which was an abbreviation of Caracalla's name, Antoninus. The whole project required about 2 million tiles and 300 tonnes of stone. Transportation alone was a major operation. This would have provided much wholesome employment for the Cornovii and their friends. It would also have kept the army busy and out of mischief for several years. That may have been the intention.

Caracalla was assassinated in AD 217.[17] He is best remembered now for having constructed the colossal baths in Rome that bear his name. Eutropius describes them as Caracalla's principal achievement.[18]

2. THE MID-THIRD CENTURY (AD 217–284)

By the end of Caracalla's reign, the conquest of Britain was effectively complete. The northern boundary of Britannia had been firmly established and there would be no further attempts to annex Scotland during that century. Conversely all territory to the south of Hadrian's Wall was, for the time being, reasonably safe from the threat of Scottish incursions.

We have noticed in Chapter 12 the cultural change that swept across the Roman Empire in the third century. Britain was not immune from those forces.[19] Public authorities were no longer erecting grand public buildings, as they had done in the first and second centuries. Few Corinthian columns or entablatures were carved after the beginning of the third century.[20] Town defences and gates no longer received embellishments. People were more interested in decorating temples and private houses. Some public buildings decayed, for example at Wroxeter. There was stone robbing at Verulamium. In Colchester, the prestigious Balkerne Gate was closed off.[21] It mattered less whether a community had the status of 'civitas'. Fewer people carved inscriptions. Perhaps they were less bothered about what future generations thought of them. One of the latest inscriptions in Roman Britain is a dedication slab to Jupiter Dolichenus set up at Chesters (a fort on Hadrian's Wall) in AD 286.[22]

In the first and second centuries there had been a tradition of munificence. Wealthy individuals might fund the building of a bathhouse or the restoration of a temple. This was how people made their mark or showed loyalty to the government. There was also an element of civic competition between benefactors. By the third century that tradition was dying out. Also there was not much left to build, since most Romano-British towns had the full suite of public buildings.

As part of the changing attitudes in the third century, people were less willing to hold public office.[23] Accordingly membership of town councils was made compulsory for anyone who was eligible and nominated. In practice, membership of the councils was almost hereditary. The sons of decurions inherited their fathers' property and then followed in their footsteps. There was little social mobility in third-century Britain.

---

[17] Dio, *Roman History* 79.4 and Herodian, *History* 4.13.
[18] *Breviarium ab Urbe Condita* 8.20.
[19] Cleary (2013b) chapter 1; Reece (1981); Webster (1981).
[20] Blagg (2002) 186.
[21] Gascoyne and Radford (2013) 109.
[22] Found in a riverbed near the bathhouse in 2004: RIB 3299.
[23] Jones (1964) 739.

Both in Britain and across the Empire there was a shift from public to private expenditure. The élites spent more of their wealth on their own villas and estates. They also spent more of their time there. The 'great man' liked to hold court in his villa, where lesser folk might come with their requests. This shift from town or city to the individual was a trend that gathered pace in the fourth century, as we shall see.

The principal exceptions to the general trend were York and London (see Chapter 17 below). York gained a new lease of life in the third century, having become capital of *Britannia Inferior*; London remained, as it always had been, the main administrative hub of Roman Britain.

In the early third century the territory of the Carvetii was established as a 'civitas', although by then that status less significant. The capital was at Carlisle (*Luguvallum*), a key town on the northern frontier. We know little about Carlisle's civic affairs, except that one of its senators was Flavius Martius who died at the age of 45. The picture on his tombstone shows a dignitary in a toga, holding what looks like a Harry Potter wand.[24] A milestone has been found at Langwathby in Cumbria, recording that the distance to Carlisle was 19 miles. This stone can be dated to AD 223. Possibly the town had become an administrative centre by that date. Carlisle was the last civitas capital to emerge and the only one to be created as late as the third century.

During the third century Britain sharply diminished in importance. It was no longer the stamping ground for generals seeking glory or politicians seeking high office. As Britannia shrank in importance, so it dropped below the horizon of contemporary historians. Dio's *Roman History* (insofar as it survives) covers the period up to 229, but he has little to say about Britain after the reign of Caracalla. Herodian's *History* extends up to 238, but he too tells us little about Britain after Caracalla's death. The *Historia Augusta* continues up to 284, but largely ignores Britain after the death of Severus.

The main focus attention during the period 217 to 284 was upon the endless struggles for imperial power. During this period there were 41 different emperors, all holding power at different times either singly or jointly. Few of these emperors enjoyed their power for long and most were murdered by their successors.

Roman society, like Chinese society, was intensely hierarchical. During the first and second centuries this had enabled the Roman emperors, like their contemporaries in the Han Dynasty, to administer a massive empire effectively. In both continents that started to break down in the third century,[25] with a regionalization of imperial power.[26] In the Roman Empire multiple emperors emerged, each with territorial responsibilities. This led to the construction of magnificent imperial palaces dotted around Europe, such as those at Trier, Split, Arles and Cordoba. Trier became the capital of the Gallic Empire (discussed below) and also the seat of a mint. The emperors were also generals, so their palaces were well fortified. Rome remained at the heart of the Empire, but it was no longer the sole seat of power. The Senate lost much of its political and military power, but it remained a social élite with immense influence.

The almost constant strife between emperors and aspirant emperors during the third century was played out against a background of major wars around the Empire. The Persian (Sassanian) Empire was attacking from the East. The Goths were pressing in on the Danube

---

[24]RIB 933.
[25]Cleary (2013b) chapter 5.
[26]Fairbank (1994) chapter 3, in particular the analysis at 72. 'The basic mechanism of the Han Dynasty's decline was the usual one: the rise of local or regional power to eclipse that of the central dynasty.'

frontier. Germanic peoples were invading across the Rhine. Seaborne raiders, including Saxons and pirates from the North Sea and the English Channel were beginning to attack coastal areas.

Decline of long-distance trade

The Empire facilitated long-distance trade by reason of its excellent road network and communications. Despite that facility, the volume of such trade diminished during the third century.[27] Here are three examples:

(i) In the first and second centuries Samian ware, manufactured in Gaul, was widely distributed across the Empire and much reached Britain. In the third century a new style of pottery emerged in the Argonne region of Gaul, derived from the Samian tradition. Argonne products were widely distributed around Gaul, but relatively little arrived in Britain.

(ii) The major British pottery industry, which was centred in the area of Poole Harbour, produced Black Burnished Ware ("BBW"). There was a widespread distribution of BBW across Britain, largely following the road network. On the Continent BBW was confined to the north coast of Gaul and probably attributable to occasional cross-Channel contact.

(iii) Less overseas produce passed through London in the third century. The quayside of this major port was now mainly used for local trade.

The cause (or perhaps the consequence) of the decline in trade was regionalization of production. Provinces, including those on the frontiers, tended to produce what was required for their own domestic consumption. Most goods no longer needed to be transported across long distances. Obviously, there were exceptions and some exports continued. For example, figs, dates, olives and grapes were exported to Britain from southern Europe.[28] But Britain was not an exporting province. Coarse pottery such as BBW did not usually travel far. It is slightly surprising that BBW reached as far as Hadrian's Wall. Military use of BBW is probably the explanation. Overall the drop in long-distance trade during the third century might be seen as a sign of entrenched economic prosperity.

Town walls

The effort, which in earlier centuries had been poured into creating fine civic buildings, was now redirected towards defence.[29] Massive city walls sprang up across Gaul and Britain, usually replacing earlier earthwork defences.

A massive town wall was built around Silchester in the late third century. This wall is particularly well preserved and still dominates the landscape: it is about 2.4 kilometres long and the base is 3 metres wide. The original height was probably 7 to 8 metres. Even now some sections of the wall rise to about 4.5 metres. The core of the wall comprises flints set in lime mortar, with stone levelling courses. Greensand and limestone blocks are set into the wall

---

[27] Reece (1981) and Cleary (2013b) chapter 7.
[28] Van der Veen, Livurda and Hill (2007) 205–6.
[29] Cleary (2013b) chapter 3.

around critical points such as gateways. These blocks came from the Bath/Cirencester region and their transport would have been a substantial task. It is estimated that the wall originally contained about 40,000 cubic metres of construction material.

A similarly massive wall was built around Chichester in the late third century,[30] but less of this survives because of medieval and later development. The foundation of the Roman wall was about 3 metres wide and the masonry superstructure was about 2.4 metres wide. The original height is unknown. The Chichester wall, like the Silchester wall, is about 2.4 kilometres long. You can have a very pleasant walk around this wall, although most of what you see is medieval, not Roman. If you need a rest, the Bishop's Garden (open to the public) is a rather more tranquil stopping-off point than the bus station.

A city wall was built around Verulamium in about 265 to 270. At the same time the river Ver was canalized by building an embankment.[31] Only a small section of the Verulamium wall now survives. This is in an area of parkland by the children's playground. But there is enough to see that the original walls were on the same scale as those of Silchester and Chichester.

During the third century substantial stone walls were built around a number of other towns in the south including Caistor St Edmund, Caerwent, Canterbury, Carmarthen and Cirencester.

There were probably two motives for the wall building. The first was insecurity. As noted earlier, by the third century the Roman Empire was on the defensive and fearful of invasions from the east and the north. In Gaul general insecurity led to the construction of circuit walls around small parts of towns, but not to wall building on the scale of Britain. There must have been a second motivation in Britain. That was probably civic pride. No town wanted to be outdone by its neighbours. Ironically, at a time when expenditure on general public buildings was in decline, the citizenry and the Roman authorities devoted huge resources to the construction of prestigious town walls.

The north

During the third century the Roman government used scouts (*exploratores*) to gather intelligence on all frontiers of the Empire.[32] In Britain scouts were posted at High Rochester, Risingham and other sensitive locations. The scouts were not like MI5 agents, who kept their activities secret. They often formed into military units and declared their role with some pride in inscriptions.[33]

As previously noted, the third century was a time of relative peace on the northern frontier.[34] Many turrets on Hadrian's Wall became unoccupied; the gates of milecastles were narrowed to let only pedestrians through. The forts at Rudchester and Halton Chesters show signs of abandonment towards the end of the century. There was reduced occupation of the forts in the Pennine region. Infantry barracks were reconstructed in a new style between AD 225 and 250, to hold *contubernia* (squads) of 5 or 6 men instead of 8. This implies that the centuries in northern Britain were reduced in size (ten *contubernia* constituted one century, commanded

---
[30] Westman (2012) chapter 3.
[31] Frere (1981) 391.
[32] Mann (1979) 146.
[33] RIB 1235, 1243, 1262, 1270.
[34] Hodgson (2009a) chapter 2; Jones (1981); Mann (1979) 145.

by a centurion). Cavalry barracks also changed, to hold fewer and larger *contubernia*. At Netherby a drill hall inscription was re-used as drain cover. There are signs of looting in certain forts. At Bewcastle there appears to have been violent destruction: the strongroom was filled with military debris. The fort at Carrawburgh seems to have come to a violent end in the late third century.

Other forts in the north remained operational[35] and continued to maintain civilian settlements outside their walls.[36] There was a flourishing *vicus* at Chesters in the third century. At Benwell the *vicus* buildings spread over the area where the *vallum* had been filled in. At Housesteads and Wallsend, the *vici* even had walls around them. This illustrates the symbiotic relationship between the forts and the *vici*. The soldiers needed somewhere to spend their money and the civilians were exploiting business opportunities. Also, the soldiers' families were living in the *vici*. Corbridge and Carlisle developed into civilian towns. A large residential building in Corbridge, which some archaeologists classify as a *mansio*, was in full use during the third century.

York, the provincial capital, was pre-eminently a military town. Up until the end of the third century the governor was always a senior army officer. New forts were built at Newton Kyme and Ribchester. These and several others, such as the Baimbridge fort, were occupied throughout the third century and beyond.

As we saw earlier, the Twentieth Legion built themselves a fine new fortress at Chester in the early third century. They were still there during the reign of Decius,[37] an Emperor who survived for all of two years between AD 249 and 251. But by then the number of legionary soldiers in Chester had diminished.[38] Inscriptions record that detachments of the Twentieth Legion were serving on Hadrian's Wall. Others were posted to the Rhine/Danube frontier. The epigraphic record of the Twentieth Legion in Britain ends in about 260. Many buildings inside the Chester fortress were demolished between about 270 and 300, but the *principia* and *praetorium* survived. The latest reference anywhere to the Twentieth Legion is on the coins of Carausius (AD 286–293). It is possible that the legion or parts of it remained at Chester until the end of the third century or beyond. Alternatively, the legion may have been disbanded, since there is no reference to it in the *Notitia Dignitatum*. As we shall see in the next chapter, there was a major reformation of the Roman army at around the beginning of the fourth century.

A substantial civilian settlement (*canabae*) had grown up around the fortress at Chester during the first and second centuries, complete with its own elected council and officials.[39] The community included soldiers' families, as well as merchants, traders, developers and many others seeking to earn an honest *denarius* or two. By the third century, forts and fortresses tended to be mixed communities. There was no longer a clear distinction between Romans, Gallic or Germanic peoples, Britons and other races. After two hundred years of intermingling and intermarriage, the boundary between ethnic groups was blurred.

The *canabae* at Chester flourished in the mid third century and remained vibrant after the Twentieth Legion had gone. Civilians gradually took over the fortress and established Chester

---

[35]Jones (1981) 400–5; Hodgson (2009a) 33–4.
[36]Jones (1981) 400; Hodgson (2009a) 35.
[37]RIB 449.
[38]Strickland, (1981); Mason (2012) chapters 11 and 12.
[39]Strickland (1981); Mason (2012) chapters 7 and 11.

as a major town. They did some rebuilding and improved the defences. The quayside and harbour on the river Dee, which once had served the army, now became a general trading route. We do not know whether Chester was ever a civitas capital or a *municipium*. It certainly had good 'Roman' credentials.

In about the mid-third century the military rebuilt the fort at Piercebridge on a grand scale.[40] The remnants of that fort now lie beneath the village green and surrounding houses, but parts have been exposed. You can see where the east gate once stood. The lower courses of a wall around the bathhouse and a courtyard building are also on display. This fort stood next to Dere Street, the main arterial road running north from York up to Corbridge. It overlooked a vital strategic area, namely the bridge where Dere Street crossed the river Tees. In about AD 260–280 defensive ditches were added around the fort. Such was the importance of the Piercebridge fort that it remained in occupation right through the fourth century and the early fifth century.

Legionary soldiers from Germany served at Piercebridge during the third century, possibly replacing units redeployed to shore forts in the south. They left a fine collection of altars and tombstones.[41] One altar to Jupiter Dolichenus was dedicated 'for the welfare of the detachments of the Sixth Legion Victrix and of the army of each Germany'.[42] The presence of legionary soldiers at Piercebridge, including reinforcements from Germany, emphasizes the significance of that location.

Some units of Germanic troops were transferred from the Lower Rhine to serve on Hadrian's Wall during the same period. They brought their family groups with them and also, of course, their gods. The soldiers needed some home comforts, so they brought their own pottery. Thus, a new style emerged on Hadrian's Wall, now known as 'Housesteads ware'. It is found mostly at Housesteads but some reached Birdoswald.

The Gallic Empire

In AD 260 Marcus Cassianius Latinius Postumus, a successful general and the governor of Lower Germany, set himself up as Emperor.[43] The provinces in Germany, Gaul, Britain and Spain fell under his control, but the rest of the Empire did not. For a period of thirteen years one section of the Empire was effectively hived off. It was known as the 'Gallic Empire' and administered in an entirely Roman fashion. There were consuls elected each year, subordinate officials, a senate and even a Praetorian Guard to protect the Gallic Emperor. The provincial governors in Germany, Gaul, Britain and Spain were appointed by and reported to the Gallic Emperor. Postumus ruled the Gallic Empire from 260 until his death in 269. After Postumus the second Gallic Emperor was Victorinus, who reigned from 269 until his murder in 271. The third and final Gallic Emperor was Gaius Pius Esuvius Tetricus, formerly governor of Aquitania.

In AD 273 the Roman Emperor Lucius Domitius Aurelianus ('Aurelian') arrived in Gaul with a formidable army.[44] Tetricus submitted to Aurelian and his life was spared. The Gallic

---

[40] Cool and Mason (2008). There is conflicting evidence as to the date of the rebuilding. It may have been during the Gallic Empire: Casey (1994) 143–4.
[41] RIB 1021–6 and 3253–8.
[42] 'pro salute vexillationum legionis VI Victricis et exercitus Germaniae utriusque': RIB 3253.
[43] Eutropius provides a brief account of the Gallic Empire: *Breviarium ab Urbe Condita* 9.9–10.
[44] Eutropius, *Breviarium ab Urbe Condita* 9.13.

Empire was absorbed back into the main Roman Empire. There appear to have been no reprisals against the errant provinces. Tetricus went on to become governor of southern Italy.

The governors of the two British provinces and the troops that they commanded did not play an active part in the events unfolding on the Continent. In AD 260 Britannia Superior and Britannia Inferior became part of the Gallic Empire. Realistically there was no alternative course. The names of the Gallic Emperors appear on several milestones, which survive from this period. In 273, following the surrender of Tetricus, Britannia Superior and Inferior reverted to their former status as provinces of the Roman Empire. Britain's entry into the Gallic Empire and subsequent exit probably had little, if any, impact on the way the country was run. The average Briton would have noticed no difference, except that there were new faces on the coins.

The province generally

Probus served as Emperor from AD 276 to 282. According to the *Historia Augusta* he granted Gaul, Spain and Britain permission to cultivate vines and make wine.[45] Although Gaul and Spain have an excellent climate for viticulture, it must be doubted whether Roman Britain had much success as a wine producer. There were probably a few vineyards in the south.

Archaeobotany involves analysing carbonized plant assemblages and faecal remains.[46] Archaeobotanists have built up a picture of what Romano-Britons were growing and what they were eating in the third century. Crops included wheat, barley, peas and beans. Vegetables such as turnips, carrots, cabbages and leeks were probably grown in gardens, because they needed more intensive cultivation and weeding. If you could step back in time and visit Roman Britain in the spring, you would see the colourful blossoms of apple, pear, cherry, plum, damson and walnut trees. People often say that 'the Romans introduced' this plant or that. While such comments may brighten up a dull cocktail party, we do not really know if they are true. There is little information about what Britons were growing in the Iron Age. Certainly, crab apples are native to Britain. But as to most of the other vegetables and crops, the most we can say is that if they were not already here, then the Romans brought them over. Sweet chestnut trees may have arrived here during the Roman period, but the evidence for this is uncertain.[47]

The panegyrics delivered at the end of the third century enthuse about Britain's fertility. The panegyric delivered to Constantius at Trier in 297 speaks of Britain as 'a land so abundant in crops, so rich in its numerous pastures'.[48] The panegyric delivered to Constantine at Trier in 310 is even more ecstatic and at one point addresses Britannia herself:

> Justly has Nature given you all the good things of heaven and earth; a land in which neither the winters are too cold, nor the summers too hot; in which there is such fertility as to supply the gifts of both Ceres and Bacchus.[49]

---

[45]'Gallis omnibus et Hispanis ac Britannis hinc permisit, ut vites haberent vinumque conficerent.' *Probus* 18.8.
[46]Van der Veen et al. (2007).
[47]Jarman et al., 'Sweet chestnut (*castanea sativa* Mill.) in Britain: re-assessment of its status as a Roman archaeophyte', *Britannia* 50 (2019) 49–74.
[48]'tanto frugum ubere, tanto laeta numero pastionum:' *Panegyrici Latini* 8 (5), 11.1.
[49]'Merito te omnibus caeli ac soli bonis Natura donavit, in qua nec rigor est nimius hiemis nec ardor aestatis, in qua segetum tanta fecunditas ut muneribus utrisque sufficiat et Cereris et Liberi' *Panegyrici Latini* 6 (7), 9.2.

The panegyric goes on to extol the peaceful herds of cows bursting with milk and the tranquil flocks of sheep laden with fleeces.

These and similar passages must have been gratifying to the Emperor, as he took his ease with an amphora of (Gallic) wine at his side. But they hardly reflect the harsh reality of agricultural life in Roman Britain. Nor do they mention that there was some grain loss in Britain due to infestation with pests, which the Romans had unwittingly introduced.[50] The province may have been self-sufficient in food by the third century but there is no evidence that it was exporting surplus produce to the Continent at this stage. The only recorded instance of that happening was in the mid-fourth century, as discussed in Chapter 15 below.

At some point in the third century the *classis Britannica* ceased to exist. The fort used by the fleet at Dover was abandoned in about AD 210.[51] The latest mention of the fleet was in the 240s. We do not know how long the fleet continued after that, nor do we know how it came to an end. Possibly the fleet was disbanded. Possibly it simply dwindled and then fell apart. Alternatively, the Romans may have divided the ships up and sent them to different ports. The disappearance of the fleet was probably linked to the development of the shore forts.

The disbanding of the fleet was a defence cut, which probably caused much grumbling. After the fleet had disappeared, there was a marked growth of piracy in the North Sea and other waters around Britain.[52] In particular, Franks and Saxons were 'infesting' the Channel between Britain and Gaul[53] and raiding the coasts on both sides.

3. THE TETRARCHY

In AD 283 the Emperor Marcus Aurelius Carus died while campaigning in Persia. His son, Numerianus, was proclaimed Emperor by the troops, but soon afterwards was murdered. By now many in the Empire were despairing because of the chaos that had surrounded the centre of government for so long. There was a yearning for effective administration and for restoration of the stability which Rome and her provinces had enjoyed in earlier centuries. It was against this background that in November 284 a group of army officers in Bithynia took the momentous decision to propose one of their number, Diocletian,[54] as Emperor. Diocletian was proclaimed Augustus by the troops. In AD 285 he defeated the forces of Carinus, the Emperor in the west, and emerged supreme.

Diocletian did not cling to his position as sole Emperor for long. He recognized that, given the size of the Empire and the scale of the threats along its frontiers, the job of emperor was too big for one man. In AD 285 he appointed Maximian[55] as his Caesar. Diocletian entrusted to Maximian the defence and administration of the Western Empire, including Britain. As Augustus, Diocletian was the senior Emperor and he dealt with the defence and administration

---

[50] Smith and Kenward (2011) 243–62.
[51] Millett (2007) 179; Philp (1981) chapter 4.
[52] Casey (1994) 153.
[53] 'quod Franci et Saxones infestabant': Eutropius, *Breviarium ab Urbe Condita* 9.21.
[54] His original name was Valerius Diocles. His full name became Gaius Aurelius Valerius Diocletianus.
[55] Marcus Aurelius Valerius Maximianus.

of the Eastern Empire. In AD 286 Diocletian promoted Maximian to the rank of Augustus, but it was still recognized that Diocletian was the senior Emperor and took precedence. In AD 293 Diocletian appointed two Caesars, namely Constantius[56] and Gaius Galerius. Constantius was assigned to the Western Empire, Galerius to the Eastern Empire. Constantius and Galerius were junior partners in the imperial college. This system of government was known as the 'Tetrarchy'. Working together Diocletian, Maximian, Constantius and Galerius ruled the Empire for twelve years.

The establishment of the Tetrarchy marked a major shift in the evolution of the Empire. The period up until AD 284 is known as the Principate. The period after the accession of Diocletian in 284 is generally referred to as the later Roman Empire or Late Antiquity. Rome became less important, as centres of power spread outwards.

The Tetrarchy proved a highly effective form of government in the early years. The four Tetrarchs concentrated on their own assigned areas, but assisted one another as and when necessary. Collectively the Tetrarchs warded off many hostile attacks upon the frontiers of the Empire, for example from the Persians in the East and from Germanic peoples along the Rhine. The Tetrarchs also dealt effectively with rebellions. These included a rebellion in Egypt and – more relevantly – a rebellion in Britain. Economic policy proved more challenging: Diocletian's attempt to control prices was not a success.[57] Overall, however, the twenty years of Diocletian's reign must have been a welcome period of stability after the turbulence of the previous century.

4. THE SHORE FORTS

Progressively through the third century, a line of forts appeared along the coasts on both sides of the English Channel. In northern Gaul and the Rhineland, a military-style identity assumed growing importance. Military installations and paraphernalia dominate the archaeology of the third century. Several forts were established in Wales, including one at Cardiff and one at Caer Gybi (Holyhead) with a fortified landing place.[58]

At least eleven stone forts appeared around the coastline of south-east England,[59] which became known as the 'Saxon Shore'. The forts were built progressively between about AD 200 and 300. The original purpose of the forts is much disputed. The traditional view was that they formed a front-line defence against Saxon raiders and other pirates. Some commentators now say that the original purpose of the forts is obscure, but later they came in handy as a defence against Saxon invaders. This is not a convincing analysis. The purpose of the shore forts must always have been defence against sea-borne attacks. For an account of the individual shore forts and their dates of construction, see the Online Appendix.

Although the architectural design varied from fort to fort, the method of construction was generally uniform. First, the builders dug out and filled the foundation trenches with appropriate materials. For example, at Reculver they used small flint cobbles; but at Pevensey they laid

---

[56]Flavius Valerius Constantius, also known as Constantius Chlorus.
[57]Du Plessis et al. (2016) 48–9 and 617–18.
[58]Nash-Williams and Garrett (1969) 27–8.
[59]For an excellent account of the forts and their history, see Pearson (2010).

successive layers of flint and chalk at depth, which they rammed into place. The Romans showed good understanding of the principles of foundation engineering, unlike some modern contractors. They then built the inner and outer faces of the wall with small stones or flint blocks. They filled the cavity between the two faces with rubble and mortar. Once the wall was above standing height, they worked from scaffolding set into small holes in the wall (putlogs).

Since the forts were military installations, the army must have played a major part in the construction. That required re-deployment of troops from the north of Britain to the south. Stamped tiles of the First Cohort of the Baetasii have been found at Reculver and stamped tiles of the First Cohort of the Aquitani at Brancaster. Both those units had previously been serving on Hadrian's Wall. The sheer scale of the fort-building operation means that there must have been much civilian labour as well, under military supervision.

So far as possible the builders used local materials. At Lympne they used limestone from quarries a few hundred metres away. When materials came from further afield, such as Kentish ragstone, the usual method of transport was by water, for the obvious reason that all the shore forts were by the sea. The *classis Britannica* may have been involved in transport operations for the earlier forts. Re-used building materials were also an important resource. For example, re-used tiles can be seen in the west wall of the fort at Reculver. It has been estimated that the whole shore-fort operation required 6,570 boatloads and 51,750 cartloads of materials.[60]

After the Second Legion Augusta had spent 200 years at Caerleon, it was time to move on. In either the late third century or in the fourth century they moved to Kent and made the new fort at Richborough their headquarters.[61] By then the legionary soldiers had no connection with Rome. The soldiers of the Second Legion Augusta were simply men who had grown up in south Wales and joined the army. Many had wives and children. The relocation of the entire legion to Kent must have been an upheaval for the families, although familiar to army wives of every age.

The *Notitia* tells us who was garrisoning each of the shore forts in the late fourth century, but there is no record of who was there in the third century. If the First Cohort of the Baetasii were involved in building the fort at Reculver, as suggested above, then they probably formed the first garrison in that fort. We know from the *Notitia* that the same Baetasii, or more probably their great-great-great-grandsons, were there in the late fourth century. Such was the level of job security in Roman Britain.

By a similar process of inference the First Cohort of the Aquitani may have formed the initial garrison of the fort at Brancaster. But they had moved on by the time that the *Notitia* came to be written. Overall, we know little about the occupants of any of the shore forts. Unlike the troops at Vindolanda, they have not left behind any caches of correspondence.

Obviously the first duty of the garrisons was to ward off invaders and raiders. Finds of spear heads, crossbow brooches and similar artefacts show that there was plenty of military activity on site. But on days when there was no invading or raiding (and there must have been many such days) what else did they do, apart from training? First, the forts probably functioned as ports. That must have generated all the usual quayside activities such as unloading and storing. Second, there seems to have been a fair amount of industrial activity both inside and outside

---

[60] Pearson (2010) 84–5.
[61] Millett (2007) 143.

the forts. This included bone and antler working, animal butchery and meat processing. The forts close to the Fens may have become large-scale meat processing centres.

Many of the shore forts had adjoining civilian settlements. They were probably not traditional *vici*, of the kind that grew up around inland forts. The shore forts generally stood close to harbours and ports, where civilian settlements were likely to exist in any event. These would have served the needs of sailors and traders passing through. The settlements would have expanded when the shore forts came, but they would not have been mere appendages to the military. Brancaster had the largest settlement. Extensive enclosures around the fort have been traced and much Samian pottery has come to light. Other forts on the east coast had substantial settlements, especially Burgh Castle. That is hardly surprising. If soldiers were going to stay in the same place for a century or more, and face repeated attacks from pirates, they were entitled to some home comforts.

One puzzle for historians is: who was the 'Count of the Saxon Shore' and when did he first come into existence. The first appearance of the phrase in any surviving document is in the *Notitia Dignitatum*. The *Notitia* reveals that during the fourth century there was an established post known as *Comes Litoris Saxonici*, which is generally translated as 'Count of the Saxon Shore'. The next question concerns the phrase 'Saxon Shore'. Does this mean (a) coastal areas that Saxons were attacking or (b) coastal areas in which Saxons had settled? It would be highly unusual for the Romans to name a frontier region after its attackers. On the other hand, there is no evidence of substantial Saxon settlement in Britain by the fourth century. The conclusion must be that the 'Saxon Shore' comprised coastal areas that were the subject of raids by Saxons.

According to chapter 28 of the *Notitia*, the commanding officers of nine out of the eleven shore forts were 'under the command of the Count of the Saxon Shore'.[62] It appears from chapters 37 and 38 of the *Notitia* that initially the Count also commanded the defence of the north coast of Gaul against raids by Saxons and others. In other words, he had a cross-Channel role. Subsequently his command was limited to the British coasts.[63]

It is not easy to say when the Count of the Saxon Shore first came into existence. Possibly this office was created as part of the massive military reorganization at the end of the third century. By then the full suite of shore forts was in existence. On the other hand, all that we can glean from the *Notitia* is that the office existed by about 390. It may be, therefore, that the office of Count of the Saxon Shore was created during the course of the fourth century. Whenever this official came into existence, he would have co-ordinated the operations of the shore forts. His prime function was to see off Saxon invaders and other unwelcome visitors.

There were probably other shore forts in addition to the eleven identifed above, but we do not know much about them. The Roman fort at Cardiff (which now lies underneath a Norman castle) was probably part of the original coastal defence system. It protected the Severn Estuary and was of similar design to the other shore forts discussed above. Interestingly, there is no reference to the Cardiff fort in the *Notitia Dignitatum*. It is possible that when the *Notitia* was compiled the 'card' for Wales had been lost or there was a copying error. Alternatively, by that

---

[62]'Sub dispositione viri spectabilis Comitis Litoris Saxonici per Britanniam'.
[63]See 'Channel Commands in the Notitia' by Stephen Johnson, at pages 81–102 of *Aspects of the Notitia Dignitatum*, Papers presented to the Oxford Conference, December 13–15, 1974: British Archaeological Reports, Supplementary Series 15, 1976.

time Wales may have been demilitarized; hence there is no reference to the Cardiff fort as being within the 'Saxon Shore' jurisdiction.

The obvious conclusion is that all the shore forts were built as defences against seaborne attacks. They developed piecemeal in response to a growing problem, rather than as the result of a single strategic decision. Nevertheless, the shore forts all had a common purpose. The similar methods of construction support this interpretation. By the end of the third century the forts formed a coherent defence system.

5. THE USURPATION OF CARAUSIUS AND ALLECTUS

Aurelius Victor and Eutropius (both writing in the fourth century and apparently using the same source) tell the story of the usurpation briefly:[64] Maximian instructed Carausius, a skilled naval commander, to assemble a fleet at Boulogne and deal with pirates. Carausius set to work and killed many of the 'barbarians'. He intercepted several pirate raids and seized the property that they had stolen. Unfortunately, he kept much of the booty for himself, instead of handing it over to the Roman treasury. Maximian was not amused. He ordered Carausius' execution. Carausius hastily crossed to Britain and established himself as Emperor of the two British provinces. Carausius appointed Allectus as his chief minister of finance.[65] After six or seven years Allectus murdered Carausius and made himself Emperor. Three years later Constantius sent Asclepiodotus, the praetorian prefect, who killed Allectus and ended the usurpation.

There is clearly quite a complicated story, which spans some nine or ten years. Further details can be gleaned from coinage and archaeology. Three panegyrics also shed some light on events, namely the panegyrics delivered to Maximian in AD 289, to Constantius in 297 and to Constantine in 310.

Carausius came from Menapia, now northern Belgium. His full name was Marcus Aurelius Mausaeus Carausius. The names Marcus Aurelius were popular in the third century, because Caracalla (Marcus Aurelius Antoninus) had granted Roman citizenship to everyone within the Empire. Apparently Carausius was 'of very humble origin',[66] but he probably couldn't help that. Alternatively, the reference to his 'humble origin' may be a literary device, in order to magnify his later achievements. Carausius became an experienced helmsman and distinguished himself in war.

Saint Jerome's *Chronicle* ascribes the usurpation to the fourth year of Diocletian, namely September 287 to September 288. The saint was writing a century later and dates were not his strong point. Coinage suggests 286. The best we can say is that the usurpation was in either 286 or 287. According to the panegyric of 297, Carausius recruited both legionary and auxiliary troops to his cause. He built a new fleet and trained the sailors. Gallic merchants also provided support.

Carausius asserted dominion over Britain and much of northern Gaul. His coins commemorated several legions based on the Continent. These included I Minerva at Bonn,

---

[64] Aurelius Victor, *De Caesaribus* 39; Eutropius, *Breviarium ab Urbe Condita* 9.21.
[65] Aurelius Victor states 'summae rei praeesset'. 'Summa res' was a financial department of state in the second and third centuries.
[66] Eutropius says Carausius was 'vilissime natus'.

VIII Augusta at Strasbourg, XXII Primigenia at Mainz and XXX Ulpia Victrix on the northern Rhine. It is clear that the provincial officials and the legions stationed in those provinces accepted Carausius' authority. He must have been a remarkable and charismatic individual to spring up through the ranks and attract such widespread support.

Carausius made London his capital. According to Aurelius Victor, he proved to be a competent administrator. The governors of Britannia Superior and Britannia Inferior reported to him and were subject to his general oversight. This was neither a 'rebellion' nor a nationalist uprising. It did not involve a provincial governor trying to take over the Empire, as Albinus had done a century earlier. It was simply the case of a senior Roman officer setting himself up as a mini-emperor in one segment of the Empire.

There were precedents for what Carausius was doing. In AD 260 Postumus had established the Gallic Empire, which lasted for thirteen years. In AD 269 Queen Zenobia did much the same in Syria. She had led an uprising against the Roman authorities and established herself as head of the Palmyrene Empire, which included both Syria and Egypt. Zenobia ruled this section of the Empire until AD 274, when she was defeated and taken as a hostage to Rome. Carausius was following the examples set by Postumus and Zenobia. He was not challenging the authority of the Tetrarchic Emperors, but rather seeking to align himself with them.

Carausius ruled as mini-emperor from AD 286 or 287 until his assassination in 293. According to Eutropius, he was highly skilled in military matters. He certainly needed to be. The coasts were under attack from marauders and the armed forces of the Western Empire were preparing for a full scale invasion. Carausius organized ship-building.[67] He maintained and extended the system of shore forts previously discussed. He probably built the fort at Portchester. Carausius appears to have reduced the strength of the garrisons on Hadrian's Wall and concentrated more of his troops in southern Britain.[68] There were several reasons for this. First, the raiders were most active around the south and east coasts. Second, Carausius must have anticipated an attack by Maximian across the Channel. Third, given the extent of his Continental domains, London and the south-east of Britain lay at the centre of his mini-empire.

In the late third century fine town walls went up around Canterbury.[69] These may been defensive or they may have been a civic gesture. Garrisons at the four shore forts in Kent would have brought much prosperity to the area. Canterbury had roads leading directly to Lympne, Dover, Reculver and Richborough. The town may have become a 'rest and recreation' centre for troops based at those forts. Parts of the Roman defences still stand. They are most obvious at Northgate where they form part of St Mary's church wall.

A single milestone of Carausius' era survives.[70] The inscription reads: 'For the Emperor Caesar Marcus Aurelius Mausaeus Carausius Pius Felix Invictus Augustus' All public references to Carausius were banned after the end of his usurpation. So obviously that milestone had to go. On the other hand it was a shame to waste a good piece of sandstone, which had already been cut to size. So an enterprising stonemason simply turned it upside down and carved a dedication to Constantine I at the other end. He then stuck it back in the ground, duly burying

---

[67] Casey (1994) 149.
[68] Casey (1994) 104.
[69] Casey (1994) 126.
[70] RIB 2291: 'Imperatori Caesari Marco Aurelio Mausaeo Carausio Pio Felici Invicto Augusto'.

the dedication to Carausius. That ruse was successful at the time. But our cheating stonemason did not get away with it for ever. In 1894 the milestone was found in a river bed at Gallows Hill, near Carlisle. The milestone now stands in Tullie House Museum, with the prohibited inscription clearly visible.

In order to secure his position Carausius needed to pay the troops. He therefore resorted to minting his own money or, in modern parlance 'quantitative easing'. Carausius also introduced a system of mintmarks.[71] These reveal that he had mints at Rouen (*Rotomagus*) and London. There was also a 'C' mint, probably at Colchester. Some coins have no mintmark. These could have come from a separate 'unmarked' mint or they may be early coins before the introduction of mintmarks. The London mint was the most productive. It continued in operation until the time of Constantine.

The idea of mintmarks was a good one. It makes life much easier for historians. Later Roman emperors copied the idea shamelessly. Carausius would have been gratified to learn that his system of mintmarks became standard practice across the Empire. Unfortunately, he was assassinated before anyone could tell him.

Carausius struck coins struck in gold, silver, billon (bronze/silver alloy), bronze and copper. The normal practice of the Roman authorities was to recover gold, silver and other coins through taxation, to melt them down and then re-use the metal to mint fresh coinage. Carausius probably followed that practice. He may also have recycled some of the silver plate and other precious metals that he had seized from pirates. It was Carausius' failure to hand in those treasures that had caused the original rift with Rome. Another possibility is that Carausius exploited the gold mines at Dolaucothi, the copper mines in Anglesey and the silver mines in Wales if those mines were still in operation.

Burying coin hoards became prevalent in the late third century. At first sight, this seems odd because the late third century was a relatively tranquil period in Britain. In some cases, people may have been burying coins, simply because they had ceased to be legal tender.[72] In all about six hundred hoards from the period have come to light. A huge hoard found at Frome, Somerset in April 2010 contains over 700 coins issued by Carausius.[73]

Carausius' coinage served two vital purposes. First, it stimulated economic activity. The soldiers received donatives in addition to their regular salaries. Their spending power boosted the local economy, especially in southern Britain. Second, coinage was a medium of mass communication, indeed the only such medium. Coins circulated freely and everyone saw what was written on them. Coinage was the internet of the ancient world.

Carausius' coinage

Carausius' coins portray him as someone who has saved Britain, presumably by warding off pirate attacks and by efficient administration. On some Carausius included lofty quotations from Virgil, usually with reference to himself, such as 'expectate veni' ('come expected one'). One of Carausius' medallions bears the letters INPCDA, standing for:

---

[71] Casey (1994) chapter 6.
[72] Bland (2018) 61–2.
[73] Described in Moorhead et al. (2010).

'Iam nova progenies caelo demittitur alto' – a quotation from Virgil's *Eclogues* meaning: 'Now a new progeny is sent down from high heaven.'

Many coins are inscribed 'RSR', which may stand for 'redeunt Saturnia regna' – an earlier line from the Eclogues, meaning that the reign of Saturn is returning, i.e. the good times are coming back. Carausius was clearly well read and determined to emphasize his own importance in the grand scheme of things.

Peace, stability and prosperity are a recurrent theme. Carausius' silver coinage indicated a new level of monetary prosperity. Many of the coins minted at London or Colchester bear the legend 'pax Aug' – 'the peace of Augustus'. Another legend, 'Concordia Aug' is to the same effect. There are also references to 'felicitas Aug' (good fortune) and 'ubertas' (plenty). In summary, Carausius thought that both he and his government were marvellous, and he did not beat about the bush in saying so.

Carausius' currency emphasizes both the legitimacy of his regime and its continuity with the past. One coin shows Romulus and Remus suckling beneath a wolf, with Carausius' portrait on the other side. That links Carausius directly with the foundation of Rome. On occasions he is described as *renovator Romanorum*, meaning restorer of the Romans. For good measure Carausius appointed himself consul three times and celebrated that honour on his coinage. There are also references to Carausius' *adventus*. The *adventus* was a formal ceremony celebrated when a new Emperor arrived. On some coins the abbreviation 'AUGGG' appears: that denoted Carausius as one of three equal Augusti, with Diocletian and Maximian being his brothers. Sadly, the two 'brothers' did not take quite the same fraternal view.

In about AD 289 Maximian launched a most unbrotherly attack on Britain. His object was to overthrow Carausius and bring Britain back under the control of the western Emperor. Little is known about this ineffective campaign, apart from brief references in the panegyrics. Unsurprisingly the panegyrists did not dwell on the Emperor's military disasters. We are lucky that this matter was mentioned at all. The panegyric of AD 289 makes it clear that an invasion of Britain has been planned in detail. The next panegyric, delivered in AD 291, says nothing at all about the campaign – a sure sign that things went badly wrong. The panegyric of AD 297, in a brief reference, says that the sea was 'difficult'. Perhaps the Imperial fleet came second in a sea battle with Carausius. We simply do not know what happened and the Romans are not going to tell us.

The British coinage that followed the defeat of Maximian repeatedly portrayed Carausius as one of the three legitimate Emperors. 'AUGGG' appeared frequently. Some aureii were even issued in Maximian's name alone. One famous coin shows the heads of Diocletian, Maximian and Carausius together. The inscription reads 'Carausius et fratres sui', meaning Carausius and his brothers. Probably these coins were part of a diplomatic overture. Carausius was a vain man who craved official recognition. The 'triple Emperor' coins stopped abruptly when Constantius was appointed Caesar in AD 293.

The first task of Constantius, upon his appointment as Caesar in AD 293, was to deal with Carausius. He began by invading northern Gaul, which he quickly recovered and reintegrated into the Roman Empire. According to the panegyric of AD 310, Constantius captured Boulogne

Figure 13.1 Coin showing Carausius with his two 'brothers' RIC 1[mdc]. © Wildwinds.

(*Bononia*) after blockading it by land and sea.[74] Having regained Gaul, Constantius paused before launching an attack against Britain. This would be a formidable operation, involving both the navy and the army.

It is not unknown for heads of government to fall out with their finance ministers. Geoffrey Howe stabbed Margaret Thatcher in the back, but only metaphorically. Thatcher has ruefully described 'the very brilliance with which he wielded the dagger'. Relations between Tony Blair and Gordon Brown were hardly more cordial.[75] Things were no different in AD 293. In the words of the panegyrist, Allectus killed the 'archpirate' thinking that imperial power would be his reward.[76] He then stepped into Carausius' shoes and proclaimed himself Emperor of Britain.

The transition of power seems to have been a smooth one, apart from the minor detail that Allectus murdered his predecessor. Allectus continued the form of government that had been established by Carausius.

The London and Colchester mints continued to function smoothly. The mints issued coins in the same style as before, except that they now depicted Allectus, not Carausius. The busts of both usurpers faced left, which was unusual in the ancient world. Allectus' coins included phrases such as 'Pax Aug', 'Providentia Aug' and even 'Hilaritas Aug' (a reference to the Hilaria festival). The distribution of his coins in Gaul was just as wide as the distribution of Carausius' coins, but it is unclear whether he had any presence in Gaul after the fall of Boulogne.[77] Allectus introduced a new coin, the quinarius. He appointed himself consul and proudly recorded his consulship on the billon coinage. In a nutshell, Allectus was just as pleased with himself as the late Carausius.

Allectus seems to have carried on with Carausius' building programme. Work continued on the shore forts. The southern defences of the York fortress were rebuilt to include towers. In London, as discussed in Chapter 17 below, Allectus may have been responsible for a monumental building, which was erected during the early 290s. Some archaeologists suggest that this was intended to be a sumptuous palace for the rebel Emperor, but that is unlikely. The building may have been a sanctuary and temple complex.

Allectus continued Carausius' policy of redeploying troops towards the south. He made substantial withdrawals of soldiers from the northern frontier. He also withdrew some garrisons

---

[74]*Panegyrici Latini* 6 (7), 5.2.
[75]Thatcher (1993) 839–40; Blair (2010) chapter 16.
[76]'archpiratam satelles occideret et illud auctoramentum tanti discriminis putaret imperium.' *Panegyrici Latini* 8 (5), 12.2.
[77]Casey (1994) 129–33.

from forts in the Pennines.[78] The top priority in the 280s and 290s was to meet any invasion that may come from the Continent.

Allectus had several fleets,[79] which he may have allocated as tactical units to individual shore forts. He continued Carausius' ship-building policy. The coins of both usurpers proudly display their ships. These were frame-constructed in the Celtic style, unlike Mediterranean ships which were built on the shell principle. The English Channel and the North Sea were a harsher environment than the warm Mediterranean basin.

Hadrian's Wall may have been allowed to deteriorate during this period. An inscription records that buildings inside Birdoswald fort were 'covered in earth and fell into ruin'.[80] This event must have occurred (if it did occur) in the last years of the century, because a cohort of Dacians had erected an altar to Jupiter at Birdoswald in AD 270–273, when presumably that fort was still a going concern. There is a need for caution about the Birdoswald inscription. First, it was a convention to say that 'bad' emperors let buildings decay and 'good' emperors restored them. Second, the Birdoswald inscription was part of a dedication slab, which commemorated the later restoration of the fort by one Aurelius Arpagius. Such inscriptions often tended to exaggerate the extent of the previous disrepair.[81] The classic example of this tendency is a rebuilding inscription of AD 202 on the Pantheon in Rome, which grossly exaggerated the extent of the restoration works. In general, however, rebuilding inscriptions were embellishments of the truth, rather than downright lies.[82] So there must have been some dilapidation at Birdoswald fort, but perhaps things were not quite as bad as Arpagius would have us believe.

In AD 296, after three years of careful planning and preparation, Constantius launched his invasion of Britain.[83] Asclepiodotus, the praetorian prefect, leading an expeditionary force crossed to Britain from the River Seine. He joined battle with Allectus' army and soundly defeated the rebels. Allectus was killed in the conflict. Constantius followed from Boulogne, leading a second expeditionary force: he sailed up the Thames and rapidly crushed the garrison in London. Constantius had little difficulty in reinstating Roman rule and bringing Britain back under the control of the 'official' Emperors. This glorious victory clearly called for a special issue of commemorative coins.

Some of those commemorative coins unexpectedly turned up in 1922.[84] Workmen in clay pits at Arras in northern France found a glittering hoard of Roman jewellery, silverware and coins. Disputes over ownership gave rise to much litigation and were hugely profitable for the legal profession of the 1920s. Ultimately a variety of museums, including the Ashmolean and the British Museum, acquired the treasures.[85] The most famous item in the hoard is the so-called 'Arras Medallion', a 10 aurei coin. This shows Constantius riding proudly into London.

---

[78]Jones (1981); Casey (1994) 136.
[79]Casey (1994) 144–54. A fourth century mosaic at Lower Ham villa shows one of these ships.
[80]'humo copertum et in labem conlapsum': RIB 1912. Jones (1981) has reservations about this evidence: see 399.
[81]Thomas and Witschel (1992), 135–78.
[82]Fagan (1996).
[83]The main sources for the re-conquest are Aurelius Victor, *De Caesaribus* 39, Eutropius, *Breviarium ab Urbe Condita* 9.22 and the panegyric delivered to Constantius at Trier in 297.
[84]Abdy (2006).
[85]Bastien and Metzger have produced the definitive catalogue, *Le trésor de Beaurains (dit d'Arras)*. The famous 'Arras medallion' is item 28. The two 5 aurei medallions are item 221.

Figure 13.2 The Arras Medallion. © The Trustees of the British Museum.

The horse seems to be trotting. A grateful citizen, representing all the citizenry of the city, kneels in front of the mighty Emperor to greet him. Beneath Constantius' horse is a picture of a Roman warship, presumably crossing the Channel. Two other medallions in the hoard, each 5 aurei, portray Constantius raising Britannia from her knees. These medallions were part of a well-managed PR exercise. The authorities were careful to portray recent events as the liberation of Britain from usurpers, rather than a Roman conquest.

The panegyric delivered to Constantius in AD 297 was part of that exercise. It emphasized that only ringleaders of the conspiracy and barbarian mercenaries were killed in the course of the operation. There is no reference to the killing of Roman soldiers who were serving under Allectus, although that must have happened. The panegyric states that the British people were delighted by the arrival of Constantius. Apparently, the Britons shouted for joy, pledging that they and their descendants would support the Emperor for ever more.[86]

The Roman authorities (like the usurpers whom they had recently crushed) were manipulating the media for their own ends.

---

[86]*Panegyrici Latini* 8 (5), 19.

CHAPTER 14
THE EMPEROR CONSTANTINE LAUNCHES HIS CAREER IN BRITAIN

1. Britain at the beginning of the fourth century
2. The momentous events of AD 305–306 and their aftermath
3. Britain during the reign of Constantine
    (i) Military control
    (ii) Civil administration of the four British provinces
    (iii) Urbanism and local government
    (iv) Villa culture
    (v) Social and religious life

The fourth century was a watershed. Rome ceased to be capital of the Roman Empire. Byzantium became the top city and, in effect, the centre of a new Empire that would last for a thousand years. Christianity emerged from the shadows and became a major world religion, which it still is. These developments had a profound effect on Britain. This chapter, therefore, will deal with events on the wider stage as well as in Britain.

1. BRITAIN AT THE BEGINNING OF THE FOURTH CENTURY

There was extensive construction activity at the beginning of the fourth century. Much of this work was along Hadrian's Wall and at forts in the north,[1] including Wallsend (*Segedunum*).[2] There is also evidence of building work at the legionary bases in York and Chester at about this time. Some archaeologists say that this was a period of 'restoration', but the label is unimportant. It may be that the authorities were simply catching up with outstanding maintenance and repairs after the turbulent years of Carausius and Allectus.

It is probable that Constantius instigated the programme of works. After all, he was 'Caesar' and had the power to make things happen. It was important to get everyone working together during Britain's reintegration into the Roman Empire.

---

[1] Casey (1994) 145–6.
[2] Bidwell (2018) 101–5.

At about the beginning of the fourth century, there was a restructuring of provinces across the entire Empire, to reduce their size. As part of that exercise Britain was divided into four provinces. They were:

- *Maxima Caesariensis* – South-East Britain
- *Britannia Prima* – South-West Britain and Wales
- *Britannia Secunda* – Midlands
- *Flavia Caesariensis* – the North.

We cannot date the restructuring precisely, but all four provinces are included in the Verona List, which means that the sub-division of Britain must have occurred before AD 314.[3] It is quite possible that the administrative reforms followed the re-conquest of Britain by Constantius in AD 296.[4] This may have been part of an operation to re-assert Roman authority in a troublesome part of the Empire. The northern province *Flavia Caesariensis* was clearly named after Constantius (whose first name was Flavius).

The governor of each new province was responsible for civil administration.[5] The four British provinces together formed a diocese, headed by a *vicarius*. The *vicarius* reported to and took his orders from the praetorian prefect in Gaul.[6] *Vicarius* literally means 'vicar', but that office has changed greatly over time. A vicar nowadays does not rule the whole of Britain, nor does he or she have powers of summary punishment. The conventional translation of *vicarius* is 'deputy'.

This was the biggest restructuring of Britain since Caracalla had divided the territory into two provinces in around AD 212. The Britons could count themselves lucky that they only underwent local government reorganizations once a century.

2. THE MOMENTOUS EVENTS OF AD 305–306 AND THEIR AFTERMATH

In AD 305 there were two events of great moment for the Roman Empire. The first was the abdication of Diocletian and Maximinian. The second was Constantius' campaign in Britain accompanied by his son Constantine, the future Emperor.

On 1 May 305 Diocletian and Maximian both retired from their positions as 'Augusti': Diocletian abdicated willingly, Maximian less so. This brought the first Tetrarchy to an end. After 21 years at the head of government Diocletian was ready for some 'me time'. He went off to live in a vast palace at Split with colonnades, quadrangles, halls and gardens overlooking the azure Adriatic Sea. That was quite some retirement home. Even now – seventeen centuries later – much of Diocletian's palace still stands. It is occupied by offices, shops, restaurants, banks, hotels and a souvenirs arcade.

---

[3] Hassall (1996) 24.
[4] Casey (1994) 149.
[5] The new administrative arrangements were recorded in the *Notitia Dignitatum*, which underwent periodic amendments during the fourth century. Hence the *Notitia* includes an additional province, which was added later.
[6] Zosimus, *Historia Historia* 2.33.

In accordance with the new constitutional arrangements, the two former 'Caesars', Constantius and Galerius, ascended to the rank of 'Augusti'. Thus Constantius[7] became the senior Emperor responsible for the Western Empire. Galerius became the senior Emperor responsible for the Eastern Empire. The first task of the new Augusti was to appoint their junior colleagues. They selected Galerius Valerius Maximinus (assigned to the East) and Flavius Valerius Severus (assigned to the West). The two new Caesars did not last long, since the sons of Constantius and Maximian both had their eyes on the top jobs.

Constantius set off for Britain. The details of his campaign in Britain are not important (which is just as well, as we don't know them). What is important is that Constantius' eldest son, Constantine, came over and a few months later succeeded his father as Emperor

Constantine is one of the giants of antiquity, who reconfigured the Roman Empire and left a lasting imprint on both the medieval and modern world. For a summary of our sources and an account of his journey to Britain, see the Online Appendix.

According to a panegyric delivered four years later both Constantius and Constantine were engaged in warfare against 'the Caledonians and other Picts'.[8] This suggests that they penetrated deep into Scotland. Apparently, they won numerous victories during AD 305 and 306, but failed to annexe that territory as a province. Constantius took the title *Britannicus Maximus*. Whether he earned the title is more doubtful. It is a recurrent feature of Romano-British history that great generals campaign in the Highlands, they allegedly win glorious victories, but the fearsome Scottish peoples remain independent. The northern frontier of the province always stubbornly remains roughly along the line of Hadrian's Wall. We must view with some scepticism the panegyrist's claims about military successes achieved in the campaign of 305/6.

The term 'Picts'[9] first appeared in the panegyric of AD 297. The Romans probably applied the slang term '*picti*' (meaning painted people) to bands of indigenous people who they thought looked weird. During the fourth century, Ammianus and others use '*picti*' as a collective noun for people living to the north of the Clyde/Forth isthmus. The overall picture is one of growing unity amongst the Scottish peoples, probably in response to the presence of Rome in the south.

After completing their Scottish campaign both father and son returned to York. Constantius was now in poor health and near the end of his life. Who would succeed him? There was no constitutionally established procedure for appointing new members to the Tetrarchy: succession had become a matter for discussion behind closed doors. Constantine had been shut out in 305. He did not want the same thing to happen again. By July 306 Constantine had established his credentials as both a dutiful son and a warrior. This was probably his best chance to seize power.

On 25 July 306 Constantius died at York. According to Eusebius, on his deathbed he nominated Constantine as his successor.[10] That may be true or it may be spin. Whatever the dying father may or may not have said, Constantine moved swiftly to secure his position. He put on the Emperor's purple robe before anyone revealed the death. He then went out to face the troops and announced that his father had died. The soldiers saw Constantine arrayed in

---

[7]He was Constantius I, to distinguish him from later emperors of that name.
[8]*Panegyrici Latini* 6 (7), 7.2.
[9]Hunter (2007) 3–6; Mann (1979) 149–50; Foster (2014) 1–2.
[10]*Life of Constantine* 1.21–22. See also *Panegyrici Latini* 6 (7), 8.2.

imperial purple and took the hint. They at once proclaimed him as the new 'Augustus'. The new emperor played his cards cautiously: in the initial period he claimed only to be 'Caesar'.

In the winter of 306 Constantine was campaigning in Gaul against the Franks, but by AD 307 he was back in Britain.[11] The London mint issued '*Adventus*' coins to mark the Emperor's return to Britain. In the same year Constantine married Maximian's daughter, Fausta, hoping that Maximian would accept him as the second 'Augustus'.

The dramatic events in Britain disrupted the system of government so recently established by Diocletian. Under that system Flavius Valerius Severus should have automatically been promoted from 'Caesar' to 'Augustus' with responsibility for the West, but that did not happen. A period of prolonged civil war followed. In AD 308 Diocletian came out of retirement and chaired a conference, hoping this would resolve the conflict. The upshot of the conference was that a new tetrarchy was established. Galerius and Licinius[12] became Augusti. Maximinus[13] and Constantine became Caesars. Maximinus and Constantine were far from pleased at their junior status. Meanwhile Maxentius,[14] the son of Maximian, was much aggrieved at being omitted altogether. This is not an easy period of history to disentangle. The task would be simpler if fewer players had names beginning 'Max . . .'.

In AD 310 Maximian committed suicide. This was a turning point for Constantine.[15] It marked his break with the tetrarchic ideology. He was now set upon his own personal and dynastic claim to power. He made Trier his base. That was not a bad choice. It was a strategic location. It was also the city where Constantius had built a luxurious palace, complete with baths and ornamental gardens.[16] It was in this comfortable setting that Constantine sat back and listened to the panegyric of AD 310.

The panegyric included a eulogy of Britain. The anonymous orator used the exotic conception of a far-away island to emphasize Constantine's claim to power and the favour of the gods. He praised Constantine's clemency to those who had fought against him in the recent conflict with Maximian. This was a carefully crafted speech with an obvious political purpose. Yet again a new Emperor in a tenuous position was using military adventures in Britain to buttress his authority. No doubt Constantine and his advisers had a hand in the drafting.

The complicated internecine struggles that ensued did not directly involve the British provinces and so need not be rehearsed in detail. There were two crucial episodes. In AD 312 Constantine marched south to Italy and defeated Maxentius at the Battle of the Milvian Bridge, just outside Rome.[17] The Arch of Constantine in Rome (erected in AD 315 and still standing) commemorates the Emperor's triumphant entry into the city after that victory. In AD 324 Constantine defeated Licinius in a series of battles in the East. Thus, eighteen years after he had been proclaimed 'Augustus' by the troops at York, Constantine finally achieved supreme power.

---

[11]Cameron (2006a) 23.
[12]Valerius Licinianus Licinius, a career soldier and friend of Galerius.
[13]Gaius Julius Verus Maximinus.
[14]Marcus Aurelius Valerius Maxentius.
[15]Cameron (2006a) 23.
[16]Rebuilt by Constantine. One part, known as the *Aula Palatina*, still stands.
[17]According to Lactantius, Maxentius declared war on Constantine to avenge the death of his father, Maximian: *De mortibus persecutorum* 43.3–4. This may have been a gloss to defend Constantine against the charge of making war against a colleague.

The Emperor Constantine Launches His Career in Britain

Figure 14.1 Bronze statue of Constantine I at York. © Wikimedia/Gernot Keller.

He ruled as sole Augustus from then until his death in AD 337. He is known to historians as Constantine I or Constantine the Great (Fig.14.1).

Constantine was a busy man and, in one guise or another, served as Emperor for 32 years, but this is not the place to give a full account of his career. The Online Appendix summarizes Constantine's two principal reforms, namely (i) establishing Christianity as the pre-eminent religion of the Empire; (ii) restructuring the Empire and moving the imperial capital from Rome to Byzantium (modern Istanbul).

3. BRITAIN DURING THE REIGN OF CONSTANTINE

(i) Military control

According to Eusebius, early in his reign Constantine 'crossed to the British nations, which lie enclosed by the edge of the Ocean'[18] and he brought them to terms. This snippet of information is, of course, most interesting. It would have helped, however, if the bishop had condescended to tell us whom Constantine was fighting and what terms he secured. Archaeological evidence

---

[18] 'τέως μέν ἔπι τά Βρέττανων ἔθνη διεβαίνεν ἔνδον ἐν αὐτῷ κείμενα ὠκεανῷ': *Life of Constantine* 1.25.2.

(principally coinage) suggests that Constantine was present in Britain several times between AD 306 and 314. Presumably he was here for military purposes, but it does not follow that there was any serious unrest. As previously noted, 'trouble in Britain' was a favourite topos of Roman historians writing about recently appointed emperors.

Insofar as there was any unrest in Britain, it is likely to have been in the north. One oddity, however, is that very little Constantinian coinage has come to light in Scotland. The Roman authorities were no longer making diplomatic gifts on any large scale. Also, most of the forts in Scotland are Severan or earlier. If there was trouble in the far north during the early fourth century, it may not have been too serious.

Constantine took the title 'Britannicus Maximus'. This reflects some sort of victory in Britain. Whether that victory was sufficient to merit a title is more dubious. The Roman bureaucracy did not include an Honours Committee. The Emperor could distribute to himself and his friends whatever honours he fancied. The Senate would faithfully rubber stamp them.

It has been estimated that the army garrisoning Britain in the fourth century was about 10,000 to 15,000 men.[19] That was less than half the size of the second-century garrison. The fourth-century garrison was largely effective in defending Britain. Some of the troops stationed here could be, and on occasions were, redeployed to operate in the wider Empire. For most of the fourth century up to AD 367, the northern frontier remained relatively peaceful.[20]

In relation to the structure of the army under the later Roman Empire, the most important source is, of course, the *Notitia Dignitatum*. But, as previously discussed, the problem with the *Notitia* is that we cannot be certain when each section was prepared or what passages may be missing. Subject to those doubts, the *Notitia* provides a valuable account of the military dispositions in Britain during the fourth century.[21] There were essentially three separate commands.

First, the Count of Britain (*comes Britanniae* or *comes Britanniarum*) commanded a field army of six cavalry units and three infantry units. This was a mobile force, which operated wherever it was required within the four British provinces. These *comitatenses* were probably brigaded in towns within the interior of the provinces. They may sometimes have been billeted on local citizens, as happened elsewhere in the Empire.[22]

Second, the Duke of the Britains (*dux Britanniarum*) commanded the *limitanei* who garrisoned the region around Hadrian's Wall. He was probably based at the fortress in York.[23] These troops comprised the Sixth Legion stationed at York and an assortment of other troops. The *Notitia* lists the prefect of the Sixth Legion and the prefects of thirteen units of late Roman formation as serving under the duke. The *Notitia* lists 'along the line of the Wall'[24] eleven tribunes of cohorts, four prefects of *alae* and one prefect of a *numerus*. All that should have been quite enough to keep the duke busy. He clearly needed some help with the paperwork. Luckily, he had a bevy of office staff. These included a chief of staff (*princeps*), a record-keeper (*commentariensis*), a judicial officer (*regerendarius*), accountants and other more junior officers.

---

[19] Gerrard (2013) 28.
[20] Mann (1979) 147.
[21] Birley (2005) 401–3; Gerrard (2013) 27.
[22] Jones (1964) 631.
[23] Bidwell (2006) 33–4.
[24] 'item per lineam valli'.

The *Notitia* reveals what was probably always the case: running the Roman Empire involved a vast amount of back-office work.

Third, there was the Count of the Saxon Shore (*comes litoris Saxonici*),[25] whom we met in Chapter 13. It is probable that mobile units, under the Count's command, garrisoned the forts along the south and east coasts of Britain. They would have moved around as required. When necessary, they may have stayed in walled towns such as Canterbury and Rochester. Although the shore forts have impressive stone defences, there is little evidence of any substantial buildings within them, except at Richborough and Reculver. Even there, the accommodation was only of modest size. The shore forts are unlikely to have housed the troops on a long-term basis. Few fourth-century coins have come to light at Reculver. Coinage at Lympne suggests that the Romans abandoned that fort by about AD 350.

For a period, the Count of the Saxon Shore also commanded units stationed along the north coast of Gaul. This dual command made good sense, since both southern Britain and northern Gaul were facing attacks from the same raiders. At some point in the fourth century or early fifth century (we do not know when) the Count's command was limited to the troops garrisoning the coasts of Britain. Chapter 28 of the Western *Notitia* states that the following were under the Count's command: the commanders of the units at Bradwell, Dover, Lympne, Brancaster, Burgh Castle, Pevensey and Portchester;[26] the tribune of the First Baetasian cohort at Reculver and the prefect of the Second Legion Augusta at Richborough.[27]

The history of the northern and southern frontier commands was different.[28] The northern frontier had been created in the second century. After the peace terms negotiated by Caracalla in AD 211, that frontier had remained relatively quiescent. As a result, the garrison had reduced in size; the maintenance of forts and military accommodation in the north had declined. On the other hand, the Saxon Shore command and the Saxon Shore forts had grown up piecemeal during the third century in response to increased raiding and attacks from the sea. All this led to a transfer of military activity from the north of Britain to the south.

Turning to Wales,[29] a fort was built at Cardiff on the east side of the river Taff at around the end of the third century. It closely resembles some of the Saxon Shore forts. Coin evidence suggests that it was occupied for most of the fourth century. The large fort at Caernarfon (*Segontium*) had existed since the first century and occupied a key position overlooking the entrance to the Menai Strait. This was the richest fourth-century military site in Wales. Its function probably included protecting the mineral wealth of the area: copper mines in Anglesey and the Ormes, silver-lead ores in Flintshire. The fort even had its own Mithraeum.[30] Probably mobile units occupied the Welsh forts, but we do not know who commanded them. Wales does not feature in the *Notitia Dignitatum*.

Some of the units stationed on the frontiers of the Empire became so well settled that they were virtually immobilized. That was one reason why Constantine needed to recruit new field armies for the defence of the Empire. In Britain, this particularly applied to the

---

[25] Millet (2007) 180.
[26] There is doubt about the correct identification of some of these place names.
[27] The *Notitia* describes him as: 'Praefectus legionis secundae Augustae, Rutupis'.
[28] Cleary (1989) 50–3.
[29] Nash-Williams and Garrett (1969) 28 and 59–73.
[30] For a discussion of Mithraea, see Chapter 19, Section 7.

northern frontier. Many of the units on Hadrian's Wall in the third century were still there throughout the fourth century. Such ossification was not a sign of failure: it showed that the units had successfully maintained the frontier. This is another reason for doubting the scale of any campaign that Constantine may have waged against Scotland early in his career.

In the fourth century Richborough became a centre of power in south-east England.[31] It was probably adorned with embellishments to link the site with the Emperor. The Count of the Saxon Shore may have been based there. As noted in Chapter 13, the Second Legion Augusta was transferred from Caerleon to Richborough in the late third or the fourth century.[32] It had probably reduced in size, unless part was stationed elsewhere. Once established in the Richborough fort, the Second Legion Augusta stayed there and came under the command of the Count of the Saxon Shore.

The Roman authorities made major improvements to the fortress at York in the early fourth century:[33] they rebuilt the *principia*, while retaining the original plan; they also created a grandiose aisled hall with sunken bases for statues. A larger-than-life statue of Constantine probably stood there, just to remind everyone who was Emperor.[34] These magnificent headquarters were now fit for a duke. This was just as well, as the Duke of Britain was based there.

At the same time, projecting towers were added to the walls of the Cardiff fort. It used to be thought that the towers added to the York fortress date from this period, but these now appear to be much earlier.[35]

By the early fourth century there was a general problem of reluctance to join the army. Imperial legislation, therefore, made it compulsory for the sons of serving and veteran soldiers to enlist. These rules applied to all provinces, including Britain. Army pay in AD 300 was the same as it had been in AD 235. The shortfall was made up by handouts on special occasions, such as emperors' birthdays and accession days.[36] In an age of multiple emperors, the troops were increasingly dependent on imperial favour and discretion.

Fashions change over time, even in military dress.[37] In the fourth century helmets became simpler and more utilitarian for soldiers, but increasingly elaborate and ostentatious for officers. Shields were now circular or oval with a central boss, unlike the oblong curved shields of earlier centuries. The belt (*cingulum*) became more important. This was a broad girdle equipped with buckles and decorative plates.

Under Constantine, there was a significant change in the arrangements for billeting troops. Many soldiers were no longer required to live in forts. Instead they could, and usually did, live in nearby towns. Zosimus was strongly critical of this reform, since he considered that it softened the soldiers and made them accustomed to luxury.[38] Luxury is, of course, a relative term: it is doubted that the modern reader would find life in a frontier town of Roman Britain

---

[31] Gerrard (2013) 126–30.
[32] Millett (2007) 143 and Cleary (1989) 57.
[33] Bidwell (2006) 34; Ottaway (2013) 299–300.
[34] The head still survives. As noted earlier, heads were often preserved even when statues were smashed.
[35] Bidwell (2006) 34; Ottaway (2013) 123.
[36] Abdy (2006) 55.
[37] Cleary (2013b) 55–60.
[38] *Historia Nova* 2.34: 'τοὺς στρατιώτας ἐκδόντας ἑαυτοὺς θεάτροις καὶ τρυφαῖς ἐμαλάκισε'.

unduly luxurious. Be that as it may, the archaeological evidence in Britain is consistent with soldiers relocating from forts to towns at about this time: towns were expanding; the accommodation available for troops inside forts and fortresses was diminishing. Also, there were reductions in overall troop numbers.[39]

The north

Corbridge and Carlisle[40] were very much 'military' towns (rather like Aldershot in modern times). Both those towns prospered in the fourth century. This reflects the vitality of many small towns at that time, as discussed in Chapter 17 below.

In the fourth century there were no flourishing *vici* attached to the Wall forts.[41] Instead, all activity including markets took place within the forts.[42] At Vindolanda the market was held on a wide street in front of the granaries. There was even a market in the fort at Carlisle, although that fort stood right next to the town. Living quarters inside the forts were more like chalets than barrack blocks. There were no more imports of Continental pottery or amphorae. Nobody bothered writing inscriptions, like they used to. There was not much to inscribe about. By AD 314 the outposts north of the Wall were abandoned. The army had poorer artefacts than in earlier times. The general impression is that the soldiers were lacking the wealth and the Mediterranean culture that their ancestors had enjoyed. Furthermore, since many of the units stayed in the same place for two centuries or longer, they did not get much change of scenery.

Although the soldiers were earning less in real terms, they spent their money locally.[43] This meant an economic boost for the civilian communities both inside and outside the forts.

(ii) Civil administration of the four British provinces

As previously noted, Constantine created separate structures of civil and military authority. The provincial governors in Britain no longer had any control over the troops serving in their respective provinces.[44] The most senior province was *Maxima Caesariensis* and its governor was *consularis*; the other three provinces were lowlier and their governors were *praesides*. The *vicarius* of the diocese of the Britains was based in London, which was in effect the diocesan capital. We know that in AD 319 the *vicarius* was a man called Pacatus, because Constantine addressed a rescript to him.[45] It is likely that the Emperor appointed the *vicarius*, the governors and the senior civilian officials. The *vicarius* had a chief of staff (*princeps*), a principal secretary (*cornicularius*), two accountants (*numerarii*), a registrar (*ab actis*), a secretary in charge of correspondence (*cura epistularum*), an adjutant (*adiutor*), assistants (*subadiuvae*), shorthand

---

[39]Cleary (1989) 58–62.
[40]Hodgson (2009a) 37.
[41]Hodgson (2009a) 36–8; Cleary (1989) 59.
[42]Patterns of coin loss fit with cash-based markets being held inside the forts on Hadrian's Wall.
[43]Mann (1979) 151.
[44]Cleary (1989) 47–8.
[45]*Codex Theodosianus* XI, 7, 2.

writers (*exceptores*), guards (*singulares*) and other officials (*reliqui officiales*).[46] The provincial governor in London had a similarly large staff.

London remained the financial centre of Britain, as it had been since the first century (and still is): the treasury was in London and an imperial mint stood there for about ten years. The *Notitia Dignitatum* helpfully lists the financial officials. The chief accountant of the Britains (*rationalis summarum Britanniarum*) was in charge. He was comptroller of the finances for the diocese of the Britains. Immediately below him came the head (*praepositus*) of the treasury (*thesaurus*). There was also a bevy of clerical staff. These officials and their staff took over what had historically been the role of the procurator. They collected in the taxes from all four provinces. They oversaw payment of the troops and of the (now numerous) civil servants within the diocese.

(iii) Urbanism and local government

The Roman Empire was an empire of cities and towns. It was through these conurbations that the Empire was administered and taxed.[47] By the fourth century a hierarchy of towns in Britain had emerged.[48] At the apex was London, the diocesan capital. Below London came the provincial capitals. Next came the civitas capitals, most of which had been established since the end of the first century. Finally, there were numerous small towns, which had developed more recently and were now flourishing.

As previously noted, the character of Romano-British towns gradually changed. Maintenance of the – now antiquated – civic buildings was becoming increasingly burdensome. The established aristocratic families were less keen on public duty and more inclined to retreat to their country villas. Councillors and magistrates continued to be elected each year, but there was little competition for the vacancies. These social changes led to the flourishing of villa culture in the early fourth century. At the same time a different form of civic governance emerged in the towns.

The new bureaucracy established by Constantine was not only to be found in the provincial capitals.[49] There was also an expansion of local government. The general system was as follows, although it is not clear how universally the system was deployed. The imperial authorities appointed a special commissioner, the *curator civitatis*, for each city. This superior official was above all the other magistrates. He regulated the city's finances and had wide powers over most departments of civic life. Two senior magistrates, the *duoviri*, presided at council meetings. The local council appointed a range of officers to assist the imperial administration. These included *susceptores* (who collected levies and taxes) and *praepositi horreorum* (who had charge of the state granaries). Other officials levied recruits for the army or labourers and craftsmen for public works. Many towns had drainage, a public water supply and communal baths. Two aediles and their officials were in charge of these amenities. The only public buildings whose upkeep no longer mattered were pagan temples, now that Christianity was the favoured religion. An increasing number of official positions carried (local) senatorial rank, which became hereditary.

---

[46] Hassall (1996) 25; Gerrard (2013) chapter 4.
[47] Cleary (2013b) chapter 3.
[48] Cleary (1989) 41.
[49] Jones (1964) chapter 19.

Top local officials usually do well for themselves, especially where there are no media to hold them to account. The new urban élites of the fourth century appear to have occupied commodious town houses, although few have survived in recognizable form. There is a fine example of a fourth-century town house in Dorchester. It had winter and summer dining rooms, spacious accommodation, hypocaust heating and colourful mosaic floors. Archaeologists have recovered numerous luxury items from the house, including a beautiful glass bowl which is still intact. Envious visitors can now admire these items in the nearby County Museum. Ironically, the Dorchester town house is still associated with local government. It stands in the grounds of the Dorset County Council offices.

Another fine town house of the same period survives at Malton (*Derventio*).[50] It had an impressive façade of limestone blocks. The lintel over the door had a sculpture of Victory. Inside the main doorway was a large room, approximately 110 square metres. Some of the rooms had mosaic floors and hypocaust heating. The walls had painted plaster. There was also an elegant dining room, complete with apse.

During the early fourth century, local authorities strengthened and extended many of the town walls. They added projecting towers to the walls around Cirencester and Caerwent:[51] some of the towers at Caerwent still stand proud for visitors to clamber around. It is not clear why the authorities took these elaborate precautions, since there was no obvious military threat (away from the south-east coast). The towers and fortifications may have been ostentation. Also, wall building was a good way to keep both soldiers and civilians busy; the Roman authorities distrusted idleness since that usually led to trouble.

(iv) Villa culture

The first half of the fourth century was the golden age of villa culture. Some of the finest Roman villas enjoyed their heyday during the reign of Constantine and his dynasty. These were now places for the display of power and wealth. Villas became a major investment for the aristocracy of Spain, Gaul and southern Britain.[52] During this period southern Britain may almost be seen as an extension of Gaul.[53]

A large proportion of the luxury items and artefacts recovered from villa sites or hoards can be dated to the fourth century.[54] They include gold and silver items, such as ear-rings, bracelets, necklaces, buckles and finger rings; jewellery made from metal, bone, antler, glass and workable stones. There was far more female than male adornment. Clearly the élites were starting to enjoy the good life.

There are several reasons why this was the heyday of villa culture. First, despite the upheavals elsewhere across the Empire, Britain was left largely at peace. Second, there was a shift of power: many of the leading families had a diminished role in local government, as the new bureaucrats

---

[50] Ottaway (2013) 254–5.
[51] Bidwell (2006) 34.
[52] Cleary (2013b) chapter 5.
[53] Cleary (2013b) chapter 7. Apart from the shared villa culture, Mayen ware from Gaul also appeared in southern Britain.
[54] Gerrard (2013) chapter 4.

were taking over. In those circumstances the traditional aristocracy withdrew to the countryside, focusing their energies on home improvement and elegant living.

Most villas were in the south-east.[55] Depending on what you classify as 'villa', there were about a thousand villas south of a line running from York to Exeter. These ranged from magnificent residences, such as Woodchester, down to more simple farmhouses built in Roman style. There were architecturally ambitious octagonal bath suites in the villas at Holcombe in Devon, Lufton in Somerset and Teynham in Kent. Anyone who built a luxurious bathroom like that nowadays could expect a write-up in *Homes and Gardens*.

A significant proportion of the surviving fourth-century mosaics outside Italy come from Britain.[56] Some of these are of exceptional size and workmanship, which suggests they must have been part of a wider array of decorative elements. The walls had painted plaster, although little survives: the faded remnants of Romano-British murals in museums hardly reflect their original vitality. The grandest villas had top-quality furnishings. These included stone tables with polished marble and wooden furniture with inlays. Such glamorous items seldom survive. Luckily, one piece of fourth-century furniture with bone inlay has been preserved in a well at Hayton.

Interestingly, even the militarized north of England embraced the villa culture in the early fourth century.[57] The villa at Beadlam comprised stone buildings ranged around a courtyard. It included a reception room with hypocaust heating and mosaic paving. There was a winged corridor on the west side and a bathhouse to the south. Yorkshire's most famous villa is at Rudston. This too reached its final form in the early fourth century. There were stone buildings around a spacious yard. The bathhouse included a row of rooms through which bathers progressed, enjoying the varied decor. The mosaics in these rooms are well preserved. The floor at the north end depicts Venus, standing stark naked with enlarged genitalia; there is a curious figure on the left with a human head and a fish's tail. The goddess is understandably surprised by her visitor and has dropped her mirror. The mirror is shown falling towards the floor. The surrounding panels depict a lion, a bull, a deer and a leopard. The next room has a fine mosaic portraying the god, Oceanus, and sea creatures. These scenes must have put visitors in a good mood for bathing and also, perhaps, for amorous encounters.

Mortality is a tricky problem for high achievers. They want to go on impressing people, but that is not so easy when they are dead. Modern man usually settles for a memorial plaque plus the hope of a favourable obituary. Romano-British aristocrats commissioned mausolea for a similar purpose. One fourth-century mausoleum now sits in the middle of a cornfield, just outside Ospringe in Kent. It appears to have been part of a villa estate. The lower sections of all four walls survive complete with tile courses and facing stones. Anyone driving along this part of Watling Street (now known as the A2) can easily stop off and visit this charming little site.

(v) Social and religious life

Following Constantine's conversion, the people of Britain, like everyone else in the Empire, were suddenly encouraged to stop believing in their own gods and to start worshipping the Christian

---

[55]Cleary (2013b) 256–8; (1989) 41.
[56]Gerrard (2013) 133–43.
[57]Ottaway (2013) 256–77.

God. As a matter of cognitive psychology, it is almost impossible to change your beliefs to order, unless you happen to be the White Queen in *Alice Through the Looking Glass*.[58] Nevertheless, from the reign of Constantine until the Romans departed a century later, Christianity was a religion with semi-official status in Britain. Some Christian artefacts and decorations started to appear, as the villa-owning élites duly nodded to the latest religious fashion.

A few archaeological finds from the fourth century confirm arrival of Christianity. For example, a lead tablet found at Bath curses a malefactor 'whether pagan or Christian'. At Mildenhall in Suffolk a quantity of silver tableware dating from the fourth century has been recovered. The 'Mildenhall Hoard' includes three spoons with the Chi-Rho motif. A number of lead tanks have been found, which may conceivably have been used for baptisms, although this interpretation has been questioned.[59]

Within a year of the Edict of Milan Britain had its own episcopal hierarchy.[60] When Constantine convened a church council at Arles in AD 314, Britannia was well represented. The records of this council[61] show that three bishops from Britain attended, namely the bishops of York, London and Lincoln. The British delegation also included a priest and a deacon.

British bishops attended the Council of Nicaea in AD 325, the Council of Serdica in AD 343, the Council of Rimini in AD 359[62] and no doubt other overseas conventions. The network of Roman roads – which now spanned Europe, the Middle East and North Africa – played a vital role in establishing Christianity as an international religion. Foreign travel, presumably with all expenses paid, was becoming one of the attractions of a career in the church.

Despite the dramatic conversion of the Emperor, it was unrealistic to expect the entire army stationed in Britain or the indigenous population to 'convert' to Christianity. Nor did they do so. In fourth-century Britain, traditional pagan practices and beliefs remained dominant. Coins continued to be placed at pagan shrines.

Archaeological evidence indicates that the British provinces flourished during the reign of Constantine. Coinage from the early fourth century is substantially more plentiful than that minted under Carausius and Allectus.[63] This was a time of prosperity. Major construction works were carried out: for example, new buildings were erected inside the fortress at Chester, probably for civilian use.[64]

In the previous chapter we noted the decline of long-distance trade in the third century. This decline continued into the fourth century.[65] Shipwrecks in the Mediterranean became rarer. Examination of amphorae contents and similar studies in Britain show that imports were rarer than in earlier centuries. The decline in foreign trade is not inconsistent with prosperity. Britain, like other provinces, was thriving on local production.

---

[58] She could believe 'as many as six impossible things before breakfast'.
[59] Crerar (2012) 135–66.
[60] Petts (2003) 36–9.
[61] Acta Concilii Arelatensis.
[62] For which the Emperor provided free transport: Salway (1993) 536.
[63] Jones (1981) 397.
[64] Strickland (1981) 434.
[65] Reece (1981).

CHAPTER 15
TURMOIL IN THE MID-FOURTH CENTURY

1. Constantine's dynasty (AD 337–363)
2. Britain in the mid-fourth century
    (i) Urbanism
    (ii) Generally
3. The 'barbarian conspiracy'
    (i) The story as told by Ammianus
    (ii) Did it really happen?
    (iii) Aftermath
4. The empire under attack

This chapter will cover the period AD 337–378. It will address two controversial issues, first whether there was a 'barbarian conspiracy' in 367, and second when and where a new province called Valentia was established. The conclusion is that there was such a 'conspiracy' in 367 and that Valentia was created soon afterwards as a new province abutting Hadrian's Wall with its capital at York.

1. CONSTANTINE'S DYNASTY (AD 337–363)

By the end of his reign Constantine was hugely popular and his death was widely mourned. For three months his body lay on display at his palace in Constantinople, while the normal court ceremonial continued as if the Emperor were still alive. Clearly this could not continue indefinitely. By acclamation of the army, Constantine's three surviving sons became Augusti, ruling jointly. They were Constantine II, Constans and Constantius II. We now enter a period of history which would be easier to follow if all emperors did not have names beginning 'Con...'

The three brothers divided up the Empire between them, but they did not remain on good terms. In AD 340 Constantine II invaded the territory of Constans. The invasion failed and Constantine was killed in an ambush.[1] That left just two sons of Constantine I, who reigned as joint Augusti for the next ten years – Constans in the West and Constantius II in the East.

---

[1] Zosimus, *Historia Nova* 2.41.

While Constantine's sons were carving up the Empire, back in Britain the golden age of peace and prosperity was drawing to a close. Although few details survive, it appears that hostile forces were threatening the diocese from the north. The Emperor decided to attend in person. His decision was probably based on political expediency, not military necessity.

In early 343 Constans crossed the Channel and campaigned in Britain. Unfortunately, the relevant books of Ammianus' history, which describe this expedition, have been lost. All that we have are some tantalizing references in later books, where Ammianus promises not to weary the reader by repeating his previous account. It is likely that Constans was campaigning in the north.

The Scottish peoples had formed into loose confederations, whenever that was expedient, as discussed in earlier chapters. Even so, they remained divided and frequently in conflict.[2] The proximity of the Empire stimulated social change and relations with Rome must have dominated internal politics. Those allied with Rome were playing off hostile groups against each other. Ammianus tells us that at the time of Constans' campaign a group of people called 'Arcani' had the duty of hurrying over long distances, in order to report the clashes of neighbouring tribes to the Roman generals.[3]

Ammianus is not specific about geographical details. The trouble was probably not confined to Scotland: Constans may also have been dealing with unrest in Wales. The Roman fort at Caernarfon (*Segontium*) was reconstructed during the mid-fourth century.[4]

Although the details of the British campaign of AD 343 are obscure, it is clear that Constans prevailed: coins were minted recording his victory. We know from a passing reference in book 20 of Ammianus' history that at the end of Constans' campaign the 'savage tribes of the Scotti and the Picts'[5] promised to maintain peace.

In his thoughtful book, *The Ruin of Roman Britain*, James Gerrard challenges the conventional view of these events.[6] He argues that people read too much into the fleeting references in the surviving portions of Ammianus. Other writers of the period (such as Libanius) concentrate on the difficulties that Constans faced in crossing the Channel during winter, rather than his military exploits on land. The bronze medallion struck in Rome at that time shows Constans victorious and levelling a spear at a figure in the water. The Theodosian Code[7] records that Constans was at Boulogne in January 343. Therefore, Constans' visit to Britain may have been imperial bravado or an out-of-season inspection of the British garrison.

There are difficulties with Gerrard's analysis. The fleeting references in Ammianus are summaries of what he has described more fully in the lost passages. They are likely to be the most important points. Also, Ammianus was one of the 'great' historians, who checked his sources and was writing about his own time. The bronze medallion was presumably recording a victory overseas. The most plausible interpretation of events is that Constans did campaign in northern Britain and he did achieve some degree of success. But contemporary reporters

---

[2]Mann (1979) 149.
[3]'Id enim illis erat officium, ut ultro citoque, per longa spatia discurrentes, vicinarum gentium strepitus nostris ducibus intimarent.' *Res Gestae* 28.3.8.
[4]Nash-Williams and Garrett (1969) 59–64.
[5]'Scottorum Pictorumque gentium ferarum': *Res Gestae* 20.1.1.
[6]Gerrard (2013) chapter 2.
[7]*Codex Theodosianus*, 11.16.5.

probably exaggerated the scale of Constans' success. As noted in earlier chapters, it is a topos of ancient historians to postulate 'victories in Britain' at the start of each emperor's reign.

The Scotti (to whom Ammianus refers) do not feature in any literature before the fourth century. They were an Irish community, some of whom appear to have been present in Scotland and making trouble during this period. They are referred to in the Verona List (*Laterculus Veronensis*) as one of the barbarian peoples on the fringes of the Empire. Rather more surprisingly, they were known to a fourth-century bishop in Cyprus called Epiphanius, who wrote treatises about the nations of the world, as divided up by Noah after the Flood. Epiphanius refers to them as 'Σκόττοι'. He does this in two places, once in a list next to Britons and once in a list next to Franks. This suggests that their attacks on Britain may have gained some notoriety.[8] As we shall see in Chapter 20, in later years the Scotti returned and settled in Argyll. Eventually, they imposed their ethnicity and their name on the whole of Scotland.

The Scotti would have readily found allies north of Hadrian's Wall. But there is no reason why they should have limited their incursions to northern Britain. That would be carrying nominative determinism too far. If there was trouble in Wales in the mid-fourth century, as suggested above, this may have been due to raiding by the Scotti.

Constans was by all accounts a cruel and unpopular emperor. In AD 350 a pretender to the throne, Magnentius, overthrew him. Constans fled and was killed soon afterwards. For the next three years Magnentius functioned as Emperor in the West. Britain fell within his domain. During the period 350 to 353 Magnentius must have appointed the governors and officials of the four British provinces, although there is now no record of who they were.

There was bitter conflict between Magnentius and Constantius II. As in earlier civil wars, this led to huge loss of life within the army because legion was pitted against legion. These losses came at an unfortunate time, when threats to the Empire were gathering in the East. Magnentius was defeated at the battle of Mursa in AD 352 and he died the following year.[9] Thus in AD 353 Constantius emerged as the sole Augustus, with the whole of the Roman Empire under his control. This was, no doubt, what he had always wanted.

Constantius II began his reign as sole Emperor by taking revenge on those who had supported Magnentius. He sent an unscrupulous official called Paulus to Britain with instructions to bring back all supporters of Magnentius to face justice. According to Ammianus, Paulus detained many who were innocent. Martinus, the *vicarius* of Britain, protested but to no avail. Eventually after failing in an attempt to kill Paulus, Martinus committed suicide. Paulus brought back a large number of suspects to the Emperor in chains. Many were completely innocent, but acquittals were not a feature of the criminal justice system under Constantius. They all confessed under torture. Some of the British prisoners were executed, others sent into exile.[10]

By the mid-fourth century the Empire was under attack from barbarians on several frontiers. Constantius II needed a junior colleague to share the burden of military command: only a descendant of Constantine the Great was likely to be acceptable. There was just one surviving member of Constantine's immediate family, a 23-year-old philosophy student in Athens called

---

[8] Rance (2012) 227–42.
[9] Zosimus, *Historia Nova* 2.53.
[10] Ammianus, *Res Gestae* 14.5.

Julian.[11] By all accounts Julian was an outstanding pupil, who outshone his tutors in all subjects.[12] Despite that promising academic career, in AD 355 Julian was summoned from his studies, appointed Caesar and given responsibility for defending the Western Empire.[13]

A modern expert in war studies might say that this was a foolish appointment, since any general worth his salt requires Sandhurst-style training rather than a PhD. But the modern expert would be wrong. As a grandson of Constantine, Julian automatically commanded the loyalty of his troops. The study of philosophy seemingly prepared the young man to master military strategy. Julian led the army in Gaul with considerable success. In separate battles he defeated the Franks and the Alamanni, both of whom had launched invasions across the Rhine. Julian re-established Roman control of Western Europe up to the Rhine and the Danube. These were the traditional frontiers of the Empire.

Provisioning the army is a crucial part of all campaigns, but seldom discussed by the historians of antiquity. Ammianus does tell us, however, that in AD 359 grain was being brought over from Britain to sustain the army in Gaul.[14] According to Zosimus, Julian built 800 ships for the purpose of transporting grain from Britain to granaries along the Rhine.[15] Zosimus explains that this was a one-off arrangement, to deal with a food shortage. That is probably correct.

There is however an alternative view, powerfully advocated by Sam Moorhead, that this was anything but a one-off arrangement.[16] By the mid-fourth century Britain had become the breadbasket of the Western Empire. Following the devastation of much agricultural land in Gaul and Germany by barbarian invaders, Britain had a vital role for provisioning the *limitanei* in the Rhineland. Rome was extracting grain and wool from Britain on an industrial scale, probably through the *annona militaris* with military support. Moorhead has based his research on the concentration of late Roman coins in distinct parts of lowland Britain, the distribution of zoomorphic buckles and fortification of small towns in the late Roman period. It is hoped that future published work on late Roman quern stones, and further interrogation of the Portable Antiquities Scheme database (www.finds.org.uk) will further elucidate the picture. If this theory is correct, it might well explain why small towns were being fortified in the late Roman period, as discussed in Section 2 below. It may also explain why Rome went to considerable lengths to retain Britain as a province during the fourth century, despite all the other demands on its military and financial resources.

In AD 360 the Scotti and the Picts, in breach of their treaty made with Constans in 343, launched an attack and laid waste the territories 'near to the frontiers'.[17] That must be a reference to Hadrian's wall. According to Ammianus, terror seized the British provinces, which were already exhausted by a mass of past disasters.[18]

---

[11] Flavius Claudius Julianus.
[12] 'τοῖς αὐτόθι φιλοσοφοῦσι συνόντα καὶ ἐν παντὶ παιδεύσεως εἴδει τοὺς ἑαυτοῦ καθηγεμόνας ὑπερβαλόμενον': Zosimus, *Historia Nova* 3.2.1.
[13] Zosimus, *Historia Nova* 3.2.
[14] In AD 359 barbarians from across the Rhine burnt down the granaries in which British grain was stored; Julian took urgent steps to re-build the granaries: *Res Gestae* 18.2.3.
[15] *Historia Nova* 3.5.
[16] Moorhead (2001) 85–105; Moorhead and Stuttard (2012) 206–8, 226–7. See also Libanius, *Oratio* 18.82–83.
[17] 'loca limitibus vicina': Ammianus, *Res Gestae* 20.1.1.
[18] 'Implicaret formido provincias, praeteritarum cladium congerie fessas': Ammianus, *Res Gestae* 20.1.1.

Julian decided not to cross to Britain himself.[19] It was more important to remain in Gaul, so that he could co-ordinate the defence of the Rhine frontier against the Alamanni, who were threatening another invasion. Instead Julian sent Lupicinus, his commander-in-chief, together with several detachments of auxiliaries.[20] They sailed from Boulogne to Richborough in midwinter, which was not an ideal time for any army to cross the Channel. From Richborough they marched up Watling Street to London, where Lupicinus took stock of the situation and planned his campaign. Ammianus does not tell us what happened in that campaign. He does, however, state that Lupicinus was a warlike man, skilled in military affairs. It is reasonable to assume that the campaign was successful. No doubt the Picts and the Scotti, for all their ferocity, were driven back once more to their icy mountains and marshes in the far north. One colourful detail which Ammianus has recorded for posterity is that Lupicinus was in the habit of 'raising his eyebrows like horns'.[21] This probably added some panache when he was dictating terms of surrender or passing death sentences.

There may have been an ulterior motive behind Julian's decision. Lupicinus was loyal to Contantius II. Therefore Julian, who had his eye on the top job, may have viewed Lupicinus with suspicion. Sending Lupicinus to Britain might have been a convenient means of getting him out of the way. Lupicinus was arrested on his return to the Continent, which lends some support to the theory.[22]

Julian's success in the European wars was such that his troops proclaimed him Augustus. On hearing this news Constantius II was furious, but there was little he could do whilst enemies were pressing on the eastern frontiers. The two rival Augusti would no doubt have loved to embark on a full scale civil war, but they were both too busy. In November 361 fate intervened. Constantius II died whilst campaigning in Cilicia. Thus Julian (better known as 'Julian the Apostate') became sole Emperor without any opposition.

Not every successful general makes a good head of government, even if (like Julian) they are experts on philosophy. Julian began his career as Emperor with a purge. He dismissed many government officials and, for good measure, had some of them executed. He also announced a change of direction in religious affairs. Julian set about suppressing Christianity and re-instating paganism. He ordered some rapid temple repairs. He organized large-scale public sacrifices to the traditional Roman gods: unfortunately, these gory spectacles did not make a favourable impression on the populace. Julian was shocked by the lack of public enthusiasm for ritual sacrifices.[23] His religious campaign was a failure. So was his next military campaign.

In AD 362 Julian embarked upon a disastrous war against Persia. In June 363 he was killed in battle whilst his army was in retreat.[24] Julian was the last member of Constantine's dynasty to serve as Emperor. Following Julian's death, the army proclaimed Jovian, the commander of the imperial guard, as Augustus.[25] Jovian secured the army's safe return to Rome by ceding to Persia much of the territory that Rome had previously conquered. He also reinstated Christianity as the official religion of the Empire. In AD 364 Jovian died after eight months in

---

[19] Ammianus, *Res Gestae* 20.1.
[20] Aeruli, Batavians and Moesians.
[21] 'supercilia erigentem ut cornua': *Res Gestae* 20.1.2.
[22] Gerrard (2013) 21–2.
[23] Maxwell (2016) 855–6.
[24] Ammianus, *Res Gestae* 25.3; Zosimus *Historia Nova* 3.29; dramatized by Ibsen in *Emperor and Galilean*.
[25] Ammianus, *Res Gestae* 25.5.

office and was succeeded by another soldier, Valentinian.[26] Valentinian ruled the Western Empire and appointed Valens, his younger brother, as Augustus to rule in the East.

2. BRITAIN IN THE MID-FOURTH CENTURY

(i) Urbanism

The improvement of town defences continued in the mid-fourth century. At many towns, projecting external towers were added. These may have been fashionable embellishments, rather than functional improvements, as generally they were not large enough to hold artillery. Some small towns, such as Horncastle and Mildenhall, acquired walls for the first time.[27]

During the fourth century, economic activity became more localized. Larger towns – especially London – went into decline with major public buildings changing in use. Élite housing increasingly dominated the urban landscape. Many smaller towns emerged as hubs for commerce and industry.

The creation of mosaics was a highly skilled art. A small number of regional centres specialized in the manufacture and laying of *tesserae* for mosaic floors.[28] The Corinian school based at Cirencester produced some brilliant work, including the great pavement at Woodchester depicting Orpheus. The Durnoverian school at Dorchester produced the famous 'chi rho' mosaic at Hinton St Mary. Other mosaicists were based at Water Newton (the largest small town) and possibly York.

Metal working continued in many urban centres:[29] bronze-workers at Wroxeter produced intricate crossbow brooches;[30] there is evidence of iron-working at the north-east corner of the basilica at Caerwent between AD 330 and 360. There is also evidence of fourth-century iron-working in the basilicas at Silchester and Cirencester. There was bronze-working in the basilicas at Leicester and Exeter. Following the decay of those great civic buildings, it made good sense to put them to practical use.

There was a late Roman industrial site at Ickham by the Little Stour river. This has produced lead sealings of AD 317 to 337 and 361–363.[31] These came from breaking open bales or sacks, which were probably being processed on behalf of the state.

Production and distribution of leatherwork, pottery, woodwork and textiles were commonplace in both large and small towns.[32] Pottery receives disproportionate attention nowadays, because it survives far better than other products. The artisans typically worked and lived with their families in strip buildings, often keeping an open area at the front, where they displayed and sold their goods.

---

[26]Ammianus, *Res Gestae* 26.1–2; Zosimus, *Historia Nova* 3.35–36.
[27]Cleary (1989) 63.
[28]Witts (2010) 21.
[29]Rogers (2011) chapter 7.
[30]White and Barker (2011) 105, 117.
[31]Millett (2007) 182.
[32]Cleary (1989) 74–5.

Figure 15.1 Crambeck pottery. © Wikimedia/Photographed by: York Museums Trust Staff.

In around AD 360 a new pottery industry emerged at Crambeck in Yorkshire,[33] based on local clays. The product was whitish-buff ware, which was often painted red. You can see examples at the Yorkshire Museum in York (Fig. 15.1). The manufacturers were remarkably successful for about 40 years. Their distribution network covered most of England north of the Humber. Crambeck ware was extremely useful both for soldiers and civilians in the fourth century. It is now extremely useful for archaeologists: any deposit containing Crambeck pottery must be dated after AD 360.

Serving in local government can be tiresome. By the mid-fourth century, leading families were reluctant to waste their time sitting in committee meetings. Many readers would sympathize with that point of view, but the Emperors did not. In AD 364 Valentian and Valens introduced a new policy, whereby decurions had to perform civic offices before they could become senators. Also, they had to leave one or more sons to carry on work in the *curia*. In AD 371 Valens made a law that any decurion who had no son was barred from the local senate.[34]

There is a sense that as the fourth century wore on, towns were losing their vitality: the number of strip buildings occupied by artisans gradually reduced and there was a diminution in the level of commercial activity.[35] The wealth of the most enterprising council members was curtailed. Civic patriotism declined. There was increasing interference by the provincial authorities.[36]

---

[33]Ottaway (2013) 290–1.
[34]Jones (1964) 741.
[35]Cleary (1989) 81.
[36]Jones (1964) 757.

(ii) Generally

As previously noted, during the fourth century Christianity achieved an official status. The church structure became aligned with the administrative structure of the state. Christian practices, instead of being hushed up, were positively encouraged and became visible. By the middle of the century there was an established church structure in Britain, with bishops, deacons and priests in place. Several villas displayed Christian décor. Even so, it is unlikely that the general population took up Christianity. Because of the incentive to be visible, the archaeological evidence may give an exaggerated picture of the spread of Christianity.

In the fourth century, the imperial government and the civic authorities required payment of taxes in cash.[37] Therefore, tenants and smallholders needed towns where they could convert their produce to coinage. The state was a major purchaser. The need for local markets may have been another reason for the growth of small towns in the fourth century. Large landowners increasingly took on the burden of paying taxes on behalf of their tenants, who then made lump sum payments to their landlords covering both rent and tax.

The size of the occupying army had shrunk from about 55,000 in the first century to less than half that size in the fourth century. The state still had to feed and clothe the soldiers, so it remained a significant purchaser of agricultural produce. The main consumers, however, were the civil population, which numbered about four million. The state controlled the direction of flow for all goods, since the army created and maintained the network of main roads.

The supply of coinage to Britain fluctuated over the years.[38] In the 350s there was a substantial drop in the delivery of coins, which continued up to 364. Between 364 and 378 there were huge issues of coins by the House of Valentinian, so that money was plentiful once more in the British provinces. After that there was another trough. Any modern banker would be horrified by such a casual approach to monetary policy. But the function of money in the ancient world was not the same as in our world – luckily for them. There was no concept of liquidity. Coinage was mainly used for paying salaries and state debts. The authorities minted bronze coinage for the purpose of buying back gold and silver coins. This is all very unsatisfactory to modern eyes, but it worked.

When money was in short supply, the counterfeiters usually set to work and produced lots more coins. No-one was unduly fussed about that. Probably it was the civilian or military officials who did much of the counterfeiting. 'Copying' may be a better term than counterfeiting, since this was done quite openly. 'Unofficial coin production' seems to have been a feature of economic life throughout the history of Roman Britain.[39]

Interestingly, coinage loss in the countryside was higher in the fourth century than in earlier centuries. This suggests that the rural economy was becoming more monetized. The effects of Romanization were gradually spreading outwards from the towns.

Britain as a place of banishment

Britain was not directly involved in the struggles of Constantius II and Julian, but it remained a suitable place of exile for those who incurred the Emperor's displeasure. In the second century

---

[37] Cleary (1989) 73.
[38] Cleary (1989) 93–6.
[39] Hall (2014) 165–94.

an errant satrap, Tiridates, had been banished to Britain.[40] In AD 361 a senior palace official, Palladius, was deported to Britain because he was 'suspected' of making accusations against a member of the Constantine family.[41] In those days mere suspicion of criticizing the imperial family was quite sufficient for the purpose of imposing severe punishment. There was no question of freedom of speech. Nor was there any question of proving guilt or treating suspects fairly. Modern investigative journalists, who rightly protest when they are muzzled, would have found life even more uncomfortable in the ancient world.

Another miscreant who was banished to Britain was one Valentinus, a man 'of arrogant spirit'.[42] The intention was that such exiles would live quietly wherever they were sent, reflecting on their past misdeeds and not making a nuisance of themselves. As we shall see, Valentinus had other ideas.

3. THE 'BARBARIAN CONSPIRACY'

According to Ammianus, in AD 367 the various communities and warlords who were hostile to Roman Britain mounted a concerted attack on the diocese. There is some debate as to whether Ammianus was gilding the lily. It may therefore be helpful to set out his version of the story first, before turning to the archaeology and the views of revisionist historians.

(i) The story as told by Ammianus

In AD 367 the Picts, the Attacotti, the Scotti, the Franks and the Saxons co-ordinated their operations in what Ammianus describes as a 'barbarian conspiracy'.[43] The Scottish peoples invaded northern Britain; the Franks and the Saxons attacked the coastal regions of southern Britain and Gaul. The barbarians captured a Roman general, Fullofaudes, and either held him prisoner or killed him. They also killed Nectaridus, who was the general commanding the coastal defences. Ammianus describes Nectaridus as count of the maritime territory,[44] which probably means that he held the office of Count of the Saxon Shore.[45]

In their coastal raids the Franks and the Saxons stole all items of value, including cattle; they burnt down properties and murdered everyone whom they caught. The army stationed in Britain was rapidly losing control and soldiers were deserting from the ranks. In short, says Ammianus, the British provinces were descending into lawlessness. There is probably an element of exaggeration or literary licence in this passage.

Valentinian was horrified by the news coming from Britain. The first general whom he sent had to be recalled for other duties. He then sent Jovinus to deal with the problem. With only

---

[40] Dio, *Roman History* 72.14.2.
[41] Ammianus, *Res Gestae* 22.3.3.
[42] Ammianus, *Res Gestae* 28.3.4.
[43] 'Britannias ... barbarica conspiratione ad ultimam vexatas inopiam': See Ammianus, *Res Gestae* 27.8.1.
[44] 'comitem maritimi tractus': *Res Gestae* 27.8.1.
[45] Gerrard (2013) 27.

the troops stationed in Britain at his command, Jovinus was no match for the enemy. Finally, Valentinian sent over a highly able general, Count Theodosius, with instructions to crush the insurgents at all costs. Theodosius brought with him an army of auxiliaries.

Count Theodosius duly set off for Britain, which Ammianus describes as 'the ends of the world'. Having crossed from Boulogne to Richborough, Theodosius marched his army up Watling Street to London, 'an old town'.[46] Theodosius then divided his troops into smaller detachments, which he sent off to the coastal regions under attack. The Roman troops rapidly came to grips with the raiding parties, killing the barbarians, releasing their captives and recovering much stolen property. The soldiers apparently kept only 'a small part'[47] of the stolen property for themselves and handed the rest back to the victims.

Meanwhile the Roman fleet engaged the Saxons at sea. According to the panegyric delivered to Theodosius' son twenty years later, the Saxon vessels were annihilated in the naval warfare.[48] Theodosius' next task was to deal with the deserters from the army. Very sensibly, he issued proclamations offering an amnesty to all deserters who now returned to their posts. Most took up this offer and, somewhat shamefacedly, returned to their barracks.

Having restored some semblance of order to Britain, Theodosius sent word to the Emperor that these unruly provinces would benefit from better discipline and firm government. Valentinian responded by sending out Dulcitius (a distinguished general) to take command of all troops stationed in Britain, and Civilis, as deputy prefect, to oversee all the British provinces. Apparently, Civilis had a fiery temper but was committed to justice and upright conduct.[49] Woe betide those who stepped out of line.

Count Theodosius then set off with his troops for the North. He confronted the Scotti and the Picts, who according to Ammianus had had the 'insolence' to attack Roman territory.[50] The insolent Scottish peoples were duly put in their place and driven back well to the north of Hadrian's Wall. In the words of the panegyrist, 'the Scots were forced back into their own swamps'.[51] Theodosius organized the restoration of the towns and forts that had been overrun by the unwelcome visitors from Scotland.

(ii) Did it really happen?

There is no archaeological evidence of widespread destruction in the mid-fourth century. Nor are there indications of general dereliction of civic buildings in Britain, as there are in fourth-century Gaul. Gerrard goes so far as to say 'There is no archaeological horizon that marks the events of 367'.[52] That, with respect, is an overstatement.

A line of buildings, which appear to have been signal stations, have been found along the Yorkshire coast.[53] They are at Huntcliff, Goldsborough, Scarborough and Filey. Each appears to

---

[46]'Lundinium, vetus oppidum': *Res Gestae* 27.8.7.
[47]'partem exiguam': Ammianus, *Res Gestae* 27.8.8.
[48]'Saxo consumptus bellis navalibus offeretur': *Panegyrici Latini* 2 (12), 5.2.
[49]'virum acrioris ingenii, sed iusti tenacem et recti': Ammianus, *Res Gestae* 27.8.10.
[50]*Res Gestae* 28.3.2.
[51]'Redactum ad paludes suas Scotum': *Panegyrici Latini* 2 (12), 5.2.
[52]Gerrard (2013) 22.
[53]Ottaway (2013) 295–8.

have comprised a rectangular courtyard, with a wall around it and a tower in the centre. At the base of each tower were substantial stone socketed blocks, into which wooden uprights could have been set. Inferences from what remains suggest that the walls were about 4.5 metres high and the towers reached a height of about 12 metres. There was probably a similar structure at Ravenscar, because a tablet has been found there with the following inscription: 'Justinianus, commander; Vindicianus, *magister*, built this fort from ground level.'[54]

Coin deposits indicate that the signal stations (if such they be) were constructed in about the 360s. If seaborne attacks were harassing Britain in AD 367, it would make obvious good sense to build a line of signal stations along the north-east coast. It is a possible conclusion that these structures were linked to the events that Ammianus describes.

There is a need for caution here. The dating of the signal stations is not entirely clear, nor is it certain that they had a single cause. The linking of archaeological evidence to known historical sources is often speculative. P. J. Casey has suggested that Magnus Maximus (a self-proclaimed Emperor, whom we shall meet in Chapter 16) was responsible for building the signal stations.[55] Casey admits, with good reason, that this view is heretical. Overall, and despite the scepticism of some historians, it is suggested that linking the signal stations to the barbarian conspiracy remains the most likely explanation for their existence.

Ammianus' reference to Theodosius restoring towns after quelling the barbarian conspiracy fits with some of the evidence. The formidable fort at Caer Gybi, which overlooked (and still overlooks) Holyhead harbour, was built or rebuilt in the second half of the fourth century.[56] As noted in the previous section, during this period smaller towns were acquiring walls, and projecting towers were being added to existing walls. By the end of the fourth century most towns were defended by stone walls.

Shortly after AD 367 the authorities rebuilt Stanegate Road.[57] This work can be dated because sealed coins of Valentinian and bits of Crambeck pottery have been found within the road material.

James Gerrard has put forward an interesting interpretation of events.[58] This is that Valentinian was planning to campaign in Britain, in order to secure a much-needed victory and to demonstrate his military mettle, but events prevented him from doing so. We know that at some point in 367 Valentinian fell ill at Amiens, so this part of the theory may be right. Next, Gerrard argues that Ammianus greatly exaggerated the barbarian conspiracy. The so-called conspiracy may have been little more than a few chance raids 'suppressed by a junior general with a limited number of troops'.

That is an extreme view. Ammianus was a generally careful and reliable historian, who would not peddle such blatant lies. It is accepted that there was probably some embellishment. At the time when Ammianus was writing, Count Theodosius' son was Emperor; it was a wise move for any ambitious historian to emphasize the achievements of the Emperor's father.

---

[54]'Iustinianus praepositus Vindicianus magister turrem et castrum fecit a solo': RIB, 721.
[55]Casey (1979) 75–6.
[56]Nash-Williams and Garrett (1969) 135–7.
[57]Hodgson (2009a) 37.
[58]Gerrard (2013) chapter 2.

A fourth century dice tower has been found near Cologne, bearing the inscription: 'Pictos victos hostis deleta ludite secure'.[59] That means: 'The Picts are beaten, the enemy is destroyed, so play without a care.' This inscription probably relates to the events of AD 367. Seemingly, the dice players of Cologne were satisfied that a serious Scottish uprising had been crushed, even if some modern historians are more sceptical. The dice players were probably correct.

(iii) Aftermath

As noted earlier, an unpopular individual called Valentinus was banished to Britain to keep him out of the way. Valentinus set about organizing a revolt against the Roman administration. He secured the support of other exiles and then started enticing soldiers away from the Roman army, to join his cause. News of these plans reached the Romans shortly before the rebellion was launched. Theodosius ordered the arrest of Valentinus together with his associates and sent them all to Dulcitius for immediate execution. It appears from Ammianus' account[60] that Theodosius proceeded straight from arrest to sentence, with no intervening formalities such as a trial. With due respect to Theodosius, it might have been fairer just to check who was guilty, and who wasn't, before they were all put to death.

The *Notitia Dignitatum* reveals that during the fifth century a new British province, Valentia, came into existence, obviously taking its name from the Emperor Valentinian. The governor was *consularis*, i.e. a man of high status. Logically, Valentia must have been created by hiving off one section of an existing province. Some scholars have argued that Valentia was simply the new name for an existing, province, but that must be wrong. You cannot have five governors (2 *consulares* + 3 *praesides*) for only four provinces. Precisely when Valentia was created and where it was located are the subject of much debate.[61] The crucial sentence of Ammianus' history reads as follows:

> He recovered a province which had passed into the control of the enemy and he so restored it to its former condition that (in the words of his report) it had a lawful governor and thereafter at the Emperor's behest it was called Valentia.[62]

The above sentence strongly implies that Valentia was in the region of Hadrian's Wall. That after all is where the insolent Scotti and Picts had been causing all the trouble. Despite the use of the word 'recovered' ('recuperatam'), it seems probable that the new province was first created during Theodosius' campaign. This territory was 'recovered' (in the sense of recaptured from the enemy), even though it was not previously a separate province. On the other hand, if the new province had been established at an earlier date, as some have suggested, what was it called? Clearly not Valentia. Also, the creation of a new border province made good sense in the aftermath of the barbarian conspiracy and its suppression. There was no obvious reason for

---

[59]Hunter (2007) 4–5.
[60]*Res Gestae* 28.3.6.
[61]For an excellent summary of the conflicting views, see Birley (2005), chapter IV.2.
[62]'recuperatamque provinciam, quae in dicionem concesserat hostium, ita reddiderat statui pristino, ut eodem referente et rectorem haberet legitimum, et Valentia deinde vocaretur arbitrio principis': *Res Gestae* 28.3.7.

doing so at an earlier date. Since the governor was *consularis*, not a mere *praeses*, it is likely that the provincial capital was at York. It is therefore suggested that Valentia was created in or soon after AD 367 by hiving off the top part of the province Flavia Caesariensis. The prestigious city of York fell within this area and, naturally, became the capital of the new province.

The Arcani were the spies who had provided much useful information during Constans' British campaign, as recounted earlier. Unfortunately, their enthusiasm for the Roman cause had waned over the following quarter century. They were gradually corrupted and, in effect, became double agents. In return for handsome rewards they started to betray the Roman plans to the Scottish peoples. Theodosius dismissed the Arcani from their posts.[63] Curiously he seems not to have had them all executed, but perhaps this was an oversight.

Count Theodosius headed home. According to Ammianus the British provinces were dancing for joy at the thought of Theodosius' victories, but that must be an overstatement. Upon return to Rome the Count was received with equal adulation and much praise from the Emperor. In the world of power politics, however, gratitude is a temporary phenomenon. A few years later Theodosius fell out of favour and was executed.

In the years following Theodosius' campaign, the British provinces appear to have stopped dancing for joy. Instead they entered a state of progressive decline. After AD 367–368 Rome seems to have lost control of territories north of Hadrian's Wall. The outpost forts were no longer occupied and Ammianus does not suggest that there was any punitive raid against the Picts.[64] As discussed in Chapter 18 below, there was a steady reduction in the number and size of occupied villas.[65] New forms of pottery had flourished earlier in the fourth century, but this dropped off dramatically in the second half of the century. The major pottery producers contracted and some went out of business altogether.[66]

There was a large scale re-flooring of the basilica at Wroxeter in the late fourth century.[67] The floor must be dated after 367, because it contains a coin of Gratian, minted between 367 and 375. The fact that some local authorities were undertaking major new works during this period cautions against adopting a simplistic view of history. Although the general pattern was one of decline, we cannot say that everything was going downhill at the same time.

The regular arrangement inside the barracks of forts along Hadrian's Wall was abandoned in the 370s.[68] There are signs of reduced occupation of the forts. There was a similar decline at South Shields, where the commanding officer's house was poorly maintained after AD 350–380. At Wallsend (*Segudunum*), silt accumulated against both faces of the fort walls containing pottery post-dating 360.[69]

Coin loss in forts along the northern frontier substantially diminished after about AD 380. This reflects the reduced money supply discussed earlier. It does not mean that people stopped holding markets. Other methods of trading were available, including barter and credit. The reduced coin loss along the northern frontier in the last part of the century was symptomatic of a breakdown of existing systems.

---

[63] *Res Gestae* 28.3.8.
[64] Mann (1979) 147–8.
[65] Ottaway (2013) 307–10.
[66] Faulkner (2010) chapter 6.
[67] White and Barker (2011) 115.
[68] Hodgson (2009a) 38–9 and 70.
[69] Bidwell (2018) chapter 9.

It is a reasonable inference from the archaeological evidence that Britain went into recession in the last quarter of the fourth century. This was probably for two reasons. First, the Empire was under attack from the east and Continental Europe was in turmoil so that cross-Channel trade would have diminished. Second, during the late fourth century, troops were being progressively withdrawn from Britain and re-deployed on the Continent. The Roman army stationed in Britain had been integral to its economy and a stimulus for economic growth over the previous four centuries. As soldiers departed, the industries that they promoted and the shops where they spent their earnings would all have suffered.

4. THE EMPIRE UNDER ATTACK

Valentinian died in AD 375, having designated his sons, Gratian and Valentinian II, as successors. Valentinian II was aged four and, despite his father's optimism, did not yet have any great grasp of statesmanship. Gratian was in his mid-teens. That was still a bit young to run an empire, but at least he understood what was expected of him. For all practical purposes there were two Emperors, namely Gratian and his uncle, Valens. The Empire was divided between them, with Valens taking the larger portion.[70]

In this confused situation Rome's enemies sensed an opportunity for smashing the frontiers of the Empire. The Huns, who had recently swept down central Asia in vast numbers seeking lebensraum, displaced the Ostrogoths. The Ostrogoths asked Valens to let them settle inside the Empire. Valens had little choice but to agree and the Ostrogoths swarmed into Thrace. They were not the only new arrivals. The Visigoths and some of the Huns followed in their path, without troubling to seek permission before they smashed through the Rhine/Danube frontier.

Valens recognized that there was now a serious threat in the east and decided to confront the invaders. In the spring of 378 he hastened to the Balkans at the head of an army. The two sides joined battle at Adrianople in Thrace on 9 August 378. The Roman infantry were no match for the hordes of barbarian horsemen. The result was an overwhelming victory for the barbarians: most of the Roman army were killed. Valens himself died, having been struck by an arrow.

The invaders of the Empire tend to be identified by ethnicity – Huns, Visigoths, Ostrogoths, Vandals and others.[71] These terms describe people who were felt at the time and are still considered to be separate from each other. But ethnicity may not have been innate. It could also be opted for or changed. The familiar classifications may be cognitive. Ethnicities were fluid and constantly being manipulated. The Huns, Visigoths, Ostrogoths and Vandals all came from the east and they perceived themselves as being separate ethnic groups.

By the autumn of 378 the Empire was now in a desperate position. Nominally it had two Emperors. They were Valentinian II, who was aged only seven, and Gratian, who was aged nineteen. Running the Roman Empire was not a task for children, so for the time being

---

[70]Zosimus, *Historia Nova* 4.17–19.
[71]Cleary (2013b) chapter 8; Maas (2012) 74–7.

Valentinian was out of the picture. Thus Gratian found himself as the sole effective Emperor, with responsibility for a vast empire under attack on all sides.

The defence and welfare of Britain were no longer high on the imperial agenda. The threats accumulating in Continental Europe had the first claim on Rome's resources and the Emperor's attention. Britain's days as a Roman diocese were drawing to a close.

CHAPTER 16
THE FINAL YEARS OF ROMAN BRITAIN

1. Introduction
   (i) Historical sources
   (ii) Archaeology

2. The beginning of Theodosius' reign

3. Maximus' rebellion and the consequences for Britain

4. The end of Theodosius' reign

5. The decline of Rome after the death of Theodosius

6. The end of Roman Britain

1. INTRODUCTION

The three decades from AD 379 to 409 are a crucial epoch in British history when Roman rule came to an end. This chapter seeks to reconstruct the events of that period from fragmentary sources. It argues that our exit from the Empire was due to a combination of internal and external causes.

(i) Historical sources

Ammianus' excellent history stops in 378. The historian, Zosimus, gives only a partial account of subsequent events. The other historical sources are fragmented. They include the writings of the court poet, Claudian, and the panegyric delivered to Theodosius on his visit to Rome in 389.[1] Such sources can hardly be regarded as unbiased.

Gildas was a sixth-century monk of gloomy disposition, who wrote a brief history entitled 'On the Ruin of Britain' (*De Excidio Britanniae*). The title says it all. He regarded the Britons as thoroughly awkward and opposed to everyone in authority.[2] If Gildas were alive today, he might take a similar view. He was particularly bitter about the end of Roman rule in Britain. He regarded the Roman period as a golden age of abundance and of freedom for the common

---

[1] This is Panegyric II delivered by Latinus Pacatus Drepanius. It is the latest of the surviving panegyrics, but for reasons best known to the ancient editor (possibly Pacatus himself) was designated as number two in the series.
[2] *De Excidio Britanniae* 4.1.

people.³ Gildas' writings were apocalyptic: he was writing about the end of the world, as he saw it. Despite his clarity of purpose, the wrathful monk was none too particular about dates and details. It is not easy to match up his comments with the other historical sources.

(ii) Archaeology

Because of the sparsity and poor quality of the written records for this period, we are heavily dependent on the archaeological record. Unfortunately, as a result of the diminished coin supply from the Continent and the reduced local pottery production, dating of material relating the last three decades of Roman rule becomes increasingly difficult. All in all, this is a tricky phase of history to disentangle and there is room for varying interpretations of the evidence.

The overall picture⁴ is one of continuing decline. In towns many buildings, both public and private, fell into disuse. Public amenities decayed through lack of proper maintenance or renewal. In the countryside villas were downsized or abandoned. As noted in the previous chapter, no new villas were built in the last quarter of the century. Hearths were sometimes built on top of mosaic floors. This suggests that utilitarian considerations were taking precedence over elegant living. Romano-British bracelets of this period were often cut down and re-used as smaller rings.⁵ Pottery production declined, and many smaller pottery manufacturers went out of business.

At Verulamium occupation of the strip buildings along Watling Street receded in the late fourth century. Few coins from Valentinian or later have come to light in that area. Overall, the number of occupied buildings in Verulamium was substantially reduced by AD 380. There was a similar pattern in Chichester. Excavations in the north-west corner show that occupation of the houses and public baths reduced in the last quarter of the century. There was abandonment and non-replacement of many large buildings in Colchester and Exeter during this period. In Canterbury, some large buildings were reduced to shells. The public drainage system broke down, so that there was flooding of foul water.

The same picture emerges in the small towns. At Brampton, Ilchester and Water Newton, for example, the extramural areas were contracting. Buildings were abandoned and drains were silting up. There was little new construction work. People were filling in pits. The coins that they dropped were no later than Valentinian.

Temples were decaying for two reasons. First, Christianity was now the official religion of the Empire, so temples to the old gods were not entitled to public support. Second, people with pagan beliefs (probably most of the population) lacked the resources for temple restoration. For goddesses such as Sulis Minerva, all this must have been intensely irritating. The people of Bath were extremely fortunate that the hot springs continued to flow.

The imperial authorities had better use for their money than paying the army in Britain.⁶ Bronze coinage stopped arriving in 402. Gold and silver coins stopped coming in bulk during

---

³Faulkner (2014) 41.
⁴Cleary (1989) chapter 4 provides an excellent summary.
⁵Swift (2012) 167–215.
⁶Cleary (1989) 140–1.

409, although a few coins still reached these shores after that date. (Possibly Rome was paying off a state debt or rewarding specific individuals.) Silver *siliquae* continued in circulation for some time after 409, but they progressively reduced in size because users were clipping off the edges. There was no longer any central authority controlling the currency.

A significant feature is that people did not start making copies of bronze coinage as they had done during previous financial squeezes. This indicates that by the turn of the century the British economy was no longer monetized. The old ways of barter and exchange were replacing payments for goods and services.

On a brighter note, the Britons stopped paying tax bills. The revenue authorities must have ceased functioning altogether at some point in the first decade of the fifth century. The ending of taxation and the drying up of the money supply led to the collapse of the British economy. There were no bulk purchases by the state to sustain the army. Prosperous traders saw their livelihoods drain away.

Many of the hoards[7] that have come to light in recent years are dated to the late fourth/early fifth century.[8] It is a feature of late Roman hoards that, in addition to coinage, they often contain luxury items such as silver tableware. Some of the silver plate may have been donatives to officials to mark special occasions, such as the accession of an emperor. The Thetford hoard contains 33 silver spoons and 22 gold finger rings. The Hoxne hoard contains a fabulous array of silver tableware, together with 569 gold coins and 14,272 silver coins. The Mildenhall hoard contains 34 items of silver tableware. The wealthy classes were burying their treasures for good reason. They could see troubled times ahead. Their intention was obvious: the hoards should remain buried until it was safe to dig them up again. Unfortunately, it was not safe to dig them up again for many centuries. So, the new owners are museums and private collectors.

There may also have been a religious dimension to the burying of hoards, especially the deposition of silver plate. The late fourth century/early fifth century was a worrying time. People had little confidence in new-fangled Christianity. They probably wanted to keep the traditional gods and the local gods on side. Burying offerings was a good way of doing that. Significantly, many hoards from this period have come to light in the same areas where Iron Age hoards had been buried, especially East Anglia.

2. THE BEGINNING OF THEODOSIUS' REIGN

In late 378 Gratian was in the predicament described at the end of Chapter 15. He urgently needed the support of an older man with military experience. Gratian wisely sought the help of one of his father's former generals, Flavius Theodosius. Flavius Theodosius was the son of Count Theodosius, who had campaigned so successfully in Britain. Unlike his father, the younger Theodosius had escaped execution and was still available to serve the Empire. Flavius Theodosius rapidly proved his worth as a general. In January 379 Gratian promoted Theodosius

---

[7]Gerrard (2013) 59–61.
[8]Bland (2018) 98–9, tables 6.1 and 6.2.

to the rank of Augustus and entrusted to him some of the eastern provinces. There were now three Emperors, namely Valentinian II (aged seven), Gratian and Theodosius.

The immediate problem facing Theodosius was how to deal with the Goths: many had poured across the eastern frontier of the Empire to settle in Thrace and surrounding provinces.[9] Theodosius devoted his first three years as Emperor to achieving a sensible accommodation with the Goths. He enrolled large numbers of them into the Roman army. The *Notitia Dignitatum* records that units of Visi and Tervingi (both Gothic peoples) formed part of the army of the Western Empire. A treaty of AD 382 allowed the Tervingi and some of the Greuthungi to settle in Thrace and Dacia. From then on, the Goths became major players in imperial politics. On occasions they provided vital support to the Empire. The panegyric to Theodosius hails all this as a masterstroke: 'What an event worthy to be remembered! The former enemies of Rome were now marching under Roman leaders and banners.'[10]

Theodosius was determined to have no more nonsense about paganism. He banned sacrifices to the ancient gods and ordered the closure of temples.[11] Like a nineteenth-century public school headmaster, he made Christianity compulsory. He disbanded the college of vestal virgins and sent those virtuous ladies packing.[12] Some pagan temples were smashed, others were left to decay. The remaining augurs and *pontifices* were unceremoniously sacked. These religious reforms had less impact in Britain, where Roman influence and control were waning.

Theodosius was anxious to establish his own family dynasty. In AD 383 he appointed his son Arcadius, then aged six, as Augustus. He planned to elevate any future sons in the same way.

3. MAXIMUS' REBELLION AND THE CONSEQUENCES FOR BRITAIN

A senior officer in Britain called Magnus Maximus was not amused when he learnt of Theodosius' appointment as Emperor.[13] Maximus had campaigned with distinction in Britain under Theodosius senior and was rather expecting that he himself would be elevated to the imperial throne. In AD 383, as *dux Britanniarum*, he took matters into his own hands. With a little encouragement from their leader, the troops in Britain proclaimed Maximus as Augustus; Maximus hastily put on a purple robe and graciously accepted the appointment. He obviously needed to do something imperial to consolidate his position. So, he established a mint in London. This issued gold *solidi* and silver *siliquae* with which to pay an accession donative to the troops. The reverse of the coins described the new Emperor as *restitutor reipublicae*, which was a somewhat dubious claim. But no matter. With a name like Magnus Maximus (meaning 'the greatest great man'), he was clearly cut out for the job.

---

[9]Zosimus, *Historia Historia* 4.24.
[10]'O res digna memoratu! Ibat sub ducibus vexillisque Romanis hostis aliquando Romanus': *Panegyrici Latini* 2 (12), 32.4.
[11]Jones (1964) 166–9 and 725.
[12]Lindner (2015) chapter 14.
[13]Zosimus, *Historia Nova* 4.35; Gerrard (2013) 25–6; Casey (1979) 67–72.

Maximus then set off for the Continent, taking with him part of the troops stationed in Britain. The army in Germany declared for Maximus. In the meantime, Gratian was in Gaul preparing to oppose the pretender. At this point, somewhat inconveniently, a large part of Gratian's army decided to change sides. First the Moorish cavalry deserted and then other soldiers followed suit. Gratian realized that his position was hopeless: he fled, taking with him those troops who had remained loyal. Maximus sent soldiers in pursuit, who caught up with Gratian and killed him. Poor Gratian, after eight stressful years as Augustus, died at the age of 24.

Maximus now controlled all the western provinces north of the Alps. Gildas, who regarded Maximus as an abomination, describes this as a 'criminal kingdom'.[14] Maximus set up his imperial court at Trier and established another mint there.

Theodosius was confronted with a fait accompli. In AD 384 Theodosius recognized Maximus as Co-Augustus but had it in mind to eliminate him as soon as circumstances permitted.[15] There were now three Emperors, namely Valentinian II in Italy, Theodosius in the East and Maximus based at Trier.

One consequence of Maximus' rebellion was that soldiers were withdrawn from Britain to support his campaigns on the Continent. These troops probably came from the *comitatenses*. Possibly some came from the *limitanei* on Hadrian's Wall. It is unlikely that any could have been spared from the south and east coasts. The troops withdrawn by Maximus would never return to these shores.[16] In view of the repeated barbarian invasions along the eastern frontier, the Empire probably could not spare any troops to bring the British garrison back up to strength. In hindsight, Maximus' rebellion may be seen as a first stage in the process whereby Britain became detached from the Roman Empire.

The *Notitia Dignitatum* describes the Count of the Saxon Shore as *comes litoris Saxonici per Britannias*. In other words, his remit was limited to the British coastline. As previously noted, at some point this officer must have lost his authority over the north coast of Gaul. If it had not happened earlier, it is likely that this reduction in his remit occurred during the rebellion of Magnus Maximus.[17]

The south and east coasts were coming under increased attacks from the sea. These were now the most vulnerable part of the diocese. Subject to the doubts about dating previously discussed, the *Notitia* records the following as garrisoning the Saxon Shore forts:

- A unit of Fortenses at *Othona* (possibly Bradwell);
- Tungrecanian troops at Dover;
- A unit of Turnacenses at Lympne;
- Branodunensian Dalmatian cavalry at Brancaster;
- Gariannonsensian Stablesian cavalry at Burgh Castle;
- First Baetasian cohort at Reculver;
- Second Legion Augusta at Richborough;

---

[14]'facinoroso regno': *De Excidio Britanniae* 13.2.
[15]Zosimus, *Historia Nova* 4.37.
[16]Gildas, *De Excidio Britanniae* 14.1.
[17]See 'Channel Commands in the Notitia' by Stephen Johnson (1974), at 81–102 (in particular, 91).

- A unit of Abulci at Pevensey;
- A unit of scouts (*exploratores*) at *Portus Adurni* (possibly Portchester).

By the turn of the century the Second Legion Augusta would have been much reduced in size. Martin Millett estimates that the total number of troops garrisoning the Saxon Shore forts was about 2,000 men.[18] Most of these units were long established in Britain. Even the Turnacenses, a unit raised from *Turnacum* (now Tournai in Belgium) around AD 360, had been here for two generations.

In AD 387 the opportunity that Theodosius had been waiting for arrived. Maximus unwisely invaded Italy, causing Valentinian II to flee. Valentinian and Theodosius then joined forces. In AD 388 they defeated and killed the upstart Emperor at Aquileia. As Gildas gleefully puts it, his evil head was cut off.[19] This victory is recorded in glowing terms in Pacatus' panegyric[20] to Theodosius, which was delivered the following year. The oration is so biased against Maximus and so oleaginous towards Theodosius that even after sixteen hundred years it still makes the reader cringe. The only ancient author who had a good word to say about Maximus was the church historian Osorius, who regarded Maximus as energetic and a worthy Augustus.[21]

As a result, by the late fourth century Britain remained a diocese comprising five provinces, the most important being Maxima Caesariensis with its capital at London. The Count of Britain commanded the diminished field army in Britain, the *comitatenses*. The few troops garrisoning the northern frontier were still under the command of a duke based in York. The troops defending the south and east coasts of Britain were commanded by the Count of the Saxon shore. The structures established many years earlier remained in place, but the occupying troops were substantially depleted. External threats to the diocese were growing.

4. THE END OF THEODOSIUS' REIGN

Following his victory in AD 388, Theodosius was now the senior Emperor with Valentinian II as his junior colleague. Valentinian established his court at Trier. In practice, Valentinian was dominated by Arbogast, a Frankish general whom Theodosius had appointed. Arbogast acted as governor of Gaul during periods when Valentinian was accompanying Theodosius in Rome and Milan.[22]

Valentinian II died in May 392, possibly by his own hand. He was aged just twenty-one. Shortly afterwards a senior official, Eugenius, asserted his own succession as Augustus. Arbogast supported this claim. Theodosius was not willing to countenance Eugenius as Co-emperor. In AD 393 Theodosius appointed his younger son Honorius, then aged eight, as Augustus. The curious practice of appointing children as Roman emperors was by now well entrenched. After

---

[18]Millett (2007) 180.
[19]'capite nefando caeditur': *De Excidio Britanniae* 13.2.
[20]*Panegyrici Latini* 2 (12), 23–45.
[21]Moorhead and Stuttard (2012) 231.
[22]The famous conflict between Theodosius and Bishop Ambrose of Milan in 390 lies outside the scope of this book.

appointing his youthful Co-emperor, Theodosius prepared for war. The army that he assembled included twenty thousand Goths. The second in command was Flavius Stilicho, a man who was ethnically half-Vandal and half-Roman. One of the Gothic officers was an able young man called Alaric. Both Stilicho and Alaric were destined to play a major role in Roman history over the years to come.

The armies of Theodosius and Eugenius met in early September 394 on the banks of the River Frigidus, just north of Trieste. There was massive loss of life on both sides, but Theodosius prevailed. Eugenius was taken prisoner and duly beheaded. Theodosius was now the sole effective Emperor. Indeed, he was the last Emperor before the fall of Rome to rule over the entire Empire. He is known to historians as Theodosius I or Theodosius the Great. Sadly, he only had four months in which to savour the pleasures of supreme power. In January 395 Theodosius died and Rome entered a state of terminal decline.

5. THE DECLINE OF ROME AFTER THE DEATH OF THEODOSIUS

On his death Theodosius bequeathed the Eastern half of the Empire to his elder son, Arcadius, and the western half to his younger son, Honorius. At the time both boys were in Constantinople. Arcadius remained in Constantinople and reigned as eastern Emperor from AD 395 until his death in AD 408. Honorius reigned as western Emperor from 395 until his death in AD 423; he was based initially at Milan and later at Ravenna.

Honorius was aged ten when he came to power and still in need of guidance. At the behest of Theodosius on his deathbed, this role was entrusted to Stilicho.[23] For the next thirteen years Stilicho was the most powerful figure in the western Empire. In AD 408, however, Stilicho fell out with the Emperor, which was not a wise move. He was promptly murdered by Honorius' guards.

The Gothic soldiers who had fought on Theodosius' side at the battle of the river Frigidus were much aggrieved that their loyalty and their sacrifices had not been properly rewarded. Alaric, who became king of the Visigoths after the battle, was particularly irritated not to be appointed commander-in-chief of the Roman army.[24] There was now a third force to be reckoned with. This was a large and disaffected Gothic army, roaming within the frontiers of the Empire and looking for somewhere to settle. The Goths first marched towards Constantinople, before being diverted to Greece, where they sacked all the major cities. In AD 401 Alaric and his troops invaded Italy. Complex negotiations followed between Alaric, the Roman Senate and Honorius. To make matters worse, over the next few years hordes of Vandals, Huns and other barbarians crossed the Rhine/Danube frontier and added to the Emperors' woes.

Finally, in AD 410 the Goths under Alaric swarmed through the gates of Rome and sacked the eternal city. They spent six days seizing items of value and raping Roman women.[25] They then withdrew, laden with their spoils.

---

[23]Stilicho was also appointed guardian to Arcadius, who was now aged eighteen. In practice Rufinus, the praetorian prefect in Constantinople, assumed this role.
[24]Zosimus, *Historia Nova* 5.5.
[25]Gibbon (1783) describes the sack of Rome in colourful terms at vol 5, 308–22.

The decline and fall of the Roman Empire is a large subject, which Gibbon has recounted in twelve majestic volumes. For present purposes, however, perhaps a paragraph will suffice. After the sack of Rome in AD 410 the western Empire steadily waned. During the first four centuries AD the Roman system had provided a significant measure of integration. This applied in the political, fiscal, administrative, economic and cultural spheres. All of that changed in the fifth century. The archaeology shows signs of general disintegration across western Europe.[26] Societies and the resources at their disposal became smaller in scale. There were repeated barbarian invasions of Italy. In 476 the last western Emperor was deposed and the whole of Italy fell under barbarian control. The eastern part of the Empire lasted longer, indeed for another thousand years, but in 1453 Constantinople fell to the Ottomans and became Istanbul.

6. THE END OF ROMAN BRITAIN

There are two views about how Roman rule came to an end in Britain:

(i) The first hypothesis is that the causes of decline were internal. Britain was unable to deal with raiders. On top of that, the economy was failing and Britons increasingly resented their subjection to Roman authority: they were getting precious little benefit from membership of the Empire. The Britons therefore rejected the trappings of Roman rule at every opportunity and deliberately dropped out of the Empire.

(ii) The alternative view is that the causes were external. Britain was becoming ever more expensive to maintain and Rome could not spare the resources to sustain the British provinces. Therefore, the Roman authorities faced up to reality: the game wasn't worth the candle. They made a conscious decision to let the province go. Britain's decline was a direct consequence of Roman government policy.

It is suggested that the correct analysis is a synthesis of the two views. The first set of causes were probably dominant. Internal pressures were pushing the Britons towards secession, particularly their inability to deal with raiders and their disillusionment with the distant Roman authorities. More generally, people wish to determine their own futures. They would not submit to a colonial authority unless they were compelled to do so. That compulsion was now receding. At the same time, external pressures were sucking resources away from Britain, as Rome needed troops to defend the heartland of the Empire. A combination of internal and external pressures brought about Britain's decline and eventual detachment from the Empire.

The principal problem that Britain faced at the turn of the century was the endless cycle of raids on her coasts by Saxons and other pirates. The Britons only had small boats powered by about 20 oarsmen on each side to protect their coastal waters.[27] These were hardly sufficient to

---

[26]Cleary (2013b) 395–6.
[27]"Scafae...quae vicenos prope remiges in singulis partibus habebant, quas Britanni pictas vocant." Vegetius, *Epitome of Military Science* 4.37.

ward off the invaders. Gildas, in his usual gloomy way, says that as a result of the raids Britain 'was aghast and groaned for many years'.[28]

In around AD 398 Stilicho sent a task force to combat Saxons and Irish raiders who were attacking the British coastline.[29] According to Gildas, the task force killed many of the invaders and drove the rest away.[30] Gildas then rather confusingly adds that the Romans told the Britons to build a wall across the island linking the two seas. That appears from the following sentence to be a reference to either Hadrian's Wall or the Antonine Wall. At this point the monk becomes hopelessly muddled.

Claudian, a fashionable court poet never guilty of understatement, heaped praise on the enterprise.[31] In elegant verses he described how Stilicho rescued Britain from hostile Saxon, Scottish and Irish invaders. Unfortunately, the Saxons were not readers of Claudian's poetry and they were not minded to go away.[32]

The Roman authorities were probably still using diplomatic gifts to maintain peace in the north. As noted in earlier chapters, diplomatic gifts were generally more effective if targeted on the hinterland, rather than the frontier. The 'Traprain Law' treasure found in 1919 may be evidence of such a policy. It was in the territory of the Votadini, about 20 miles east of Edinburgh. The treasure comprises a collection of coins and silver plate. Three of the coins depict Arcadius and one shows Honorius, which dates them to the early fifth century. There are 152 pieces of silver, mostly plate, which had been cut into pieces, some coming from a jug that depicted Old Testament scenes.[33] Apparently the Scottish recipients of fine Roman tableware were only interested in its value as raw silver. This would have been disheartening for the original silversmith, but hopefully he never knew.

It appears from both Claudian and Gildas that in and after AD 402 more of the troops garrisoning Britain were recalled to the Continent to help in resisting barbarian invasions. The *Notitia Dignitatum* records several British units in locations around the Empire: for example, soldiers from Caenarvon were serving in Illyricum. In the eyes of the imperial government, the defence of Rome and the heart of the Western Empire was a matter of top priority. Certainly, that was more important than the maintenance of order on an island that had brought nothing them but trouble for four centuries. Gildas adds for good measure that Britain was an island numb with cold ice and far removed from the sun's light.[34]

The soldiers remaining in Britain were far from happy with their lot and in AD 406–407 decided to rebel.[35] They first proclaimed a man called Marcus as Emperor, but soon changed their minds and killed him because he 'did not suit their temperament'.[36] They next selected one of their number called Gratian, kitting him out with a fine purple robe and imperial crown.

---

[28] 'multos stupet gemitque annos': *De Excidio Britanniae* 14.
[29] Gerrard (2013) 26.
[30] *De Excidio Britanniae* 15.2.
[31] *De Consulatu Stilichonis* 2.247–55 and 3.146–9.
[32] Gildas, *De Excidio Britanniae* 16.
[33] Collins (2006) 229–30.
[34] *De Excidio Britanniae* 8.
[35] The rebellion can be dated because Zosimus says it occurred in the seventh and second consulships of Honorius and Theodosius respectively.
[36] 'οὐχ ὁμολογοῦντα τοῖς αυτῶν ἤθεσιν': Zosimus, *Historia Nova* 6.2.

This appointment lasted for as long as four months. The troops then became 'displeased with Gratian'[37] and duly executed him.

It may be thought that any sensible man would keep his head down when the selection committee was looking for a third candidate. Not so. An officer called Constantinus stepped forward and was proclaimed Emperor. Having donned the purple robe and crown, Constantinus did not hang around in Britain waiting to be murdered in the usual way. Instead, taking the best available soldiers with him, he headed south to Richborough and embarked for Boulogne.

It is likely that Constantinus took with him the remaining *comitatenses* and the Second Legion Augusta.[38] These troops did not return to Britain. That left only some *limitanei* who were garrisoning Hadrian's Wall and the Saxon Shore.

Once on the Continent, Constantinus quickly rallied the troops in Gaul to his cause. Stilicho, much alarmed, sent an army commanded by a general called Sarus to put down the usurper from Britain. Sarus did not achieve success or cover himself with glory. He even stooped to the expedient of murdering an ambassador called Nebiogastes, who came from Constantinus to negotiate peace terms. Meanwhile Constantinus appointed two able generals to command sections of his army. These were a Briton called Gerontius and a Frank called Edobinchus. Constantinus marched southwards to the Alps, where he placed garrisons to prevent barbarian invaders from penetrating Gaul. From there he sent his son, Constans, together with Gerontius to Spain. This expedition was successful and the army in Spain declared its support for Constantinus. Constantinus was now in a powerful position and Honorius was left with little room for manoeuvre. Accordingly, Honorius recognized Constantinus as co-Augustus. Thus the usurper from Britain became the official Emperor of the West. He enters the history books as Constantinus III. The new Emperor established his court at Arles and reigned over a steadily diminishing Empire from AD 407 until his defeat and execution in AD 411.[39]

As the money supply slowly dried up, the existing economic systems of Britain disintegrated.[40] The state was no longer a bulk purchaser. The wealthy potters of Crambeck, whom we met in Chapter 15, no longer had a market for their goods. Other industries collapsed or shrank in the same way. Buildings in many of the large towns show signs of abandonment at the start of the fifth century.

A layer of 'dark earth' formed over the rubble at Canterbury, Gloucester, Lincoln, Winchester, London and Southwark. The causes and significance of the dark earth are the subject of much debate, into which we need not enter. In some instances, the cause may simply be rotting vegetable matter or rubbish. When states are failing, waste disposal systems are not at their best. Whatever the precise causes of the dark earth in different towns, it signified that society was crumbling.

Some *limitanei* remained along Hadrian's Wall in the early years of the fifth century. Interestingly, a group of eight copper *nummi* has been found at Great Whittington, the latest of which is dated AD 406–408. It is stamped *Gloria Romanorum* with three emperors visible on the back. These coins were the product of an illegal eastern mint.[41] Although the

---

[37] 'δυσαρεστήσαντες δὲ καὶ τούτῳ': Zosimus, *Historia Nova* 6.2.
[38] Millett (2007); Cleary (1989) 142.
[39] Wood (2007).
[40] Cleary (2016) 138–40 and (1989) 143–8.
[41] Collins (2008) 256–61.

monetized economy was now collapsing, there was still some coin exchange with Continental Europe.

Kent appears to have been the main Roman stronghold in the final years.[42] Richborough was one of the last places to continue receiving supplies of Roman coinage in the fifth century. Many coins have been found there dated AD 388–402. Richborough remained a key government installation until the end. Coinage also indicates continuing use of Dover into the fifth century.

A hoard of silver found in Canterbury appears to have been buried in the second decade of the fifth century.[43] Now on display in the Canterbury Roman Museum, it includes twelve spoons and three ingots. Two of the ingots are stamped to show that they were produced in Trier.[44] Other stamped ingots have been found at Reculver and Richborough.[45] These finds suggest that in the early fifth century, officials were gathering in north-east Kent. Lullingstone villa, which was not far away, remained in occupation until the early fifth century. Whether any hapless officials took refuge there, perhaps yearning for a bit of luxury, must be speculation.

By about 408 or 409 the troops garrisoning Britain were so depleted that they could no longer maintain control; nor were they being paid, which hardly improved morale. Saxon and other raids on the coasts were increasing. The Britons, for their part, were receiving precious little benefit from membership of the Roman Empire. Without even the formality of a referendum, they decided to expel their European masters and enjoy some independence. In a famous passage Zosimus records that the Britons resolved to 'throw off Roman rule and live by themselves, no longer obeying Roman laws'.[46] That sentence has the ring of truth. Zosimus continues that the Britons took up arms and, braving danger, freed their cities from the barbarians who were threatening. He adds that this defection took place during the tyranny of Constantinus, who had failed to protect Britain against barbarian attacks.

Although we are grateful to Zosimus for that account, it is a trifle short, being only one sentence. Much detail is lacking. We do not know the precise year in which independence was achieved, although it was probably around AD 409. Nor do we know how things actually happened. Did the Britons massacre the Eurocrats or politely ask them to leave? Did some of the officials stay to help the Britons cope with independence? Was any thought given to the power vacuum that would follow when the Romans packed their bags and headed south? History is replete with examples of independence movements that end in tears.

Shortly after 'independence day', someone buried a massive hoard at Whorlton in the Cleveland Hills. The hoard included silver bars and ornaments, as well as several thousand coins.[47] These were probably the treasures of a wealthy Yorkshire estate. The owner must have hoped, forlornly, that the good times would return, so that he could dig it all up and carry on as before. Unfortunately for him, the good times did not return. The hoard lay hidden until the nineteenth century, when some light-fingered antiquarians got to work. Only a few pieces now survive: they are in the British Museum.

---

[42] Millett (2007) 143 and 180–3; Cleary (1989) 143.
[43] Millett (2007) 180–3.
[44] RIB 2402.9; 2402.12.
[45] RIB 2402.6; 2402.8.
[46] 'τῆς Ῥωμαίων ἀρχῆς ἀποστῆναι καὶ καθ' ἑαυτὰ βιοτεύειν, οὐκέτι τοῖς τούτων ὑπακούοντα νόμοις': Zosimus, *Historia Nova* 6.5.
[47] Ottaway (2013) 314.

When any long-established political order collapses, there are winners as well as losers. The lucky few may seize opportunities and do well for themselves, as the oligarchs of Russia did after the fall of the Soviet Union. In the early fifth century, Britain retained a thriving agricultural sector although farming patterns changed.[48] Small towns in agrarian communities continued to prosper.[49] Some landowners may have used their freedom from taxation wisely. They could share the surplus with their workers and still live in comfort.[50] With due respect to Gildas, life after AD 409 may not have been doom and gloom for everyone.

And what about the army? Where did they go? Probably nowhere. By the fifth century the 'Roman' soldiers in Britain were men who had lived here for generations. It is a reasonable inference that when their salaries dried up, they stopped being soldiers. The military units who were still present in AD 409 were probably *limitanei* serving on the northern frontier and around the south-east coast. The archaeology of forts along Hadrian's Wall suggests a change from coherent organization to a series of smaller scale groups becoming increasingly self-reliant.[51] On the south and east coasts some of the shore forts were abandoned.[52] The former soldiers would have merged into the general population. No doubt they made a valuable contribution to the local economy as well as to the gene pool.

The Britons may have had mixed feelings about independence. When they were not busy burying hoards or celebrating their new tax holidays, perhaps they worried about foreign affairs. There was good reason to worry. Other hostile nations had set their sights on the British Isles. According to Gildas, after independence the Romans occasionally gave Britain military support in warding off invaders.[53] According to Zosimus, on the other hand, Honorius merely sent a letter advising the British cities to defend themselves,[54] but it may be that this passage in Zosimus has been corrupted.[55] That is not the only source of confusion: the Dark Ages had arrived.

---

[48] Cleary (1989) 158–9.
[49] Fitzpatrick-Matthews (2014).
[50] Gerrard (2016) 860–2.
[51] Cleary (2016) 138.
[52] Cleary (1989) 143–4.
[53] *De Excidio Britanniae* 17–18.
[54] *Historia Nova* 6.10.
[55] Birley (2005) 461–2.

CHAPTER 17
TOWNS AND URBAN LIFE

1. Introduction

2. Civitas capitals
   (i) The civitas system
   (ii) Specific towns that served as civitas capitals

3. Colonies

4. London

5. Small towns

1. INTRODUCTION

The towns that emerged in Roman Britain were radically different from the former Iron Age *oppida*. They had much in common with the towns that developed across the rest of the Empire.[1] This chapter will review the different categories of towns and how they developed over time.

The basic plan for a Roman town[2] was that two main roads would cross in the centre at right angles: the *cardo maximus* ('biggest hinge') and the *decumanus maximus* ('largest street, which divides the area into tenths'). Other streets would then be set out in straight lines, crossing at right angles, so as to form a grid of rectangular islands (*insulae*). Plots were allocated for the construction of houses and shops. Although this was the basic scheme, local conditions such as rivers, contours or pre-existing roads required many variations. The people who laid out the new towns in Roman Britain were probably military surveyors. They possessed technical skill but would have won few prizes for originality.

Town defences started to appear in the late second century. These took the form of massive walls, often with bastions added later. Typically, there would be four gates, one at each end of the two major roads. Their locations are often recorded in modern place names: Chichester, for example, has four suburbs known as Northgate, Southgate, Eastgate and Westgate.

Every substantial Roman town had a *forum* near the centre. This was an open area where people could meet and traders could market their wares. There were usually rows of shops or

---
[1] As to which, see Zuiderhoek (2017).
[2] See the street plans for each town in Wacher (1995); De la Bédoyère (2010a) 24–9.

colonnades around three sides. A *basilica* generally stood on the fourth side, which was in effect the town hall, where councillors could meet and magistrates could sit. It was also a convenient place to store public records and documents. Other major public buildings to be found in Roman towns were temples and communal baths. Both played an important role in civic life.

Turning to entertainment,[3] several Romano-British towns possessed an amphitheatre, usually standing on the outskirts. Amphitheatres were venues for public games, fights between animals, and gladiatorial contests. Gladiators were expensive because they had to be maintained and trained, so it was tiresome when too many got killed. Animal fights on the other hand were cheaper and more frequent. One popular and inexpensive form of entertainment was the public execution of criminals, condemned to be eaten alive by wild animals (*damnatio ad bestias*).[4] A smaller number of towns possessed a theatre, the best preserved being at St Albans. Theatres were semi-circular, with a stage at the back, and used for drama, musical or other performances. Amphitheatres were oval shaped. Since few towns possessed both, there may have been some interchange of functions. Finally, a circus was used for horse races. The remains of a circus have been found at Colchester, some 500 metres to the south of the Roman town,[5] and are on display with a small museum attached. So far, this is the only known circus in the province.

The Romans built a series of inns (*mansiones*) around the Empire, so that those travelling long distances could stay in comfort overnight. Archaeologists have a tendency, whenever they excavate the foundations of a grand town house, to identify it as a *mansio*. In truth there is no way of knowing whether it was the house of a local grandee or a genuine *mansio*. The 'painted house' in Dover has a reasonable claim to be a *mansio* because of its location. Bacchic murals adorn its walls.[6] Other suggested *mansiones* are at Catterick and Wall, but these could equally well be opulent town houses. Unlike modern hotels, *mansiones* were only open to those travelling on official business.

Vici were small civilian settlements that grew up around forts.[7] The soldiers had money to spend. Shopkeepers, craftsmen, itinerant traders, prostitutes and others were eager to meet the needs of the army and welcomed a steady source of income. Military families also lived there. Some *vici* grew into small towns but they did not have civic institutions, instead remaining under the control of the local commanding officer. The *vicus* adjoining the fort at Vindolanda has been the subject of particularly thorough excavation: it includes shops, houses, baths, lavatories and craft areas.

Canabae were civilian settlements that grew up around legionary fortresses and served the needs of the military. For obvious reasons, they were larger than *vici*. The *canabae* had facilities, such as bathhouses, which both soldiers and civilians used. The day-to-day administration of *canabae* could be in the hands of elected councils and the officials whom they appointed. But there were limits to democracy in the ancient world; the legionary legate exercised ultimate

---

[3] Wilmott (2010).
[4] Wilmott (2010) 162; Wacher (1995) 55.
[5] Fulford and Holbrook (2015) 74–5.
[6] Philp (1989) and (2007).
[7] De la Bédoyère (2010a) 146–8.

control over all matters. The *canabae* at Chester provide a good example of how such communities functioned.[8]

The towns of Roman Britain may be divided into four broad categories:

- Civitas capitals
- Colonies (*coloniae*)
- London
- Small towns.

It is helpful to consider these four categories separately, even though there is overlap and the distinctions between them diminished as time went on.

2. CIVITAS CAPITALS

(i) The civitas system

The Roman authorities and the indigenous élites established a system of local government for Britain, which was based on the Roman model, suitably scaled down for use in the provinces.[9] They identified what were believed to be existing communities capable of self-government and treated each as a *civitas*, meaning a community of provincial citizens. We do not know the details of the civitas system, but it appears to have worked like this. The landowners and wealthiest members of a district became decurions (*decuriones*), who formed the senate (*ordo*) of the civitas. There was a governing council (*curia*), whose members were appointed from the senate. Magistrates were elected annually from the senate, usually in pairs and had administrative responsibilities, such as overseeing the water supply and public works. They also presided in courts.

As explained earlier, the Romans and the indigenous élites established civitas capitals progressively, as and when they considered that local communities could be trusted to govern themselves. If a civitas capital reached a certain level of Romanization, it was given the status of *municipium*. It is not entirely clear what this meant in practice; probably the residents were given a scaled-down form of Roman citizenship. Tacitus states that St Albans was a *municipium*.[10] There must have been a charter from the emperor conferring this honour. It is a matter of speculation which other towns achieved this status.[11]

What is the evidence of this system of local government in Britain? Not a lot. No manual of local government practice survives from the Roman age. We do, however, know how civitates were administered in other provinces, in particular from inscriptions recovered in Spain. There are occasional helpful references to British towns in the literary sources. In addition, there are inscriptions recording the status of individuals. The relics of public buildings are also evidence

---

[8] Mason (2012) chapter 7.
[9] De la Bédoyère (2010a) 19–22; Millett (1990) 65–6.
[10] *Annals* 14.33.
[11] Wacher (1995) 18–19.

Figure 17.1 Tombstone of Volusia Faustina, Lincoln. © Flickr/Michaël Martin.

of what was going on. There was no point in building grand town halls, unless important people met in them and took significant decisions.

A few inscriptions found in Britain record that individuals had served as local councillors or magistrates. A tombstone found at Old Penrith commemorates Flavius Martius.[12] Apparently Flavius was a senator in the civitas of the Carvetii. He had also served as a quaestor. A tombstone found in Lincoln records that the deceased, Volusia Faustina, was the wife of a decurion called Aurelius Senecio.[13] Her hairstyle suggests that she lived in the mid-third century. A stone coffin found in Scarborough records that the deceased, Flavius Bellator, was a decurion of the colony of York.[14] Bellator cannot have served for long, since he died at the age of 29.

A statue base recovered from Caerwent (which now stands in the church porch) is evidence of the civitas system in operation. It reads:

> To Tiberius Claudius Paulinus, legate of the Second Legion Augusta, proconsul of the province of Gallia Narbonensis, imperial governor of the province of Lugudunensis, by decree of the senate, the republic of the civitas of the Silures set this up.[15]

---

[12]RIB 933.
[13]RIB 250.
[14]RIB 674. The sarcophagus of another decurion in York is described by Hassall and Tomlin in *Britannia* 18 (1987) at 367.
[15]RIB 311: 'Tiberio Claudio Paulino legato legionis II Augustae proconsuli provinciae Narbonensis legato Augusti propraetore provinciae Lugudunensis ex decreto ordinis res publica civitatis Silurum'.

Paulinus was legate of the Second Legion Augusta, based at Caerleon. He was promoted to be governor first of Narbonensis, then of Lugudunensis (both provinces in Gaul) and finally, in AD 220, of *Britannia Inferior*. Paulinus obviously did something of great benefit for the Silures, probably while he was the legate at nearby Caerleon. The erection of a statue with this handsome inscription on the base was a thank you from the local people to their benefactor. There is no reference to Paulinus' final governorship in the text, so probably the statue was erected shortly before AD 220. The inscription is graphic evidence that the Silures were a self-governing community – it describes them not only as a civitas, but also as a 'republic'. The inscription refers to the local senate (*ordo*) as having passed a decree that the statue be set up. That illustrates the powers (including capital expenditure) that indigenous leaders possessed, once they had become local senators within the Roman system of administration.

The civitas system did not continue unchanged for four hundred years. Towns were constantly evolving. Many went into decline during the third century, as discussed in Chapter 13. The status of civitas capital mattered less by then. Following the reforms of Diocletian and Constantine in the fourth century, new bureaucrats arrived in the provinces and the old élites lost much of their power. As a result, civitas capitals seem to have waned further in the fourth century. There is less evidence of continuing opulence in those towns, although out-of-town villas flourished.

(ii) Specific towns that served as civitas capitals

Earlier chapters have identified towns that became civitas capitals as part of the chronological narrative. Given the limited sources, it is not always easy to be certain about the status of individual towns. Subject to that, Table 17.1 is a reasonably comprehensive list of civitas capitals.

Archaeologists have carried out detailed excavations at all of the civitas capitals. In respect of each town, vast masses of data are available in the professional journals. These include street layouts, lists of coin finds, inscriptions, dendrochronological analysis, location of post holes and much other fascinating detail. Any recitation of all this material might try the patience of the reader and it would certainly try the patience of the author. For discussion of some civitas capitals, see the Online Appendix.

3. COLONIES

Coloniae were in origin settlements for veterans.[16] The three principal *coloniae* were Colchester, Lincoln and Gloucester, each built on the site of a legionary fortress. The veterans took over, almost intact, the structures that the legions had left behind, using the existing streets and buildings as the basis for their new towns. Gloucester and Lincoln never had the same status as Colchester, nor could they rival its monumental buildings: they had to make do with more ordinary temples, baths and basilicas. Gloucester was overshadowed by the civitas capital at Cirencester. Lincoln fared better. It became a centre for administering the Corieltauvi, at least until Leicester was established as civitas

---

[16] Mann and Dobson (1996) 44–5; Millett (1990) 85–7.

Table 17.1 Civitas Capitals Throughout Roman Britain

Community	Capital town	Latin name of town
Cantiaci[a]	Canterbury	Durovernum Cantiacorum
Regni	Chichester	Noviomagus Reginorum
Belgae	Winchester	Venta Belgarum
Atrebates	Silchester	Calleva Atrebatum
Durotriges	Dorchester	Durnovaria
Dumnonii	Exeter	Isca Dumnoniorum
Catuvellauni	St Albans	Verulamium
Dobunni	Cirencester	Corinium Dobunnorum
Corieltauvi	Leicester	Ratae Corieltauvorum
Iceni	Caistor[b]	Venta Icenorum
Cornovii	Wroxeter	Viroconium Cornoviorum
Silures	Caerwent	Venta Silurum
Demetae	Carmarthen	Moridunum Demetarum
Brigantes	Aldborough	*Isurium Brigantum*
Parisi	Brough	Petuaria Parisorum (uncertain)
Carvetii	Carlisle	Luguvallum

[a] Referred to by Ptolemy as 'Cantii'.
[b] Caistor St Edmund, near Norwich.

capital. As time went on, fewer retired soldiers chose to move to *coloniae*. They tended to stay in the areas where they had served. Like many old people nowadays, they often preferred to spend their autumn years close to family and friends. The three principal *coloniae* were too few to form part of any comprehensive policy of Romanization. Over time their character merged with that of other towns. After the first century, the status of *colonia* was sometimes given to a town as an honorific, York being an example.

Colchester

Chapters 4–7 have outlined the development of Colchester (*Camulodunum*) in the first century. The Roman settlers prospered: they had an extensive agricultural hinterland and enjoyed a healthy trade with the Continent. A building in Insula X, which can be dated to the 50s (because it is below the layer of Boudica's destruction) appears to have been a store. It was laden with flagons, amphorae, unused mortaria and carbonized wheat. An impressive town house from the same period has been identified at Lyon Walk. It had fine painted wall plasters. There were three ranges of rooms around a gravel courtyard, bounded by oak-lined drains. Veteran soldiers may have sat in the courtyard on summer evenings, reminiscing about the conquest of Britain.

Colchester was one of the most Romanized towns in the province. It was the location of the first legionary fortress, the site of the temple to Claudius, the first provincial capital, the first colony and the first town to acquire walls. The Balkerne Gate, on the west side, was a monumental structure with two pedestrian passageways and a guard chamber. Unlike any other city gate in Roman Britain, it stood apart from the main wall. This was, in effect, making a statement about the power of Rome. The Balkerne Gate is still there, remarkably well preserved. You can walk through the passageways or even have a picnic in the guard chamber. Colchester remained a town of strongly Roman character throughout the Roman period.[17] During the first and second centuries it acquired a full suite of monumental buildings: forum, basilica, administrative buildings, temples and baths. It had an aqueduct, pumping house, fountains, water storage facilities and drainage. There was a theatre (the largest in Britain)[18] and probably an amphitheatre there. Large town houses were built in the second century. From the mid-first century onwards, Colchester was a major centre for manufacturing and distribution. There was a vibrant pottery industry, as well as metal working. Unusually, there was also glass manufacture, rather than mere recycling of broken glass. Unlike any other town in Britain, Colchester had a circus.[19] This was a massive structure designed for serious chariot racing, 448 metres long and 71–74 metres wide, with starting gates at the west end.

When Christianity arrived in the fourth century, a church was built on the south side of the town, the remains of which can still be seen next to Butt Road. There is also a fourth-century cemetery there, with burials aligned east/west in accordance with Christian practice. There is even evidence that the temple of Claudius was adapted for Christian worship. This would have been the ultimate insult for the divine Emperor who was so proud of his British adventure.

Lincoln

In about AD 72 the Ninth Legion headed north to York and the Second Legion Adiutrix moved into the Lincoln fortress. During the 80s, after the army had finally moved out, the site became available for other uses. The Roman authorities established Lincoln (*Lindum*) as a *colonia* for veterans, probably including many from the Ninth Legion.[20] They laid out an initial settlement at the top of the hill, covering the same area as the previous fortress, which was fine to begin with but inadequate in the long term. The Romans subsequently extended the colony across lower ground to the south, so that the town ended up as an oblong shape running north–south. Inevitably, in both the top half and the bottom half there was a neat grid of streets crossing each other at right angles. Most unusually, the side wall of one of the buildings within the town is still standing: it is known as the 'Mint Wall' and rises 7 metres above the present ground level (which is probably 2 metres above the Roman level).[21]

In the second century Romano-Britons erected stone defences, some of which remain. Parts of the east gate of the upper town and the west gate of the lower town are still intact, although you must go into the grounds of City Hall to inspect the latter. At the north gate the original

---

[17]Gascoyne and Radford (2013) 108–65.
[18]The outline of the theatre is marked on the ground at Gosbecks Archaeological site.
[19]Crummy (2008), 15–31.
[20]Jones (2011) 52.
[21]Jones (2011) 62–3.

Figure 17.2 Roman arch, now known as Newport Arch, Lincoln. © Wikimedia/Keith Ruffles.

stone arch (now called 'Newport Arch') still stands, albeit with medieval masonry around it (Fig.17.2). This is the only Roman arch in Britain through which traffic still passes. All this is a testament to the skill of the military engineers. It is highly doubtful whether any twentieth-century buildings will still be standing in two thousand years' time.

Ermine Street passed straight through the town from the north to the south gate. The junction with Fosse Way lay a short distance to the south. A sophisticated aqueduct, including lifting devices, delivered water to the town from a source downhill.[22]

In Roman times, as now, Lincoln lay in a fertile farming area.[23] Excavations at the nearby waterfront have revealed large quantities of cattle bones, which must have resulted from the butchery process. There is also evidence of granaries there. It is likely that Lincoln and its hinterland were yielding surplus agricultural produce. This may well have been despatched to army units elsewhere in Britain. Probably the Roman authorities, rather than private traders, controlled the distribution of any agricultural surpluses.

Following the reforms of Diocletian and Constantine, the Midlands became a separate province known as *Britannia Secunda*. It is generally assumed that Lincoln became the provincial capital and that the governor had his seat there.[24] Unfortunately, there is no epigraphic or other evidence to confirm the position.

---

[22]Jones (2011) 96–8.
[23]Rogers (2011) 124.
[24]Jones (2011) 119–24.

York

As described in Chapter 7, one of the final acts of the Ninth Legion, before it departed, was to construct a massive fortress at York[25] (*Eburacum*) on the north side of the river Ouse. A surviving pair of timber piles, which supported the north-west corner of the fortress, have been dated to *c.* AD 80–120.[26] This fortress (much of which now lies beneath York Minster) became the base of the Sixth Legion, when it came to Britain with Hadrian. The legion made substantial improvements to the defences during the second century.[27] A large civilian settlement grew up around the fortress.

The north of Britain was a heavily militarized zone. As the only fortress in the top half of Britain, York was at the centre of a huge fort system and had responsibility for overseeing the defence of the vital northern frontier. In addition, York stood on neutral ground forming the boundary between two communities, the Parisi and the Brigantes. All these factors combined to make York in effect the capital of the north.[28] When Caracalla divided Britain into two provinces, York formally became the capital of the northern province, *Britannia Inferior*.

More significantly, as noted in Chapter 11, York served as capital of the Empire from AD 208–211. This would have had a transformative effect upon the city. We can visualize the scene: numerous officials bustling around; messengers coming and going; embassies seeking audiences with Severus or his sons; petitions, letters and other documents arriving from all parts of the Empire. In the short term, the presence of the Emperors must have stimulated economic development. Over time it transformed York from a fortress with a surrounding settlement into a major, prestigious town. The very fact that an imperial cremation was held there in AD 211 is evidence of the town's high status.

We know that by AD 237 York was a *colonia*, which was the highest status any provincial town could enjoy. In that year one Marcus Aurelius Lunaris dedicated an altar at Bordeaux, describing himself as a *servir augustalis* (priest of the imperial cult) at the *coloniae* of York and Lincoln.[29] It is likely that York acquired colonial status while the Emperors were in residence there. If the local council had petitioned Severus or his sons for that privilege, it may have been awkward for them to say no.

The reforms of Diocletian and Constantine at the beginning of the fourth century led to a wholesale reorganization of provinces, as well as a shake up of civil and military administration. York now became capital of the newly created province, *Flavia Caesariensis*. The commander of the troops in northern Britain was based at York.

There are intriguing signs of Christian worship at York after Constantine's conversion. Beneath the Minster a tile was recovered from the fortress with a chi-rho symbol scratched on it. The records of the Council of Arles, which was held in AD 314, show that a bishop from York attended. So there must have been a Christian congregation in York to whom the bishop preached, except when he was attending overseas conferences.

---

[25] For a delightful account of Roman York, see Higgins (2013) chapter 9.
[26] Ottaway (2015) 49.
[27] Ottaway (1993) chapter 3.
[28] Millett (1990) 91.
[29] Ottaway (1993) 64–5.

Figure 17.3 York, Roman wall and tower. © Wikimedia/Kaly99.

The city retained its pre-eminence after the fall of Rome. The Vikings made it the capital of their Northumbrian kingdom and re-named it 'Yorvick', a name which mutated to 'York' over time. The modern city of York retains the pre-eminence that it acquired in the Roman era (Fig. 17.3). It is the religious capital of northern England and the only city outside Canterbury to have an archbishop.

4. LONDON

The site of Roman London was the most easterly point of the Thames where the river could conveniently be bridged. In about AD 47–48 the Romans built a wooden bridge across the Thames roughly where London Bridge now stands. This bridge became the single focal point from which roads linking the principal settlements in south-east Britain fanned out: to Silchester, St Albans, Colchester, Chichester, Canterbury and, of course, the port at Richborough. As Lacey Wallace points out in her excellent study of pre-Boudican London,[30] there seems to have been some central road planning authority in the early period after the conquest.

---

[30]Wallace (2014) 14–16.

A civilian trading port probably developed around the area of the bridge in the mid-first century.[31] How it gained the name *Londinium* is unknown. The new town was established in the area of Ludgate Hill and Cornhill. The Walbrook stream flowed down into the Thames through the valley between those two hills. In other words, ancient *Londinium* was established roughly where the City of London now is. The bridge over the river gave access to a suburb which developed on the south side. Watling Street crossed the river at this point and then branched off to the west. The development of London was swift and appears to have been planned.

London was not a civitas capital. Instead it straddled community boundaries: to the north lay the domains of the Catuvellauni and the Trinovantes; to the south the territories of the Atrebates, the Regni and the Cantiaci. Situated at a crossing point of the Thames, London was ideally placed to function as a trading centre and in due course as an administrative hub. It was removed from the major power bases that had been established in the Iron Age. The indigenous élites were therefore less likely to control economic exchange.[32]

Because of its strategic location London rapidly became a major centre for traders and merchandise.[33] There is evidence of metal working, wood working, pottery production, butchery, grain dealing and other trades during the 50s. Numerous coins from the Claudian period have been found in the area to the north of London Bridge. Admittedly most of those coins were forgeries, in the sense that they were not official issue from the imperial mints, but the fact that so many coins (whether genuine or forged) were lost shows that there was a great deal of commerce in the early years. It is quite likely that Gallic traders spotted a business opportunity and came over. They had the experience of trading inside the Roman Empire for a century and their presence could well account for London's rapid emergence as a boom town. By AD 60 three high-status buildings were standing in London: a proto-forum building, an aisled hall and an apsidal building with a complex substructure. There was also a public water supply. Not bad for a new town less than twelve years old. Tacitus says that by 60 London was: 'an important centre with a large number of businessmen and much merchandise'.[34] This remains the position today, as London approaches its 2000th anniversary.

The neutral location of London brought with it other advantages. Because London was removed from the established civitas capitals, it was ideally placed to become the capital city. At some point in the late first century (we do not know precisely when) London became the centre of provincial administration, with both the procurator and the governor based there.

The logic of designating London for this role was essentially the same as the logic that led to the establishment of both Washington and Canberra as federal capitals. The District of Columbia, which was created in 1790 to accommodate Washington, lay on the boundary between the powerful states of Maryland and Virginia. The Australian Capital Territory, created in 1911 to accommodate Canberra, lay between Sydney and Melbourne, the two most prosperous cities in Australia. If you are creating a state with strong regional government, it makes sense to locate the capital on neutral ground away from the regional centres.

---

[31] Wallace (2014) chapter 3.
[32] Millett (1990) 89.
[33] Wallace (2014) 88–93, 114–20; Perring (2015) 23–6.
[34] 'Copia negotiatorum et commeatuum maxime celebre': *Annals* 14.33.

As noted in Chapter 6, Queen Boudica of the Iceni was not a supporter of the Roman administration. In 60-1 she took the opportunity to invade London, slaughter the inhabitants and set fire to all buildings. Archaeological evidence suggests that everything was burnt to the ground. This was not a good start for the Londoners of that period, but the strategic and geographical considerations identified above meant that the city had to survive. The Romans and other entrepreneurs set about rebuilding it on a grander scale during the Flavian period, monumentalizing the city.[35] They constructed a forum at the heart of the new city and a timber amphitheatre in the area where Guildhall now stands.[36] They developed the waterfront to create a major port, with public baths on the higher ground above. They established the full complement of public buildings, as well as a new water supply system.[37] A cynic might say that Boudica had done the Romans a favour: by carrying out such a thorough demolition job, she had cleared the ground for comprehensive re-development.

The centrepiece of the new city was a large rectangular forum,[38] which was established on Cornhill. It was just over 100 metres long and 50 metres wide. A perimeter wall defined the area. The forum seems to have comprised a higher level piazza at the north end, with a larger courtyard beneath it to the south. Both of these areas could have been used for public meetings or markets, as occasion required. On the south, east and west sides of the forum there were narrow ranges of rooms, which might have been shops or offices.

A substantial basilica stood at the top of the forum. This was a long, covered rectangular hall. It was an imposing building, which dominated the London skyline. Built of stone, it included both a nave and aisles. The basilica housed council offices and meeting rooms, archives for records, storerooms for valuables, courtrooms where magistrates sat and so forth. The Roman basilica was the precursor of the modern City Hall, which now stands on the opposite side of the river.

The Romans and others built a prestigious set of public baths at Huggin Hill,[39] just to the south of Mansion House tube station. The baths stood on one of the newly formed terraces above the Thames. The bath complex was built on two levels, with water tanks on the higher level. A series of drains and culverts conveyed water from nearby springs to be stored in the tanks and adjacent reservoirs. The actual baths and heated rooms were on the lower level. A large section of the hypocaust survives with over 100 *pilae* still in situ. The furnace room lay to the east of the main buildings. A separate set of pipes conveyed waste water down into the Thames. There appears also to have been a lavatory block on the lower level. This too conveniently discharged into the Thames.

A fort was necessary to accommodate the soldiers who had been detached from their legions and auxiliary units to serve on the governor's staff. The remains of such a fort have been found at Cripplegate. It was built of stone and appears to date from the early second century. Rows of barrack blocks, separated by corridors, occupied the southern half of the fort. The fort

---

[35] Perring (2011) chapter 2 and (2015); Hingley (2018) chapter 7.
[36] Wilmott (2010) 93–5.
[37] Hingley (2018) 63–4.
[38] Marsden (1987).
[39] English Heritage are now responsible for this site (which is not open to the public) and provide a description on their website.

housed both cavalry and infantrymen,[40] who served as the governor's bodyguards as well as doing clerical work. We know from the Vindolanda tablets that they were retained on the books of their regiments, but they were recorded as 'at London'. The Cripplegate fort replaced an earlier temporary fort, which had stood on the south-eastern slope of Cornhill.[41]

As discussed in Chapter 10, London's building boom continued through the first half of the second century: the baths at Huggin Hill were substantially restructured; the amphitheatre was rebuilt in stone. Along the north bank of the river the terraces and the quays were extended. A large official building went up on the south bank. The élite classes built fine masonry houses for themselves, fragments of which have been found around Bishopsgate and Watling Court. During the 120s or 130s the western and central areas of the city survived a substantial fire.[42]

In about AD 120 developers erected a large building[43] on the south bank at Southwark.[44] The dating is based on sherds of black burnished ware found in the demolition debris overlying an earlier building. The new building included a well-appointed suite of heated rooms and a substantial bathhouse. It continued in use through the second, third and fourth centuries. The presence of fine wall paintings[45] confirms that the occupants were of high status. An early third-century marble inscription found there lists the members of a vexillation[46] of legionary soldiers, identifying the cohort from which each man came. Possibly they were *beneficiarii* – they must have been important to get their names carved in marble: their presence would have been linked with London's status as provincial capital. Two tiles recovered from the site are stamped 'PPBRILON', which stands for *procurator provinciae Britanniae Londinii*: 'the procurator of the province of Britain at London'. All the evidence suggests that this was a prestigious building with both military and official uses.

Around AD 125 the Romans rebuilt the amphitheatre partly in stone.[47] The rebuilt amphitheatre had capacity to hold between 7,000 and 10,000 people. The walls of the arena and the entrance passageways were 1.2 metres thick – in places they survive to a height of 1.5 metres. The surface of the arena was rammed gravel mixed with hard mortar. Timber-lined drains took away surface water. The eastern end of the amphitheatre lies beneath the Guildhall Art Gallery and is now on display in the basement. Remarkably, much of the wood has survived because it has lain in wet anaerobic conditions for the last two thousand years. You can walk on thickened glass above the drains and study the original woodwork at close quarters. The Guildhall display is so excellent that it is easy to imagine the amphitheatre in its heyday: Londoners in those times much enjoyed the spectacle of wild animals fighting, condemned men being eaten alive and gladiators fighting to the death. All of these frivolities were excellent spectator sport. Modern West End theatre is tame by comparison.

At some point in the second century a fine town house was built at Billingsgate. The builders terraced into the hillside to achieve a level ground floor; they included a hypocaust system as central heating. Unusually, this house remained in occupation throughout the Roman period

---

[40]Hassall (1973).
[41]Dunwoodie et al. (2015).
[42]Hingley (2018) 116–20.
[43]Yale (2005); Hassall (1996) 22–3; Hingley (2018) 137–9.
[44]Where Winchester Palace, the medieval London residence of the bishops of Winchester, was later built.
[45]Recovered from room B of building 13.
[46]See Chapter 1, Section 3.
[47]Bateman et al. (2008); Hingley (2018) 126–8.

and beyond. A coin hoard was hidden in the furnace wall soon after AD 395 and a Saxon brooch has been found amongst the collapsed roof tiles. The foundations have survived intact: they are now on display at 101 Lower Thames Street, an English Heritage site.

One major project in the late second century was the construction of the London wall. That apart, the city seems to have gone into decline.[48] The volume of imported luxury goods reduced and some of the buildings destroyed by fire (more of a hazard in ancient times than now) were not reinstated. The Huggin Hill baths were abandoned and demolished; other buildings fell into disuse. A layer of dark earth started to form over parts of the city, which may be evidence of gardening or farming.[49] There is controversy as to when the dark earth was deposited and what it signifies,[50] but we can safely bypass this debate.

There was something of a revival in the third century.[51] The building of the city wall continued during the early years of the century. The engineers created a set of gateways, commemorated in place names familiar to every Londoner: Ludgate, Newgate, Bishopsgate and Aldgate. In the mid-third century they extended the city wall, so that it ran along the riverfront. This seems odd, as it restricted access to the quays, but no doubt the designers had their reasons. The Romans also erected a monumental arch with a screen of the gods on top[52] and a temple to Mithras.[53] They constructed new quays on the north bank of the river and the volume of imported luxury goods started to increase once more. As previously noted, the Emperor Severus took up residence in Britain for several years in the early third century. That may have triggered a revival in the fortunes of the province.

The population of London during the third century seems to have been smaller and richer than before.[54] The élites were building ever grander town houses, often with fine mosaics. Many of these were located in the Walbrook valley, which seems to have been the Roman version of Mayfair or Belgravia.

In the late third century the forum was demolished and not rebuilt. This may have been due to the political upheavals of that time (see Chapter 13). On the other hand, somewhat incongruously, a new monumental building was erected at St Peter's Hill.[55] Dendrochronology dates the timbers for this structure as having been felled in AD 293 and 294. Possibly, therefore, Allectus the rebel emperor ordered the building works; alternatively, the Roman authorities might have built this after Constantius regained control of Britain in AD 296. It is unlikely that the building was a palace, as some have suggested. The building may well have had a religious function, as an extension to the nearby temple complex. That would have been a fitting precursor to St Paul's Cathedral, which now overshadows that site.

As previously explained, at the beginning of the fourth century Britain was divided into four provinces and London became capital of the principal province, *Maxima Caesariensis*. The administrative reforms introduced by Constantine led to a substantial increase in bureaucracy. New officials took up residence in London, many no doubt occupying the fine

---

[48] Perring (2015) 32–3; Hingley (2018) 170.
[49] Perring (2011) 78–81.
[50] Rogers (2011) 10.
[51] Hingley (2018) chapter 8.
[52] Perring (2011) fig 41; Hingley (2018) 186–7.
[53] Hingley (2018) 183–5.
[54] Perring (2011) 100–2.
[55] De la Bédoyère (2010a) 93–4; Perring (2011) 110–12.

houses which sprang up during the early fourth century.[56] It is a tradition of bureaucracies that those at the top pay themselves handsomely. The new bureaucrats of fourth-century London were loyal to that tradition.

The fourth century saw few major building works in London. In the latter half of the century the Empire was under threat and Rome progressively cut back the forces that were garrisoning Britain. One project of the late fourth century, which may not be surprising, was the strengthening of London's defences. The city authorities constructed a set of D-shaped bastions on the eastern side of the city and along the waterfront wall from Walbrook to where the Tower of London now stands.[57]

Was Britannia too London-centric? The short answer is no. In the Roman era London was the seat of the governor and the procurator, a thriving sea port and the point from which most major roads fanned out. But Londinium did not dominate Britannia in the way that London now dominates England. One problem for modern Britain is that London is pre-eminent in all spheres: it is the political, administrative, commercial, financial and legal capital. Sadly, we cannot blame these developments on the Romans – they made quite a good choice at the time.

5. SMALL TOWNS

'Small towns' is the term that historians use to describe settlements or communities that did not have civic institutions and were generally much smaller than civitas capitals. Some had their origins in the Iron Age, but most developed in response to the demands and opportunities generated by Roman occupation. Generally, these small towns were in existence by the end of the first century, but the peak of their prosperity came in the third and fourth centuries,[58] which was the period when civitas capitals started to wane.

Roads and buildings in small towns did not follow a standard pattern: there were no grids of streets neatly crossing each other at right angles. The small towns seem to have grown up in a haphazard manner. Very few of them had defences.

On main roads

Some small towns developed along the main roads as places where travellers might stop off. For example, Crayford in Kent was located at a convenient point on Watling Street between London and Rochester. Other small towns were dotted along Fosse Way between Exeter and Lincoln.

An interesting example is Wall (*Letocetum*), which stood on Watling Street, a few miles north of Birmingham. In the mid-first century the Fourteenth Legion built a vexillation fortress there and a small civilian settlement grew up, originally serving the needs of the military. The army moved away in about AD 70, but the town remained. It seems to have prospered, no

---

[56] Perring (2011) 118.
[57] Perring (2011) 124.
[58] Millett (1990) 143–7.

doubt because it stood on a major thoroughfare. In about 120, developers built a fine courtyard house there with thick walls, suggesting that it was two stories high. Someone has recently labelled this building as a *mansio*, but that identification is not secure. It could equally well be a grand town house. A substantial set of public baths stood nearby. The big house seems to have been destroyed by the end of the second century, although *Letocetum* retained its strategic importance. In about 300 a wall and rampart were built round part of the town. Wall is now a peaceful village with a congenial public house. There is an English Heritage site in the centre of the village, where the remains of the big house and the bathhouse are on view. Within the baths you can see where the furnaces and hypocausts were located. Several courses of stonework still stand and are fun for children to climb over.

Ilchester (*Lindinis*) stood at a nodal point on the Fosse Way and developed into a relatively small urban centre, probably with its own civic institutions.[59] The remnants of eight buildings have been found in the area, which could be classified as modest villas. Probably the occupants of these properties served as councillors, sat as magistrates and generally ran the show. In such towns there were complex webs of power and social mobility was not on the agenda.

Ports and industrial centres

Small towns developed around all the major ports for obvious reasons. Richborough was the first Roman port established in Britain: a large township developed on the site overlooking the harbour.[60] This flourished from the first century onwards, acquiring an amphitheatre as well as temples and housing. During the second century the Romans established a port and barracks at Dover, where another small town grew up principally to serve the needs of the navy.

Many small towns were centred around specific industries. Camerton and Nettleton, both on the Fosse Way, became manufacturing centres. Mining communities also generated new towns. At Charterhouse in the Mendips a settlement for lead miners was established in the mid-first century. This became one of the larger 'small towns', as it attracted traders and others whose business was related to the mines. Charterhouse even possessed a small amphitheatre with earth banks, which was an unusual luxury.

At religious centres

Some small towns were clustered around shrines or holy places. For example, Wycomb in Gloucestershire was centred on a temple precinct.

By far the best-known town to develop around a shrine was Bath (*Aquae Sulis*).[61] This began as a military base, guarding the point where two major roads crossed the river Avon: Fosse Way leading from Lincoln to Exeter and the great west road running from London to *Portus Abonae* (the Roman port at Bristol). It was also a centre of religious significance, because the Celtic goddess Sulis discharged some 250,000 gallons of hot water per day through the hot spring. The Romans identified Sulis with their own goddess Minerva and established a magnificent

---

[59]Gerrard (2013) 230.
[60]Millett (2007) 141–3.
[61]Cunliffe (1995) chapter 8.

temple to honour both deities during the early Flavian period. Stonemasons from north-east Gaul probably did the stonework – the single surviving column head is remarkably like one found in Cologne.[62] The Gorgon's head in the pediment is a dominant feature. Carved oak leaves surround the head to form a roundel. Since oak leaves were linked with the image of the Emperor[63] and oak trees were common across Europe, including Britain, the choice of motif was diplomatic. The roundel resembles others at provincial centres in Gaul and Spain. They, in turn, echo designs found in the Forum of Augustus at Rome.[64] The Bath temple is a graphic example of the cultural exchange between provinces, discussed in Chapter 9 above.

The baths linked to the temple were a remarkable engineering achievement.[65] The Roman authorities and legionary engineers probably had a direct input. They created a reservoir round the sacred spring, from which piping took water into a 'great bath' (measuring 22 × 8.8 metres, lined with lead sheets) and a series of smaller baths (Fig. 17.4). A separate massive drain took surplus water down to the river Avon. Over the last two thousand years, these works have survived much devastation, including a collapse of the superstructure. You can still see them functioning effectively.

Figure 17.4 The great bath at Bath. © Flickr/Matthew Hartley.

---

[62]Blagg (1979) 101–7.
[63]Cousins (2016) 102.
[64]Cousins (2016) 99–118.
[65]Cunliffe (2012) chapters 1–6.

Wealthy individuals from around the Empire left relics of their presence in Bath. Peregrinus from Trier was typical. In fulfilment of a vow to Loucetius Mars and Nemetona, he established an elegant altar, which still stands close to the sacred spring.[66] From the first century onwards, Bath was a busy cosmopolitan centre. The temple and the warm healing waters attracted many visitors, so that the tourist trade boomed and local businesses flourished, just as they do today.

Vagniacis (Springhead) stood on the main road between Rochester and London; it was built on the site of eight springs which fed the River Ebbsfleet.[67] The springs and their nearby pool were, of course, sacred. The indigenous people revered them; so did the invaders. The Romans built a temple complex around the springs and the pool. By the end of the first century the town had a population of 1,000 to 2,000.[68] It was an ideal spot for those taking the waters or worshipping the local gods. The town was also a convenient stopping off point on Watling Street. It must have been visited by many travellers en route between Britain and Gaul. It still is. Ebbsfleet International Station (the best place to catch Eurostar) now proudly stands at *Vagniacis*.

---

[66] RIB 140: 'Peregrinus Secundi filius civis Trever Loucetio Marti et Nemetona votum solvit libens merito'.
[67] Millett (2007) 160–1.
[68] See the Wessex Archaeology website.

CHAPTER 18
LIFE IN THE COUNTRYSIDE

1. Introduction
2. Roman villas in Britain
3. Some specific villas
4. The deep countryside
5. Rural development in the late Roman period

1. INTRODUCTION

If you leaf through the pages of *Country Life* you might conclude that the English countryside is teeming with wealthy landowners, enjoying a comfortable lifestyle and a range of leisure pursuits. That is, of course, only a small part of the picture. Likewise, if you visit the sites of Roman villas, what you will see is just one aspect of country life in the first to fourth centuries. Even so, this chapter will look at villas first. They were an important feature of Roman Britain (especially in the south-east) providing an array of comforts for the élites and regular employment for many others. Indeed, those who worked there may have welcomed the career opportunity, unless they happened to be slaves.

Although villas were home to only a small proportion of the rural population, they are now the public face of Roman Britain. Most people have visited a villa, if only because they were dragged round one on a school trip.

After that we shall look at the deep countryside. This is where most of the Romano-British population lived and worked. Obviously, there was not a sharp divide between 'villa land' and 'deep countryside'. There were country houses and rich farmers' houses built of stone, which fell short of the grand villas. So, the divide was blurred, especially in the later period. Finally, we shall look at events in the late Roman period and how they affected the countryside.

2. ROMAN VILLAS IN BRITAIN

'Villa' is the term that we use to describe the rural retreats or country houses of the élite classes in Roman Britain. Except for Fishbourne, the villas in Britain did not achieve anything like the scale or magnificence of those built in Italy for top Romans. Nevertheless, they were a complete departure from the Iron Age dwellings that they replaced. The villas were built in stone, usually to a rectangular plan, and had solid floors often decorated with mosaics.[1] They included bathhouses, which required skilful plumbing and engineering. Villas also had under-floor heating, known as hypocausts. These houses were designed for the wealthy classes, who had sufficient leisure to enjoy the pleasures of gracious living.

The remains of many smaller country houses from the Roman period have also been found across Britain. They were not villas in the sense described above, though may well now be described as such in tourist literature. A country house in this category would be built in stone and perhaps comprise a single range of rooms. A farm would have been attached and the house would probably have belonged to a well-to-do farmer. These smaller country houses did not have hypocausts or mosaics. The owners probably spent their time doing real work on their estates, rather than taking baths or sitting around reading Virgil.

The construction of Roman-style villas for the local élites was one of the defining features of the Empire. They were built across Germany, Belgium, Gaul and other provinces, although with strong regional variations. In relation to the larger villas, two main styles have been identified, namely those built round a central hall and those built round a central yard. It is not easy to distinguish between the two types, because the roofs have long vanished. The question becomes: was the central area a courtyard or a hall? Sometimes it is possible to discern the presence of post holes, indicating that posts once stood there to support a roof. In summary, most villas in Germany and Belgium were built around halls, whereas most villas in Britain and Gaul were built around yards.[2] The German halls tended to be wider and almost square. In the case of British villas, the halls (where they existed) were usually narrower and more elongated.

Farmland was attached to the villas, although it is now impossible to discern the extent of the land belonging to any particular property. The affluence of Romano-British villas came from agricultural production or nearby commercial enterprises.[3] Farming was an incidental activity, not the principal purpose of villas. The real function of villas was the display and consumption of wealth, rather than its production.[4]

The villa owners were generally leading Britons who held senior positions in civitas capitals. In the Roman political order and probably in Iron Age society as well, wealth and power were inextricably linked. Wealth generally meant ownership of land. The wealthy were deemed the best people to hold power. Those in power were best able to maintain and accumulate wealth. Local leaders who held sway in the Iron Age retained their dominance in the Roman era. They carried out local administration and tax collecting on behalf of the Roman authorities, with the opportunity to build and occupy Roman-style villas as their reward.

The head of the family occupying a villa was the *dominus*, which roughly means lord and master. He was not only a great man in the local community, he was also a powerful figure at home. Everyone including his family, servants and slaves did what the *dominus* ordered. Many a henpecked husband in the modern world may envy the position of the Roman *dominus*.

---

[1] For a clear description of the mosaics and explanation of their background, see Witts (2010). Better still, go and look at them!
[2] Smith (1978) 351–8.
[3] Reece (1981) 27–38.
[4] Millett (1990) 91–9.

It is obvious from a brief visit to any Romano-British villa, that a great deal of work was needed to keep the place going. This included washing, cleaning, maintaining, repairing, portering and waiting upon diners at mealtimes. It also included tending the adjacent farmland to serve the needs of the great house. Finally, someone had to sell off the surplus produce to the nearby urban population. It is reasonable to suppose that some of those who worked in or around the villas were slaves, some were freedmen and some were employed servants or workers. We simply do not know how the staff and workers were divided between these categories.[5] Possibly family members of the villa owner did some of the work. It may have been a good move to keep the younger generation busy, rather than making a nuisance of themselves. The large number of buildings in villas such as Chedworth suggests that an extended family could have lived there. Some villas seem to have housed mixed communities.[6] The complex of aisled halls at North Warnborough (near Silchester) is an example: that was probably in group ownership.[7]

Naturally enough the élite classes wanted their rural retreats to be reasonably close to the civitas centres where they held power, so villas tended to cluster around the major towns. For reasons that are not entirely clear, they were mainly confined to the south and east of Britain. For example, several villas clustered around Dorchester, but there were few of any significance around Exeter or in the south-west peninsula.

The one major town in south-east Britain that did not have many villas in its surrounding countryside was London.[8] This is not surprising, since London was not a civitas capital, but rather the seat of Roman government and a major trading centre. Senior Romans, not Celtic leaders, were in charge. The governor, the procurator and their respective officials had urban residences. They did not need or desire rural retreats.

In the first half of the fourth century there was a boom in villa building. New villas were appearing, and existing villas were being extended. Chedworth Roman Villa reached its zenith in the early fourth century. This period is generally regarded as the golden age of villa culture, as discussed in Chapter 14. In the second half of the century the number of villas reduced and any new villas were smaller. After about AD 375 there was very little construction work on villas.[9] The number of villa rooms occupied dropped dramatically in the second half of the fourth century.[10] And many villas were abandoned altogether.

3. SOME SPECIFIC VILLAS

Fishbourne – a provincial 'palace'

Fishbourne is a modest village in West Sussex. It lies between a railway line and the main road into Chichester. Not an obvious place to put a palace.[11] Two thousand years ago, however,

---

[5]Salway's introduction to Cleary (2013a).
[6]Gerrard (2013) 143.
[7]Wallace (2018) 231–52.
[8]Millett (1990) 193.
[9]Faulkner (2010) figure 33.
[10]Faulkner (2010) figure 34.
[11]Barry Cunliffe, who oversaw the excavation, calls it a palace and this chapter will follow suit. Some scholars say that it is only a large villa, since it is not on the scale of Nero's palace and other great palaces in Italy.

things were different. The sea stretched further inland and Fishbourne was a major harbour. It served the needs of both Chichester and the wider province.

A spacious and comfortable timber house was built at Fishbourne in AD 45, a couple of years after the original invasion. In about 65 the timber house was demolished and replaced by a substantial masonry building, described by Cunliffe as a 'proto-palace'.[12] Seemingly no expense was spared. There was much decorative stone inlay: some was Purbeck marble from Dorset, some was red silt-stone from the Mediterranean region. A separate bathhouse served this mansion. The remnants of the proto-palace have been reburied and are no longer visible.

This was a remarkably elaborate and expensive house for anyone to build at such an early date. Britain had only been under Roman occupation for 20 years. The province had recently been devastated by Boudica's rebellion, with massive loss of life and property damage on both sides. This was an unlikely period for either the Romans or Britons to start investing in luxury housing. Even if nothing else had been built at Fishbourne, one would wonder why this magnificent house was built and who it was for. But the proto-palace is not the end of the story.

Between AD 75 and 80 the existing mansion was demolished and a colossal palace was built in its place.[13] This was like none other that the Romans built either in Britain or anywhere else in northern Europe. The building comprised four massive wings, surrounding a courtyard laid out to gardens.

The west wing was built on an upper terrace, so that it dominated the gardens below. The principal room was a large square audience chamber with a high ceiling, seemingly designed to strike awe into whoever was received. The pediment in front of the audience chamber was supported on four huge columns, with a flight of steps leading down to the garden. Anyone walking in the gardens had access to all the main rooms of the west wing, which suggests that they had a public function. They may have been offices and meeting rooms for public officials.

The north wing was 70 metres long, 21 metres wide and built in the shape of an 'E'. It incorporated colonnaded gardens, suites of large rooms and much elaborate decoration. This wing may have served as accommodation for VIP visitors, such as senators or even occasionally the governor. Nowadays this wing is less exclusive. It is open to the general public, who can walk along raised pathways and see what remains of the mosaic floors.

Less is known about the south wing because modern roads and houses lie above it. Unsurprisingly, the homeowners do not favour demolition and excavation. This wing, which appears to have been the private residence of the palace owner, was designed on a grand scale. A bathhouse stood in the south-east corner. On the south side of this wing was a fine landscaped garden, which swept down towards the sea.

The east wing was some 150 metres long. At its centre was the impressive entrance hall through which all visitors would pass on arrival. This was the largest room in the palace, being approximately 25 metres wide and 30 metres long. The front and back entrances had pedimented facades, each supported on six columns 8 metres high. At the north-east corner was a separate aisled hall, also with an imposing façade.

---

[12]Cunliffe (2010) chapter 5.
[13]Cunliffe (2010) chapters 6–8.

An obvious question to ask is who lived at Fishbourne and why did the Romans build a palace fit for a king at such an unprepossessing location in a distant province? The most likely explanation is that both the proto-palace and the palace were built for Togidubnus.[14] He supported Rome from the start of the Claudian invasion. According to Tacitus, Togidubnus remained loyal to Rome throughout his reign and he was still alive in the late first century.[15] The kingdom of the Atrebates, the Regni and the Belgae remained peaceful throughout the first century. This was in marked contrast to the other client kingdoms. Togidubnus certainly earned whatever reward he received.

The cost of labour and materials for constructing the palace must have been vast. The Atrebates did not have that sort of money, even if all their coin hoards were put together. One possibility is that Togidubnus personally amassed enough wealth to pay for his palace. Individuals can make fortunes rapidly in developing countries: for example, African dictators in the years following independence or Russian oligarchs after the collapse of the Soviet Union. In the Roman world there was no progressive taxation. Powerful people controlled the tax system. Taxation was, if anything, regressive. Alternatively, funding for the construction project may have come from Rome. Vespasian, who was Emperor at the time, took a keen interest in Britain. Having commanded the Second Legion Augusta during the conquest, he probably knew Togidubnus and respected him. Vespasian may have personally authorized the lavish expenditure on Togidubnus' palace, as a reward for an old friend and faithful ally. Such munificence with public money was perfectly acceptable in those times. Anyone who tried to do that now would be hauled before the Public Accounts Committee for a grilling.

After the death of Togidubnus, the client kingdom came to an end and the king's former territories became conventional civitates, as previously described. Fishbourne palace became one of the many villas owned by the indigenous élites in south-east England. It was too far big and too expensive for an ordinary Celtic aristocrat to maintain. Subsequent owners lived principally in the north wing and neglected the remainder, which fell into disrepair. In the second century the north wing of the former palace served as an extremely grand villa for a well-to-do family. They built new accommodation within the existing shell.

In the centre of the north wing the new owners, or rather their craftsmen, laid a truly magnificent mosaic (Fig. 18.1). This has survived almost entirely intact. The central roundel depicts Cupid winged and riding on a dolphin, holding reins in one hand and a trident in the other. Around the side, enclosed in four semi-circles are two winged sea horses and two winged sea panthers. Other decorative motifs are dotted in the spaces. The choice of such themes at Fishbourne is typical. The villa-owning élites in Britain consciously espoused Roman culture. Whether or not classical mythology is your idea of art, the whole composition is stunningly beautiful and technically impressive. Taking care of such a precious work of art on the dining room floor must have been quite a challenge for the villa owners, especially if they had children.

The second century villa continued into the third century with only moderate changes. Sadly, in the third century the north wing caught fire and was destroyed. The damage was such that no-one attempted re-building. Over the centuries that followed, the site was plundered by

---

[14] Both (Cunliffe 2010) 109 and Wacher (1995) 259 tentatively support this view.
[15] *Agricola* 14.

Figure 18.1 Dolphin mosaic at Fishbourne palace. © Flickr/Leimenide.

stone-robbers. All that remained were foundations, sections of floor, low bits of wall and some building debris. The achievement of Barry Cunliffe and his team of archaeologists has been to reconstruct from these clues what the original palace looked like. This is shown in a model at the entrance to the site.

Chedworth – a fourth century villa

A modest villa was built at Chedworth early in the Roman period (Fig. 18.2). Around AD 300 the villa was substantially rebuilt and extended. What you see when you visit Chedworth now are the remains of a fine fourth-century villa, a typical example of the golden age of the villa culture. The National Trust has taken over and restored the site. There are raised walkways and clear signs to explain everything as you walk round. Simon Esmonde Cleary has written an excellent account of the villa.[16] The following paragraphs draw heavily on that account.

The villa was built around a central courtyard. On the inside of the north, south and west wings there are galleries, which face the courtyard. A cross gallery on the east side of the courtyard links the north and south wings, with the main entrance in the middle. The villa stands on a hillside, with the north wing at the top, projecting some way to the east beyond the rest of the villa, to capture fine views over the valley. At the north-west corner there is a gap between wings, giving access to a small nymphaeum, which stands right at the top of the site.

The nymphaeum is an elegant apsidal basin, built around a spring. The spring was (of course) sacred and presumed to be the home of a nymph. Nymphs were small divinities, who busied themselves looking after springs and other local amenities. The Chedworth nymph did

---

[16] Cleary (2013a).

Life in the Countryside

Figure 18.2 Chedworth villa. © Wikimeedia/National Trust/Tony Kerins.

a splendid job: she provided enough water for the entire villa operation, including the kitchen, baths, lavatories and so forth. A lead pipe (part of which survives) took the sacred spring water down from the nymphaeum into the villa complex. In return for her services the nymph was given her own shrine. No doubt the occupants of the villa attended from time to time, to pay their devotions and keep the little nymph on side.

Unfortunately for the nymph, Christianity came to Britain in the fourth century. The *dominus* and his household dutifully adopted, or at least nodded to, the new religion. They had the 'chi rho' symbol carved into at least three of the basin coping stones. There were probably more stones with a carved 'chi rho', but these have now been lost. Such carvings could quickly be obliterated if there was another change of official religion. The nymphaeum may have become a shrine for Christian worship. Even so, all was not lost for the nymph. It is probable that members of the household continued to worship her, just to be on the safe side. The Romans liked to hedge their bets in matters of religion.[17]

There was a bathhouse in the west wing. This had its own separate entrance up a flight of steps. The cold room (*'frigidarium'*), the warm room (*'tepidarium'*) and the hot room (*'caldarium'*) can all be identified. There was a furnace attached for heating both the water and the hypocausts. The flooring throughout the bathhouse was polychrome mosaic. The mosaic in the changing room is still well preserved. It comprises intricate geometric patterns with a circular medallion at the centre, containing a two-handled cup. The bathers probably enjoyed the odd drink when getting dressed, so this was an appropriate motif.

Another bath suite stood in the north wing at the western end. This had its own separate furnace and a full range of baths. Whereas the west bathhouse offered wet heat (like a modern

---

[17] When Goths were besieging Rome and the Christian God was not doing much to help, many Romans returned to worshipping pagan gods: Gibbon (1783) vol 5, 290–1.

Turkish bath), the north bathhouse offered dry heat (like a modern sauna). It was a mark of considerable luxury that the villa provided baths of both types for the comfort of the owners and their guests.

The main dining room (room 5) stood in the west wing. It was of substantial size and had a hypocaust system with its own dedicated furnace. The floor surface was an elaborate, high-quality mosaic. Figures representing the four seasons are in triangles around the side. The winter figure is perfectly preserved: he is well wrapped up in cloak and hood, holding a leafless branch in one hand and a hare in the other. The central panel, which would have faced the diners directly, portrays Bacchus and Ariadne. Bacchus was a common feature of villa decoration because of his association with the good life. The myth of Ariadne was also popular: she rescued Theseus from the Minotaur's maze with the aid of a thread, but her plans for a long-term relationship with Theseus came to an abrupt end soon afterwards. He unceremoniously dumped her on the island of Naxos. Happily, Ariadne then met and married Bacchus. In the Chedworth mosaic she sits in the centre of the dining room, gazing lovingly into her husband's eyes.

Another fine dining room (room 32), probably intended for summer use, was built in the north wing. It had a mosaic floor (now lost) and a slightly raised area for couches and tables. A hypocaust system was provided in case the weather grew chilly. Because the north wing projected outside the villa, this room commanded fine views to the south. The diners would have looked out through windows or openings across the Coln Valley to the landscape beyond – a perfect setting for dinner on summer evenings.

The lavatories were built in a small room adjoining the south wing. This meant that they were right next to the kitchens and service block, hardly an ideal arrangement. There was a seat built of stone, immediately above a sewer running along the south wall. This may have been a malodorous building in its heyday, but now it is much loved by archaeologists. Valuable objects lost down lavatories were not always retrieved, for obvious reasons.

For a discussion of the villas at Lullingstone and Bignor, see the Online Appendix.

4. THE DEEP COUNTRYSIDE

The silent majority

Between 80 per cent and 90 per cent of the population[18] of Roman Britain did not live in towns and were not attached to villas. They lived and worked in the deep countryside. No historian troubled to report their doings. No mosaics or murals depict their homes. They got on with their lives as they always had,[19] but they were now ineluctably drawn into the Imperial system. The bulk of the countryside showed continuity from the late Iron Age, although the context was changing.[20]

---

[18]Taylor (2013) 173. On the calculations in Millett (1990) at 181–5, the figure would have been about 90 per cent. See also Gerrard (2013) 55.
[19]Russell and Laycock (2010) 119–29.
[20]Millett (1990) 120.

Agricultural practice was central to the lives of the silent majority. The matters that structured their relationships with neighbouring communities were field boundaries, traditional routes of access to grazing and so forth. More generally the prime concern of these communities was maintenance of the rural landscape upon which they depended for their livelihood. Status symbols were the ownership (or at least occupation) of land and the well-being of their livestock.[21]

Two direct consequences of the Roman occupation were the obligation to pay taxes usually at modest rates[22] (often in kind) and the need to provide surplus produce to the occupying army.[23] Money appeared on the scene, at least in areas where soldiers were making purchases. The new transport system also had a transformative effect. Roman artefacts began to penetrate the countryside, certainly in the immediate vicinity of roads. People started to use different ranges of pots. Their diet changed as well.

Regional variations

The deep countryside cannot be regarded as a single homogenous mass, engulfing the whole of Britannia beyond the curtilage of forts, villas and towns. As discussed in Chapter 2, there were distinct regional variations in domestic life and agricultural practice during the LPRIA. These regional variations were accentuated during the Roman period, in part because of the differing impact of the invaders. In the north and west the landscape was largely open. In the south and east the landscape was more intensely divided up. In some areas the fourth-century field systems can still be traced from upstanding earthworks and infilled ditches.[24] The Roman army played a significant role: it controlled movement; also, it offered an alternative career for those who did not fancy a life of subsistence farming.

In the north and west of Britain, material culture[25] was significantly restricted. By contrast, the distribution of coinage, pottery and metalwork was far greater in the south and east. The same was true of personal adornment. Far more women were wearing brooches in the south and east than elsewhere.[26] There were also differences in architectural styles. The dominant architecture in the north and west was the roundhouse. In the south and east roundhouses were much rarer. There was a tendency towards rectangular buildings.[27] Villas and stone-built farmhouses were more prolific.

The territory of the Cornovii roughly comprised modern Shropshire and the Welsh Marches. Unsurprisingly a substantial amount of Samian ware has been recovered from Wroxeter. Samian ware was mass-produced pottery, widely used across the Roman world and not unduly expensive. Despite that circumstance, very little Samian ware has been recovered from settlements across the hinterland of Wroxeter and virtually none more than five kilometres from the town.[28] Almost all the pottery finds in the hinterland were the products of local kilns,

---

[21] Taylor (2013) 175.
[22] Kehoe (2018) 37.
[23] Breeze (2013).
[24] Gerrard (2013) chapter 6.
[25] Gerrard (2013) chapter 6.
[26] Smith et al. (2018) 44–7.
[27] Smith et al. (2018) 76–7.
[28] Gaffney and White (2007).

mainly in the Severn Valley. Likewise, the use of Roman coins in Shropshire was sparse and may have been limited to meeting tax demands. Beyond the town boundaries there seems to have been a clear rejection of Roman culture.

Examination of pottery recovered from Exeter and York shows a similar trend.[29] The townsfolk were happily using Samian ware. In the surrounding countryside, however, the picture is more varied. Whilst some of the farming communities did start to use Roman pottery, others had no wish for such imported nonsense. They continued to use rural coarse ware, perhaps pointing out that what was good enough in the Iron Age was good enough for them.

The East Midlands roughly comprises Leicestershire, Lincolnshire and Northamptonshire. Here the impact of Rome was felt more directly. There was a colony in the north, Lincoln, and a civitas capital in the south, Leicester. The farming communities in this region appear to have continued with gradual changes during the first and second centuries. Facilities for processing and storing agricultural produce slowly emerged. More prosperous families started to occupy aisled halls. They used one end, usually the east, for domestic life. There they cooked, ate and slept. They used the other end for agricultural processing, such as corn drying, malting and crafts. During the third and fourth centuries some of these halls were built in stone.[30]

The greatest concentration of farmhouses, trackways and nucleated settlements was across the 'Central Belt', a region stretching from the Wash to the Bristol Channel.[31] Settlement across the Central Belt peaked in the late second century.

Agricultural production increased during the Roman period.[32] The widespread introduction of corn-dryers across southern and central England is an indication that by the third century those regions were generating grain surpluses.[33] There were also improved storage facilities. The surpluses were probably sent to the troops garrisoning Hadrian's Wall. Even so, that did not make the province self-sufficient. Storage deposits of foreign origin in the granaries at South Shields show that the army was continuing to import grain from the Continent.

Livestock grew fatter in the Roman period,[34] especially in central and southern England; there was an increase in cattle numbers.[35] Full-time specialist butchers appeared in towns and on military sites. More people kept chickens. There was a shift from sheep farming to cattle farming in certain areas. Cattle were used for ploughing, as well as being a source of meat. As discussed in Chapter 10, in an age without refrigeration, the best way to preserve meat was to treat it with salt. The salt industries of the Fens, Droitwich and Cheshire were vital to the agricultural economy.[36]

The investigation of 'ecofacts' involves analysing plant and animal remains, bits of bone, faecal remains and so forth. Some archaeologists love sifting through such material. They have

---

[29]Taylor (2013) 181.
[30]Taylor (2013) 177–9.
[31]Smith et al (2016) 172.
[32]The promotion of efficient agriculture was vital to the stability of the Empire: Kehoe (2018) 34–43.
[33]Allen et al. (2017) chapter 2.
[34]Allen et al. (2017) chapter 3.
[35]Smith et al. (2018) 118.
[36]Allen et al. (2017) 212–16.

demonstrated a significant increase in the availability of nutrients and flavourings throughout the province,[37] at least for the benefit of the élites.

Despite all the agricultural improvements, the mass of the rural population did not benefit. Diets in the countryside deteriorated during the Roman period, leading to an increase in tooth decay and diseases.[38] The countryside suffered a general decline in health compared with the Iron Age.[39]

Areas near forts

Agricultural communities sprang up around forts to meet the needs of the occupants. Farming was probably one of the main activities of a *vicus*. The extramural settlement at Housesteads is a good example.[40] It flourished during the second and third centuries and the remains of the buildings are clearly visible to anyone who visits the fort today. A dedication slab to a man called Julius was erected there 'by decree of the villagers'.[41] A coin hoard has been recovered from the site, as have two clay moulds used by coin counterfeiters. It seems that, in addition to farming, the villagers turned their hands to forgery.

Wherever cavalry were based there was a demand for fodder. Several cavalry units were stationed at forts along Hadrian's Wall, including Wallsend and Vindolanda. Analysis of plant and animal remains shows that many of the horses were kept in stalls over winter and fed with a mixture of hay and grain.[42] Hay is bulky to transport, so as a matter of practicality it must have been produced and supplied locally. This would have kept the local farmers busy. It was also a source of income, since the Britons charged for their services.[43]

East Yorkshire study

The lowlands of East Yorkshire provide an interesting case study, since Roman occupation did not reach this area until the 70s.[44] The army established a forward legionary base at York and, at some point during the 70s, forts at Brough-on-Humber and Hayton. They occupied the fort at Hayton for about 20 years and then abandoned it. They did not, however, abandon Brough; instead they made it the civitas capital of the Parisii, *Petuaria Parisiorum*. Marcus Ulpius Januarius funded the construction of a small theatre at Brough and has won perpetual glory: the dedication slab recording his munificence has survived largely intact.[45] In the early second century the Romans established the section of Ermine Street, which ran from Brough to York via Hayton.

Martin Millett and Peter Halkon have conducted a detailed investigation over some 30 years in order to establish the impact of the Roman presence on the countryside around

---

[37] Scheidel (2018) 67–9.
[38] Smith et al. (2018) 343–5.
[39] Smith et al. (2018) 356–7.
[40] Allason-Jones (2013).
[41] 'Decreto vicanorum': RIB 1616.
[42] Huntley (2013).
[43] *Tab Vindol* II, 649 records payment to Britons for delivering a cartload of grain.
[44] Millett (2015b).
[45] RIB 707.

Hayton.[46] It is not easy to distil the results of 30 years painstaking research into a couple of paragraphs. In essence, however, what Millett and Halkon have established is as follows. There are two distinct periods to consider. These are (i) the short military phase while the Hayton fort was occupied and (ii) the period after the road was constructed.

(i) Military phase. The fort size suggests that it held an auxiliary cohort, some 500 men. The occupying troops and their commanding officer would have become the *de facto* authority in the area. It seems that the local farmsteads were providing their best sheep meat to the army. The soldiers had healthy appetites and money to spend, so Roman coinage started to appear in the vicinity of the fort in the 70s–90s. The men also had other appetites and must have formed relationships with local women. Despite about a generation of occupation, no *vicus* developed around the fort. There are, however, the remains of a large roundhouse nearby, which suggests that a local potentate moved his home to be next to the new centre of power. As noted previously, the general effect of the occupation was to strengthen the position of the pre-existing élites, so long as they threw in their lot with Rome.

(ii) It is uncertain who built the road. Possibly the army did, in the usual way. Alternatively, since the road appeared in the early second century, it is possible that the local Parisii did the construction work as a civic duty. If so, army officers and surveyors would have supervised the operation, dealing appropriately with any slackers. Ermine Street was a major thoroughfare leading towards the northern frontier, which was then under development. The arrival of the road had a substantial effect on the landscape: roadside settlements sprang up; many coins and much imported Samian ware were scattered along the line of the road. Since Hayton was about half-way between Brough and York, it formed a natural stopping point. A large settlement developed there during the second century, covering an area of about 7 hectares. Some sixty families came to live in the new settlement, which probably comprised most of the local population. They appear to have embraced the full range of Romano-British culture. Metal detectorists have recovered many brooches, tools, fitments and other artefacts from the area of the settlement. Housing styles changed and aisled timber halls began to appear. In the later Roman period, the Hayton settlement even boasted a small bath building. The hardy Yorkshire farmers began to enjoy the luxury of hot and cold baths.

5. RURAL DEVELOPMENT IN THE LATE ROMAN PERIOD

Archaeology reveals a number of changes to the countryside in the late Roman period. In particular, taxes were paid in cash rather than kind; there were changes to farming methods; villages started to emerge. Also, the 'colonate' system developed.

New farming methods

There was an expansion of arable farming in the late Roman period.[47] Arable farmers started to use asymmetric ploughshares and coulters. They also appear to have adopted full crop

---

[46]Millett (2015a) and (2015b).
[47]Allen et al. (2017) 172.

rotation. Long balanced sickles and scythes were introduced. All this would have led to more efficient agriculture. It appears from animal bones recovered that there was a decrease in sheep farming and an increase in the use of woodlands for hunting and pasturage of pigs. The changes in agricultural methods and greater efficiency achieved in the fourth century may be part of the reason for the flowering of villa culture at that time.

There seems to have been an increase in the size of estates and land holdings in the fourth century. Certainly, this was the case elsewhere in the Empire. Any substantial increase in size would be likely to lead to greater efficiency. There is evidence that many rural sites prospered during the fourth century, although the increased productivity did not always benefit British workers. We know that in AD 359 the authorities sent surplus grain across the Channel in order to feed the Roman army on the Rhine.[48] There is debate as to whether this was an exceptional measure or a regular arrangement. The former is more likely, unless the theory being developed by Sam Moorhead (summarized in Chapter 14) prevails. When it was necessary to meet a particular exigency, the Roman authorities levied an *annona*, which was a compulsory requisition in kind. The supply of grain to the Rhine army during the late 350s was probably an *annona*.

Increased tax burden

The tax burden probably increased during the fourth century. There were three major heads of public expenditure. First, a new enlarged bureaucracy was administering Britain and other provinces. These bureaucrats had to be paid and they may have claimed lavish expenses as well. Second, the imperial treasury had to finance major wars on the eastern front. Third, there was the mounting cost of defending Britain against barbarian invaders. Overall it seems likely that the peasants who toiled to improve agricultural output ended up paying more taxes.

Colonate system

The colonate system developed during the fourth century.[49] Under this system tenant farmers or workers (*coloni*) cultivated the land on great estates and were completely under the control of the *dominus*. Unlike modern agricultural tenants and workers, who have a raft of statutory rights and protections, the unfortunate *coloni* had no such rights. They just had duties. They were required by law to stay on the estates where they worked.[50] Their children and grandchildren were also required to stay and work on the same estates. 'What are you going to do when you grow up?' was not a tactful question to ask in the households of the *coloni*. The status of *coloni* was similar to that of Russian serfs before their emancipation in 1861.

Our knowledge of the colonate system is mainly derived from other provinces. However, a reference in book XI of the *Theodosian Code* confirms that this system operated in Britain. The *Theodosian Code* is a digest of the Emperors' decrees and the laws of Rome from AD 313 to 438, compiled during the reign of Theodosius II. Book XI of the Code dealt with the taxation of country estates. It is replete with fascinating details. For example, a senator was let off paying

---

[48] Ammianus, *Res Gestae* 18.2.3.
[49] Millett (1990) chapter 8; Faulkner (2010) chapter 6.
[50] Kehoe (2018) 44–5.

fiscal dues in respect of any land from which the *colonus* had fled.[51] Provincials were liable to 'suffer lashes with leaded whips' if they failed to pay their taxes on time.[52] Modern revenue authorities, including HM Revenue and Customs, may look back with envy at Roman procedures for enforcing tax payments.

Villages

In the late Roman period 'small nucleated settlements', as they are described by archaeologists, emerged.[53] These were in effect villages, since they comprised clusters of timber houses and farms. There is also evidence of craft activity there. Some of these villages developed from earlier settlements, while others sprang up in the fourth century. Examples of such villages have been found at Chalton in Hampshire, Kingscote in Gloucestershire, Catsgore in Somerset and Stanwick in Northamptonshire. Sometimes country houses of modest size were associated with these villages. It is debatable whether or not these houses should be called 'villas'.

---

[51] *Theodosian Code* XI.1.7.
[52] A decree of 5 December 353 banned this method of tax collection: *Theodosian Code* XI.7.7.
[53] Millett (1990) 205–11; Faulkner (2010) chapter 6.

CHAPTER 19
RELIGION IN ROMAN BRITAIN

1. Introduction
2. Roman religion and mythology
3. The Roman Gods
4. Army religion
5. The indigenous religions of Britain
6. The mingling of Roman and Celtic religions
7. Mithraism
8. Christianity
9. Curse tablets
   (i) The sacred spring at Bath
   (ii) Elsewhere in Britain
10. Summary

1. INTRODUCTION

In this chapter we will look at the religions of the Roman Empire and of Iron Age Britain. We will examine how those religions commingled, the impact of Mithraism and the advent of Christianity. We will come finally to 'curse tablets'. Most of the available evidence relates to religious practice, which will be the focus of this chapter. What people believed must be a matter of inference from those practices.

'Religion' is a complex web of beliefs and practices, by which humans seek to make sense of the world and to influence whatever invisible forces govern their lives. Religions are traditional in the sense of being transmitted between generations with successive adjustments, so that each is the product of history and the expression of a particular national, regional, local or ethnic culture.

When peoples migrate, they may keep their religious practices intact, as in the case of Judaism. Alternatively, fusion occurs: there is a mingling of the religion of the newcomers and the host country. For example, African slaves transported to Brazil brought with them their own spiritual traditions, known as Candomblé and these became fused with Catholicism. The

Church of Bonfim in Salvador exhibits elements of both religions. In the Roman Empire there was much migration and ample scope for fusion.

Believers often portray their gods in statues or other art forms, which can themselves become objects of veneration. Anyone who doubts this should visit the Hong Kong New Territories: a bronze statue of the goddess Guan Yin (erected in 2014 at a cost of HK $1.5 billion) stands 76 metres high and dominates the area. You can see Chinese worshippers looking up to her statue and praying.

Religion has always been a powerful force in politics, driving people to extremes of virtue or evil. Both are in evidence today. Lucretius, the Richard Dawkins of the ancient world, cynically observed: 'Tantum religio potuerit suadere malorum', meaning 'so great are the evils which religion could induce'.[1] Augustus appreciated the political value of religious ritual and belief; it strengthened social cohesion and reinforced patriotic sentiment. He appointed himself Pontifex Maximus (equivalent to Archbishop of Canterbury) and promoted a religious revival.[2]

In many societies, religion is used as a means of naturalizing power structures: it legitimates the position of the leaders. The divine right of kings asserted by the Stewart kings of England (supported by Archbishop Laud and others) was a classic example. Druidism as practised in Iron Age Britain was another example. Empire builders usually claim to have God or the gods on their side: their dominion over foreign lands may be presented as part of a divinely ordained historical process.

In the ancient world rational scientific explanations for the origins of the universe and life were unavailable. Almost all ancient peoples believed in a god or gods.[3] Even the sceptical Lucretius believed in gods, although he maintained they were unconcerned with human affairs. Many gods were associated with particular places: for example, Vulcan made thunderbolts inside Mount Etna; Sulis inhabited a hot spring in Somerset. The ancients felt close to their gods and maintained regular two-way contact with them. This contact involved:

- ceremonies on appointed days;
- sacrifices;
- prayers at shrines or other appropriate places;
- consultation about future decisions by questioning oracles, reading omens or divination;
- giving thanks for successful outcomes attributed to divine intervention.

2. ROMAN RELIGION AND MYTHOLOGY

Rome gained mastery of Italy early in its history, taking over the gods of conquered communities. Much 'Roman' religion is of Etruscan origin. As Rome rose to power in the Mediterranean world, it absorbed Greek culture, including religion and mythology. Most Roman gods had

---

[1] *De Rerum Natura* 1, 101.
[2] Scullard (1963) 241–4.
[3] There were a few rare instances of atheism: Whitmarsh (2016) chapter 14.

Greek equivalents. They were a strange assortment of immortals, with many human foibles. That is not surprising. The peoples of the ancient world created the pantheon of classical gods and projected onto them their own ambitions, anxieties, lusts, fears and faults.

In the modern world most religions have authoritative texts, setting out what their adherents are expected to believe. The texts of the three great Abrahamic religions are, of course, the Old Testament, the New Testament and the Koran. Greece never had anything like that; nor did Rome under the Republic or the Principate. The stories of the gods were part of an oral tradition, which poets and playwrights elaborated as they saw fit. Homer, Aeschylus, Sophocles, Euripides, Ovid, Horace, Virgil and other authors described the gods and their doings. They had no authority to pronounce on religious doctrine, but their texts became the best-known repositories of classical mythology and religion. The boundary between myth and religion was blurred.

Virgil's epic poem, the *Aeneid*, became a text of supreme importance because it traced the origins of Rome right back to the Trojan War and provided a moral basis for Rome's imperialism. Early in the poem there is a discussion between the gods, in which Jupiter says that he has given imperial power without limit to the Romans.[4] The storyline is that Aeneas, a Trojan hero, flees to Italy after the fall of Troy and founds Lavinium, the predecessor of Rome. On the way he stops off for a visit to the Underworld, where he meets the spirits of numerous celebrities and, more importantly, learns Rome's destiny. The ghost of Anchises, Aeneas' father, points to the souls of future Roman heroes who are waiting to be born, including of course Augustus. Warming to his theme, Anchises explains that some people are fine artists and sculptors; some are powerful advocates in court; some are skilled astronomers. But Rome has a special talent – to rule the world. Anchises explains Rome's destiny to Aeneas in three famous lines:

'tu regere imperio populos, Romane, memento
(hae tibi erunt artes), pacisque imponere morem,
parcere subiectos et debellare superbos.'[5]

'But you, Roman, remember that you must rule other nations by your authority (for this will be your particular skill). Impose a peaceful way of life upon them. Spare the conquered. Crush the arrogant in warfare.'

This is an example of the process discussed above. Religion is being used to naturalize power and legitimate imperialism. The lines quoted above must have resonated across the Empire and made many a Roman general feel good after massacring the opposition.

3. THE ROMAN GODS

Jupiter (Greek equivalent Zeus) was king of the gods. Jupiter exercised supreme power in the heavens. This included organizing thunderstorms and hurling bolts of lightning at those who

---

[4]'Imperium sine fine dedi': *Aeneid* 1,279.
[5]*Aeneid* 6, 851–3.

annoyed him. He was not a god to be crossed. The Roman Empire teemed with altars intended to placate Jupiter. Such altars were inscribed 'Iovi Optimo Maximo', meaning 'to Jupiter, the best and the greatest'. This was usually abbreviated to 'IOM'. In view of the great cost and labour that inscribing into stone involved, Jupiter graciously tolerated this use of initials. There is certainly no evidence that the sculptors were struck by lightning.

According to the *Aeneid* Jupiter was the protecting deity who kept Aeneas in the path of duty towards gods, the state and his family. It was only fitting that the top god should guard and guide the founder of the world's top nation.

Juno (Greek equivalent Hera) was Jupiter's wife and Minerva (Greek equivalent Athene) was his daughter. Juno was associated with women and childbirth; Minerva was the goddess of wisdom, arts and crafts. Jupiter, Juno and Minerva together formed the patron deities of Rome. They shared a magnificent temple on the Capitoline Hill. An annual festival was held in their honour on 13 September, when the consuls thanked Jupiter for preserving the state over the last year and took an oath to perform their duties. They also sacrificed an ox, which was Jupiter's favourite meat.

Mars (Greek equivalent Ares) was the god of war. The Field of Mars (Campus Martius) was named after him because soldiers trained there. March was also named after him, because festivals were held that month in Mars' honour: it was vital to get the god of war on side at the beginning of the campaigning season. There were more festivals for Mars in October to mark the end of the campaigning season.

Apollo (a Greek god whom the Romans adopted) was god of the sun, who drove his chariot of fiery horses across the sky every day to light up the world. He was multi-talented, being an accomplished lyre player as well as the god of music and poetry.

Neptune (Greek equivalent Poseidon) was god of the sea, also known as earth-shaker because he caused earthquakes when in a bad mood. He carried a trident and usually rode on a dolphin. His festival, Neptunalia, was celebrated on 23 July.

Pluto (Greek equivalent Hades) was god of death and king of the Underworld.

Diana (Greek equivalent Artemis) was goddess of the hunt and of the moon, normally portrayed carrying a bow.

Venus (Greek equivalent Aphrodite) was goddess of love and the mother of Aeneas. She led an exciting and varied love life, enjoying intimate relationships with both gods and men.

Cupid (Greek equivalent Eros) was god of love. He was the son of Venus and Mercury, usually portrayed as a winged child carrying a bow. Anyone pierced by his arrows fell deeply in love.

Mercury (Greek equivalent Hermes) was god of merchants and travellers; also the messenger of the gods. He and his mother Maia (goddess of growth, who gave her name to the month of May) were honoured at a festival on 15 May.

Ceres (Greek equivalent Demeter) was earth goddess and goddess of corn. Festivals were held in her honour to ensure a good harvest.

Proserpine (Greek equivalent Persephone), the daughter of Ceres and wife of Pluto, was goddess of the Underworld. She spent the summer months with her mother and the winter months with her husband; hence crops do not grow in winter.

Vulcan (Greek equivalent Hephaestus) was god of fire and volcanoes, as well as the smith of the gods. He had a forge in Mount Etna, where he made thunderbolts for Jupiter. His chief festival, the Volcanalia, was held on 23 August in order to placate Vulcan and avert fires. Sadly, this did not work in AD 79, when Vesuvius erupted destroying Pompeii and Herculaneum.[6]

Bacchus (Greek equivalent Dionysus) was god of wine, ecstasy and the theatre. The festival in his honour, 'Bacchanalia', was always a jovial occasion.

Saturn (Greek equivalent Cronus) was god of time and sowing or seed. Being the father of Jupiter, Neptune and Pluto, he was quite elderly. He always carried a scythe. His great festival, the Saturnalia, began on 17 December and lasted for seven days. All work and business stopped, while people enjoyed parties and exchanged presents. This was the precursor of Christmas.

Vesta (Greek equivalent Hestia) was goddess of the home. She was the protector of the sacred flame which Aeneas had brought from Troy to Italy. Six priestesses, known as Vestal Virgins,[7] guarded this flame inside the Temple of Vesta in the Forum. They had many privileges and quite a jolly time, unless they lost their chastity (or were suspected of doing so) – whereupon they were buried alive, thus abruptly ending their merriment.

Silvanus (no Greek equivalent) was the god of forests, woods and fields. He was associated with hunting.

Janus (no Greek equivalent) was god of beginnings, gates and doors. He had two faces, one looking forwards and one looking backwards. The shrine of Janus stood in the Forum: the doors were open when Rome was at war and closed on those rare occasions when Rome was at peace. January is named after Janus.

New gods were appointed at regular intervals, including recently deceased emperors whom the Senate deified. These nouveau gods all required their own temples, shrines and priests.

Festivals for the traditional Roman gods were regular and important events. The deified emperors' birthdays and accession dates were also marked by religious festivals. These occasions were splendid opportunities for gladiatorial contests, theatrical performances and circus races.[8]

Imperial Rome was a vibrant multi-cultural city with a population of about a million drawn from all parts of the Empire. The influence of immigrants, including freed slaves, traders and others was substantial.[9] Unsurprisingly the immigrants brought with them their own religions and forms of worship.[10] The cults of Isis, Mithras, Jahveh, *Magna Mater* and Christ all had their adherents in Rome. The remains of temples and shrines used for those and other cults have been found within the city. Some of the emperors were from overseas and zealously promoted their own religions. In the third century the Emperor Marcus Aurelius Antoninus Augustus worshipped the Egyptian god Elagabalus. He even married her off to the Carthaginian goddess Tanit.

The traditional Roman gods became established in provinces across the Empire. In Britain there were countless altars and columns with dedications to Jupiter, usually in the form 'IOM'.[11] There were also altars and dedications to Silvanus, because of the help he gave to huntsmen. Temples and shrines for other Roman gods sprang up across Britain from the first century onwards, although not as many as in other more pious provinces.

---

[6]Pliny the Younger, book 6, letters 16 and 20.
[7]Lindner (2015).
[8]Beard et al. (1998) vol 1, 262.
[9]Prag and Quinn (2013).
[10]Beard et al. (1998) vol 1, 245–53.
[11]For example, the Jupiter column found at Cirencester, RIB 103.

4. ARMY RELIGION

The relationship between military and divine authority is too vast a topic for this book. A problem in many European wars has been that both sides were worshipping the same God, so it was not clear who He was supporting. In the ancient world life was simpler. Each side had their own gods and Jupiter's team usually won.

Dura-Europus is an abandoned Hellenistic, Parthian and Roman city on the banks of the Euphrates. A Roman garrison was stationed there between the mid-second century and AD 256, when Sasanian Persians destroyed the city. Amongst the remains was a calendar[12] of religious festivals, which an auxiliary cohort from Palmyra had left behind. This calendar sets out the festival days of the traditional Roman gods and deified emperors.[13] 41 entries survive. Here are two examples:

- 1 March: birthday ceremonies of Mars *Pater Victor*: a bull to be sacrificed.
- 10 July: anniversary of the accession of Antoninus Pius: an ox to be sacrificed.

Even Commodus, who was a very bad emperor, gets an ox on his birthday.

Interestingly, the festival dates celebrated at Dura were the same as or very close to corresponding festival dates celebrated at Rome.[14] We do not know whether this was typical of all the auxiliary units across the Empire. It is likely that there were local variations, depending upon where the troops originally came from. Nevertheless, the Dura calendar suggests that the celebration of official Roman religious festivals was an important element of army life. We know that up at Vindolanda, the Ninth Cohort of the Batavians celebrated the Saturnalia in style.[15]

The sheer volume of religious art in forts suggests that the army took religion seriously. That included celebrating official religious ceremonies. Particularly important was the annual sacrifice in January, when Jupiter and other gods were invoked to protect the Roman state in the coming year.[16] Any religious ceremony generates a 'feel good' factor. There can little doubt that these ceremonies fortified the troops for the hardships which lay ahead. As an additional precaution some soldiers had prayers to Jupiter inscribed on their belts.[17]

Under Augustus, the official religion of the Roman state became a unifying force across the Empire. It connected the troops to their mother city, since they were celebrating the same festivals at about the same time. Also, as a shared heritage, it bound together disparate army units serving in provinces far removed from one another.

A large volume of inscriptions and sculptures found within forts across all provinces relate to the traditional Roman gods, especially Jupiter. There were shrines, figurines and substantial statues. Fragments from Housesteads and Risingham indicate that fort gates were sometimes

---

[12]Dated *c*. 225–7.
[13]See Fink et al. (1959); Fink, *Dura Military Records on Papyrus*, American Philological Association, 1971, No. 117; Haynes (2013) chapter 12.
[14]Haynes (2013) chapter 12.
[15]*Tab Vindol* III, 622.
[16]Henig (1995) 88–9.
[17]'(Jupiter) Optime Maxime, conserva numerum omnium militantium', meaning 'Jupiter, Best and Greatest, keep safe all this band of soldiers'.

adorned with images of Roman gods.[18] That made good sense: the gods would want to keep an eye on who was coming and going. As time went on, more and more emperors died and went to Heaven; they too kept an eye on things and needed to be worshipped. So, the forts contained a growing number of dedications to deified emperors.

Army units and individual soldiers erected altars and other objects with votive inscriptions. These were principally in the north and west of Britain, which was the militarized zone. Almost half of the votive inscriptions have been found along or close to Hadrian's Wall,[19] including 25 dedications to Mars, 10 to Mercury and 10 to Minerva. No less that 63 altars to Jupiter have been found; there would have been far more in antiquity. This was an extremely sensible policy. Hadrian's Wall was a vital frontier and sometimes a theatre of war. The troops guarding the wall needed all the help they could get from the king of the gods. Perhaps cynically, the Romans deified military virtues such as strength, victory and discipline. The army dedicated altars[20] around Britain to *Virtus*, *Victoria* and *Disciplina*.

Taking the omens before going into battle was an important religious procedure. A shrewd priest would announce that the results were favourable. This did wonders for the soldiers' morale.

People from every province were cajoled or conscripted into military service in distant lands. They continued to worship their own gods as well as the Roman ones.[21] Individual army units dedicated altars in Britain to all sorts of foreign deities, such as the Eastern god Jupiter Dolichenus.[22] At Birrens fort in Scotland Tungrian soldiers set up altars to the German goddesses Ricagambeda and Viradecthis.[23] The Batavians brought with them their god, Magusanus, who became quite popular. His worship spread and he was sometimes identified with Hercules.[24] This may have been gratifying for Magusanus but Hercules, that mighty hero of Greek and Roman mythology, must have hated being associated with an obscure little god from the Rhine.

Every legion and auxiliary unit had its own standard, which was kept in a special room known as the shrine of the standards (*aedes principiorum*).[25] These standards acquired a powerful symbolic or even religious significance and they featured prominently in religious ceremonies.

Roman soldiers, like the Celts whom they conquered, were intensely superstitious. They were inclined to believe that minor deities protected specific places such as woods, springs and hills. It was important for any invader to keep these mini-gods on side, so the soldiers erected altars to them. If the army did not know the name of a local god, they inscribed *Genius Loci* on the altar, meaning 'Spirit of the Place'.[26] One particularly enterprising centurion called Marcus Cocceius Firmus dedicated an altar *Genio Terrae Britannicae* meaning 'To the Spirit of the Land of Britain'.[27] This was a wise move. Marcus was serving in Auchendavy at the time, but

---

[18] Haynes (2013) 192.
[19] Zoll (1995) 129–37.
[20] RIB 1791, 990, 2144 and many others.
[21] Haynes (2013) chapter 14.
[22] RIB 1330.
[23] RIB 2107 and 2108.
[24] RIB 2140 is an altar dedicated to Hercules Magusanus.
[25] An inscription at the Reculver fort records the construction of the *aedes principiorum*: RIB 3027.
[26] RIB 450, 647.
[27] RIB 2175.

liable to be deployed anywhere in the province. Hopefully Marcus' altar kept him safe wherever he was posted.

5. THE INDIGENOUS RELIGIONS OF BRITAIN

The only religious practice of Iron Age Britain that contemporaneous writers troubled to record was Druidism. As previously noted, there are limits to what we know about Druidism, because the ancient authors were relying on hearsay and they were interpreting what they were told against the background of Roman religion. Nevertheless, it is clear that Druidism involved human sacrifice; there was also a brighter side to Druidic worship, which centred upon oak trees. According to Pliny the Elder,[28] the Druids revered oak trees and believed everything growing on them was sent from heaven. Any mistletoe growing on an oak tree was the subject of special ceremony: a priest cut it down and distributed the pieces. Interestingly, mistletoe has retained its pre-eminence long after the demise of Druidism. When Christianity spread across the Western world, mistletoe remained the subject of mystical respect. Even now it is an essential Christmas decoration, as well as an excuse for the occasional kiss.

The whole of nature was a mystery in the ancient world[29] and inspired people with religious awe. Britain was a thickly wooded island with heavy rainfall and surging rivers. Hills, groves, springs and rivers were sacred places which the Britons revered.[30] With one or two exceptions, such as Bath, we now know nothing of the gods and goddesses who inhabited these holy places. Iron Age communities also venerated animals and birds. The migration of birds was a particular puzzle; it seemed possible that in winter they flew off to the realm of the gods.[31] According to Caesar[32] the Britons regarded it as sacrilegious (*non fas*) to eat hares, fowl or geese. Very wisely, they did not regard everything in nature as divine and untouchable. Otherwise they all would have starved.

In the late Iron Age, formal temples or shrines started to appear in southern Britain, similar to shrines and temples of the same period in Gaul. They were probably the product of cross-Channel interchange, rather than any new religious movement in Britain. One of the best examples has been found on Hayling Island: this was a circular shrine, surrounded by a series of enclosures. Worshippers deposited votive offerings such as coins, mirrors and jewellery, which suggests that the Hayling deity was female. The Romans later took over the site and built a fine stone temple there.

There is little doubt that the Iron Age peoples of Britain worshipped a vast pantheon of gods. Generally, they were linked to the landscape or the natural world. Although most of those gods have now vanished into oblivion, a few names are recorded in Roman inscriptions. These include Verbeia (whose name means winding river), a goddess in Yorkshire;[33] Arnomecte,

---

[28] *Natural History* 16.95.
[29] Henig (1995) chapter 1.
[30] Gildas, *De Excidio Britanniae* 4.2–3.
[31] Henig (1995) 18.
[32] *Gallic War* 5.12.
[33] RIB 635.

a goddess in Buxton;[34] Cocidius, a warlike god in northern Britain; Coventina, a water goddess;[35] Brigantia, a goddess widely worshipped in the north. There is a serious issue, however, as to when and by whom these gods were named. The only evidence which we have for the names of the Iron Age gods comes from Roman sources, usually inscriptions at military sites. When the Romans arrived they would have expected all the indigenous gods to have names, because that was how the Romans did things. It is perfectly possible that until then the Celts were treating springs, forests, rivers and other natural features as divine without actually personifying them. Many early societies had a nebulous view of their religion. On this hypothesis the Romans would have attributed names to the local gods. Brigantia may be the name that the Romans gave to the goddess who was worshipped in the region of the Brigantes; and so on.

6. THE MINGLING OF CELTIC AND ROMAN RELIGIONS

Unsurprisingly the Britons continued to believe in their own gods during the period of Roman occupation[36] and maintained their traditional religious practices. The Brigantes continued to worship their goddess of the north who was, or became known as, Brigantia. At Uley in Gloucestershire there are signs that Iron Age religious cults continued to be followed at a shrine within the hillfort. The Catuvellauni established a dynastic cult centre at Folly Lane near Verulamium, which served as a centre for traditional religious worship long into the period of Roman occupation. In addition, many of the auxiliaries who garrisoned Britain came from Celtic areas of Germany. They brought with them their own deities and rituals, which they maintained with local adaptations.

The only Celtic religion that the Romans stamped out was Druidism. Ironically, that is the one Iron Age religion that has been reinvented in modern times,[37] but with the omission of human sacrifice. Modern Druids are allowed to parade around Stonehenge on 21 June and they have their own website, none of which reflects the ancient practice of Druidism.

We can recover fragments of temples and other evidence of formal public worship. It is much harder to explore the private beliefs of individuals and to see how such beliefs intersected with daily life. There does, however, seem to have been a practice of burying valuable items in pits or at the bottom of wells as a form of ritual deposition. Excavations at Silchester have revealed unbroken pots in wells and pits. Also dogs' skulls and two metalwork hoards (excluding coins) have been found in those locations.[38] At Housesteads fort a large number of pits have been found, in 37 of which significant objects seem to have been deliberately buried. The objects include human bone, altars, weapons and armour.[39] At a well near Leeds a human skull and mundane items of pottery seem to have been the subject of ritual deposition.[40] Similar

---

[34] RIB 281.
[35] RIB 1524 and many other altars.
[36] Laycock (2008) 81–3.
[37] The British Druid Order now has 7,000 members: *Times*, 14 September 2019.
[38] Fulford (2001) 199–218.
[39] Haynes (2013) 197.
[40] Cool and Richardson (2013) 191–217.

finds have been made at other urban and rural centres. Possibly the intention was to propitiate the chthonic gods or to ensure fertility.

From time to time irate Celts or Romano-Britons smashed up statues, usually as a protest.[41] Other possible reasons for iconoclasm were changes in religious belief or a former emperor having fallen out of favour. The iconoclasts usually melted down bronze statues and re-cycled the valuable metal; they smashed stone statues and re-used the rubble as infill. But the heads of statues (even hated statues) seem to have become objects of veneration: they were often buried separately. This continued even when Christianity arrived. For example, at Uley Christians appear to have demolished a pagan temple and built a church on the site. They duly smashed the cult statue and used the fragments as foundation material, but they preserved the head and buried it later probably as a form of ritual deposition. It may be that in the ancient world people saw statue heads as imbued with magic or divine powers.

When building forts or towns close to Iron Age settlements, the Romans tended to adopt any existing gods and add them to their own pantheon. At Benwell an army unit dedicated three altars to the local god, Antenocitius.[42] At Carrawburgh thirteen dedications have been found to Coventina.[43] Along Hadrian's Wall there are eight dedications to Belatucadrus. The Roman army erected many altars to Cocidius,[44] no doubt anxious to appease the local god of war. The result was often a fusion of Celtic and Roman religions.

There was a marked difference between the two halves of Britain, namely the north-west and the south-east, which impacted on religious practice. In the north and west of the province the principal evidence of fusion was the erection by soldiers of altars and other dedications to the local gods, with occasional instances of twinning Roman and Celtic deities. In the south and east of Britain religious practice was more formalized. Many Romano-Celtic temples sprang up.[45] In Chichester King Togidubnus ordered the construction of a column to Jupiter (the bottom part survives, with elegant water nymphs around the base) as well as a temple to Neptune and Minerva. The ceremonial at such temples probably included elements of both Roman and Celtic practice. Some Iron Age sacred sites were adapted to suit new developments in religion, as happened at Hayling Island. At Maiden Castle in Dorset a Roman temple was built on top of an earlier shrine. Another Iron Age religious site that the Romans, or more probably Romanized Britons, took over for their own purposes is at Marcham.[46]

On occasions the Romans identified indigenous gods with their own deities. The army had no difficulty in twinning Cocidius with Mars and sometimes erected altars jointly to Mars Cocidius.[47] The Celtic god Ocelus was also twinned with Mars: altars and other dedications to Mars Ocelus have been found at Caerwent and Carlisle.[48] This merging of Roman religion with indigenous gods occurred elsewhere across the Empire. Archaeologists call this 'double-naming' and they enjoy counting how often it happened. Double-naming occurs in 4 per cent of the votive inscriptions in the Hadrian's Wall region and in 3 per cent of the votive inscriptions

---

[41] Croxford (2003) 81–95.
[42] RIB 1327, 1328 and 1329.
[43] Zoll (1995) 129–37 at 132.
[44] RIB 993, 1961, 1963 and many others in the Hadrian's Wall region.
[45] Millett (1995) 93–100.
[46] Kamash, Gosden, and Lock (2010) 95–125.
[47] RIB 602, 1017, 2015, 2024.
[48] RIB 309, 310 and 949.

in Lower Germany.⁴⁹ Where it did occur, the Romans were adopting local gods as part of their strategy for gaining control of the region.⁵⁰ Ironically an altar, which was dedicated to Mars Ocelus two thousand years ago, now stands in the porch of a Christian church in Caerwent. The inscription reads: 'To the god Mars Ocelus, Aelius Augustinus, *optio* [a junior officer] willingly and deservedly fulfilled his vow'⁵¹

The city of Bath now provides the most famous example of double-naming. Bath was an Iron Age Centre for the worship of Sulis, a Celtic goddess who presided over the hot spring. As discussed in Chapter 17, the Romans identified Sulis with Minerva and erected a temple to Sulis Minerva. Seven blocks of stone survive from the temple's pediment, including the famous Gorgon's head, which now adorns most tourist brochures for Bath (Fig. 19.1). In Greek mythology, a Gorgon was a fearsome monster which turned to stone all who caught its eye. Classical Greek sculptors generally portrayed a Gorgon as a female with her hair made of snakes and horrifying visage. The Bath Gorgon has glaring eyes and a fierce expression. It appears to be a conflation between the monster of classical mythology and the Celtic goddess Sulis.⁵²

Whether 'Sulis' and 'Minerva' were different names for the same goddess or were two different goddesses temple-sharing is a tricky theological question. Probably the latter is correct, because Sulis was a local goddess whereas Minerva was international. The two deities graciously accepted this arrangement. So the hot springs continued to flow and the city's tourist trade has continued to prosper for 2,000 years.

One way for the élite classes to maintain their superiority was to adopt the religion of their conquerors. Local chieftains duly studied the lives and loves of the Roman gods. As we saw in

Figure 19.1 Gorgon's head, Bath. © Flickr/Brian Snelson.

---

⁴⁹Zoll (1995) 129–37.
⁵⁰Millett (1995) 93–100.
⁵¹RIB 310: 'Deo Marti Ocelo Aelius Augustinus optio votum solvit libens merito'.
⁵²Cunliffe (2012) 41.

the previous chapter, scenes from classical mythology adorned the villas of well-to-do Britons from the earliest days of Roman occupation.

In summary, Britain became a hotchpotch of different religious practices and beliefs. Ancient Celtic rituals and imported Roman religions sometimes merged and sometimes continued separately. Auxiliary units from across the Empire were spreading their own cults and erecting monuments to overseas deities. Throughout the Principate, the religious policies of Rome were fluid and there was no attempt to standardize religious belief or practice.

7. MITHRAISM

Mithras was an ancient Persian god, associated with treaties and oaths. He features in a cuneiform tablet of the fifteenth century BC, recording a treaty made by the Hittites. He was also the god of the sun and acquired other functions over the centuries. No religious texts survive recording his exploits or what his followers believed, but Mithraic art reveals that he was born from a rock. Young Mithras clearly meant business, because he was carrying a dagger and a flaming torch. In adult life Mithras is portrayed as slaying a sacred bull, an event known as the 'Tauroctony'. There are also banquet scenes where Mithras and the sun god feast on the bull's carcass.

It might be thought that the Romans already had enough gods to be getting on with, but apparently not. In the second century AD Rome adopted Mithraism with enthusiasm. Traces of the Mithraic cult dating from the second or third centuries have been found across the entire Empire, with a particular concentration in the Rome/Ostia region and along the European frontier from Britain to the Danube. Mithraism rapidly went out of fashion in the fourth century, once Constantine had opted for Christianity.

Temples to Mithras, known as Mithraea, were small, generally sunk below ground level and windowless. These gloomy surroundings represented the cave in which Mithras had slaughtered the sacred bull. The army built an unusually large Mithraeum[53] at London during the 240s,[54] in the valley of the Walbrook stream. In the fourth century the building suffered a structural collapse. Also, the Romans stopped believing in Mithras, which hardly helped. They hastily buried the Mithraic sculptures at depth and re-dedicated the temple to Bacchus. The temple remained buried until the Second World War, when it was revealed as a result of the Blitz. The remains are now on display in the basement of the Bloomberg Building. The Mithraeum was about 18 metres × 8 metres with a nave, two aisles and an apse. Columns separated the aisles from the nave, which had a lower floor. In the south-west corner there was a water container, probably used for ritual ablutions. A white marble relief of the Tauroctony[55] has been recovered from the site, showing Mithras astride the sacred bull, apparently strangling it (Fig. 19.2). Two attendants are nearby watching, and a dog is excitedly up on its hind legs. Everyone in the carving seems very cheerful, except the bull. A carved head of Mithras has also been retrieved, which shows the god with a Phrygian cap, long rippling hair, a beard and an anxious expression.

---

[53]Shepherd (1998) 104–5.
[54]The approximate date can be deduced from coin finds and pottery.
[55]RIB 3 and plate 2.

Figure 19.2 Marble relief of Mithras slaying the bull, found at Bloomberg site, London. © Wikimedia/ Carole Raddato from FRANKFURT, Germany.

The Mithraeum at Carrawburgh in Northumberland was of more modest size, about 8 metres long and 5 metres wide. The lower part of the temple has been excavated and is well preserved: it follows the standard design of nave and two aisles, with altars at the top end. This was a typical Mithraeum, which suggests that the congregations were generally small.[56] A Mithraeum found at Rudchester in Northumberland contains a well-preserved altar with a relief of Mithras leading the sacred bull by its horns. Carvings round the side show daggers and a Phrygian cap. The inscription reads: 'To the god. Lucius Sentius Castus, (centurion) of the Sixth Legion, set this up as a gift.'[57]

There was a flourishing Mithraeum at Housesteads, on Hadrian's Wall. This included several altars dedicated to the Persian god.[58] There was also a stone relief of Mithras sitting inside what looks like an egg or a space capsule. The signs of the Zodiac are carved around him.

8. CHRISTIANITY

Christianity began as an offshoot of Judaism. It was one of many cults circulating around the Empire, given the extensive migration between provinces.[59] Tacitus described Christians as 'a

---

[56] Henig (1995) 108.
[57] RIB 1398.
[58] RIB 1599–1601.
[59] Price, 'Religious Mobility in the Roman Empire' *JRS* 102 (2012) 1–19.

group hated for their shameful conduct, whom the people called Christians'.[60] He then added a brief explanation: 'Christ the originator of that name [i.e. "Christians"] was executed during the reign of Tiberius by order of the procurator Pontius Pilate'.[61] This is one of the earliest authoritative historical records of Jesus' execution.

Tacitus described the early spread of Christianity in scathing terms: 'Although initially suppressed, the deadly superstition broke out again not only in Judaea (where the evil started) but also in Rome, where vile and shameful practices from all quarters come together and flourish.'[62]

According to Tacitus,[63] Nero blamed the followers of Christ for the great fire of Rome in AD 64. Nero ordered the execution of Christians on a large scale as a form of public entertainment: some were fed to wild animals in the Circus Maximus; others were made into human torches and burnt at night to illumine the Emperor's gardens. A recent article suggests that none of this really happened,[64] but the analysis unconvincing.

Up until Constantine's reign, the authorities saw Christianity as subversive. It involved the worship of a crucified criminal as Son of God. Christianity, being a monotheistic religion, was a denial of the rituals and festivals of the Roman state.[65] It was also implicitly a challenge to the position and the power of the Emperor. In Roman eyes Christianity was even more objectionable than Judaism. Judaism was the religion of an ethnic group. Christianity was a matter of belief and it was evangelical.

There were periods of persecution during the second and third centuries, in particular under Marcus Aurelius and Diocletian. During these periods Christian scriptures were burnt and the faithful were executed. Some of those condemned welcomed martyrdom, just as modern religious fanatics do today. The Christian faith and its associated practices had their own dynamic and spread progressively across the Empire, aided by Rome's excellent transport system. Church structures were created, and bishops were appointed. The periodic persecutions seemed to attract ever more converts to the new religion.

Estimating the numbers of practising Christians[66] at any given time is not easy. Until the third century there were no purpose-built churches. Adherents met in house-churches. House-cult groups in each town were linked into notional communities under the overall leadership of bishops. The best approximate estimate is that there were less than 10,000 Christians in AD 100 and about 200,000 Christians in AD 200. That was about 0.3 per cent of the total population of the Roman Empire. By AD 300 there were about 6 million Christians. That was about 10 per cent of the total population of the Empire. It was this growth in numbers that led to the great purges of the third century and early fourth century.

The spread of Christianity in the Roman Empire, despite periodic persecutions, is similar to what has happened in China in recent years.[67] Despite periodic clampdowns by the authorities,[68]

---

[60] 'quos per flagitia invisos vulgus Christianos appellabat': *Annals*, 15.44.
[61] 'auctor nominis eius Christus Tiberio imperitante per procuratorem Pontium Pilatum supplicio adfectus est.'
[62] 'repressaque in praesens exitiabilis superstitio rursum erumpebat, non modo per Iudaeam, originem eius mali, sed per urbem etiam quo cuncta undique atrocia aut pudenda confluunt celebranturque': *Annals* 15.44.
[63] *Annals* 15.44.
[64] Shaw (2015) 73–100.
[65] Hopkins (1999) 78.
[66] Hopkins (1999) chapter 3.
[67] 'Religion in China', *Economist*, 1 November 2014, 23–7.
[68] Increasing under Xi Jinping: 'New commandments', *Economist*, 17 March 2018, 55–6.

Christianity has steadily spread across that vast country. As at November 2014, estimates for the number of practising Christians in China ranged between 40 and 90 million. There are predicted to be 250 million Christians in China by 2030, but how anyone knows that is even more of a mystery than Mithraism.

Christianity shared many elements with other cults of the period: communal prayers were almost universal; hymn singing was commonplace, as most gods enjoyed a musical performance. The theme of death and resurrection featured in many religions. The cults of Bacchus and Mithras were centred around a sacred meal, as was Christianity. Mithraism and other cults made use of water, as Christianity did in baptisms. The Christian God was of course the God of the Old Testament, whom the Jews worshipped.

The Christian scholars Tertullian and Origen both record that Christianity arrived in parts of Britain by the early second century,[69] but the evidence of Christian worship then is sparse. Christianity was probably very much a minority cult during the second and third centuries.

An intriguing piece of red wall plaster has been found in Cirencester. It comes from a second-century town house and has the following letters carved into it:

ROTAS

OPERA

TENET

AREPO

SATOR

The sentence means 'Arepo the sower holds the wheels with force'. There is nothing terribly profound about that, you may think. But look at the letters. The sentence is the same whether you read it sideways or vertically. The word 'TENET' is in the middle both horizontally and vertically, thus forming a cross. The whole piece is an anagram. The letters can be rearranged to form APATERNOSTERO twice. PATER NOSTER are the first two words of the Lord's Prayer ('Our Father'). The letters at each end (A and O) represent Christ, who said that he was alpha and omega, the beginning and the end. Such acrostics are rare. This may be evidence of a Christian community that was secretly operating in second-century Cirencester. The little piece of wall plaster now sits in the Corinium Museum, transmitting its coded message across eighteen centuries to the modern world.

Saint Alban, a fervent Christian after conversion, was beheaded by the Roman authorities at Verulamium. The fact of Alban's martyrdom is reasonably well attested, but the date is in dispute. The two periods canvassed are AD 208–209 during the reign of Severus and AD 303–304 during the persecution of Diocletian. The earlier period, namely AD 208–209, is probably correct.[70] Bede provides a much embroidered account of Alban's execution.[71] Alban's martyrdom caused a sensation and the site of his burial became a cult centre. An Abbey was built there in the eighth century. Subsequently, a magnificent Norman cathedral replaced the abbey, standing on the edge of a city that bears Saint Alban's name.

---

[69]Tertullian, *De adversus Iudaeos* vii.
[70]Frere (1991) 321.
[71]*Ecclesiastical History of the English People* 1.7.

Diocletian issued an edict outlawing Christianity in AD 303. A period of intense persecution followed. According to Gildas two practising Christians, Julius and Aaron, were put to death because of their faith. Bede[72] says that they were tortured and executed in the 'City of the Legions', which was probably a reference to Caerleon: archaeological evidence indicates that this is where Saint Aaron and Saint Julius were commemorated. They now share a feast day with Saint Alban in the Roman Catholic calendar, 22 June.

The game changer was Constantine's conversion to Christianity in AD 312. Christianity was no longer banned – it became the favoured religion and included the Emperor among its adherents. The imperial family instigated and funded the building of churches. All subsequent emperors were Christian, except for Julian the Apostate who only reigned for two years. In AD 391 Theodosius banned paganism altogether and set about destroying pagan temples. This completed the Christian revolution: Churches replaced temples; prayers to God and Jesus replaced animal sacrifices.[73]

Once Christianity was authorized, Christian priests could go about their business openly. Archaeologists have recovered some fine-looking crowns and diadems from sites in Norfolk. It has been suggested that these were priests' headgear – bishops and vicars (like judges) do enjoy dressing up. But there is no basis for this speculation.

As noted earlier, Christian decorations and motifs started to appear in well-to-do villas during the fourth century: finger rings, strap ends and other personal ornaments were sometimes decorated with Christian motifs.[74] Despite the outward signs of Christianity, the élite classes may have been hedging their bets. In AD 312 Christianity had suddenly changed its status from persecuted cult to top religion. Who was to know when there would be another religious revolution? That would have happened in the mid-fourth century, if Julian had survived as Emperor. The symbols of Christianity in Roman Britain were for the most part either disposable, like the silver spoons with engraved with 'chi rho' found at Canterbury, or ambiguous.

The classic instance of such ambiguity is the famous mosaic at Hinton St Mary, which shows a young male head with a pomegranate on each side. Behind the head is the 'chi rho' symbol. For many years archaeologists have identified the head with Christ and assumed that the villa owner was a practising Christian. But now doubts are growing.[75] The face is unlike other depictions of Christ from that period, but remarkably like the faces of Constantine and his son Constantius II, as they appear on statues. The 'chi rho' symbol was closely associated with Constantine, because of his vision before the battle of Milvian Bridge. Constantine and his successors frequently used the 'chi rho' symbol as a means of self-identification or authentication. All in all, the mosaic may best be seen as a sign of loyalty to the Emperor and more generally to the Roman state. The villa owner may well have professed the Christian faith, at least so long as that was in fashion, but his mosaic was not an enduring religious statement.

The impact of Christianity on the general British population was slight: there is little evidence of widespread Christian worship. By the fourth century most of the occupying army was hereditary, so it was more closely connected with Britain than the imperial capital. In AD 391, when Theodosius banned paganism, Britain was fast slipping away from the Empire.

---

[72] *Ecclesiastical History of the English People* 1.7.
[73] Hopkins (1999) chapter 3.
[74] Petts (2003) 109–14.
[75] Pearce (2008) 193–218.

Given all the other crises of those final years, it is unlikely that the Britons took much notice of imperial edicts on spiritual matters. It is notable that in Italy Christianity only becomes visible in buildings and architecture during the early fifth century. By that time Britain had fallen out of the cultural ambit of Rome.

Against that background, it is hardly surprising that paganism continued to flourish alongside Christianity during the fourth century. The London Mithraeum was re-dedicated not to Christ, but to Bacchus. The governor of Britannia Prima erected a column dedicated to Jupiter, the Best and the Greatest.[76] There are some signs of a shift towards Christianity at the end of the fourth century and in the early fifth century, but the evidence is not conclusive.[77]

9. CURSE TABLETS

In an age when there was no police force or prosecution service, many crimes went unpunished. Luckily help was at hand in the form of divine retribution: all the aggrieved person needed to do was to invoke the help of a suitable deity. Jupiter, despite being the Greatest and the Best, probably would not be bothered about petty crimes. He had ceremonies to attend across the Empire and much other important Olympian business. One of the other gods or, better still, a local god was more likely to respond. The real question therefore was how to contact the relevant god.

Curse tablets (*defixiones*) were the answer. These were little prayers to gods, reporting crimes and requesting punishment. Long before the annexation of Britain the practice had grown up in the Mediterranean of writing out formal curses and putting them in places where the gods were likely to read and act on them. Archaeologists have recovered many hundreds of curse tablets from across the Graeco-Roman world. About 300 curse tablets have been recovered from British sites, generally in Latin but two in Celtic. The language tends to follow set formulae, such as 'whether man or woman, slave or free' and to include quasi-legal phraseology.[78] Like a modern day indictment, any ancient curse tablet required careful drafting: it was important that the gods caught the right person and punished him or her for a clearly identified offence.

(i) The sacred spring at Bath[79]

In 1978 archaeologists were given a chance to explore the Roman spring that lies beneath the Pump Room at Bath.[80] There they found a mass of Romano-British curse tablets. This is the largest cache of such tablets ever found in one place.

The authors or their scribes wrote messages of varying length on small sheets of lead. They then rolled up the sheets into little tubes and threw them into the spring. These tablets may have been legible to the goddess when they first fell into her spring but sitting under flowing

---

[76] RIB 103.
[77] Henig (1995) 215–16.
[78] Hobbs and Jackson (2010) 78–80.
[79] See generally Oxford Committee for Archaeology (1988); Tomlin (1988); Bradley (2011).
[80] Higgins (2013) 103–5.

water for two thousand years is not a good way to preserve lead engraving. Luckily some can still be deciphered. Unlike the Vindolanda tablets, which were mainly written by soldiers, the authors of these tablets were ordinary people who lived in or visited Bath. They were usually reporting thefts.

The authors addressed most requests to Sulis or Sulis Minerva. This was obviously sensible. Sulis was the protective goddess of the hot spring and had a lovely temple on site. Sulis could be trusted to take an interest in local affairs – she would probably be affronted by crimes committed on her patch. Only one tablet was addressed to Minerva alone. Of the other tablets two were addressed to Mars and one to Mercury.[81]

Annianus suffered the loss of six silver coins. He wrote a tablet calling upon Sulis to punish the thief:

> ... whether pagan or Christian, whoever it is, whether man or woman, boy or girl, slave or free.[82]

Unfortunately the tablet is incomplete. A later reference to 'his blood' ('sanguinem suum') suggests that Annianus was proposing a fairly painful form of punishment. The most interesting feature is the reference to 'pagan or Christian'. This tablet, presumably written in the fourth century, shows that Christianity was a recognized religion, at least in the Somerset area.

Docilianus had his cloak stolen and demanded severe punishment (Fig. 19.3):

> I curse him[83] who has stolen my hooded cloak, whether man or woman, slave or free, that ... the goddess Sulis inflicts death upon ... not allow him sleep or children now and in the future, until he has brought my cloak to her temple.

One tablet refers to oaths that had been sworn before the sacred spring, probably in the name of Sulis. The author demands that those who committed perjury should pay for it with their lives.

> Whosoever there has perjured himself you are to make him pay for it to the goddess Sulis in his own blood.[84]

Perjury before the gods was one of the gravest crimes in the ancient world.

An incomplete tablet reads:

> To the goddess Sulis Minerva from Docca. I give to your holiness the money which I have lost by theft, namely five denarii and he who has stolen it, whether slave or free ... is to be compelled ...[85]

We do not know what fate lay in store for this thief. Five denarii was a significant sum – the equivalent of several days' pay for a legionary soldier.

---

[81] Bradley (2011) 46, table 1.
[82] *Tabulae Sulis* (hereafter, *Tab Sulis*) 98.
[83] 'Devoveo eum ...': *Tab Sulis* 10.
[84] 'Quicumque illic periuraverit deae Suli facias illum sanguine suo illud satisfacere.': *Tab Sulis* 94.
[85] *Tab Sulis* 34.

Figure 19.3 Curse tablet, Tab Sulis 10. © The Roman Baths, Bath and North East Somerset Council.

Basilia lost her silver ring. She decided that gruesome punishments were appropriate for all involved. Her tablet reads:

> Basilia gives to the Temple of Mars her silver ring and asks that if anyone, whether slave or free, has been involved or knows anything about it, he may be cursed in his blood, eyes and all his limbs; or even – if he has stolen it – may he have all his guts eaten away.[86]

This is one of the few Bath tablets that were not addressed to Sulis. Probably Basilia feared that the goddess would be too soft on the offender. Warlike Mars was the god for the job.

Deomiorix suffered a burglary. He cursed the offender: 'Execro qui involaverit', meaning 'I curse him who made a forcible entry'. After referring to the theft, Deomiorix continued:

> Whoever is guilty may the god find him and recover it with his blood and his life.[87]

---

[86] *Tab Sulis* 97.
[87] *Tab Sulis* 99.

(ii) Elsewhere in Britain

The temple of Mercury at Uley in Gloucestershire has yielded the second largest cache of curse tablets. Unsurprisingly, these tablets are addressed to Mercury. As messenger to the gods, Mercury could be trusted to visit regularly and read his mail.

Saturnina wrote what she called a memorandum ('commonitorium') to Mercury concerning some linen that had vanished. She instructs:

> Let he who stole it have no rest unless/until he has brought the aforesaid things to the aforesaid temple, whether he is man or woman, slave or free.'[88]

On the back of the tablet Saturnina sets out her side of the bargain. She will give one third of the linen, when recovered, to Mercury. She will also give one third to Silvanus (god of the forest), provided he exacts the necessary punishment. This whole tablet comes across as a business-like memo from an efficient woman to a busy god. Saturnina very sensibly stipulates a handsome reward for Mercury, to spur him into action. She also enlists the help of Silvanus; he too gets a handsome reward. As a shrewd businesswoman, Saturnina appreciated the need to incentivize people (or in this case gods) whom she employed.

Biccus, the victim of theft, proposed that the culprit should suffer a novel form of punishment until he returned the stolen goods to Mercury's temple. The specified punishment was that the thief should not be able to urinate, defecate, speak, sleep or wake. Nor, Biccus added, should the thief enjoy good health. Given the previous impositions, good health would seem unlikely.

Both Bath and Uley were in the territory of the Dobunni. A smaller number of curse tablets have been found at other locations around Britain, principally in the south. They are addressed to a variety of gods, including three to the Christian God.[89] Four curse tablets were addressed to Neptune. Wisely, the authors threw all of the Neptune tablets into water: they have been found in riverbeds at Brandon, Caistor St Edmund, the Hamble Estuary and London.

The frequent use of the formula 'whether slave or free' suggests that slavery was widespread in Roman Britain. It also suggests that slaves were allowed to go out and about (unlike many slaves in southern USA pre-1865). Otherwise they would not have been suspected of committing so many opportunistic thefts.

10. SUMMARY

The official Roman religion played a vital role in unifying the Roman state and could properly be described as 'civic religion'.[90] Religious ceremonies were public affairs, often with high attendance. The rules governing religion were part of public law.[91] As we have seen, different

---

[88]'Ille qui hoc circumvenit non ante laxetur nisi quando res s dictas ad fanum s dictum attulerit si vir si mulier si servus si liber.' 'S' is an abbreviation for 'supra', so the phrase is a short way of saying 'the aforesaid things to the aforesaid temple'.
[89]Bradley (2011) 45–6.
[90]Scheid (2013).
[91]For example, no-one could sacrifice on the Capitol without official authorization.

military units across the Empire celebrated the same religious festivals at roughly the same time, which tied them to the mother city and to each other. Augustus encouraged traditional religious practices, to promote political stability.

Religious myths, especially those articulated by Virgil, provided a justification for imperialism: Rome was destined by the gods to crush other nations and to rule the world. The resounding verses of the *Aeneid* would have soothed any doubts that generals may have felt about mounting invasions or mass slaughter. That was what the gods wanted Rome to do.

As the Empire expanded, Rome welcomed the gods of conquered nations into a broader unofficial pantheon. In Britain and elsewhere, Roman soldiers cheerfully built altars and sometimes temples to the local Celtic gods. This policy of inclusivity and religious tolerance was one of the stratagems by which Rome converted its enemies into friends. At the same time, the élite classes in the provinces espoused the official Roman religion: scenes of Jupiter, Bacchus, Cupid and other classical deities adorned their walls and floors. All these developments strengthened Rome's grip on the provinces.

New religions from the east, such as Mithraism and Christianity, swept across the Empire from the second century onwards. After a bumpy start, Christianity finally triumphed. Like most successful religions, it evolved into a means of naturalizing existing power structures. It still does this, as evidenced by Papal ceremonies, coronation services or bishops sitting in the House of Lords.

Religion involves personal dealings between the individual and whatever deities they believe in. There were many deities circulating during the first four centuries AD. Rome's general policy of religious freedom let people worship their own gods in their own way. This contributed to social cohesion.

The curse tablets found in Britain should not be dismissed as supernatural nonsense. They may well have been highly effective. The general population of the province, both indigenous, Roman and others, were extremely superstitious. If the culprit learnt that he had been made the subject of a formal curse, the news could have been devastating, especially if he looked up at the Gorgon's head. There can be little doubt that these curses sometimes led to the restitution of stolen property, but perhaps not to the dire penalties proposed.

The gods of the ancient world served their people well.

CHAPTER 20
THE ROMANO-BRITISH LEGACY

1. Introduction
2. To what extent and how was Britain Romanized during the Roman occupation
    - (i) The military community
    - (ii) Urban dwellers
    - (iii) Rural societies
    - (iv) Conclusions
3. What did the Romans gain from their British adventure?
4. What did Britain gain from the colonial experience?
5. Subsequent British history – a very brief summary
6. Long-term impact of the Roman occupation
    - (i) London
    - (ii) Other towns
    - (iii) Ports and coastal defences
    - (iv) Scotland
    - (v) Wales
    - (vi) National identity
    - (vii) Religion and culture
    - (viii) Brexit

1. INTRODUCTION

In this chapter we will first consider the extent to which Britain was Romanized during the four centuries of Roman occupation. Building on the analysis in Chapter 9, it will be argued that towns, villa owning élites and communities around military units were highly Romanized, but the rural population was less so.

The chapter will then consider what Rome gained from its British adventure. As we shall see, an accountant's answer to that question is 'not very much', but the political benefits were substantial. We will then consider what Britain gained from the colonial experience. The answer to that is much grief and little benefit. After a brief survey of later British history, we will consider the long-term effect on Britain of the Roman occupation.

2. TO WHAT EXTENT AND HOW WAS BRITAIN ROMANIZED DURING THE ROMAN OCCUPATION?

In Chapter 9 we defined Romanization as a continuous process and examined its effects in Britain during the first fifty years after the conquest. We must now stand back and look at the topic more broadly – to what extent and how was Britain Romanized during the four centuries of Roman occupation?

The first point to note is that there was a high degree of mobility between all countries under Roman control. This was due to the road system, established sea-routes, long-distance trading and the posting of auxiliary units overseas. There was large-scale migration of people and objects around the Empire.[1] The Romanization of Britain took the form of cultural exchanges with Gaul, Germany, Spain, Italy, Greece, the Balkans, the near East and North Africa.[2]

An important aspect of that process was the spread of countless religions across the Empire. As we saw in Chapter 19, Mithraism, Christianity, the worship of dead emperors and other faiths circulated freely around all provinces, including Britain. Auxiliaries from overseas brought their own gods with them, erecting altars to record their names along Hadrian's Wall and elsewhere.

In his excellent account of Roman Britain,[3] David Mattingly (although he does not believe in Romanization) argues that we must approach this question by looking separately at three distinct communities, namely (i) the military community, (ii) urban dwellers and (iii) rural societies. Drawing on post-colonial research into modern imperialism, he says that we should examine the 'discrepant experience' of each section of society. That is a sensible approach, which this chapter will follow.

(i) The military community

Auxiliaries

In the years following AD 43, many young Britons were conscripted into the army, usually for service overseas. They could bypass the local hierarchy to achieve wealth and status through serving as auxiliaries.[4] After 25 years' service they retired as Roman citizens. They may or may not have returned to Britain with that new status.

Auxiliary units were drawn from all parts of the Empire, but once established in Britain they tended to recruit locally. Nectovelius provides an example. His tombstone reads:

> To the spirits of the departed: Nectovelius, son of Vindex, aged 29, of 9 years' service a Brigantian by tribe, served in the Second Cohort of the Thracians[5]

---

[1] Hingley, Bonacchi, and Sharpe (2018) 284.
[2] Reece (1988) 9.
[3] Mattingly (2006) 18.
[4] Millett (1990) 60.
[5] RIB 2142: 'Dis Manibus Nectovelius filius Vindicis annorum IXXX stipendiorum VIIII nationis Brigans militavit in cohort II Thracium'.

Veterans often retired in the area where they had served, with successive generations joining the same regiment. It is probable that most auxiliaries were Roman citizens long before Caracalla granted universal citizenship. In the third century, some Germanic units were drafted in to support the northern frontier.[6] That apart, it is probable that from the third century onwards almost all auxiliary soldiers were recruited in Britain.

Legions

In the first century and early second century, legions were normally raised in Italy, but after that the legions usually recruited locally.[7] The legions in Britain generally recruited from the areas where they were based,[8] often with sons following their fathers. They may have secured further recruits from the sons of military families in the *coloniae* at Colchester, Lincoln and Gloucester.

Generally

The original annexation of Britain required four legions and a large auxiliary force, but by the fourth century, the size of the occupying army was substantially reduced. That coincides with a period of high prosperity within the province. Rome had less need to 'squeeze' the province, when there was no longer a large and expensive occupying army.[9]

The army garrisoning Britain operated within a Roman military structure.[10] The life of every soldier was conducted primarily within his regiment and subject to the commanding officer. Below the level of centurion, soldiers rarely changed units. During the Principate, the provincial governor was at the top of the pyramid: there was no military authority above the provincial level; the Roman government had no department like a ministry of war or ministry of defence. The layout of fortresses and forts emphasized the hierarchy within the legion or the cohort.[11] This rigid hierarchy backed by violence was crucial to the structure of military life: ruthless discipline was a feature of Romanization affecting all military units across the Empire.

Many soldiers had specialist skills and specialist roles, which defined their identity. A typical example is Julius Vitalis. His tombstone, which you can see at Bath Museum, reads:

> Julius Vitalis, armourer of the Twentieth Legion Valeria Victrix, of 9 years' service, aged 29, a Belgic tribesman, with funeral at the cost of the Guild of Armourers; he lies here.[12]

---

[6] RIB 920 (Old Penrith), 1036 (Binchester) and 1593–1594 (Housesteads).
[7] Mann and Dobson (1996).
[8] See RIB 357, 361, 365 and 369 for soldiers from Caerleon in the Second Legion Augusta.
[9] Mattingly (2006) 528.
[10] James (2001).
[11] Gardner (2013) 11–14.
[12] RIB 156: 'Iulius Vitalis fabriciensis leg XX VV stipendiorum IX annorum XXIX natione Belga ex collegio fabricensium elatus hic situs est'.

Julius' role as armourer defined him both in life and in death. Not many modern arms manufacturers will still be remembered two thousand years from now.

The soldiers put their engineering skills to use in establishing military installations, roads and such infrastructure as they needed. They were also, apparently, proficient at local government. There is much evidence from elsewhere in the Empire of centurions acting as regional administrators (*centuriones regionarii*). The records of two such regional administrators survive in Britain, one at Bath and one at Carlisle.[13] There was probably an extensive network of centurions administering different regions of Britain before the civitas capitals were functioning. Soldiers known as *beneficiarii* undertook surveillance and policing functions: their names appear on altars and tombstones around the province.[14] Non-combatants were integrated closely into the lives of soldiers and the regiment. Most cavalrymen had grooms and they often feature on tombstones. Some soldiers had servants or slaves.

Augustus had banned soldiers from marrying, but that was too much to ask of healthy young men on active service. They took wives unofficially and founded families, a practice that the authorities tolerated. On his visit to Britain Hadrian granted certain veteran soldiers 'the right of marriage to the wives they already had when citizenship was granted to them',[15] without any suggestion that the soldiers had been out of order in acquiring wives previously. Serving soldiers became heads of households with mothers, sisters and other dependants to support.

As a result, fully fledged social communities usually grew up around military units. The soldiers and their families had money to spend; shopkeepers and visiting traders had wares to supply; prostitutes offered their services. Former slaves lived there as freedmen. There was not a rigid military/civilian dichotomy. There is no evidence that civilians were banned from entering forts. On the contrary, children's shoes have been found in the Vindolanda fort;[16] women's and children's clothes or items for their use have been found in many forts.[17] Some civilian support staff would have had duties within the forts. The communities were a complex social mix. The commander of the local regiment was in overall charge of the adjoining civilian community.

In summary, all those serving in the army and the civilian settlements attached to military units were Romanized to a high degree.

(ii) Urban dwellers

As Martin Millett points out in *The Romanization of Britain*:

> The most characteristic phenomenon related to Romanization is the emergence of towns of a particular character, which are seen right across the Empire.[18]

---

[13] RIB 152 and *Tab Vindol*, I, 250.
[14] RIB 88 (Winchester), 235 (Dorchester, Oxon), 602 (Lancaster), 725 and 726 (Thornborough-on-Swale), 745 (Great Bridge), 1085 (Lanchester), 1225 (Risingham), 1599 (Housesteads).
[15] CIL XVI 69.
[16] Birley (2009) 57.
[17] Van Driel (2011) 115–22.
[18] Millett (1990) 69.

Millett goes on to argue that the impetus for this development came from local élites, who were keen to emulate Roman ways. He refers to differences in town layout between Gaul and Britain: in Gaul a temple abutted the forum, whereas in Britain temples were located separately, away from the forum and basilica. This leads to the suggestion that the inspiration and expertise were drawn from local areas, rather than from the army.[19] Whilst this is all true, it may be only half the picture: the impetus to develop Roman-style towns may have come from both the local élites and the occupying power, since they both had much to gain from the process.

Chapter 17 has outlined the formal classification of towns as civitas capitals, *municipia*, *coloniae* and so forth. As discussed earlier, civitas capitals were towns where the old aristocracy of the Iron Age retained their power but exercised it with the backing of the Roman state. They also controlled trading operations.[20] Local officials must have conducted censuses, although little evidence of that now survives.[21] The townspeople used Roman-style public buildings and amenities. They worshipped at Romano-Celtic temples dedicated to a range of Celtic and other deities, not just the classical Roman gods.[22] There was a rich blend of cultures in the civitas capitals, reflecting both indigenous and Roman aspirations.

The extent of Roman influence varied greatly from one town to another. St Albans (*Verulamium*) was perhaps the most Romanized civitas capital.[23] In the mid-first century, it became a *municipium* and acquired a masonry forum. During the late first century and the second century, the full suite of public buildings appeared, including baths, a *macellum* (indoor market), a theatre in Insula XV and an unusually large number of temples. The town seems to have been a hive of religious activity. A bronze statuette of Venus has been recovered from the cellar of a house fronting Watling Street. *Verulamium* boasted fine town houses, many with painted wall plaster and mosaic floors. Some had kitchens, dining rooms, bedrooms, latrines, shrines and stables. The town benefited from proximity to London. There was a flourishing line of kilns where Watling Street entered *Verulamium*. The potters there probably did a brisk trade with the Roman authorities in the capital. The forum/basilica complex was rebuilt after fires in the mid-second century. The town may even have had a monumental arch, reflecting its status as *municipium*.

The Romanization of British towns was not simply a matter of super-imposing the architecture and customs of the mother city on Iron Age *oppida*. British urban centres received migrants from across the Empire throughout the Roman period,[24] leading to cultural exchanges with all provinces. As we saw in Chapter 9, the public buildings in many civitas capitals were the work of Gallic designers and stonemasons in conjunction with local people.

From the first century onwards, artistic styles of the Roman Empire progressively replaced the abstract designs of the Iron Age. The statues and sculptures of Roman Britain are attempts to emulate the classical forms, but the results are often second rate.[25] The

---

[19] Millett (1990) 72.
[20] Millett (1990) 123–5.
[21] Mattingly (2006) 495.
[22] Millett (1990) 107–11.
[23] Niblett and Thompson (2005) chapter 4.
[24] Hingley et al. (2018) 292.
[25] Millett (1990) 112–16.

various carvings of mother goddesses (usually in threes) dotted around the province are not impressive.

The one area where Romano-British artists and craftsmen excelled was mosaics.[26] The workshops of Central Southern Britain produced some stunning works, such as the 'Four Seasons' mosaic in Cirencester or the 'Dido and Aeneas' mosaic at Low Ham Roman villa. The latter is now in the Somerset Museum. It depicts the story of Dido and Aeneas in five panels: Venus stands commandingly in the centre; in two of the panels Dido and Aeneas make eye contact – their erotic attraction is obvious. These mosaics stand comparison with some of the finest mosaics found across the Empire.

Relatively few textiles have survived from Roman Britain.[27] However, a few rags have been recovered from the late first century/early second century fort buildings at Vindolanda; there is some material from Corbridge, dated about AD 120, which was used to wrap weapons; there are also some textiles from Colchester. These few finds are sufficient to show the technical competence of textile producers in Britain. They also show that British textiles of the Roman period have far more in common with British textiles of the Iron Age, than with the textiles of more distant provinces. The inference is that Roman occupation had relatively little impact on the textile industry.

Roman law, as developed by jurists since the second century BC,[28] was the law of the Roman Empire.[29] It applied in Britain as in all other provinces. One of the Bloomberg tablets[30] records routine commercial litigation proceeding in London in October 76. As we saw in Chapter 7, a few years later the distinguished lawyer Javolenus was in Britain trying a probate case and creating a precedent for future guidance, written up in Justinian's *Digest*.

(iii) Rural societies

Villas were the rural seats of those who held power in the civitas capitals.[31] They were a setting for the display of wealth. Most of the villa owners lived in the south-east, but there were some exceptions to the general pattern. Holme House villa, near Piercebridge in the north of Britain, was a luxury residence with élite dining.[32] Complete or almost complete glass vessels have been recovered from the site. Materials scraped from the drain reveals what the occupants ate, which included lamb, pork, chicken and oysters. The Holme House residents would have been highly Romanized – perhaps they read Latin poetry of an evening. But not many Britons lived like that, especially up in the north.

Most Britons lived in the deep countryside, as discussed in Chapter 18. These communities were the least affected by Romanization. Much less Samian ware, metalwork, glass and coinage has been found in rural areas than in towns. In many areas the advent of Rome had little impact

---

[26]Millett (1990) 175–6.
[27]Wild (2002) 1–42.
[28]Nicholas (1987) 34–55.
[29]Du Plessis et al. (2016) 261–2 and *passim*.
[30]WT 51.
[31]Millett (1990) 91–9.
[32]Cool and Mason (2008) 297.

on the values and way of life of the agricultural communities, especially in the first and second centuries.[33] Habitations and farming methods remained the same. At many rural settlements, such as Alfred's Castle in Oxfordshire, there was a continuum of development from the Bronze Age through the Iron Age and into the early Roman period.[34] Nevertheless, taxes had to be paid, new roads were appearing and the economy was becoming monetized. Over time there was an acculturation, which resulted in a fusion characterized as Romano-British.[35]

For obvious reasons, many infants died at, or soon after, birth. During both the Iron Age and the Roman period, it was common in rural settlements to bury neonatal corpses close to domestic buildings.[36] People may have seen this as a way of preserving the link between the deceased baby and its mother or its family. Whatever the thinking behind this practice, it is an indigenous practice, which continued from the Iron Age through the Roman period.

(iv) Conclusion

The broad picture that emerges from the material summarized above is as follows:

(i) Romanization involved the sharing of cultures, activities and religions between all parts of the Empire, not just the imposition by Rome of its own way of doing things. It was a form of globalization.[37] The presence in Britain of migrants from all parts of the Empire contributed to that process over some four centuries.

(ii) Army units and those serving the army were Romanized to a high degree.

(iii) In the major towns (civitas capitals and colonies) there was considerable Romanization. Roman systems of administration were set up; the courts applied Roman law; there was widespread use of Samian ware and other artefacts imported from around the Empire. Many of the public buildings in major towns were the work of Gallic designers and stonemasons, in conjunction with local people. The extent of Romanization varied from one town to another.

(iv) In the countryside the villa-owning élites readily achieved a high level of Romanization and they loved it.

(v) The communities living around auxiliary forts and legionary fortresses were in regular contact with the Roman military and were dominated by Roman culture in all its cosmopolitan forms. They traded with the soldiers; they used public baths provided by the army. Many of the local women married soldiers and their sons probably went on to serve in the army.

(vi) In the deep countryside, away from the towns, forts and villas, the agricultural population were much less affected by Roman ways and Roman culture, especially in the first and second centuries. Nevertheless, the presence of Rome was felt everywhere, not least because every community had to pay taxes.

---

[33] Taylor (2013) 171–90.
[34] Gosden and Lock (2003) 65–80.
[35] Hanson (1994).
[36] Millett and Gowland (2015) 171–89.
[37] See Versluys (2014) 11.

(vii) Archaeological evidence suggests that Roman culture had a greater impact in the deep countryside during the third and fourth centuries than in the early period. At the same time, many towns were showing signs of decline.

(viii) Romanization of the élite classes was driven by (a) their own aspirations and (b) Roman government policy as described by Tacitus. The major building and infrastructure works, which the authorities encouraged at urban centres, were a manifestation of that policy. The imperial government could not micro-manage Britain or any other province, and so needed to win over the indigenous élites, who would undertake the administration.

(ix) Insofar as the rural population in the deep countryside became Romanized, this was probably by accident rather than design. The Roman authorities would not have cared much about the British peasants, so long as they paid their taxes and did not rebel.

3. WHAT DID THE ROMANS GAIN FROM THEIR BRITISH ADVENTURE?

Strabo wrote his geography in the period following Caesar's invasions, whilst Britain was still nominally an independent island. He demonstrated with concise but compelling logic that annexing Britain to the Roman Empire would be a waste of resources and counterproductive. Augustus on at least three occasions considered invading Britain, but wisely decided against this course.

Seemingly Strabo's readership did not include Claudius. Two years after coming to power that Emperor embarked upon the formal annexation of Britain. We do not know what calculations were made or what policy discussions there were before Claudius and his advisers took the momentous decision to annexe Britain as a province. It seems likely that this project was driven not by any rational assessment of Rome's interests, but by the internal politics of the Principate. A weak and unpopular Emperor needed some spectacular military success in order to shore up his position. This led to the invasion of AD 43 and the establishment of southern Britain as a Roman province.

Once southern Britain was incorporated into the Empire the logic of imperialism took over. It was not practicable for Rome to administer and tax southern Britain, whilst leaving the north to its own devices. Withdrawal from Britain would involve massive loss of face and was politically impossible. Nero reluctantly accepted this, much though he would have liked to abandon Britannia. As a result, therefore, the Romans remained in Britain and gradually extended their reach northwards.

By the end of the first century the Romans had extended their control as far north as the Solway Firth. As set out in Chapters 5 to 7, however, they paid a high price for this modest extension to their Empire. For example, during the short period of Boudica's rebellion there was massive loss of life on both sides.

Because of its position as an island outpost, Britain unlike other provinces required its own dedicated fleet, the *classis Britannica*. This fleet was established in the late first century and remained in operation until the mid-third century. Even after the fleet was disbanded, the defence of British shores made considerable demands on the Roman navy.

The Romano-British Legacy

The preceding chapters have traced the conflicts that the Roman authorities encountered in Britain, ranging from Boudica's rebellion in the first century to the so-called 'barbarian conspiracy' in the fourth century. Britain was a troublesome province: during the first, second and early third century approximately 10–12 per cent of the entire Roman army was tied up in garrisoning 4 per cent of the Empire.[38]

Despite strenuous efforts Rome never succeeded in subduing Scotland. Thus, throughout the history of Roman Britain there was an extremely expensive northern frontier to defend.

In hindsight, we can see that the logical northern frontier for the Roman Empire was the English Channel. This was the effective frontier during the reign of Augustus. He decided that the Empire had reached its proper limits and that there should be no further expansion. The Roman concept of *limes* or frontier was not just a barrier to separate the Empire from barbarians. It was also a route along which officials and military units could travel. The Rhine/Danube frontier served that purpose well. The English Channel would also have served that purpose well.

Did Britain pay its way?

Undoubtedly, once Britannia was part of the Empire, Rome took advantage of her minerals and her grain crop. But there is no evidence that Britain was a financial asset to the Empire at any time during the first two centuries of Roman occupation. It is highly doubtful whether the taxes, tribute and minerals extracted from the province were sufficient to cover the costs of administration and maintaining order. Appian, who was writing in the second century, indicated that Britain was not paying its way.[39] The second century, it should be noted, was the most stable period in the whole of Rome's imperial history.

But is the accountancy model relevant? In the modern world we tend to assess every project from an accounting point of view. Even with the aid of top accountants and sophisticated software, that exercise is not easy. Assessments are often controversial, as illustrated by the battles over HS2 and a new runway at Heathrow Airport. In the ancient world however, *pace* Strabo and Appian, it is far from clear that people, looked at matters in that way. Accounting considerations were probably not uppermost in the minds of Roman policymakers.

The annexation of Britain and maintenance of such a distant island as a province was a source of immense prestige, regardless of the cost. It may be said that the Julio-Claudian dynasty converted capital of one form, namely cash, into another form, namely political capital. The same comment applies to the Flavian dynasty, at least until the accession of Domitian.

The position may possibly have changed during the third century, when peace was achieved on the northern frontier and the British garrison reduced in size. During the fourth century Britain achieved its highest level of prosperity and may possibly have been exporting grain to the Continent. But during that century attacks on Britain were intensifying from Scotland, Ireland and seaborne raiders. We became once again a difficult and expensive province to defend.

Britain was a steppingstone in the careers of many Roman politicians: Vespasian, Caracalla and Constantine being obvious examples. New emperors burnished their military credentials

---

[38] Mattingly (2006) 166.
[39] Preface to Appian's *History of Rome* 5.

by campaigning here and claiming great victories. Claudius was the first emperor to have this idea. Others followed his example.

Did it matter that Britain was so far away?

Well, that certainly added to the cost. Sometimes people drowned on the way here, which was a nuisance. But distance from Rome was also an asset. Britain was the ideal place of exile for miscreants such as Tiridates and Palladius. Emperors could send their rivals or other high-status troublemakers to govern Britain. Military units loyal to their commanders played a critical role in the power politics of the Empire. Any such units stationed in Britain were kept well out of the way.

The Roman annexation of Britain was, in one sense, the ultimate vanity project. It created an unnecessary northern frontier, which was difficult to defend. On the other hand, the political benefits of annexing Britain and maintaining it as a province were substantial.

The provinces collectively had a massive reverse effect on the mother city. Rome became provincialized as the provinces became Romanized.[40] But it is not easy to separate out the specific impact of Britain upon Rome. We were furthest from the centre of power; the last major province to join the Empire and the first to drop out.

4. WHAT DID BRITAIN GAIN FROM THE COLONIAL EXPERIENCE?

By the beginning of the first century AD Britain was set upon a trajectory of change that would have continued, invasion or no invasion.[41] As we saw in Chapters 2 and 3, the élites of the British communities were consciously adopting Continental fashions. Latin was the language used on coinage. Trade with the Empire was increasing. Even the Brigantes in the north were amassing Roman luxury items. In other words, many of the changes that swept across Britain in the first and second centuries AD may have happened anyway. The élites may have chosen to create Roman-style towns. Gallic stonemasons and designers would probably have crossed the Channel to provide embellishments. Gallic traders would certainly have seen business opportunities here, even if not in the London basin.

The effect of the invasion in AD 43 was to disrupt a process that was taking place naturally and to cause massive loss of life. This was followed a few years later by the Boudican rebellion, which involved even greater violence and loss of life. Once Britannia settled down under Roman rule, there were of course both winners and losers. Even so, we were a vassal state on the fringe of the Empire. Britons were obliged to pay taxes, which by all accounts they much resented. As we saw in Chapter 18, the diet of those working in the deep countryside (the vast majority of the population) declined. So did their health.

The final phase of the Roman occupation was disastrous, as we saw in Chapter 16. A feature of imperialism is that a colonial power disrupts the natural evolution of society and, upon

---

[40]Reece (1988) 11.
[41]Wallace (2016) demonstrates the continuity between the period before and the period after the invasion of AD 43.

withdrawal, it usually leaves behind chaos. That was certainly the case in Roman Britain: law and order broke down, the economy ceased to function, industries collapsed, and barter re-emerged as the means of trade.

In summary, Britain would have been far better off if it had remained a frontier region, with the Channel serving as northern boundary of the Empire. Britain would have gained many of the benefits of Romano-Gallic culture, without paying a horrendous price. The conclusion must be that the Britons of the first to fourth centuries AD gained little benefit and much grief from their colonial experience.

We will now turn to the post-Roman period and look at the long-term consequences of our subjection to Rome.

5. SUBSEQUENT BRITISH HISTORY – A VERY BRIEF SUMMARY

The so-called medieval period ran roughly from the fifth century up to the Renaissance. In the fifth and sixth centuries Germanic peoples known as Angles and Saxons settled in Britain and established control over an area that roughly equates to modern England.[42] They absorbed relatively little of the indigenous culture. They referred to the Britons as *wealas*, meaning foreigners. Contrary to the impression given by the *Anglo-Saxon Chronicle* and Bede's *Ecclesiastical History of the English People*, the Britons did not move away in some form of mass migration. They remained and formed most of the population of the territories under Anglo-Saxon control.

Cultural impact of the Germanic invasions

The impact of the Germanic invasions varied regionally. For example, few Anglo-Saxon type burials have been found in the West Midlands. In East Anglia a new and distinctive 'Anglian English' culture developed within a few generations, which included Scandinavian-style dress for women. The royal burial ground at Sutton Hoo included a splendid array of gold objects. Most cemeteries used in the fifth and sixth centuries were new, although often they were close to Romano-British burial grounds. A new style of housebuilding emerged, which was based on a module of two squares: this architectural tradition was widespread in the fifth to seventh centuries and appears to be part of 'deliberate acts of hybridization'.[43]

The major Anglo-Saxon kingdoms were Kent, East and Middle Anglia, Lindsey, Deira, Bernicia, Mercia, Sussex, Wessex and Essex.[44] Despite elements of hybridization, by and large, the Britons in those kingdoms adopted much of the culture, the language and even the ethnicity of their conquerors. As discussed in earlier chapters ethnicity is a fluid concept, which depends upon perception and choice, as much as race and heredity. In this instance, speaking English

---

[42] Hamerow (2005).
[43] Millett (2015c) 1–14.
[44] See map in Hamerow (2005) at 281.

became the crucial determinant of ethnic identity. By contrast, the Viking occupation of northern England during the ninth and tenth centuries did not have the same cultural impact.

In a well-reasoned paper, 'Why did the Anglo-Saxons not become more British?',[45] Bryan Ward-Perkins argues that the Britons made a cultural choice to adopt 'Anglo-Saxonness'. Part of the stimulus for this cultural choice seems to have been that under the law code of Ine (king of Wessex 688–726), foreigners received distinctly unfavourable treatment. Those who still identified themselves as Britons were regarded as foreigners (*wealas* or *wyliscmen*). They received only half of the *wergilds* (compensation paid by offenders to victims) that would be due to Englishmen. Under Ine's law, there was a binary ethnic distinction between *Englisc*/English ('us') and *Wylisc*/Welsh ('them'). When a single kingdom emerged in the tenth century, it took its name 'England' from the Anglo-Saxon settlers.

Wales and Scotland

The Britons who lived to the west of the emerging Anglo-Saxon kingdom remained as *wealas* or *wyliscmen*. They became known as Welshmen. They continued to speak Celtic. Other regions where Celtic languages remained in use were Brittany, Ireland, Scotland, the Isle of Man and the south-west peninsula (now Devon and Cornwall).[46] There was little urbanization in the Celtic regions. In some areas there were no towns at all. By the late sixth century, Roman Caerwent supported a monastery, but no urban life. Gildas records that there were two major kingdoms in Wales, Gwynedd in the north-west and Dyfed in the south-west.

The Picts who lived to the north of Anglo-Saxon Britain retained their separate identity, until they succumbed to Celtic invaders from Ireland. These invaders were the Scotti, whom we first met in Chapter 15. The indigenous people then adopted the ethnicity and language of their conquerors. As discussed more fully below, the northern part of Britain became Scotland. The population spoke Gaelic, the Celtic language of Ireland.

Did the Roman way of life continue?

At a superficial level, the Roman way of life did not continue in Britain during the medieval period. Roman towns and buildings fell into decay; Roman coinage ceased to circulate; existing industries closed down. Many technologies, such as use of the wheel for pottery production, vanished. The Anglo-Saxon settlers showed no desire to learn Latin and rejected the trappings of Roman culture. When Augustine arrived in AD 597 on his mission to Christianize Britain, there were few remaining traces of Christianity, the official religion of the Roman Empire.

Events on the continent took a different course.[47] The Visigoths and Ostrogoths occupied south-west Gaul and Spain. The Franks moved into northern Gaul. These peoples generally respected the Roman heritage and became Christian. The Franks in Gaul imposed their ethnic identity (*franci*, which later became *français*) and accepted much of the indigenous

---

[45]Ward-Perkins (2000) 513–33.
[46]Davies (2005).
[47]Cleary (2013b) chapters 8 and 9.

Gallo-Roman culture. They adopted Christianity and spoke a version of Latin, which evolved into modern French.[48]

6. LONG-TERM IMPACT OF THE ROMAN OCCUPATION

Although the superficial trappings of Romanitas fell away quickly after AD 409, at a deeper level the impact upon Britain of the Roman occupation was both permanent and structural.

(i) London

The Romans founded *Londinium* within a few years after the conquest. Almost immediately entrepreneurs moved in and the town became a major commercial centre. During the first century a civil service was established in London. The city acquired monumental buildings. The Roman authorities made it the provincial capital and central hub of the country's transport system. They also made London their financial centre, where the procurator gathered in taxes and oversaw public expenditure.

London has the same characteristics today. It is our capital city, the seat of government, the central hub of the national road network and the national rail network. The Treasury and the headquarters of HM Revenue & Customs are in Westminster. They perform essentially the same functions as the Roman procurator. On the commercial side, Tacitus' description of London in AD 60 is perfectly apt today: 'copia negotiatorum et commeatuum maxime celebre'[49]

Many of the first-century tablets recovered from the Bloomberg site have a distinctly contemporary feel. They record financial deals and similar matters. One tablet (WT30) advises the recipient to take care for his reputation on the London market. The city of London, its functions, its character and even its name are a central part of our Roman heritage.

The intervening history has not extinguished Rome's legacy. London fell to the Saxons at an unknown date, but by 597 when Augustine arrived the city was still of great importance. The king of Kent founded St Paul's Cathedral there (close to the site of a substantial Roman temple) and installed Mellitus as the first bishop in 604. In the seventh to eighth centuries most development was in the area of the Strand and Aldwych, 'ald wych' meaning old port or town. In the ninth century under King Alfred the original town was reoccupied, with the Roman walls serving as city defences. The city retained its importance through the Viking period. In the eleventh century, Edward the Confessor founded Westminster Abbey. A few years later William the Conqueror was crowned there and made London his capital city. London has retained that status ever since.

Despite two thousand years of development, parts of London's massive Roman wall survive, for example around Tower Hill and in the cells of the Old Bailey. Familiar place names fix the location of gates: Ludgate, Newgate, Bishopsgate and Aldgate. Some of London's major roads

---

[48]Ward-Perkins (2000) at 517 and 528–30.
[49]*Annals* 14.33: 'an important centre with a large number of businessmen and much merchandise'.

follow the line of Roman streets. The A5 running north from Marble Arch, up through Stanmore and beyond follows the line of Watling Street. Oxford Street follows the line of a road that led from Colchester to Silchester, passing through the capital. London Bridge is on the site of the first wooden road bridge over the Thames, which the Roman invaders built in AD 47/48.

In the twenty-first century, London is and remains a highly Romanized city.

(ii) Other towns

The Romans brought with them the concept of the city – an established feature of the classical world, far removed from the Iron age *oppida* of Britain. Roman town planners effectively determined the locations where many of our major cities are sited.

Their history follows a common pattern, similar to London. The Angles or Saxons settled just outside a Romano-British town. Then later in the Anglo-Saxon period, there was a reoccupation of the original town, with the Roman walls serving as urban defences. Winchester is typical in that regard.[50] The Saxons settled outside the old town. Then during the Alfredian period a new street grid was laid out within the Roman walls. Because of the location of the gates, the principal roads necessarily followed the lines of the main Roman streets.

The Anglo-Saxons adopted the Roman communications network, because roads were already in place and they fitted with the geography. That in turn dictated that the locations of most major towns should be where the Romans had put them.

As demonstrated in Chapter 17 and the Online Appendix, many modern towns and some villages bear the imprint of Rome. Colchester, Chichester, Bath, Lincoln, York, Cirencester, Silchester and Caerwent are examples.

Some of our major roads follow the lines of Roman roads laid out in the first century AD. Examples are (parts of) the A1, the M1, the A2, the A3, the A4, the A5, the M4 in South Wales and the M5 north of Exeter. More generally, a glance at the Ordnance Survey map of Roman Britain shows the remarkable congruence of Roman and modern roads.

A study[51] carried out at two Danish universities compared the road network across the Empire in AD 117 with the intensity of light emitted from towns and conurbations in 2010. The map in their report shows a clear correlation between the Roman road network and areas of modern economic prosperity. This led to their conclusion that early infrastructure development tends to persist over time and to generate economic activity. That is certainly true of Roman Britain.

(iii) Ports and coastal defences

In the seventh century, a number of royally controlled trading centres or 'emporia' were established along the coast or on major rivers.[52] They included London, York, Southampton

---

[50]Ottaway (2017).
[51]https://voxeu.org/article/roman-roads-and-persistence-development.
[52]Hamerow (2005) 285.

Figure 20.1 Pevensey shore fort: Second World War pillbox built into the Roman wall. © Geoffrey May.

and Ipswich. These trading centres generally coincided with Roman ports or harbours. Save where the coastline has changed, similar geographical considerations have governed the selection of ports in ancient, medieval and modern times.

The Romans established a port at London complete with quays, jetties and warehouses in the Flavian period. That location made sense because it was close to the Continent; the Thames was tidal and deep; London had good overland transport links. That same logic led to the use of London as a major port in medieval and modern times. It was only in the late twentieth century that the Port of London closed, because it could not accommodate container ships. The area was developed as 'London Docklands', a hub for international business in the digital age. Tilbury, which is about 20 miles downstream, became the new port.

The port of Dover was established to serve the *classis Britannica*. It continued as a port and was a bastion against invasion during the Napoleonic wars; and again, during the Second World War. It is now the main port for cross-channel ferries and Eurostar.

During the third century the Romans built a line of shore forts along the coastline of south-east England, as a defence against Saxons and other sea-borne raiders. Some of those forts were long-lasting. They continued to serve as defences long after the fall of Rome. The shore fort at Pevensey was in the front line of defence against the Spanish Armada: in 1588 the Elizabethans mounted canons along the south wall. That same fort was also in the front line of defence against German invasion during the Second World War. The British army constructed pillboxes within the walls of the ancient shore fort (Fig. 20.1). It is striking that a Roman military structure should be used for its original purpose sixteen centuries after it was built.

(iv) Scotland

It is not obvious that during the Iron Age there was any stark ethnic division between the communities of highland Scotland, the communities of lowland Scotland and the various communities in the main part of the British island.

The emergence of a separate Scottish identity appears to be a product of the Roman period. For two centuries it was Roman policy to annexe the entire British island as a province – an enterprise that the highland and lowland communities successfully resisted. That left the question of where the frontier should lie. The two serious candidates were the Tyne/Solway line and the Forth/Clyde line. Eventually the Tyne/Solway line prevailed and Hadrian's Wall became the northern frontier of the Roman Empire. The Romans did not see their Empire as bounded by Hadrian's Wall or, indeed, by any other frontier: their domination and sense of entitlement extended far into the hinterlands beyond. Even so, Hadrian's Wall marked the boundary of the formal province. The regions to the north were not subject to direct Roman rule through the machinery of civitas capitals, senates, magistrates and so forth.

The word 'Picts' (*Picti*, meaning 'painted men') was a term that the Romans used to describe the strange looking people, who lived to the north of the Forth/Clyde isthmus. The word, which may originally have been soldier-slang, first appears in the panegyric delivered by Eumenius to Constantius in AD 297: Eumenius refers to the Picts attacking Hadrian's Wall. 'Picts' was a convenient collective noun for communities to the north of the wall and that word entered general usage.

The emergence of a separate Pictish identity appears to be a product of the Roman period. As Sally Foster observes in her history of medieval Scotland:

> It is a remarkable achievement that such a geographically extended and diverse group of peoples as the Picts could have been identified as a grouping since the late Roman period. Equally extraordinary is the fact that this relationship should have survived the withdrawal of the Romans – the external threat which had first impelled the Iron Age tribes of Scotland to bond in adversity against a common enemy.[53]

In the fifth to tenth centuries there were numerous petty kingdoms in Scotland.[54] Those in central and eastern areas gradually coalesced to become a political entity, Pictland, with the shared language P-Celtic. Meanwhile Irish peoples, variously described as 'Scotti' (whom we met in Chapter 15), 'Gaels' or 'Dal Riata', settled on the western side in the Argyll area. Their language was Q-Celtic or Gaelic. They adopted Christianity, apparently following the mission of St Columba in 563. In the ninth and tenth centuries, the Irish settlers became dominant. When a single kingdom emerged in the tenth century, it was known as 'Alba' or Scotland, not Pictland. The Anglo-Saxon Chronicle referred to the kings of Alba as kings of the Scots. The language of that kingdom was Scottish Gaelic, a version of Q-Celtic.

The Picts (who were in the majority) appear to have adopted the ethnicity of the Scotti, in the same way that the Britons further south (also in the majority) adopted the ethnicity of the

---

[53] Foster (2014) 146.
[54] Foster (2014) chapters 3 and 7.

Angles and the Saxons. Two large kingdoms emerged in the tenth century, England and Scotland, both taking their names and much of their culture from minority overseas settlers.

The origin of the divide between England and Scotland lies in the Roman period. Ever since then, the separate identity of the top section of Britain has been acknowledged. Although England and Scotland were separate, the location of the boundary remained in dispute for some eight hundred years after the fall of Rome. In 1237 the Treaty of York established the Anglo-Scottish border roughly where it now is.

The issue of Scottish independence

Once Rome had resigned itself to the independence of the Picts, that meant there was a new frontier of the Empire to defend. For the reasons explained earlier, Hadrian's Wall alone was not sufficient to ward off trouble from the north. Rome therefore resorted to two expedients, namely bribery/diplomatic gifts and a strong frontier army ranged along the Wall. The problem of how to deal with an independent Scotland may be the product of the Roman period, but it is not unique to that era. It has been a recurrent issue through sixteen hundred years of English history since the fall of Rome and is no less topical today.

Hadrian's Wall symbolizes the separateness of England and Scotland, but it does not mark, and has never marked, the actual line of the frontier. Hadrian's Wall lies some way to the south of the present border. The sense of Scottish separateness from the rest of Britain and the demands for independence have their origins in the events of the Roman period.

(v) Wales

The Welsh communities, starting with the Silures, put up a stronger resistance to Roman conquest than the rest of southern and central Britain. It is possible to trace the separate identity of Wales back to the struggles described in Chapters 5 and 7 above. This was a decentralized society, which harassed the invaders with repeated guerrilla warfare through the first century.

The people of Wales were neither placid nor easy to govern. Out of the three permanent legionary bases which Rome established in Britain, two were needed to control Wales – Caerleon in the south and Chester in the north. Also, a network of auxiliary forts was established across the territory, as described in Chapter 7. The civitas system came late to Wales and did not encompass the whole of the territory. Areas in the north remained under military administration. The communities of Wales did not (and do not) welcome control from London.

As Ward-Perkins has demonstrated,[55] the Britons in Wales made a cultural choice not to adopt Anglo-Saxon ethnicity. They remained as *wealas* or *wyliscmen*. During the period AD 400 to 800 several separate Brythonic kingdoms emerged and flourished in Wales. They largely resisted conquest by the Saxons and by the Vikings. Over the same period their Brythonic language (P-Celtic) evolved into Welsh.

---

[55] Ward-Perkins (2000)

Offa, king of Mercia from 757 to 796, organized the construction of the famous Dyke which bears his name.[56] He appears to have planned the route in consultation with the kings of Powys and Gwent. Unlike Hadrian's wall (which had a military/defensive function), Offa's Dyke primarily existed to denote the boundary between England and Wales.

As noted above, a single kingdom emerged in England during the tenth century. The various Welsh kings maintained their independence but were constrained to acknowledge the suzerainty of the English king. This remained the position after the Norman conquest. The *Domesday Book* records the degree of control exercised by the English monarch: for example, the king of Deheubarth paid an annual tribute of £40 to William I and William II.

Early in the reign of Henry I (1100–1135) the March emerged as a separate territory running roughly along the boundary between England and Wales. The Marcher Lords were powerful landowners with the right to build castles and wage war against their neighbours.

The Welsh rulers bridled against the overlordship of England. After numerous battles and treaties, matters came to a head in 1282, when Edward I crushed the Welsh forces. Edward made his son (the future Edward II) Prince of Wales and established a network of castles across the principality. He substantially reformed the Law of Wales, which had been a defining feature of Welsh culture since the ninth century. Even so, the administration of Wales remained separate from that of England. A new class of officials grew up to carry out that administration.[57] The continued existence of the March emphasized the separation of Wales from England; the Marcher Lords were amongst Edward I's leading vassals.

Moving on three centuries, Henry VIII set about uniting the administration of England and Wales. Wales became subject to the same laws as England. It returned MPs to sit in the Westminster Parliament. The Marcher Lords were abolished. The use of English became compulsory in Welsh courts. This last reform was not hugely successful, since most of the Welsh population knew no English. Two statutes achieved Henry's agenda, the Laws in Wales Acts 1536 and 1543. Thomas Cromwell promoted the first of those statutes but was unable to assist with the second one, as by then he had been decapitated.

That was not the end of Wales' separate identity. Welsh continued to be the main language of Wales and heirs to the throne continued to be Princes of Wales, which emphasized the separate status of the principality. As previously discussed, ethnicity is partly a matter of choice. The indigenous people continued to see themselves as ethnically Welsh and distinct from the English. In the nineteenth and twentieth centuries the holding of eisteddfods strengthened the sense of Welsh nationhood and culture. In 1993 the Welsh Language Act repealed the last vestiges of Henry VIII's unpopular legislation. The subsequent creation of the Welsh Assembly and the return of powers from Westminster to Cardiff is the most recent stage of that story.

In summary, Wales put up stout resistance to conquest by Rome; later Wales put up stout resistance to conquest by Anglo-Saxons and Danes. The separate ethnicity of the Welsh people was a matter of cultural choice. They have fought to assert their independence for two thousand years and against high odds. The sense of Welsh separateness from England lies not in any racial divide, but in events of the Roman and medieval periods.

---

[56]Davies (2007) 62–5.
[57]Davies (2007) 163–74.

The Romano-British Legacy

(vi) National identity

The image of Britannia as a seated lady holding a javelin has long been one of the representations of Britain. It has appeared on the back of our coins since the seventeenth century. It still features on 50 pence coins. This is a Roman image, as discussed in Chapter 10: it originally symbolized both Britain as a place and the subjection of Britain to the Roman Emperor.

It may seem odd that an image that once represented Britain's subordination to Rome has come to be a projection of British sovereignty and power. This happened because when Britain moved onto the world stage in the seventeenth century, the power brokers of London – all classically educated – saw themselves as the successors of Rome. Britain was doing the same thing as Rome had done, but seventeen centuries later. So, Britannia was now the imperial power, not a lowly province.

There is also a wider point here. The concept of Britain as a country (as well as its name – an anglicized version of Britannia) has its origin in the Roman period. During the Iron Age the scattered communities described in Chapter 2 above did not see themselves as forming part of a nation state; nor did anyone else see them in that way. The conceptualization of Britain as a country is part of the Roman heritage.

(vii) Religion and culture

In the fifth and sixth centuries Christianity principally survived on the east side of Britain, to the south of York. Christian burials can be identified because generally they are oriented east–west and contain no grave goods.[58] Saint Patrick, who went on a mission to Ireland in the fifth century, was the son and grandson of British priests.[59] Christianity gradually receded from Britain, so that when Augustine arrived at the behest of the Pope in AD 597 he found a largely pagan country. There was little direct continuity of the Christian tradition in this country.

Christianity was heavily structured around Rome. The church structure came to mirror the structure of the Empire. In the emerging kingdoms of France and Spain, the kings adopted Christianity. Unlike Anglo-Saxon Britain, these kingdoms did not have a break in continuity, followed by the re-imposition of Christianity.

Despite the break in continuity, Britain later fell into line with the other former provinces. Christianity, the official religion of the later Roman Empire, became and still is the official religion of England. This will remain the case unless and until the Church of England is disestablished. We know from the records of early church councils that in the fourth century Britain had bishops, deacons and priests. That is essentially the same as the present church hierarchy.

As noted in Chapter 19, Christian worship in Britain goes back to the era of persecution, before Christianity became 'official'. St Alban's cathedral is testament to that tradition on a grand scale. On a less grand scale, but perhaps more powerful evidence of the practice of Christianity in the second century, is the little acrostic in the Corinium Museum at Cirencester.

---

[58]Stancliffe (2005) 426–7.
[59]Thompson (1985) reconstructs what little is known about St Patrick.

The Latin alphabet fell out of use in Anglo-Saxon Britain but remained in use on the Continent. The Latin alphabet was re-introduced into Britain during the late Saxon period. Once again, despite the break in continuity, our alphabet is part of the Roman legacy.

Some aspects of Romano-British history are now embedded in our national culture. Boudica's rebellion is part of folklore, even amongst people who have never heard of Tacitus or Dio Cassius. The famous statue of Boudica riding her war chariot next to Westminster Bridge epitomizes the popular image. Strong-willed female leaders, like Elizabeth I or Margaret Thatcher, tend to identify with her. Elizabeth I was a formidable classical scholar and produced her own translation of Tacitus' Annals.[60] Her address to the troops at Tilbury, as the Spanish Armada approached, has strong echoes of Boudica's famous pre-battle speech.

An analysis of 2,528 posts and comments on Facebook between 2010 and 2017 revealed a huge number of references to Roman Britain and Boudica.[61] The vessel chartered in June 2019 to commemorate the 75th anniversary of the D-Day landings was named 'MV Boudica'.

Romanization as a continuing process

We saw in Chapter 9 that the evolving cultures of Rome became blended with those of the provinces that it annexed. The ultimate proof of Romanization is that no-one knows when the Roman Empire ended. As time went on, the original 'Roman' elements of those shared cultures diminished. The Empire divided and acquired new administrative hubs. The Byzantine Empire is generally regarded as a continuation of the Roman Empire. Rightly so, since it was founded by the Emperor Constantine as the 'new Rome'. Over time the Roman features of the Byzantine Empire progressively receded. In the seventh century, Greek replaced Latin as the official language. Eventually the Roman Empire ceased to exist at all, but no-one can say exactly when that happened.

That does not mean Romanization fizzled out. Quite the opposite. Romanization was a process whereby the cultures of Rome rippled out across the known world and across time, continuously mutating as they mingled with other cultures. That process continues today. Look at the Roman elements of the US constitution, the use of Latin in scientific or literary contexts, the Roman Catholic Church worldwide, all other variants of Christianity, the plays of Shakespeare, the paintings in the Prado, 'Apollo' space missions, box sets about gladiators, the calendar, the concept of 'citizenship', the design of churches (modelled on the Roman basilica and often called 'basilicas'), current legal systems,[62] the use of 'forums' for meetings or debate, and much else besides. Even Islam has its origins in the Roman world and contains Roman elements.[63] The process of Romanization has now become unstoppable.

The Roman occupation of Britain was morally indefensible. At the time, it brought much grief to the indigenous population, who suffered many abuses. At least some of the occupying troops scathingly described the local people as 'Brittunculi' – wretched little Britons.[64] Ironically, however, later generations in Britain have positively benefited from Romanization.

---

[60] Philo (2019) 1–30.
[61] *The Times* 10 April 2018, 'Farage is Boudicca to Europe's Emperors, say cyberwarriors'.
[62] For a recent case turning on Roman law, see *King v Chiltern Dog Rescue* [2015] EWCA Civ 581; [2016] Ch 221.
[63] Hoyland (2016).
[64] *Tab Vindol* II, 164.

(viii) Brexit

As discussed in Chapter 16, Britain dropped out of the Roman Empire in the early years of the fifth century. Internal pressures were pushing the Britons towards secession, particularly their inability to deal with raiders and disillusionment with the distant Roman authorities. At the same time, external pressures were sucking resources away from Britain, as Rome needed troops to defend the heartlands of the Empire. A combination of internal and external pressures brought about Britain's detachment from the Empire.

There are no direct parallels with Brexit, but there are some interesting points of comparison:

(i) From the first to the fourth century the Roman Empire had functioned as a European super-state. There was a common currency, a broadly uniform tax regime, an integrated road system, a European army and an overarching imperial administration.

(ii) That administration became increasingly bureaucratic during the fourth century. This may have been necessary, but according to Zosimus Britain resented these arrangements.

(iii) The dominant threat to the world order in the late fourth/early fifth century came from the East.

(iv) Uncontrolled immigration of people perceived as foreigners (*barbari*) destabilized the European political order and led to its transformation.

(v) Continental Europe was wracked with conflict during much of the fourth century, while Britain enjoyed its greatest period of prosperity. Even so, any notion that Britain could prosper on its own proved to be an illusion. The comfortable middle classes enjoying villa life in the mid-fourth century had no notion of what lay just round the corner.

(vi) Britain's ambiguous position as an island state (in one sense cut off from Europe's problems and hoping to do better, but in another sense heavily dependent on the fortunes of its Continental neighbours) was as much a feature of the ancient world as it is of the modern world.

(vii) The imperial government seems to have been sorry to see us go. For some years after 409, the *Notitia Dignitatum* pretended that Britain was still part of the Empire. This may have reflected an intention that Britain would be brought back into the fold.

(viii) After dropping out of the Empire, Britain gradually declined. There was no effective maintenance of law and order. Industries collapsed. Invaders moved in. The Dark Ages had arrived.

Some of the factors mentioned in the previous paragraph, but hopefully not item (viii), have their counterparts in the early twenty-first century. Even so, surprisingly, the events of AD 409 have barely featured in the debates about Brexit. Perhaps people should pay closer attention to the history of Roman Britain – as you the reader have done.

BIBLIOGRAPHY

Ancient works

Ammianus Marcellinus, *Res Gestae*
Appian, *History of Rome*
Augustus, *Res Gestae Divi Augusti*
Aurelius Victor, *De Caesaribus*
Bede, The Venerable *The Ecclesiastical History of the English People*
Bible, the New Testament
Cicero, *Letters to his brother Quintus*, *Letters to Atticus* and *De Re Publica*
Claudius Claudianus ('Claudian'), *De Consulatu Stilichonis*
Columella, *De Re Rustica*
Dio Cassius, *Roman History*
Diodorus Siculus, *Library*
Eusebius, *Life of Constantine*
Eutropius, *Breviarium ab Urbe Condita*
Gildas, *De Excidio Britanniae*
Herodian, *History of the Roman Empire after Marcus*
Herodotus, *The Histories*
St Jerome's *Chronicle*
Julius Caesar, *Gallic War*
Justinian, *Digest*
Lactantius, *De mortibus persecutorum*
Latinus Pacatus Drepanius and others, *Panegyrici Latini* (Latin Panegyrics)
Lucretius, *De rerum natura*
Pausanias, *Periegesis*
Pliny the Elder, *Natural History*
Pliny the Younger, *Letters*
Ptolemy, *Geography*
Quintilian, *Institutio Oratoria*
Scriptores Historiae Augustae, *Historia Augusta*
Strabo, *Geography*
Suetonius, *Lives of the Caesars*
Sun Tzu, *The art of war*
Tacitus, *Annals*; *Histories*; *Agricola*
Theodosian Code
Unknown officials, *Notitia dignitatum omnium, tam civilium quam militarium*
Unknown officials, *Laterculus Veronensis*
Vegetius, *Epitomy of Military Science*
Virgil, *Aeneid*
Zosimus, *Historia Nova*

Bibliography

Inscriptions

Collingwood, R. G. and Wright, R. P., *The Roman Inscriptions of Britain*, Vol I (second edition). Oxford University Press and Sutton Publishing (1995).
Collingwood, R. G. and Wright, R. P., *The Roman Inscriptions of Britain*, Vol II. Sutton Publishing (1995).
Corpus Inscriptionum Latinarum.
Tomlin, R. S. O., Wright, R. P. and Hassall, M. C. W., *The Roman Inscriptions of Britain*, Vol III. Oxbow Books (2009).

Tablets

Bloomberg Tablets, identified as 'WT1', 'WT2', etc. ('WT' is an abbreviation for writing tablet). See Tomlin (2016) page 6.
Carlisle Tablets, are referred to as *Tabulae Luguvalienses*, abbreviated to *Tab Luguval* followed by the number of the relevant tablet.
Sulis Tablets, found at the temple to Sulis Minerva in Bath are referred to as *Tabulae Sulis*, abbreviated to *Tab Sul*, followed by the number of the relevant tablet.
Vindolanda Tablets are referred to as *Tabulae Vindolandenses*, abbreviated to *Tab Vindol* followed by the number of the relevant tablet. Published online: vindolanda.csad.ox.ac.uk/ and vto2.classics.ox.ac.uk/

Works cited

Abdy, Richard, 'In the pay of the emperor: coins from the Beaurains (Arras) Treasure' in E. Hartley, M. Hawkes, M. Henig and F. Mee (eds), *Constantine the Great, York's Roman Emperor*. York Museums Trust (2006).
Acemoglou, Daron and Robinson, James, *Why Nations Fail*. Profile Books (2012).
Allen, M., Lodwick, L., Brindle, T., Fulford, M., Smith, A., *The Rural Economy of Roman Britain*. Society for Promotion studies (2017).
Allason-Jones, Lindsay (ed.), *Artefacts in Roman Britain*. Cambridge University Press (2011).
Allason-Jones, Lindsay, 'The Vicus at Housesteads: a case study in material culture and Roman life', in Rob Collins and Matthew Symonds (eds), *Breaking Down Boundaries: Hadrian's Wall in the 21st Century* [Journal of Roman Archaeology Supplementary Series]. (2013).
Annels, Alwyn and Burnham, Barry, *The Dolaucothi Gold Mines*. APECS Press (2013).
Barnes, Timothy, *Constantine and Eusebius*. Harvard University Press, 2006.
Bateman, N., Cowan, C., Wroe-Brown, R., *London's Roman Amphitheatre: Excavations at the Guildhall*. Museum of London Archaeology Service (2008).
Bayley, Justine, Croxford, Ben, Henig, Martin, and Watson, Bruce, 'A Gilt Bronze Arm from London', *Britannia* 40 (2009) 151–62.
Beard, Mary, *Confronting the Classics*. Profile Books (2013).
Beard, M., North, J. and Price, S., *Religions of Rome*. Cambridge University Press (1998).
Berggren, L. and Jones, A., *Ptolemy's Geography*. Princeton University Press (2000).
Bidwell, Paul, *Roman Forts in Britain*. Tempus Publishing (2007).
Bidwell, Paul, 'Constantius and Constantine in York', in E. Hartley, M. Hawkes, M. Henig and F. Mee (eds), *Constantine the Great, York's Roman Emperor*. York Museums Trust (2006).
Bidwell, Paul, 'The Roman Fort at Bainbridge, Wensleydale', *Britannia* 43 (2012) 45–113
Bidwell, Paul, *Hadrian's Wall at Wallsend*. Arbeia Society and Tyne and Wear Archives and Museums, 2018.
Birley, Anthony, *The Roman Government of Britain*. Oxford University Press (2005).
Birley, Anthony, *Hadrian: The Restless Emperor*. Routledge (1997).

Bibliography

Birley, Anthony, 'Britain under Trajan and Hadrian' in Thorsten Opper (ed.), *Hadrian: Art, Politics and Economy*. British Museum (2013).

Birley, Eric, 'Britain under the Flavians: Agricola and his predecessors', in E. Birley collected papers, *Roman Britain and the Roman Army*. Titus Wilson & Son (1961).

Birley, Robin, *Vindolanda: A Roman Frontier Fort on Hadrian's Wall*. Amberley Publishing (2009).

Blagg, Thomas, 'The date of the temple of Sulis Minerva at Bath', *Britannia* 10 (1979) 101–7.

Blagg, Thomas, 'Roman civil and military architecture in the province of Britain', *World Archaeology* 12 (1) (1980) 27–42.

Blagg, Thomas, 'Architectural munificence in Britain: the evidence of inscriptions', *Britannia* 21 (1990) 13–31.

Blagg, Thomas, *Roman Architectural Ornament in Britain*, BAR British Series 329 (2002).

Blair, Tony, *A Journey*. Hutchinson (2010).

Bland, Roger, *Coin Hoards and Hoarding in Roman Britain AD 43-c.498*. Spink, London (2018).

Bowman, Alan, *Life and Letters on the Roman Frontier*. British Museum Press (2003).

Bowman, Alan, Thomas, John, and Tomlin, Roger, 'The Vindolanda writing-tablets (*Tabulae Vindolandenses* IV, Part 1)', *Britannia* 41 (2010) 187–224.

Bowman, Alan, Thomas, John, and Tomlin, Roger, 'The Vindolanda writing-tablets (*Tabulae Vindolandenses* IV, Part 2)', *Britannia* 42 (2011) 113–44.

Bowman, Alan, Thomas, John, and Tomlin, Roger, 'The Vindolanda writing-tablets (*Tabulae Vindolandenses* IV, Part 3): new letters of Julius Verecundius,' *Britannia* 50 (2019) 225–51.

Bradley, Colleen, *Romano-British Curse Tablets*. Createspace (2011).

Bray, Lee, 'Horrible, speculative, nasty, dangerous': Assessing the value of Roman Iron', *Britannia* 41 (2010) 175–85.

Breeze, David, (ed.), *J. Collingwood Bruce's Handbook to the Roman Wall* (14th edn). Newcastle upon Tyne (2006a).

Breeze, David, *The Antonine Wall*. John Donald (2006b).

Breeze, David, *The Frontiers of Imperial Rome*. Pen and Sword (2011).

Breeze, David, *The Impact of Rome on the British Countryside*. Royal Archaeological Institute (2013).

Breeze, David, *Roman Scotland*. BT Batsford (1996).

Breeze, David, 'Two Roman Britains', *Archaeological Journal* 171 (2014) 97–110

Breeze, David, *The Roman Army*. Bloomsbury Academic (2016).

Breeze D. and Dobson B., *Hadrian's Wall* (4th edn). Penguin Books (2000).

Brewer, Richard, *Caerwent Roman Town* (3rd edn). Welsh Assembly Government (2006).

Brewer, Richard, 'Dolaucothi Gold mine and Pumsaint Roman fort' in Patrick Ottaway (ed.), 'South-West Wales' [supplement to] *Archaeological Journal* 167 (2010) 27–8.

Broodbank, Cyprian, *The Making of the Middle Sea*. Thames & Hudson (2013).

Bruun, C. and Edmondson J. (eds) *Oxford Handbook of Roman Epigraphy*. Oxford University Press (2015).

Bryan, J., et al., *Archaeology at Bloomberg*. Museum of London Archaeology (2017).

Cameron, Averil, 'Constantius and Constantine: an exercise in publicity', in E. Hartley, M. Hawkes, M. Henig and F. Mee (eds), *Constantine the Great, York's Roman Emperor*. York Museums Trust (2006a).

Cameron, Averil, 'Constantine and Christianity', in E. Hartley, M. Hawkes, M. Henig and F. Mee (eds), *Constantine the Great, York's Roman Emperor*. York Museums Trust (2006b).

Campbell, Duncan, 'A note on the battle of Mons Graupius', *Classical Quarterly* 65 (2015) 407–10.

Cartledge, Paul (ed.), *Cambridge World History of Slavery*, vol 1. Cambridge University Press (2011).

Caro, Robert, *The Years of Lyndon Johnson*, volume 4, *The Passage of Power*. Bodley Head (2012).

Casey, P., *Carausius and Allectus*. B T Batsford (1994).

Casey, P., 'Magnus Maximus in Britain', in P. Casey (ed.), *The End of Roman Britain*, BAR (British series) 71 (1979).

Champion, Timothy, 'Britain Before the Romans', in Martin Millett, Louise Revell and Alison Moore (eds), *The Oxford Handbook of Roman Britain*. Oxford University Press (2016).

Claridge, Amanda, 'Hadrian's succession and the monuments of Trajan', in Thorsten Opper (ed.), *Hadrian: Art, Politics and Economy*. British Museum (2013).

Bibliography

Cleary, Simon Esmonde, *The Ending of Roman Britain*. BT Batsford (1989).
Cleary, Simon Esmonde, *Chedworth, Life in a Roman Villa*. History Press (2013a).
Cleary, Simon Esmonde, *The Roman West AD 200-500*. Cambridge University Press (2013b).
Cleary, Simon Esmonde, 'Britain at the end of empire', in Martin Millett, Louise Revell and Alison Moore (eds), *The Oxford Handbook of Roman Britain*. Oxford University Press (2016).
Collins, Rob, 'Traprain Law Treasure', in E. Hartley M. Hawkes M. Henig and F. Mee (eds), *Constantine the Great, York's Roman Emperor*. York Museums Trust (2006).
Collins, Rob, 'The latest Roman coin from Hadrian's Wall: a small fifth century purse group', *Britannia* 39 (2008) 256–61.
Collis, John, *The Iron Age*, in Blaise Vyner, (ed.) *Building on the Past*. Royal Archaeological Institute (1994).
Cool, H., Jackson, C., and Monaghan, J., 'Glass-making and the Sixth Legion at York', *Britannia* 30 (1999) 147–62.
Cool, H. and Mason, D., *Roman Piercebridge*. Architectural and Archaeological Society of Durham and Northumberland (2008).
Cool, H. and Richardson, J., 'Exploring ritual deposits in a well at Rothwell Haigh, Leeds', *Britannia* 44 (2013) 191–217.
Cousins, Eleri, 'An imperial image: the Bath Gorgon in context', *Britannia* 42 (2016) 99–118.
Creighton, John, *Coins and Power in Late Iron Age Britain*. Cambridge University Press (2000).
Creighton, John, *Britannia, the Creation of a Roman Province*. Routledge (2006).
Creighton, John, 'The Iron Age Roman transition', in Simon James and Martin Millett (eds) *Britons and Romans: Advancing an Archaeological Agenda*. Council for British Archaeology Research Report 125 (2001).
Creighton J. and Fry R., *Silchester: Changing Visions of a Roman Town*. Society for the Promotion of Roman Studies (2016).
Crerar, Belinda, 'Contextualising Romano-British Lead Tanks: A Study in Design, Destruction and Deposition', *Britannia* 43 (2012) 135–66.
Cronin, Vincent, *The Florentine Renaissance*. Folio Society (2001).
Croxford, Ben, 'Iconoclasm in Roman Britain', *Britannia* 34 (2003) 81–95.
Crummy, Philip, 'The Roman circus at Colchester', *Britannia* 39 (2008), 15–31.
Cuff, David, 'The King of the Batavians: Remarks on *Tab Vindol* III, 628', *Britannia* 42 (2011) 145–56.
Cunliffe, Barry, *Roman Bath*. BT Batsford (1995).
Cunliffe, Barry, *The Extraordinary Voyage of Pytheas the Greek: The Man Who Discovered Britain*. Penguin Books (2002).
Cunliffe, Barry, *Facing the Ocean*. Oxford University Press (2004).
Cunliffe, Barry, *Iron Age Communities in Britain* (4th edn). Routledge (2005).
Cunliffe, Barry, *Fishbourne Roman Palace*. History Press (2010).
Cunliffe, Barry, *Danebury Hillfort*. History Press (2011).
Cunliffe, Barry, *Roman Bath Discovered*. History Press (2012).
Cunliffe, B., Down, A. and Rudkin, D., *Excavations at Fishbourne 1969–1988*. Chichester District Council (1996).
Dando-Collins, Stephen, *The Legions of Rome*. Quercus (2010).
Davenport, Caillan, *A History of the Roman Equestrian Order*. Cambridge University Press (2019).
Davies, Hugh, 'Designing Roman roads', *Britannia* 29 (1998) 1–16.
Davies, Hugh, *Roman Roads in Britain*. Shire Publications (2011).
Davies, Jeffrey, 'Soldier and civilian in Wales', in Malcolm Todd (ed.), *Companion to Roman Britain*. Blackwell Publishing (2007).
Davies, John, *A History of Wales*. Penguin Books (2007).
Davies, Wendy, 'The Celtic kingdoms', in Paul Fouracre (ed.) *The New Cambridge Mediaeval History*, vol 1. Cambridge University Press (2005).
De la Bédoyère, Guy, *Roman Towns in Britain*. History Press (2010a).
De la Bédoyère, Guy, *Roman Britain: A New History*. Thames & Hudson (2010b).
Drinkwater, John, *Roman Gaul*. Groom Helm (1983).

Drogula, Fred, *Commanders and Command in the Roman Republic and Early Empire*. University of North Carolina Press (2015).
Dungworth, David, 'Metals and metalworking', in Martin Millett, Louise Revell and Alison Moore (eds), *The Oxford Handbook of Roman Britain*. Oxford University Press (2016).
Dunwoodie, L., Harward, C. & Pitt, K., *An Early Roman Fort and Urban Development on Londinium's Eastern Hill*. Museum of London Archaeology (2015).
Du Plessis, P., Ando, C. and Tuori, K., (eds), *The Oxford Handbook of Roman Law and Society*. Oxford University Press (2016).
Dyson, Stephen, 'Native revolt patterns in the Roman Empire', *Aufstieg und Niedergang der Römischen Welt*, vol II, part 3 (1975) 138–75.
Eckhardt, Benedikt, 'Romanization and Isomorphic change in Phrygia: the case of private associations', *JRS* 106 (2016), 147–71.
Fagan, Garrett, 'The reliability of Roman rebuilding inscriptions' *Papers of the British School at Rome* 64 (1996), 81–93.
Fairbank, John King, *China: A New History*. Harvard University Press (1994).
Faulkner, Neil, *The Decline and Fall of Roman Britain*. History Press (2010).
Faulkner, Neil, 'Gildas: the red monk of the first peasants' revolt', in F. Haarer (ed.), *AD 410: The History and Archaeology of Late and Post-Roman Britain*. Society for the Promotion of Roman Studies (2014).
Fell, David, 'Scotch Corner: A crossroads on the Roman frontier', *British Archaeology*, May/June (2017), 14–21.
Fincham, Garrick, *Durobrivae, A Roman Town Between Fen and Upland*. Tempus Publishing (2004).
Finley, Moses, *Studies in Roman Property*. Cambridge University Press (1976).
Fitzpatrick, Andrew, 'Ebbsfleet 54 BC', *Current Archaeology*, April (2018), 26–32.
Fitzpatrick-Matthews, Keith, 'The experience of small towns: utter devastation, slow fading or business as usual', in F. Haarer (ed.), *AD 410: The History and Archaeology of Late and Post-Roman Britain*. Society for the Promotion of Roman Studies (2014).
Forder, Simon, *The Romans in Scotland and the Battle of Mons Graupius*. Amberley Publishing (2019).
Foster, Sally, *Picts, Gaels and Scots: Early Historic Scotland*. Birlinn (2014).
Fouracre, Paul (ed.) *The New Cambridge Mediaeval History*, vol 1. Cambridge University Press (2005).
Fradley, Michael, 'The Field Archaeology of the Romano-British Settlement at Charterhouse-on-Mendip', *Britannia* 40 (2009), 99–122.
Fraser, James, *The Roman Conquest of Scotland: The Battle of Mons Graupius AD 84*. Stroud (2005).
Frere, Sheppard, 'Verulamium in the third century', in A. King and M. Henig (eds), *The Roman West in the Third Century*, BAR International Series 109 (ii) (1981).
Frere, Sheppard, *Britannia, A History of Roman Britain* (3rd edn). Pimlico (1991).
Frere, Sheppard, Hassall, Mark, and Tomlin, Roger, 'Roman Britain in 1982', *Britannia* 14 (1983) 280–356.
Fulford, Michael, 'Links with the past: pervasive 'ritual' behaviour in Roman Britain', *Britannia* 32 (2001) 199–218.
Fulford, Michael, 'Economic structures', in Malcolm Todd (ed.), *Companion to Roman Britain*. Blackwell Publishing (2007).
Fulford, Michael, *Silchester and the Study of Romano-British Urbanism* [Journal of Roman Archaeology Supplements], (2012).
Fulford, Michael, and Holbrook, Neil, *The Towns of Roman Britain: The Contribution of Commercial Archaeology since 1990*. Society for the Promotion of Roman Studies (2015).
Fulford, Michael, *Silchester Roman Town*. English Heritage (2016).
Gaffney, Vince and White, Roger, *Wroxeter, the Cornovii and the Urban Process: Final Report on the Wroxeter Hinterland Project 1994–1997*. Bradford Scholars (2007).
Gambash, 'To rule a ferocious province: Roman policy and the aftermath of the Boudican revolt', *Britannia* 43 (2012) 1–15.
Gardiner, V., 'An analysis of Romano-British lead pigs', *iams* 21, (2001), 11–13.

Bibliography

Gardner, Andrew, 'Thinking about Roman imperialism: postcolonialism, globalisation and beyond' *Britannia* 44 (2013) 1–25.

Gascoyne, A. and Radford, D., *Colchester Fortress of the War God: An Archaeological Assessment*. Oxbow Books (2013).

Gerrard, James, *The Ruin of Roman Britain*. Cambridge University Press (2013).

Gerrard, James, 'Economy and power in late Roman Britain', in Martin Millett, Louise Revell and Alison Moore (eds), *The Oxford Handbook of Roman Britain*. Oxford University Press (2016).

Gibbon, Edward, *The History of the Decline and Fall of the Roman Empire* (3rd edn), (1783).

Gibson, Catriona and Wodtko, Dagmar S., *The Background of the Celtic Languages: Theories from Archaeology and Linguistics*. Research Paper 31, University of Wales Centre for Advanced Welsh and Celtic Studies (2013).

Goldsworthy, Adrian, *The Complete Roman Army*. Thames & Hudson (2011).

Goldsworthy, Adrian, *Hadrian's Wall*. Head of Zeus (2018).

Gosden, Chris, and Lock, Gary, 'Becoming Roman on the Berkshire Downs: the evidence from Alfred's Castle', *Britannia* 34 (2003) 65–80.

Graafstal, Erik, 'What happened in the summer of AD 122? Hadrian on the British frontier – archaeology, epigraphy and historical agency', *Britannia* 49 (2018) 79–111.

Grainge, Gerald, *The Roman Channel Crossing of AD 43*. BAR British Series 332 (2002).

Gregory, Tony, 'Excavations in Thetford 1980–82, Fison Way', *East Anglian Archaeology Reports* 53 (1991).

Hachmann, R., 'The problem of the Belgae seen from the Continent', *Bulletin of the Institute of Archaeology* 13 (1976) 117–32.

Hall, Jenny, 'With criminal intent? Forgers at work in Roman London', *Britannia* 45 (2014) 165–94.

Hamerow, Helena, 'The earliest Anglo-Saxon kingdoms', in Paul Fouracre (ed.) *The New Cambridge Mediaeval History*, vol 1. Cambridge University Press (2005).

Hanson, W. S., *Dealing with Barbarians: The Romanization of Britain. Building on the Past* (149–63), Royal Archaeological Institute (1994).

Hanson, W. S., Jones, R. E., and Jones R. H., 'The Roman military presence at Dalswinton, Dumfriesshire: a reassessment of the evidence from aerial, geophysical and LIDAR survey', *Britannia* 50 (2019) 285–320.

Harris, Susan, *Richborough and Reculver*. English Heritage (2002).

Haselgrove, Colin (ed.), *Cartimandua's Capital: The Late Iron Age Royal Site at Stanwick, North Yorkshire, Fieldwork and Analysis 1981–2011*. Council for British Archaeology (2016).

Haselgrove, Colin and Millett, Martin, 'Verulamium reconsidered', in Adam Gwilt and Colin Haselgrove (eds) *Reconstructing Iron Age Societies*. Oxbow Books (1997).

Hassall, Mark, 'Roman soldiers in Roman London', in D. Strong (ed.) *Archaeological Theory And Practice: Essays Presented to Professor W.F. Grimes*. Seminar Press (1973).

Hassall, Mark, 'London as a provincial capital', in J. Bird, M. Hassall and H. Sheldon (eds) *Interpreting Roman London*. Oxbow Books (1996).

Hassall, Mark and Tomlin, Roger, 'Inscriptions', *Britannia* 18 (1987) 360–77.

Hastings, Max, *All Hell Let Loose*. Harper Press (2011).

Haverfield, Francis, *The Romanization of Roman Britain* (2nd edn). Clarendon Press (1912).

Haynes, Ian, *Blood of the Provinces*. Oxford University Press (2013).

Haynes, Ian, 'Identity and the military community in Roman Britain', in Martin Millett, Louise Revell and Alison Moore (eds), *The Oxford Handbook of Roman Britain*. Oxford University Press (2016).

Henig, Martin, *Religion in Roman Britain*. BT Batsford (1995).

Higgins, Charlotte, *Under Another Sky, Journeys in Roman Britain*. Jonathan Cape (2013).

Hill, J., 'Romanization, gender and class: recent approaches to identity in Britain and their possible consequences', in Simon James and Martin Millett (eds) *Britons and Romans: Advancing an Archaeological Agenda*. Council for British Archaeology Research Report 125 (2001).

Hind, J.G.F., 'A Plautius' Campaigns in Britain: an alternative reading of the narrative in Cassius Dio (60.19.5-71.2)', *Britannia* 38 (2007) 93–106.

Hingley, R., and Unwin, C., *Boudica: Iron Age Warrior Queen*. Hambledon & London (2005).

Bibliography

Hingley, Richard, *Londinium: A Biography*. Bloomsbury Academic (2018).

Hingley, Richard, Bonacchi, Chiara, and Sharpe, Kate, 'Are you local? Indigenous Iron age and mobile Roman and post-Roman populations: then, now and in-between', *Britannia* 49 (2018) 283–302.

Hobbs, Richard and Jackson, Ralph, *Roman Britain*. British Museum Press (2010).

Hobley, Andrew, 'The numismatic evidence for the post-Agricolan abandonment of the Roman frontier in northern Scotland', *Britannia* 20 (1989) 69–74.

Hodgson, N., 'The Stanegate: a frontier rehabilitated', *Britannia* 31 (2000) 11–22.

Hodgson, N., *Hadrian's Wall 1999-2009*. Cumberland and Westmorland Antiquarian and Archaeological Society (2009a).

Hodgson, N., 'The abandonment of the Antonine Wall: its date and causes', *Journal of Roman Archaeology, Supplementary Series* No. 74 (2009b) 185–93.

Hodgson, N., 'The British Expedition of Septimus Severus', *Britannia* 45 (2014) 31–51.

Holbrook, Neil, 'The towns of South-West England', in Michael Fulford and Neil Holbrook (eds), *The Towns of Roman Britain: The Contribution of Commercial Archaeology since 1990*. Society for the Promotion of Roman Studies (2015).

Holder, Paul, *The Roman Army in Britain*. Batsford (1982).

Hopkins, Keith *A World Full of Gods*. Weidenfeld & Nicholson (1999).

Hornblower, Simon, *The Greek World 479-323 BC* (3rd edn). Routledge, (1991).

Hoyland, Robert, 'Early Islam as a late antique religion', in Scott F. Johnson (ed.), *The Oxford Handbook of Late Antiquity*. Oxford University Press (2012).

Hunter, Fraser, *Beyond the Edge of the Empire – Caledonians, Picts and Romans*. Groam House Museum (2007).

Hunter, Fraser, 'Powerful objects: the uses of art in the Iron Age', in Julia Farley and Fraser Hunter (eds) *Celts, Art and Identity*. British Museum Press (2015a).

Hunter F., Goldberg M., Farley J., Leins I., 'In search of the Celts', in Julia Farley and Fraser Hunter (eds) *Celts, Art and Identity*. British Museum Press (2015b).

Hunter F. and Joy J., 'A connected Europe, c 500 – 150 BC', in Julia Farley and Fraser Hunter (eds) *Celts, Art and Identity*. British Museum Press (2015c).

Huntley, J., 'The world is a bundle of hay: investigating land management for animal fodder around Vindolanda based on plant remains', in Rob Collins and Matthew Symonds (eds), *Breaking Down Boundaries: Hadrian's Wall in the 21st Century* [Journal of Roman Archaeology Supplementary Series]. (2013).

James, Heather, *Roman Carmarthen, Excavations 1978–1993*. Society for the Promotion of Roman Studies (2003).

James, Simon, 'Soldiers and civilians: identity and interaction in Roman Britain', in Simon James and Martin Millett (eds) *Britons and Romans: Advancing an Archaeological Agenda*. Council for British Archaeology Research Report 125 (2001).

Johnson, Scott Fitzgerald (ed.), *The Oxford Handbook of Late Antiquity*. Oxford University Press (2012).

Johnson, Stephen, 'Channel Commands in the Notitia' in *Aspects of the Notitia Dignitatum*, Papers presented to the Oxford Conference, 13–15 December (1974).

Jones, A. H. M., 'The Roman civil service (clerical and sub-clerical grades)', *JRS* 39 (1949) 38–55.

Jones, A. H. M., *The Later Roman Empire 284-602*. Basil Blackwell (1964).

Jones, A. H. M., 'Taxation in Antiquity', [in the collection of essays by A. H. M. Jones edited and published after his death by P. A. Brunt] *The Roman Economy*. Basil Blackwell (1974a).

Jones, A. H. M., 'Inflation under the Roman Empire', [in the collection of essays by A. H. M. Jones edited and published after his death by P. A. Brunt] *The Roman Economy*. Basil Blackwell (1974b).

Jones, Duncan, *The Economy of the Roman Empire, Quantitative Studies* (2nd edn). Cambridge University Press (1982).

Jones, Michael, *Roman Lincoln*. History Press (2011).

Jones, Peter, *Veni, Vidi, Vici*. Atlantic Books (2013).

Jones, R. F. J., 'Change on the frontier: northern Britain in the third century', in A. King and M. Henig (eds), *The Roman West in the Third Century*, BAR International Series 109 (ii) (1981).

Bibliography

Joy, Jody, 'Approaching Celtic art', in Julia Farley and Fraser Hunter (eds) *Celts, Art and Identity*. British Museum Press (2015).

Kamash, Zena, Gosden, Chris, and Lock, Gary, 'Continuity and Religious Practices in Roman Britain: The Case of the Rural Religious Complex at Marcham/Frilford, Oxfordshire', *Britannia* 41 (2010) 95-125.

Kehoe, Dennis, 'The state and production in the Roman agrarian economy', in Alan Bowman and Andrew Wilson (eds) *The Roman Agricultural Economy*. Oxford University Press (2018).

Keppie, Lawrence, 'The Roman Fortress at Carpow, Perthshire: an Alternative Interpretation of the Gates and their Dedicatory Inscriptions', *Britannia* 50 (2019) 265-83.

Keynes, John Maynard, *The General Theory of Employment, Interest and Money*. Macmillan (1936).

Knight, Jeremy, *Caerleon Roman Fortress*. Welsh Assembly Government (2010).

Lancaster, Lynne, 'A new vaulting technique for early baths in Sussex: the anatomy of a Romano-British invention', *Journal of Roman Archaeology* 25 (2012) 419-40.

Laycock, Stuart, *Britannia the Failed State*. Tempus (2008).

Leins, I. and Farley, J., 'A changing world, c 150 BC - AD 50', in Julia Farley and Fraser Hunter (eds) *Celts, Art And Identity*. British Museum Press (2015).

Lindner, Molly, *Portraits of the Vestal Virgins, Priestesses of Ancient Rome*. University of Michigan Press (2015).

Lushkov, Ayelet, *Magistracy and Historiography of the Roman Republic*. Cambridge University Press (2015).

Maas, Michael, 'Barbarians: problems and approaches', in Scott F. Johnson (ed.) *The Oxford Handbook of Late Antiquity*. Oxford University Press (2012).

Magilton, John, 'RIB I, 2334: An alleged inscription from Chichester reconsidered', *Britannia* 44 (2013) 85-92.

Maldonado, Adrián, 'The early mediaeval Antonine Wall' *Britannia* 46 (2015) 225-45.

Malin, Tim, *Stonea and the Roman Fens*. Tempus Publishing (2005).

Mann, J. C., 'The frontiers of the Principate', *Aufstieg und Niedergang der römischen Welt* 2 (1974) 508-33.

Mann, J. C., 'Hadrian's Wall: the last phases', in P. Casey (ed.), *The End of Roman Britain*, BAR (British series) 71 (1979).

Mann, J. C., 'The function of Hadrian's Wall', *Archaeologia Aeliana*, fifth series 18, (1990) 51-4.

Mann, J. and Dobson, B., *The Roman army in Britain and Britons in the Roman army* in J. Mann (ed.) *Britain and the Roman Empire*. Variorum (1996).

Manning, William, 'The Conquest of Wales', in Malcolm Todd (ed.), *Companion to Roman Britain*. Blackwell Publishing (2007).

Margary, Ivan, *Roman Roads in Britain* (3rd edn). John Baker Publishers (1973).

Marsden, Peter, *The Roman Forum Site in London: Discoveries before 1985*. HMSO (1987).

Mason, David, *Roman Britain and the Roman Navy*. History Press (2010).

Mason, David, *Roman Chester: Fortress at the End of the World*. History Press (2012).

Mattingly, David, *An Imperial Possession, Britain in the Roman Empire*. Penguin Books, 2006.

Maxwell, Jaclyn, 'Paganism and Christianization', in Scott F. Johnson (ed.), *The Oxford Handbook of Late Antiquity*. Oxford University Press (2012).

Millar, Fergus, *The Emperor in the Roman World* (2nd edn). Duckworth (1992).

Millett, Martin, *The Romanization of Britain*. Cambridge University Press (1990).

Millett, Martin, 'Rethinking religion in Romanization', in J. Metzler, M. Millett, N. Roymans and J. Slofstra (eds) *Integration in the Early Roman West*. Luxembourg National Museum (1995).

Millett, Martin, 'Roman Kent', in John Williams (ed.) *The Archaeology of Kent to AD 800*. Boydell Press (2007).

Millett, Martin, 'Approaches to urban societies', in Simon James and Martin Millett (eds) *Britons and Romans: Advancing an Archaeological Agenda*. Council for British Archaeology Research Report 125 (2001).

Millett, Martin, 'Archaeological studies of the Hayton data', in P. Halkon, M. Millett and H. Woodehouse (eds), *Hayton, East Yorkshire: Archaeological Studies of the Iron Age and Roman Landscapes*. Leeds: Yorkshire Archaeological Report (2015a).

Bibliography

Millett, Martin, 'Broader perspectives on past lives', in P. Halkon, M. Millett and H. Woodehouse (eds), *Hayton, East Yorkshire: Archaeological Studies of the Iron Age and Roman Landscapes*. Leeds: Yorkshire Archaeological Report (2015b).

Millett, Martin, 'Rural settlement in Roman Britain and its significance for the early mediaeval period', *Haskins Society Journal* 27 (2015c) 1–14.

Millett, M., Revell, L. and Moore, A. (eds), *The Oxford Handbook of Roman Britain*. Oxford University Press (2016).

Millett, Martin, 'Improving our understanding of *Londinium*', *Antiquity* 90 354 (2016), 1692–1699.

Millett M. and Ferraby R., *Aldborough Roman Town*. English Heritage (2016).

Millett, Martin, and Gowland, Rebecca, 'Infant and child burial rites in Roman Britain: a study from East Yorkshire', *Britannia* 46 (2015) 171–89.

Milne, Gustav, *The Port of Roman London*. Routledge (1985).

Mitchell, Stephen, *A History of the Later Roman Empire*. Blackwell Publishing (2011).

Moore, Tom, 'Perceiving communities: exchange landscapes and social networks in the later Iron Age of Western Britain' *Oxford Journal of Archaeology* 26 (2007) 79–102.

Moorhead, Sam, 'Roman coin finds from Wiltshire' in Peter Ellis (ed.), *Roman Wiltshire and After*. Wiltshire Archaeological and Natural History Society (2001).

Moorhead, S., Booth, A. and Bland, R., *The Frome Hoard*. British Museum Press (2010).

Moorhead S. and Stuttard, D., *The Romans Who Shaped Britain*. Thames & Hudson (2012).

Mullen, Alex, 'Sociolinguistics', in Martin Millett, Louise Revell and Alison Moore (eds), *The Oxford Handbook of Roman Britain*. Oxford University Press (2016).

Nash-Williams, V.E, and Garrett, M.G., *The Roman Frontier in Wales* (2nd edn). University of Wales Press (1969).

Newman, Phil (ed.), *The Archaeology of Mining and Quarrying in England*. National Association of Mining History Organisations (2016).

Niblett, Rosalind, *Verulamium: The Roman City of St Albans*. History Press (2001).

Niblett, Rosalind, Manning, William, and Saunders, Christopher, 'Verulamium: Excavations within the Roman Town 1986–88', *Britannia* 37 (2006) 53–188.

Niblett, R. and Thompson, I., *Alban's Buried Towns: An Assessment of St Albans Archaeology up to AD 1600*. Oxbow Books (2005).

Nicholas, Barry, *An Introduction to Roman Law*. Clarendon Press (1987).

Nixon C. and Rodgers Barbara, *In Praise of Later Roman Emperors*. University of California Press (1994).

Opper, Thorsten (ed.), *Hadrian: Art, Politics and Economy*. British Museum (2013).

Oxford Committee for Archaeology, *The Temple of Sulis Minerva at Bath*. Monograph No. 16 (1988).

Ottaway, Patrick, *Roman York*, BT Batsford (1993).

Ottaway, Patrick, *Roman Yorkshire*. Blackthorn Press (2013).

Ottaway, Patrick, 'Commercial Archaeology and the study of Roman York 1990–2013', in Michael Fulford and Neil Holbrook (eds), *The Towns of Roman Britain: The Contribution of Commercial Archaeology since 1990*. Society for the Promotion of Roman Studies (2015).

Ottaway, Patrick, *Winchester: An Archaeological Assessment*. Oxbow Books (2017).

Pearce, Susan, 'The Hinton St Mary mosaic pavement: Christ or Emperor', *Britannia* 39 (2008) 193–218.

Pearson, Andrew, *The Roman Shore Forts*. History Press (2010).

Perring, Dominic, *Roman London*. Routledge (2011).

Perring, Dominic, 'Recent advances in the understanding of Roman London', in Michael Fulford and Neil Holbrook (eds), *The Towns of Roman Britain: The Contribution of Commercial Archaeology since 1990*. Society for the Promotion of Roman Studies (2015).

Petts, David, *Christianity in Roman Britain*. The History Press (2003).

Philo, John-Mark, 'Elizabeth I's translation of Tacitus: Lambeth Palace Library, MS 683', *The Review of English Studies*, New Series (2019) 1–30.

Philp, Brian, *The Roman House with Bacchic Murals at Dover*. Kent Archaeological Rescue Unit (1989).

Philp, Brian, *The Painted House and Roman Dover* (4th edn). Kent Archaeological Rescue Unit (2007).

Bibliography

Philp, Brian, *The Excavation of the Roman Forts of the Classis Britannica at Dover*. Kent Archaeological Rescue Unit (1981).
Poulter, John, 'New discoveries relating to the planning of the Antonine Wall in Scotland', *Britannia* 49 (2018) 113–46.
Prag J. and Quinn J., *The Hellenistic West*. Cambridge University Press (2013).
Ralston, Ian, 'Central Gaul at the Roman conquest: Conceptions and misconceptions', *Antiquity* 62 (1988) 786–97.
Rance, Philip, 'Epiphanius of Salamis and the Scotti: New Evidence for Late Roman-Irish Relations', *Britannia* 43 (2012) 227–42.
Reece, Richard, 'The third century: crisis or change?', in A. King and M. Henig (eds), *The Roman West in the Third Century*, BAR International Series 109 (ii) (1981).
Reece, Richard, *My Roman Britain*. Cotswold Studies (1988).
Rivet, A. and Smith, C., *The Place-Names of Roman Britain*. Book Club Associates (1979).
Roberts, Andrew, *Masters and Commanders: How Roosevelt, Churchill, Marshall and Alanbrooke Won the War in the West*. Allen Lane (2008).
Rogan, Eugene, *The Arabs: A History*. Allen Lane, 2009.
Rogan, John, *Reading Roman Inscriptions*. History Press (2006).
Rogers, Adam, *Late Roman Towns in Britain: Rethinking Change and Decline*. Cambridge University Press (2011).
Roseman, Christina *Pytheas of Massalia, On the Ocean: Text, Translation and Commentary*. Ares Publishers (2005).
Ruete, Emily, *Memoirs of an Arabian Princess from Zanzibar*. Gallery Publications (Zanzibar) (1998).
Russell, Miles, *Roman Sussex*. Stroud (2006).
Russell, Miles, and Laycock, Stuart, *UnRoman Britain*. History Press (2010).
Salway, Peter, *A History of Roman Britain*. Oxford University Press (1993).
Score, Vicki, *Hoards, Hounds and Helmets*. University of Leicester (Leicester Archaeology Monograph 21) (2011).
Scheid, John, *The Gods, the State and the Individual*. University of Pennsylvania Press (2013).
Scheidel, Walter, *The Science of Roman History*. Princeton University Press (2018).
Scheidel, Walter, and Friezen, Steven, 'The Size of the Economy and Distribution of Income in the Roman Empire', 49 *JRS* (2009) 61–91.
Scheidel, Walter, Morris, Ian, and Saller, Richard (eds), *The Cambridge Economic History of the Greco-Roman World*. Cambridge University Press (2007).
Shepherd, John, *The Temple of Mithras, London*. English Heritage (1998).
Sealey, Paul, 'Where have all the people gone? A puzzle from Middle and Late Iron Age Essex', *Archaeological Journal* 173 (2016) 30–55.
Scott, Andrew, *Emperors and Usurpers*. Oxford University Press (2018).
Scullard, H. H., *From the Gracchi to Nero* (2nd edn). Butler and Tanner (1963).
Shaw, Brent, 'The myth of the Neronian persecution', *JRS* 105 (2015) 73–100.
Shotter, David, *The Roman Frontier in Britain*. Carnegie (1996).
Shotter, David, 'Vespasian, Auctoritas and Britain', *Britannia* 35 (2004) 1–8.
Sim, David, *The Roman Iron Industry in Britain*. History Press (2012).
Smith, A., Allen, M., Brindle, T., Fulford, M. and Lodwick, L. (eds), *The Rural Settlement of Roman Britain*. Society for the Promotion of Roman Studies (2016).
Smith, A., Allen, M., Brindle, T., Fulford, M., Lodwick, L. and Rohnbogner, A. (eds), *Life and Death in the Countryside of Roman Britain*. Society for the Promotion of Roman Studies (2018).
Smith, David and Kenward, Harry, 'Roman Grain Pests in Britain: Implication for Grain Supply and Agricultural Production', *Britannia* 42 (2011) 243–62.
Smith, J. T., 'Halls or Yards? A problem of Interpretation', *Britannia* 9 (1978) 351–8.
Southern, Patricia, *Ancient Rome: The Republic 753BC-30BC*. Amberley Publishing (2009).
Southern, Patricia, *Roman Britain*. Amberley Publishing (2011).
Stancliffe, Clare, 'Christianity amongst the Britons, Dalriadan Irish and Picts', in Paul Fouracre (ed.) *The New Cambridge Mediaeval History*, vol 1. Cambridge University Press (2005).

Stead, Ian, 'The Snettisham treasure: excavations in 1990', *Antiquity* 65 (1991) 447–64.
Stevens, C. E., 'Britain between the invasions (BC 54 –AD 43): a study in ancient diplomacy', in Grimes, W. F. (ed.) *Aspects of Archaeology in Britain and Beyond*. HW Edwards, London (1951).
Strickland, T. J., 'Third century Chester', in A. King and M. Henig (eds), *The Roman West in the Third Century*, BAR International Series 109 (ii) (1981).
Swift, Ellen, 'Object biography, re-use and re-cycling in the late to post-Roman transition period and beyond: rings made from Romano-British bracelets', *Britannia* 43 (2012) 167–215.
Taylor, David, 'The forts on Hadrian's Wall' BAR 305 (2000).
Taylor, Jeremy, 'Encountering Romanitas: characterising the role of agricultural communities in Roman Britain', *Britannia* 44 (2013) 171–90.
Thatcher, Margaret, *The Downing Street Years*. HarperCollins (1993).
Thomas, Edmund, and Witschel, Christian, 'Constructing reconstruction: claim and reality of Roman rebuilding inscriptions from the Latin West', *Papers of the British School at Rome* 60 (1992), 135–78.
Thompson, E. A., *Who Was St Patrick?* Boydell Press (1985).
Todd, Malcolm, 'The Claudian conquest and its consequences', in Malcolm Todd (ed.), *Companion to Roman Britain*. Blackwell Publishing (2007).
Tomlin, Roger, 'The curse tablets', in Oxford Committee for Archaeology, *The Temple of Sulis Minerva at Bath*. Monograph No. 16 (1988).
Tomlin, Roger, 'Roman manuscripts from Carlisle: the ink-written tablets', *Britannia* 29 (1998) 31–84.
Tomlin, 'The girl in question: a new text from Roman London', *Britannia* 34 (2003) 41–51.
Tomlin, Roger, *Roman London's First Voices: Writing Tablets from the Bloomberg Excavations 2010–14*. Museum of London Archaeology (2016).
Tomlin, Roger, *Britannia Romana: Roman Inscriptions and Roman Britain*. Oxbow Books (2018).
Van der Veen, Marijke, Livurda, Alexandra, and Hill, Alistair, 'The archaeobotany of Roman Britain: current state and identification of research priorities', *Britannia* 38 (2007) 181–210.
Van Driel, Carol, 'Batavians on the move: emigrants, immigrants and returnees', *Theoretical Roman Archaeology Journal* (2011) 115–22.
Versluys, Miguel John, 'Objects in motion: An *archaeological* dialogue on Romanization', *Archaeological Dialogues* 21 (1) (2014), 1–20.
Von Clausewitz, *On War*, 1832. Published by Oxford University Press with introduction and notes (2008).
Wacher, John, *The Towns of Roman Britain* (2nd edn). BT Batsford (1995).
Wallace, Lacey, *The Origin of Roman London*. Cambridge University Press (2014).
Wallace, Lacey, 'The early Roman horizon', in Martin Millett, Louise Revell and Alison Moore (eds), *The Oxford Handbook of Roman Britain*. Oxford University Press (2016).
Wallace, Lacey, 'Community and the creation of provincial identities: a re-interpretation of the Romano-British aisled building at North Warnborough', *Archaeological Journal* 175 (2018) 231–52.
Wallace-Hadrill, *Augustan Rome* (2nd edn). Bloomsbury Academic (2018).
Ward-Perkins, Bryan, 'Why did the Anglo-Saxons not become more British?', *The English Historical Review*, Vol 115, No. 462 (June 2000) 513–33.
Warry, Peter, 'Legionary Tile Production in Britain', *Britannia* 41 (2010) 127–47.
Webster, Graham, 'The Roman military advance under Ostorius Scapula', *Arch Journal*, cxv for 1958 (1960) 49–98.
Webster, Graham, 'The military situations in Roman Britain between AD 43 and 71', *Britannia* 1 (1970), 179–97.
Webster, Graham, 'The history and archaeology of Britain in the third century', in A. King and M. Henig (eds), *The Roman West in the Third Century*, BAR International Series 109 (ii) (1981).
Welles, C. B., Fink, R., Gilliam, J. F. and Henning, W. B., *The Excavations at Dura-Europos Final Report V, Part 1: The Parchments and the Papyri*. Yale University Press (1959).
Westman, Andrew, *Chichester City Walls*. Museum of London Archaeology (2012).
White, R. and Barker, P., *Wroxeter, Life and Death of a Roman City*. The History Press (2011).
Whitmarsh, Tim, *Battling the Gods*. Faber & Faber (2016).
Wild, John-Peter, 'The textile industries of Roman Britain' *Britannia* 33 (2002) 1–42.
Williams, Jonathan, 'New light on Latin in pre-conquest Britain', *Britannia* 38 (2007) 1–12.

Bibliography

Willis, Steven, 'Samian ware and society in Roman Britain and beyond', *Britannia* 42 (2011) 167–242.
Wilmott, Tony, *The Roman Amphitheatre in Britain*. History Press (2010).
Wilson, Pete, *Lullingstone Roman Villa*. English Heritage, 2009.
Wilson, Roger, *A Guide to the Roman Remains in Britain* (4th edn). Constable (2002).
Witts, Patricia, *Mosaics in Roman Britain*. History Press (2010).
Wood, Ian, 'The final phase', in Malcolm Todd (ed.), *Companion to Roman Britain*. Blackwell Publishing (2007).
Woolf, Greg, 'Rethinking the *oppida*', *Oxford Journal of Archaeology* 12 (1993) 223–34.
Woolf, Greg, *Tales of the Barbarians: Ethnography and Empire in the Roman West*. Wiley-Blackwell (2011).
Woolf, Greg, *Rome: An Empire's Story*. Oxford University Press (2012).
Wilson, Harold, *The Labour Government 1964–70*. Penguin Books (1974).
Yale, Brian, *A Prestigious Roman Building Complex on the Southwark Waterfront*. Museum of London (2005).
Zoll, Amy, 'A view through inscriptions: the epigraphic evidence for religion at Hadrian's Wall', in J. Metzler, M. Millett, N. Roymans and J. Slofstra (eds) *Integration in the Early Roman West*. Luxembourg National Museum (1995).
Zuiderhoek, Arjan, *The Ancient City*. Cambridge University Press (2017).

Relevant journals and papers

Antiquity.
Archaeological Journal (published by the Royal Archaeological Institute).
Aufstieg und Niedergang der Römischen Welt.
Britannia (published by the Society for the Promotion of Roman Studies).
British Archaeological Reports ("BAR").
British Archaeology.
Bulletin of the Institute of Archaeology.
Classical Quarterly.
Encyclopaedia Britannica.
English Historical Review.
The Institute for Archaeo-Metallurgical Studies ("IAMS") at UCL publishes papers online.
Journal of Roman Archaeology.
Journal of Roman Studies ('JRS').
Oxford Journal of Archaeology.

Maps

Ordnance Survey Map of Roman Britain (5th edn), 2001.

Index

Note: Page numbers in *italics* indicate illustrations.

Addedomaros 49
Adimius 50, 53
administration 67–72, 99–100, 217–18. *See also* bureaucracy; local government
Adrianople, Battle of 236
Aeneid (Virgil) 127, 128, 148, 285, 286
Agricola, Gnaius Calpurnius 169
Agricola, Gnaius Julius 11, 97, 101, 102–3
    campaigns in the north 104–10
    Romanization 132–4
Agricola, Sextus Calpurnius 171–3
agriculture 34, 79, 170, 196–7, 277, 278
    around forts 279
    Lincoln 258
    new farming methods 280–1
Agrippa, M. Vipsanius 53
Alaric 245
Albinus, Decimus Clodius 174, 176–7
Allectus 201, 205–6, 264
Ammianus Marcellinus 12, 239
    barbarian conspiracy 231–2, 233, 234, 235
    Constantine's dynasty 224, 225, 226, 227
amphitheatres *118*, 252, 263
Anglesey 76
Anglo-Saxons 315–6, 318
Antonine Itinerary 12
Antonine Wall 164–7, 168, 169–70
Antoninus Pius 161–4
Antonius, Marcus Aurelius. *See* Caracalla
Apollo 286
Appian 170, 313
Arcadius, Flavius 245
Arcani 224, 235
archaeobotany 196
archaeological evidence 13–15
architecture 133, 153, 277. *See also* villas
Argonne pottery 192
Ariadne 276
army. *See* Roman army
army religion 288–90
Arras culture 32
Arras Medallion 206–7
"Arthur's Oven" 164
arts and crafts 18–19. *See also* pottery
Atrebates 21, 28–9
    Caesar's invasion in 55 BC 38
    Caratacus 50
    civitas capitals 70, *71*, 111, *256*
    Claudius' invasion in AD 43 54, 58

    client kingdom 60, 63, 64, 84
    Commius 48
    Cunobelinus 49
    Togidubnus 111, 273
Augustus 2
    autobiography 148
    British kings 51
    coins 50
    Dubnovellaunus 49
    frontiers of the Roman Empire 149, 313
    Gaul 47
    invasions 52, 312
    praetorian guard 7
    religion 284, 288, 303
    soldiers 308
Aurelian (Lucius Domitius Aurelianus) 195
Aurelius, Marcus 171–3, 296
Aurelius Victor, Sextus 11, 201, 202
auxiliary forces 7, 8, 79, 136, 306–7
    Claudius' invasion in AD 43 55, 56
    cultural exchange 142, 291
    Flavian period 99, 103, 108–9, 118
    Hadrian 145, 151
    Marcus Aurelius 172
    Septimius Severus 178, 183–4
    Vindolanda 120, 128
auxiliary forts 65, 76, 104, 138, 280

Bacchus 276, 287, 294
Balkerne Gate, Colchester 115, 190, 257
barbarian conspiracy 231–6
basilica 245, 252, 262
Batavians 120, 122–5, 289
Bath 266–8, 293, 299–301
baths 262, 263, 264
Beadlam Roman Villa 220
Belgae 28, 48, 58, 60, 70, 84, 111
Benwell 194, 292
Biccus 302
Billingsgate town house 263–4
Birdoswald inscription 206
Black Burnished Ware ("BBW") 192
Black Sea 149
Blagg, Thomas 133, 158
Bloomberg tablets 92, 98, 99, 100, 310, 317–18
Bodunni 56
Bolanus, Vettius 93–4
Boudica 64, 70, 77, 82, *88*, 262, 324
Boudican rebellion 84–9

339

Index

aftermath 89–94
background 82–4
Boudica's speech 87–8
Boulogne 53, 159, 204–5, 224
Brexit 325
Bridgeness slab *165*
Brigantes 32
    Cartimandua 72, 75
    civitas capital 158, *256*
    client kingdom 60, 65
    Flavian period 100–1, 102, 103
    Hadrian 144
    Hadrian's Wall 162–3
    raids 172
Britain
    consolidation of Roman control 59–65
    decline of Roman rule 239–41
    end of Roman rule 246–50
    gains from occupation 314–15
    long-term impact of occupation 317–25
    mid-second century map *166*
Britannia 25, 144, *145*
Britannia Inferior 188, 191, 196, 202, 255, 259
Britannia Secunda 258
Britannia Superior 188, 196, 202
British fleet. *See classis Britannica*
Britons 18
    Rome's perception of 33–5
Brittunculi 124
Brocchus, Aelius 124
bronze working 228
building projects 132–3. *See also* architecture; construction; urban development
bureaucracy 264–5. *See also* administration
burials 32, 49

Caerleon 102, 103, 116–17, 298, 321
    amphitheatre *118*
Caernarfon fort 104, 215, 224
Caerwent 158, 219, 254
Caesar, Gaius Julius 2, 10
    Belgae 28
    campaigns in Britain 37
        invasion in 54 BC 40–4
        invasion in 55 BC 38–40
        review 44–6
    coins 50
    Gaul 47
    indigenous religions 290
    Kent 28
    oppida 22
    perception of Britain 33–5
Caledonians 106–9, 179
Calgacus 108
Caligula, Gaius 53–4
canabae 252–3
Canterbury 97, 201, 215, 249
Cantii (Cantiaci) 28, 49, 64
Caracalla 180, 181, 183, 184, 185, 210
    reign 187–90
    Roman citizenship 201
Caratacus 50, 54, 56, 57, 71, 73–4
Carausius, Marcus Aurelius Mausaeus 201–4
    coinage *205*
Cardiff 198, 200, 215, 216
Carlisle 125, 155, 189, 194, 217
    civitas capital 191
    road network 105, 114
Carmarthen 158
Carpow 183, 188
Carrawburgh 292, 295
Cartimandua 72, 73, *74*, 75, 94
Carus Marcus Aurelius 197
Carvetii 32, 191
Casey, P. J. 233
Cassivellaunus 42, 43, 44, 49
Castle Cary 169
Catuvellauni 29, 49, 61, 70–1, 84
    Caesar's invasions 42, 44
    Claudius' invasion 56, 57, 58
    religion 291
Cear Gybi 233
Celtic arts and crafts 18–19, 36
Celtic languages 18, 316
Celtic religions 290–4
Celts 17–18, 23
    British communities 25–32
    contact with the Mediterranean world 23–5
Ceres 286
Cerialis, Flavius 113–14, 123, 124–5, 128
Cerialis, Quintus Petillius 83, 85, 97, 102
    campaign against the Brigantes 100–1
Charterhouse 77–8, 266
Chedworth Roman Villa 271, 274–6
"chester" suffix 139
Chester fortress 72, 117, 321
    Agricola 103, 104
    Caracalla 189
    civilian settlements 194–5
    Frontinus 102
    restoration 209
Chichester 63, 64, 193, 240, 292
Christianity 230, 240, 241, 295–9, 323
    Chedworth Roman Villa 275
    Colchester 257
    Constantine 220–1
    Flavius Theodosius 242
    Julian 227
    Uley Christians 292
    York 259
Cicero 42, 43
Cirencester 219, 228, 297
cities. *See* urbanization
city defences 172–3
civil administration 217–18
civil war 175–7, 212, 225
civitas capitals *71*, 137, 158, 191, 255, *256*, 309
civitas system 48, 69–72, 253–5

Classicianus, Gaius Julius Alpinus 68, 90, 91
classis Britannica 111–12, 159–60, 197, 199, 312
    Hadrian's Wall 150
    mining 78, 140
Claudius 52, 76, 83, 85
    bronze statue 86
    Caratacus 73
    invasion in AD 43 54–9, 312
    temple 63
client kings 60, 63–4, 103
climate change 2–3
coastal defences 318–19
Cocidius 292
Coelius, Roscius 93
coin hoards 14–15, 84
coins 19, 48–9, 50, 230, 240–1. *See also* currency
    Britannia 144, *145*
    Carausius 203–4, *205*
    Claudius' invasion in AD 43 59
    Flavian period 112, *113*
    Iron Age 26, 30
Colchester 29, 67, 70, 190, 240, 255, 256–7
    Boudica 84, 85, 86, 91–2
    circus 252
    city defences 172
    Claudius 57, 58, 61, 62–3, 97
    Cunobelinus 49–50
    Flavian period 115
    road network 139
    textiles 310
collaboration 60, 64
colonate system 281–2
colonies 8, 62–3, 69, 137, 255–60
Colosseum 96
Commius 38, 39, 40, 48
Commodus 173–4
Constans, Flavius Iulius 223, 224–5, 226, 248
Constantine 211–13, 298
    Christianity 220–1, 298
    civil administration 217–18
    military control 213–17
    panegyrics 196, 201
    urbanism and local government 218–19
    villa culture 219–20
Constantine II 223
Constantinus III 248
Constantius, Flavius Valerius 198, 201, 206–7, 209, 210, 211, 264
Constantius II 223, 225, 227
construction 141–2, 172–3, 178, 205, 209, 263–4. *See also* building projects; urban development
contemporaneous historians 9–12
copper 140
Corbridge 122, 155–6, 169, 189, 217
    civilian settlements 194
    road network 105, 114
    textiles 310
Corieltauvi 30, 64

Corio 32
Cornovii 65, 158, 277
Cornwall 24, 25, 31
Count of Britain 214, 244
Count of the Saxon Shore 200, 215, 216, 243, 244
country houses 270
countryside 269
    deep countryside 276–80, 310–1
    rural development 280–2
    rural societies 310–11
    villas 269–76
Crambeck 229
Cramond 183–4
Crayford 265
Creighton, John 51, 52
cremation 21
Cripplegate 262–3
cultural change 190–1
culture 324
culture exchange 142, 291
Cunobelinus 49–50, 56
Cupid 286
currency 33–4
curse tablets 14, 299–302

Dacians 112, 206
Dalswinton fort 113
Danebury hillfort 21
Danube 149
debt 83, 89
Deceangli 73, 102, 158
Decianus, Catus 68, 83, 84–5, 90
Decius, Gaius Messius Quintus Traianus 194
deep countryside 276–80, 310–11
Demetae 73, 102, 104, 158
dendrochronology 15
Dere Street 114, 139, 155–6, 178, 184, 195
Devon 24, 31, 61
Diana 286
Dio Cassius 11
    Antoninus Pius 162
    Boudica 82, 84, 85, 86, 89
    Caledonians 179
    Caracalla 187
    Catuvellauni 49, 56
    Claudius 57, 58, 59
    Commodus 173
    Flavian period 103, 105, 110
    Hadrian 144, 146
    Pertinax 175
    Priscus 174
    Septimius Severus 175, 180, 182–3, *183*
    Sextus Julius Severus 156
    taxes 83
    Verica 54, 55
Diocletian, Gaius Aurelius Valerius 3, 197–8, 204, 210, 212, 296, 298
diplomas 14, 79
Dobunni 30, 49, 65

Index

Dolaucothi gold mine 140, *141*
Domesday Book 322
dominus 270, 281
Domitian (Titus Flavius Domitianus) 96, 105, 110, 112, 113, 114
Dorchester 219, 228
Dorset 30, 61
double-naming 292–3
Dover 159, 160, 252, 266, 319
Druidism 34–5, 76–7, 290–1
Dubnovellaunus 49
Duke of the Britains 214–5
Dumnonii 31, 60, 61
Dura-Europus 288
Durobrivae 159
Durotriges 30, 60, 61
Dyson, Stephen 81

East Anglia 84, 103, 158, 315
East Yorkshire 279–80
Ebbsfleet 268
ecofacts 278–9
economy 77–9
Edward I 322
Elizabeth I 324
entertainment 252
Eppilus 48
equites 4
Ermine Street 139, 159, 258, 280
Essex 29, 78, 84
Eutropius 12, 201, 202
Exeter 61, 139, 240
exile 230–1

Falco, Quintus Pompeius 144, 146
farming. *See* agriculture
Fens 158–9
financial administration 68, 218
Fishbourne 28, 64
Fishbourne Roman Villa 271–4
Flavian period 95, 96–7
    Agricola's campaigns in the north 104–10
    campaigns in Wales 102–4
    Cerialis' campaign against the Brigantes 100–1
    consolidation of the province 115–18
    Domitian's reign 110–3, 114
    governors 99–100
    infrastructure 97–9
    London 262
    Trajan's reign 113–14
fleet. *See classis Britannica*
fortresses 137–8
forum 251–2
Fosse Way 65, 139, 258, 265, 266
Foster, Sally 320
Franks 231, 316–7
freedmen 68
frontiers 148–9, 313
Frontinus, Sextus Julius 97, 102

Galerius, Gaius 198, 211, 212
Gallic Empire 191, 195–6, 202
Gallic War (Caesar) 10, 33, 37, 44–5, 56
Gaul 47–8, 53, 70, 193, 309, 316–7
Genunia 163
geophysics 14
Germanic invasions 315–16
Germany 53, 89, 107, 195
Gerrard, James 224, 232, 233
Geta, Gnaeus Hosidius 56
Geta, Publius Septimus 180, 181, 182, 187, 188
Gildas 239–40, 243, 244, 247, 250, 298, 316
Gloucester 75, 100, 137, 255
Gloucestershire 30
gods 285–7
gold 140
Gorgon's head 293
Goths 242, 245
governors 4
Gratian (Flavius Gratianus) 236, 241, 242, 243
Greek mythology 293
Gross Domestic Product 170–1
ground penetrating radar (GPR) 14

Hadrian 4, 7, 11, 126, 143
    early reign 144–5
    soldiers 308
    urban development 157–8
    visit to Britain in AD 122 145–7
Hadrianic revival 156
Hadrian's Wall 126, 147–55, *166*, 167–9
    altars 292, 295
    Brigantes 162
    deterioration 206
    military units 216
    Septimus Severus 181
    shortcomings 163
Halkon, Peter 279–80
Hampshire 28
Haverfield, Francis 135, 137, 182
Hayling Island 290, 292
Hayton 279–80
Helmsdale Hoard 189
Henry I 322
Henry VIII 322
Hercules 289
Herodian 11, 191
    Caracalla 187
    Pertinax 175, 176
    Septimus Severus 180, 183, 188
Herodotus 24
Hertfordshire 29
Hill, J. 137
hillforts 20–2, 61
Hinton St Mary 298
Historia Augusta 11, 191
    Antoninus Pius 162, 163
    Commodus 173, 174
    Hadrian 144, 146, 147

Hadrian's Wall 149
Marcus Aurelius 171
Probus 196
Septimus Severus 181
historical sources 9–15, 239–40
History (Herodian) 11
Hodgson, Nick 182, 183
Holme House 116, 310
Honorius, Flavius 245, 248
Horace 33
hostages 39, 40, 41, 43, 44, 51
Housesteads 194, 291, 295
Hoxne hoard 241
Huggin Hill baths 262, 263, 264
Huns 236

Iceni 31, 58, 60, 64, 82, 84
Ickham 228
Ilchester 266
imperators 8
imperial power 191–2
imperialism 135, 314–5
Inchtutil fortress 113
indigenous religions 290–1
Indus, Julius 90
industrial centres 266
industry 77–8, 228–9, 261. *See also* salt industry; tin industry
infrastructure 97–9, 116. *See also* road networks
inns 252
inscriptions 14, 116, 206
inter-war period 47–50
    relations between Britain and Rome 50–4
Ireland 18, 105, 316, 323
Irish people (Scotti) 225, 226, 231, 232, 320
Iron Age 20–3
    British communities 25–32
    Celtic arts and crafts 18–9, 36
    Celts 17–8, 23
    contact with the Mediterranean world 23–5
    inter-war period 47–50
        relations between Britain and Rome 50–4
    religion 290–1
    Rome's perception of Britain 33–5
iron currency bars 33–4
iron ore 78, 140
iron working 228
Isle of Anglesey 76
Isle of Wight 61

Janus 287
Javolenus Priscus, Lucius 111, 112
Jovian 227
Judaism 296
Julian (Flavius Claudius Julianus) 226, 227
Julianus, Didus 176
Julius Caesar. *See* Caesar, Gaius Julius

Juno 286
Jupiter 285–6, 287, 288, 292

Kent 28, 33, 38, 49, 56, 64, 78, 249
Kingsholm 75

language 18, 316, 322
Late Antiquity 198
late Roman Empire 3
Laterculus Veronensis 12
law 310
Laycock, Stuart 132
lead 77, 78, 140, 141
legions 6–7, 307
Leicester 278
Leicestershire 30, 158
Lepidina, Sulpicia 124, 125
Licinius, Valerius Licinianus 212
Lincoln 100, 137, 255, 257–8, 278
Lincolnshire 30
literacy 119, 128
local government 218–9, 229, 308
Lollius Urbicus, Quintus 162
London 86–7, 137, 260–5, 271
    as administrative centre 72, 191
    building activity 156–7
    as financial centre 68–9, 218
    Flavian period 97–9
    long-distance trade 192
    long-term impact of occupation 317–8
    Mithraism 294
    port 319
    road network 78, 139
London Wall 172
long-distance trade 192
Longinus 62
Lucretius 284
Lucullus, Sallustius 110–11
Lullingstone villa 249
Lupus, Virius 178

Maetae 179
magistrates 3
magnetometry 14
Magusanus 289
Maiden Castle 21–2, 61, 292
Malton 219
mansiones 252
manufacturing centres 266
manumission 5
Marcellus, Lucius Neratius 113–14, 125
Marcellus, Ulpius 173–4
Marcher Lords 322
Marcianius, Vivus 99
Marcus Aurelius. *See* Aurelius, Marcus
markets 217
marriage 308
Mars 286, 289, 292, 293, 300, 301

343

Index

Mattingly, David 131–2
mausoleum 220
Maxentius, Marcus Aurelius Velarius 212
Maximian (Marcus Aurelius Valerius Maximianus) 197, 198, 201, 204, 210, 212
Maximinus, Gaius Julius Verus 212
Maximus, Flavius Magnus 233, 242–4
Maximus, Valerius 111–12
medieval period 315–7
Menai Strait 215
Mendip Hills 77–8
Mercury 286, 289, 300, 302
metal working 228
metals 140
Metchley Roman Fort 65
Midlands 30–1, 64–5
Mildenhall Hoard 221
military cemeteries 61–2
military theory 8
military training 8–9
military tribunes 4
Military Way 169
Millett, Martin 156, 244, 279–80, 308–9
Minerva 286, 289, 292, 293, 300
mining 77–8, 139–41
mining communities 266
mintmarks 203
Mithraism 294–5
money 230, 277. *See also* coins; currency
Mons Graupius 107
Moorhead, Sam 226
mosaics 228, 273, *274*, 298, 310
mythology 284–5

Narcissus 55, 68
national identity 323
native revolts 81–2
    Boudican rebellion 84–9
        aftermath 89–94
        background 82–4
navy 9. *See also* classis Britannica
Nepos, Aulus Platorius 145, 146, 155
Neptune 286, 292
Nero 76, 90, 93, 312
    Christians 296
    freedmen 5
    Prasutagus 83
Nerva Cocceius 113
Newcastle 151
Newport Arch, Lincoln *258*
Newstead 105, 113, 167, 169
Norfolk 31, 64
north of England 31–2, 72, 193–5, 217
North Street 63, 64
North Warnborough 271
Northumberland 32
Notitia dignitatum omnium 12–3
    British military units 247
    Count of the Saxon Shore 200
    Goths 242
    military control 214–15
    shore forts 199, 243–4
    Valentia 234
Numerianus, Marcus Aurelius Numerius 197
nymphaeum 274–5

Ocelus 292, 293
Octavian, Gaius. *See* Augustus
Offa's Dyke 322
offical records 12–13
Ogofau Pit 140
"On the Ruin of Britain" (Gildas) 239–40
oppida 22–3, 28, 29
Ordovices 73, 90, 102, 103, 158
Origen 297
Osorius 244
Ostorius Scapula, Publius 59, 72, 73, 75
Ostrogoths 236, 316
ovations 8
Oxfordshire 30

panegyrics 13, 196, 201
Pantheon 206
Parisi 32
Paulinus, Tiberius Claudius 254–5
Paullinus, Gaius Suetonius 76–7, 84, 85, 87, 89, 90
Pausanias 162–3
Peregrinus from Trier 268
Persia 227
Pertinax, Helvius 174, 175–6
Picts 25, 211, 226, 231, 232, 316, 320
Piercebridge 178, 195
Planning Policy Guidance Note 16 (PPG 16) 13
Plautius, Aulus 55, 56, 57–8, 59, 60, 73
plebs 4
Pliny the Elder 35, 100, 179, 290
Pliny the younger 5, 24, 25, 114
Pluto 286
poets 33
Polyclitus 5, 90
Pompey 44
Pons Aelii 146
Portable Antiquities Scheme (PAS) 14–15
ports 266, 318–19
Postumus, Marcus Cassianius Latinius 195, 202
potteries 78
pottery 15, 30, 114, 183, 188, 192, 228–9, 277–8
praetorian guard 7
praetorium 120, 124
Prasutagus 64, 70, 83
princeps praetorii 99
Principate 2, 5, 6, 7, 77, 198
principia 120
private expenditure 191
probate 111–12
Probus, Marcus Aurelius 196
procurator provinciae 68, 72, 98
procurators 4

Index

Proserpine 286
provinces 4, 210
Ptolemy 11, 25–6, 32, 179
public baths 262, 263, 264
public building projects 132–3
public office 190
Pudens, Titus Valerius 100–1
Pytheas 24–5

raiding 152, 155
RCO (Roman Climate Optimum) 2–3
Reculver 64, 215, 249
Regni 28, 48, 58, 60, 70, 84, 111
religion 227, 240, 241, 242, 283–4, 302–3
    army religion 288–90
    Christianity 230, 240, 241, 295–9, 323
        Chedworth Roman Villa 275
        Colchester 257
        Constantine 220–1
        Flavius Theodosius 242
        Julian 227
        Uley Christians 292
        York 259
    curse tablets 299–302
    indigenous religions 290–1
    long-term impact of occupation 323
    mingling of Celtic and Roman religions 291–4
    Mithraism 294–5
    Roman gods 285–7
    Roman religion and mythology 284–5
religious centres 31, 266–8
religious festivals 288
religious practices 35, 50–1
religious shrines 21
renuntia 123
revolts. *See* native revolts
Rhine 149
Richborough 64, 79, 199, 215, 216, 266
    Claudius' invasion in AD 43 56
    construction 97
    ingots 249
    road network 78, 139
road networks 53, 63, 78, 105, 114, 138–9, 277
Rochester 215
Roman army 6–9, 134, 170, 214, 306–8
    army religion 288–90
    fortresses 137–8
    payment 68
    recruitment 79, 216
Roman citizenship 188, 201
Roman Empire
    a brief account 1–6
    decline 245–6
    frontiers 148–9, 313
    gains from occupation 312–14
    Gross Domestic Product 170–1
    imperial power 191–2
Roman gods 285–7

Roman law 310
Roman occupation
    gains from 312–15
    long-term impact 317–25
Roman religion 284–5
    mingling with Celtic religions 291–4
Roman rule
    decline of 239–41
    end of 246–50
Roman towns 251–2
Romanization 131–2, 306–12, 324. *See also* Roman occupation: long-term impact
    construction 141–2
    culture exchange 142
    Haverfield 135, 137
    meaning 136–7
    mining 139–41
    road system 138–9
    Roman army 137–8
    Tacitus' account of 132–5
Rome 2, 287
    perception of Britain 33–5
    relations between Britain and 50–4
Rudchester 295
rural development 280–2
rural societies 310–1. *See also* countryside
Russell, Miles 132

Saliga, Lucius Licinius 100
salt industry 158–9, 278
Samian ware 15, 192, 277–8
Saturn 55, 287
Saturnalia 124
Saturnina 302
Saxon Shore 198, 243–4
    Count of the 200, 215, 216, 243, 244
Saxons 231
Scotch Corner 32, 100
Scotland 25, 32. *See also* Picts
    Antonine Wall 164–7, 168
    Antoninus Pius 162–4
    Caracalla 187–8, 189
    Constans 224
    Constantius and Constantine 211
    Flavian period 105, 106–9, 112, 114
    Hadrian's Wall 154
    long-term impact of occupation 320–1
    medieval period 316
    Septimus Severus 179–84
Scotti 225, 226, 231, 232, 320
scouts 193
scriba 99
Scriptores Historiae Augustae 11
Seius Saturninus 111–2
Senate 3, 40, 59, 93, 176
Senators 4
Seneca 72, 83
Severa, Claudia 124–5
Severn estuary 159, 200

345

Index

Severus, Septimius 176, 177–8, 188
   Britain under 178–80
   campaigns in Scotland 181–4
   death 183–4
shore forts 198–201
Silchester 29, 48, 97, 139, 192–3
Silures 73, 75, 76, 90, 104
   civitas 158, 255
   Frontinus 102
Silvanus 287
silver 77, 78
slaves 5, 55, 68
small towns 265–8
social life 220–1
soldiers' diplomas 14, 79
Solway Firth 32
Somerset 30, 61
South Shields 181, 189, 235, 278
South-east England 28–30, 61–4
South-west England 60–1
speculatores 99
St Alban 297
St Albans 49, 78, 85, 139, 253, 309, 323. *See also* Verlamion
St Paul's Cathedral 317
Stane Street 63, 139
Stanegate Road 114, 119, 139, 149, 151, 152, 156, 233
Stanwick 32, 72, 94, 100
Statius Priscus, Marcus 171, 174
Stilicho 245, 247, 248
Stonea 159
Strabo 10, 312
   Britons 51–2
   Druids 35
   exports 30
   perception of Britain 33
   Pytheas 24
stylus tablets (Bloomberg tablets) 92, 98, 99, 100, 310, 317–8
Suetonius (Gaius Suetonius Tranquillus) 11
   Boudica's rebellion 86, 89
   Caligula 53
   Claudius 54, 59
   Cunobelinus 50
   Hadrian 146–7
   Pliny the younger 114
   Sallustius Lucullus 110
   Vespasian 55, 61
Suffolk 31
Sulis 266, 293, 300
superstition 289–90
Surrey 28, 78
Sussex 28, 78
Sutton Hoo 315

Tacitus, Publius Cornelius 10–11, 112
   Agricola 101, 103, 104, 105, 110
   Augustus 52
   Batavians 123
   Bolanus 93
   Boudica 82
   Boudica's rebellion 85, 87, 89–90
   Boudica's speech 88
   Brigantes 32
   Britons 72
   Brittonic 18
   Caledonians 106, 107
   Christianity 295–6
   client kingdoms 84
   Colchester 63
   Decianus 68
   Frontinus 102
   Iceni 64
   London 261
   Roman army 79
   Romanization 132–5
   Scottish army 108, 109
   southern Britain 59
   St Albans 253
   taxes 83
   Togidubnus 111, 273
   Turpilianus 91
   Venutius 94
   Vespasian 61, 95
   Wales 72–7
Tasciovanus 49, 50
taxation 68, 82–3, 89, 230, 241, 273, 277, 281
   Agricola 104
   Hadrian's Wall 153
Tertullian 297
tetrarchy 3, 197–8, 210, 212
textiles 310
Theodosian Code 281–2
Theodosius, Count 232, 234, 235
Theodosius, Flavius 241–2
   end of reign 244–5
   Maximus' rebellion 242–4
   paganism 298
Thetford 31
Thetford hoard 241
Tiberius, Iulius Caesar Augustus 52, 149
tiles 141–2
tin industry 24, 25, 31
Tincomarus 48, 50
Titus (Titus Flavius Vespasianus) 105
Togidubnus 63–4, 70, 96, 111, 273, 292
Togodumnus 56, 57
tortoise formation 41
toturers 100
Towcester 172
town building. *See* urban development
town defences 172–3, 192–3, 251
town walls 251
towns 115–16, 251–3, 318. *See also* colonies; *oppida*; urbanism; urbanization
   local government 218–19
   small towns 265–8

urban development 156–8
urban dwellers 308–10
trade
    between Britain and the Empire 48, 50, 314
    between Britannia and Scotland 153, 189
    London 98, 261
    long-distance 192
trading centres 318–19
Trajan, Marcus Ulpius Nerva 113, 116–17, 149
"Traprain Law" treasure 247
Trebellius Maximus, Marcus 91, 93
tribunes 4
Trier 191, 212
Trinovantes 29, 49, 70
    Boudica 84
    Cassivellaunus 43
    Catuvellauni 44, 61
    Colchester 63
triumphs 8
Tungrians 120, 121–2, 126–8, 169
Turpilianus, Publius Petronius 91

Uley 302
Uley Christians 292
urban development 156–8
urban dwellers 308–10
urbanism 218–19, 228–9
urbanization 69–72
Urbicus, Quintus Lollius. See Lollius Urbicus, Quintus
Usipi 107

Vagniacis (Springhead) 268
Valens 228, 229, 236
Valentia 234–5
Valentian 229, 231–2
Valentian II 243
Valentinian 228, 233, 236
Valentinian II 236–7, 242, 244
Valentinus 234
Vallum 147, 151, 167–8, 169
Vardullians 169
Vegetius (Publius Flavius Vegetius Renatus) 8, 9
Venus 286
Venutius 75, 94, 100
Veranius, Quintus 76
Verecundus, Julius 121
Verica 48, 54–5
Verlamion 29, 49, 56. See also St Albans
Versluys, M.J. 132
Verulamium 58, 178–9, 190, 240, 309
    Boudica's rebellion 86
    infrastructure 97, 116
    municipium 71
    town wall 193

Verus, Gnaeus Julius 169
Vespasian (Titus Flavius Vespasianus) 6, 55, 56, 60–1, 93, 95, 96–7, 105, 273
Vesta 287
vicarius 210, 217
vici 194, 252
Victor, Sextus Aurelius. See Aurelius Victor, Sextus
Vikings 260
villages 282
villas 71, 218, 219–20, 269–71
    Chedworrth 274–6
    Fishbourne 271–4
    Holme House 116, 310
Vindolanda 217
Vindolanda forts and tablets 14, 119–21, *127*, 128–9, 141
    Batavians 122–5
    Tungrians 121–2, 126–8
Virgil 33, 125, 127, 128, 148, 203–4, 285
Visigoths 236, 245, 316
Vitellius, Aulus 93
Votadini 163
Vulcan 286

Wales 31, 72–7, 158, 198, 215
    Flavian period 102–4
    long-term impact of occupation 321–2
    medieval period 316
Wall 265–6
Wallsend 151, 194, 209, 235
Ward-Perkins, Bryan 316
Warwickshire 30
Watling Street 64, 75, 78, 97, 139, 265, 309
Welsh language 322
West Country 31
Westminster Abbey 317
Wheathampstead 29
Wiltshire 30
Winchester 318
Worcester 30
Wroxeter 75, 102, 146
    basilica 235
    decay 190
    road network 78, 139
    urban development 157–8
Wycomb 266

Y Pigwn 102
York 72, 118, 146, 191, 194, 209, 216, 259–60
    Duke of the Britains 214
    Septimus Severus 181, 184

Zenobia (Queen) 202
Zosimus 12, 226, 249, 250

'Rupert Jackson presents an excellent and comprehensive introduction to Roman Britain, which explores ancient sources as well as the diversity of modern scholarly opinion. His crisp style, punctuated by humour, will engage the reader.'
James Renshaw, Classics Teacher, Godolphin and Latymer School, UK

'In this book Rupert Jackson revisits Roman Britain, re-engaging with the written evidence, but placing it in the context of new ideas and key recent discoveries. This refreshing approach provides an excellent and rounded account of the province which will be of interest to specialist and general readers alike.'
Martin Millett, Laurence Professor of Classical Archaeology, University of Cambridge, UK

This book tells the fascinating story of Roman Britain, beginning with the late pre-Roman Iron Age and ending with the province's independence from Roman rule in AD 409. Incorporating for the first time the most recent archaeological discoveries from Hadrian's Wall, London and other sites across the country, and richly illustrated throughout, this reliable and up-to-date new account is essential reading for students, specialists and general readers alike.

Writing in a clear, readable and lively style, Rupert Jackson draws on current research and new findings to deepen our understanding of the role played by Britain in the Roman Empire, deftly integrating the ancient texts with new archaeological material. A key theme of the book is that Rome's annexation of Britain was an imprudent venture, motivated more by political prestige than economic gain, such that Britain became a 'trophy province' unable to pay its own way. However, the impact that Rome and its provinces had on this distant island was nevertheless profound: huge infrastructure projects transformed the countryside and means of travel, capital and principal cities emerged, and the Roman way of life was inseparably absorbed into local traditions. Many of those transformations continue to resonate to this day as we encounter their traces in both physical remains and in civic life.

SIR RUPERT JACKSON (a former Lord Justice of Appeal) is an independent scholar based in London, UK. Having read Classics at Cambridge before turning to the law, he has retained a lifelong interest in the subject, and is a keen and experienced academic reviewer of titles relating to classics and ancient history.

Cover image: The north wall of the Frigidarium, Viroconium Cornoviorum. Jon Lewis / Alamy Stock Photo

CLASSICAL STUDIES & ARCHAEOLOGY

BLOOMSBURY ACADEMIC

Also available from Bloomsbury Academic
www.bloomsbury.com

ISBN 978-1-350-14937-3